The Trial

Sir Roger Casement

Roger Casement,

Editor: George H. Knott

Alpha Editions

This edition published in 2020

ISBN : 9789354040429

Design and Setting By
Alpha Editions
www.alphaedis.com
email - alphaedis@gmail.com

Trial of

Sir Roger Casement

EDITED BY

George H. Knott, M.A.(Edin.)

OF THE MIDDLE TEMPLE, BARRISTER-AT-LAW

TORONTO

CANADA LAW BOOK COMPANY, LIMITED

TO

THE RIGHT HONOURABLE VISCOUNT READING

LORD CHIEF JUSTICE OF ENGLAND

WHO PRESIDED AT THE TRIAL OF ROGER CASEMENT

FOR HIGH TREASON

AND TO

THE HONOURABLE MR. JUSTICE DARLING

WHO PRESIDED AT THE HEARING OF THE APPEAL

IN THE COURT OF CRIMINAL APPEAL

THIS BOOK IS

BY THEIR KIND PERMISSION

RESPECTFULLY DEDICATED

BY

THE EDITOR

PREFACE.

This report of the trial of Roger Casement for high treason, and of the appeal to the Court of Criminal Appeal, is based on the transcript of the notes taken by the Government shorthand writers each day of the proceedings. It is a verbatim report, except for such parts of it as are of a more or less formal character, where the direct narrative form is followed instead of that of question and answer. The report has also had the additional advantage of being read by Viscount Reading, the Lord Chief Justice, who presided at the trial, and by his colleagues, Mr. Justice Avory and Mr. Justice Horridge. Mr. Justice Darling, who presided at the proceedings in the Court of Criminal Appeal, has also read the report of the judgment of that Court which was delivered by him. The Attorney-General, Sir Frederick Smith, has revised the report of his speeches. For the photograph of Roger Casement which appears as the frontispiece of this book the Editor is indebted to Mr. Michael Francis Doyle, of the American Bar, who assisted the defence throughout the proceedings, both at the trial and in the Court of Criminal Appeal. The interest of this photograph is that it was taken in Germany at the time when Casement was engaged in the mission which ultimately led him to trial and the scaffold.

Numerous documents and photographs will be found throughout the work and in the Appendices, relating to the persons who were engaged in the proceedings, or to things which were produced as evidence at the trial. Material of a personal nature relative to Casement which is available at present to a would-be biographer is very scanty. Hardly anything has been made public except the formal record of his career in the service of the British Government, which was set out in the opening speech of the Attorney-General. Perhaps no one so notorious was ever so little known in his private character. Amongst the documents in the Appendices to which attention may be drawn are the petitions which were presented by numerous persons, animated by various motives, for the commutation of the sentence. For these the Editor is indebted to Clement Shorter, Esq.

It remains only for the Editor to express his thanks to Viscount Reading, Lord Chief Justice, and Mr. Justice Darling, who have accepted the joint dedication to them of this record of a famous historic trial in which they respectively played such distinguished parts.

G. H. K.

The Library,
Middle Temple,
23rd June, 1917.

CONTENTS.

CONTENTS.

Closing Speech for the Crown.

LIST OF ILLUSTRATIONS.

SIR ROGER CASEMENT.

INTRODUCTION.

In the latter part of the month of April, 1916, the papers contained the news that Sir Roger David Casement had been arrested by the Irish police on the Kerry coast near Tralee Bay, where he had landed with several companions, in circumstances indicating an attempt to run men, arms, and ammunition with the intention of raising rebellion in Ireland. Casement had been employed in the Consular Service for twenty-one years, and in 1913 he had retired on a pension. In January, 1911, he had been knighted, and during the years 1909 to 1912, while Consul-General at Rio de Janeiro, he had been employed in making inquiries into what were known as the Putumayo atrocities, and he was in consequence very conspicuous in the public view. During all these years nothing was known of him to suggest that he was connected with any of the popular movements in Ireland. In the latter part of 1914 and the early part of 1915 Casement was reported to be moving about freely and publicly in Germany, and appearing to be treated by the German Government as a very privileged person. He was reported, too, to have been amongst the Irish prisoners in the camps, and as having made speeches to them. If the British Government knew how Casement happened to be in Germany, no disclosure was made, nor has at any time been made, public. The Government may not have received accurate information as to Casement's proceedings in the German camps until, in February, 1916, some of the Irish prisoners were exchanged, and came home, and their narratives then became available for whatever subsequent events might happen. In view of the events which did follow, especially the trial for treason which this book records, the remark may be made that it was with singular indifference to the interests of Sir Roger Casement that the German authorities allowed the exchange of the very prisoners who could tell the whole story of the happenings in Germany.

For the time being, however, it was sufficiently startling to hear that a British subject, and a former official of the Government, could be engaged in an enterprise, whatever it might be, which bore on its face the ugly look of treachery and treason. Had the fulsome letter which Casement wrote to Sir Edward Grey acknowledging the honour of his knighthood been known at the time of his German enterprise, it would have increased the anger and contempt felt for him, though it would certainly not have lessened the mystification of his proceedings.

Such was the person who was arrested in Ireland on the 21st of April, 1916, and such was the nature of the interest which the public took in him. This interest was immensely stimulated, moreover, by other facts which became known within a few days of the news of his arrest. On this 21st of April the British sloop "Bluebell," whilst patrolling in the neighbourhood of Tralee, sighted a suspicious ship flying the Norwegian ensign, and with Norwegian ensigns painted on her sides. The captain of the "Bluebell" had taken this vessel, which described herself as the "Aud," of Bergen, into charge, and had directed her to follow the "Bluebell" to Queenstown. Arrived off Queenstown, a dramatic scene was enacted. The *soi-disant* "Aud" stopped her engines. The "Bluebell" went back to her, and when about a cable's length away the crew of the "Bluebell" saw a small cloud of white smoke issue from the "Aud." At the same time two German ensigns were broken at her mast, and two boats were lowered. The "Bluebell" fired one round across the bows of the "Aud," and thereupon the boats hoisted two flags of truce, and the men put up their hands. They were then taken prisoners on board the "Bluebell," and placed under armed guard. These men were German bluejackets—nineteen sailors and three officers. The "Aud" sank almost immediately, and divers found soon afterwards that she had carried a cargo of rifles and ammunition, the rifles being Russian rifles of the 1905 pattern. Other even more surprising events quickly succeeded, and threw further light on the enterprise of Casement and the German cruiser, the "Aud." Casement had hardly arrived in England, where he had been taken in custody, when news arrived from Ireland of the Sinn Fein rebellion. Then the connection of things became clear. Casement had landed between the 20th and 21st of April; he was evidently expected by conspirators who were plotting rebellion; and they were awaiting his arrival with the German cruiser carrying the arms and ammunition which now lay at the bottom of the sea. On 24th April it was announced in England that "grave disturbances had broken out in Dublin." It is unnecessary to do more than remind the reader of the subsequent developments, of the suppression of the rebellion, and of the executing of the rebels by courts-martial. Had Casement succeeded in landing himself and the cruiser "Aud," without being intercepted, and had he arrived safely amongst his fellow-conspirators with all his German honours thick upon him, it is probable that he would have shared their summary punishment, unless, indeed, the British Government had been of opinion that in any event it was desirable in the public interest that the plotting of the German Government with Casement and the Irish rebels should be made manifest by a formal investigation of the Courts in the ordinary course of the criminal law.

On Casement's arrival in England he made to the metropolitan police the statement, "I am Sir Roger Casement, and the only person to whom "I have disclosed my identity is a priest in Tralee, Ireland." Afterwards, until the 15th May, he was kept in military custody in the Tower of London; but he was then removed by a warrant issued on the 13th May, and was brought to Bow Street Police Station to hear the charge which was to be preferred against him.

The formal charge preferred was that "on the 1st day of November, "1914, and on divers days thereafter, and between that day and the 21st "day of April, 1916, he" (with a fellow-prisoner, Daniel Julian Bailey, an Irish soldier who had been interned in Germany whilst Casement was there) "unlawfully, maliciously, and traitorously did commit high treason "without the realm of England in contempt of our Sovereign Lord the "King and his laws, to the evil example of all others in the like case "offending, contrary to the duty of the allegiance of the said Sir Roger "Casement to our said Sovereign Lord the King, and against the form "of the statute in such case made and provided."

The magisterial inquiry was held at Bow Street on the 15th, 16th, and 17th days of May, 1916, and on the last of these days Casement, who made no statement, was committed for trial.

It may perhaps be well to state here how and why it was that Casement, who had been arrested in Ireland, was brought for charge and trial to England. If the reader turns to the trial in the High Court he will find that, after the verdict of the jury, Casement made a long rhetorical statement protesting against the jurisdiction of an English Court and his trial by an English jury. He declared that the Court was to him, as an Irishman, a foreign Court, and that he had an indefeasible right, as an Irishman, if tried at all, to be tried in Ireland by an Irish Court and an Irish jury.

Considered as a legal objection to the jurisdiction of the Court, this statement was quite vain and baseless; and it could not have been with the belief that it had any legal validity that Casement made his objection. He was not simply an Irishman, but a British subject, born and bred under the British law, and the only Court of law in the United Kingdom, or the Dominions, which had jurisdiction to try him for treason committed abroad was the Court of King's Bench of England. In similar circumstances no British subject—English, Scottish, Welsh, or Irish—could have been tried by any other Court. His fellow-countryman, Dr. Lynch, had been tried and convicted in 1903 by the Court of Queen's Bench for treason committed in South Africa during the Boer War. Until, with whatever motive, Casement himself declaimed against the jurisdiction of the Court, no objection was taken to it at any point of his trial; that is to say, by any of the very competent counsel who defended him. So far from advancing any argument or plea of this kind, Serjeant Sullivan, Casement's leading counsel, a distinguished leader of the Irish bar, as well as an English counsel, began his address to the jury in these words, "If your lordships please, gentlemen of the jury, it is indeed a matter "of congratulation that such a trial as this at such a time is taking place "here in the capital of your nation in open Court, according to the "ordinary process of law regulating the lives of the civil subjects of His "Majesty." This reference, we may suppose, may have meant that on a charge of treason committed during war, in the country of the enemy, it was not altogether inconceivable that Casement might have been tried, as the Sinn Fein rebels were tried, under military law by a court-martial on his arrest in Ireland. Serjeant Sullivan may also, seeing that he had addressed so many arguments to the Court as to the procedure in trials of treason, have been referring to the fact that Casement might have been tried by a Commission issued by the Crown constituting a special Court, and not by the ordinary Courts of any of the countries of the United Kingdom, the King's Bench in England or Ireland, or the Court of Justiciary in Scotland. This power of the Crown to appoint a special Commission for the trial of treasons committed abroad was conferred on the Crown by the statute 35 Henry VIII., chapter 6; and this brings us to this statute which made the Court of King's Bench the Court, and the only one of the regular Courts of law in the United Kingdom, which could try Casement or any other British subject for this kind of offence. We are not speaking now as to the point whether Casement had, in fact, committed any offence at all. This was the only legal point raised by Casement's counsel at the trial in the King's Bench and in the Court of Criminal Appeal. The arguments and judgments in the latter Court relating to the commission of the offence will be dealt with below in this Introduction. What we are concerned with at present is the Court and the mode of trial of the offence of treason when it is committed abroad.

The statute 35 Henry VIII. enacts, "For as much as some doubts "and questions have been moved that certain kinds of treasons, mis-"prisions, and concealments of treasons done, perpetrated, or committed "out of the King's Majestie's realm of England, and other his Grace's "dominions, cannot by the common laws of this realm be enquired "of, heard, and determined within this his said realm of England, for a "plain remedy, order, and declaration therein to be had and made, be "it enacted by authority of this present Parliament, that all manner of "offences being already made or declared or hereafter to be made or "declared by any of the laws and statutes of this realm to be treasons, "misprisions of treasons, or concealments of treasons done, perpetrated, or "committed, or hereafter to be done, perpetrated, and committed, by any "person or persons out of this realm of England, shall be from henceforth "enquired of, heard, and determined before the King's Justices of his "Bench for pleas to be holden before himself by good and lawful men of "the same shire where the said Bench shall sit and be kept, or else be "before such Commissioners, and in such shire of the realm as shall be "assigned by the King's Majestie's Commission and by good and lawful "men of the same shire, in like manner and form to all intents and "purposes as if such treasons, misprisions of treasons, or concealments of "treasons had been done, perpetrated, and committed within the same "shire whereof they shall be so enquired of, heard, and determined as "is aforesaid."

This statute is still in force, and determines the law as to the procedure of charge and trial for treasons committed out of the realm; that is, out of the United Kingdom of Great Britain and Ireland. Moreover, the substantive law of treason is the same in England, Scotland, and Ireland. If Casement had been tried in Ireland the procedure would have been the same as here. The witnesses against him there would have been his own countrymen, as they were here. His pose as an Irish patriot would have led him equally to protest against any existing Irish Court trying him. His protest, in short, can only be understood as an expression of disappointment and anger that he had not been given the better chance of acquittal which he would, or supposed he would, have had if the jury had been Irish. The fact of his arrest in Ireland was quite irrelevant. Possibly a charge of treason founded on acts done in Ireland might have been formulated, but what he did there was perhaps dubious, whereas his acts in Germany were indubitably treasonable.

At the magisterial inquiry the Attorney-General had intimated that it was very desirable that the proceedings should be pushed on as quickly as possible. It was undesirable, considering the situation of Irish affairs, and with Ireland still troubled by the effects of a revolution just suppressed, that the case of Casement, the principal rebel, should be protracted. There was much speculation as to whether, supposing Casement was convicted, it would be possible in the state of Irish feeling to add another Irish name to the long list of Irishmen who had already been executed.

The Government therefore were quickly ready with their indictment, and on the 25th of May the Grand Jury of Middlesex and the county of London were summoned for the purpose of having the indictment presented to them according to the procedure under the Act of 35 Henry VIII., as above described. If the reader will turn to this document, as it was laid before the Grand Jury, it will appear to be sufficiently lengthy and laboured; yet it was the first exemplar of an indictment for treason as simplified by the new Indictments Act, 1915, which came into operation in April, 1916, its laudable aim being to simplify indictments in all kinds of criminal cases. The sort of redundancies which were pruned from the Casement indictment may be gathered by turning to the indictment on the trial of Lynch for treason in 1903. The following clause is redolent of the archaisms with which indictments until recently abounded, and which other forms of legal documents still retain in unnecessary exuberance. The Grand Jury presented that Lynch, "being a subject of our "said late Lady Queen Victoria, and well knowing the premises aforesaid, "but not regarding the duty of his allegiance nor having the fear of God "in his heart, and being moved and seduced by the instigation of the "devil, as a false traitor against our said late Lady Queen Victoria, and "wholly withdrawing the allegiance, fidelity, and obedience which every "true and faithful subject of our said late Lady Queen Victoria should "and have right ought to have borne towards our said late Lady Queen "Victoria, and contriving and with all his strength intending to aid and "assist the said enemies of our said late Lady Queen Victoria, against our "said Lady Queen Victoria and her subjects, heretofore during the said "war, to wit, on the 18th day of January in the year aforesaid at Pretoria, "in the territory of the said South African Republic, in parts beyond the "seas without the realm of England, and at other times both before and "after that day, as well at Pretoria as elsewhere within the territory of the "said South African Republic, with force and arms unlawfully, maliciously, "and traitorously was adhering to, aiding, and comforting the said "Government and the said South African Republic under the said Govern-"ment, against our said late Lady Queen Victoria and her subjects, the "said Government of the said burghers and men then being enemies of "our said late Lady Queen Victoria."

In the last treason trial before this of Casement, that of Ahlers, a naturalised German, in 1914, for the treason of adherence to the King's enemies, within and not without the realm, the same form was used. The benefit from and the simplifications of indictments may be convenient chiefly to certain lawyer officials who draw these documents, and the public may hardly be conscious of any change, except from the suppression of absurdities of language which were wont to raise a smile in Court when gravely read aloud to audiences sceptical as to mediæval views about the devil.

The assembling of twenty-three Grand Jurymen for the purpose of considering whether the indictment presented a *prima facie* case against

Casement, after a magisterial inquiry of three days, with a resulting committal, may be considered to be one of these legal anachronisms whose abolition would be a public benefit. However, this, it must be admitted, is a matter of controversy. Conceivably the Grand Jury might have considered Casement the victim of Government tyranny; might even have accepted his claim to be of the antique type of Irish patriot, and so have prevented his being put upon trial by finding "no bill," as an assertion of the people's right against the executive acts of Government. Instead of so doing, after standing listening for fifty-six minutes to an address on the facts and the law from the Lord Chief Justice, Viscount Reading, and after an hour's absence, they returned true bills both against Casement and the prisoner Bailey, who has been before mentioned.

Then followed the assignment of counsel to the prisoner. Casement was not present on this occasion, but Mr. Gavan Duffy, his solicitor, who had appeared for him at the Police Court, applied that counsel might be assigned, this being necessary under the Act 7 & 8 William III., chapter 3, passed in 1695-6, known as the Treason Act, which allows persons charged with treason to be defended by counsel, and requires the Court to assign two such persons as the accused may desire, a privilege of defence which before that date alleged traitors did not possess. They were left for their defence to the instigation of the devil! This ceremony of assignment of counsel still lingers as part of the archaic fringe of the law of treason, and is not found in connection with any other kind of trial.

It may be mentioned that it is this same Act which explains the questions put by the King's Coroner and Master of the Crown Office to Casement, as to whether he had received a copy of the indictment and a list of the jurors who were summoned to try him; and this Act also provided that an indictment must be found by a Grand Jury within three years of the commission of the treason charged—perhaps a unique privilege not known in respect of crimes other than treason.

The person assigned to Casement as his leading counsel was Mr. Alexander Sullivan, K.C., the Second Serjeant of the Irish bar, who defended Casement by virtue of being a barrister called to the English bar in 1899, but not holding the rank of King's Counsel there. As to his rank of Second Serjeant in Ireland it may be noted that while the ancient order of the coif, the Serjeants at Law, who were once, in very far away times, the only advocates in the King's English Courts, has now passed away, and only an individual may perchance survive, it still lingers in Ireland. In Victorian days some of the leading advocates were of the order, but the King's Counsel were becoming the more common figures as the leaders of the bar. In Ireland the office of Serjeant is also of great antiquity; but it was not conferred so freely as in England. Down to 1627 only one person held the dignity of Serjeant, and he was known as the King's Serjeant. In that year a second Serjeant was appointed, and the senior Serjeant was styled the prime Serjeant. In 1682 a third Serjeant was appointed; and the prime Serjeant became first Serjeant. So that Mr. Serjeant Sullivan is the second of a group of three of an ancient order of Serjeants at Law at the Irish bar. No order of Serjeants at Law is known in Scotland.

Mr. Thomas Artemus Jones, the second counsel assigned to Casement, is an able and well-known barrister—a "rising junior," to use a phrase rather gone out. Mr. John Hartman Morgan is hardly a regularly practising barrister; he is a Professor of Constitutional Law at University College, London, and a publicist and journalist. He was not assigned as counsel, and therefore had no *locus standi* in the case; but it will be seen that at one part of the proceedings this technical difficulty was evaded by the Lord Chief Justice allowing Professor Morgan to address an argument to the Court as *amicus curiæ*. As to the counsel who represented the Crown it is not necessary to do more than draw attention to the references made by Casement in his statement before sentence to Sir Frederick E. Smith, the Attorney-General. The defence on the facts, as apart from the law, set up for Casement was that he had not plotted against the Crown, but was intending to resist the armed forces that had been raised in Ulster for preventing Home Rule for Ireland. There was piquancy in the fact that the Attorney-General had taken so prominent a part in the Ulster movement, and that Casement appealed to the movement as an excuse for his treason.

The Government counsel had pressed on the Lord Chief Justice that the trial should be fixed at as early a date as possible. The defence showed some inclination to put off the trial to a later date than the Crown was inclined to accept, alleging the necessity of obtaining evidence from America. The Lord Chief Justice pointed out that it was not apparent why witnesses in America were required. There was no satisfactory answer forthcoming, and no American witnesses were, in fact, called. A member of the American bar, Mr. Michael Francis Doyle, assisted the defence; but a certain mystery remains as to why Casement needed the assistance of an expert in American law. Ultimately the trial was fixed for the 26th of June; and this was ample time for both sides. The way had already been prepared by the previous trial of Lynch. The authorities had been thoroughly examined, and all material collected for the purposes of that trial by the Crown lawyers; and the counsel for Casement had the benefit of the reported arguments, arguments they themselves adopted and elaborated as they had been used for the defence in that case.

Introduction.

The trial was what is termed a trial at bar. By a kind of fiction it is supposed that the Court of King's Bench itself, that is now the whole body of the common law judges, sits, as, in fact, in ancient days it did, to hear and determine a case. The prisoner is at the bar of the Court itself. It is not necessary by law that all crimes of treason should be tried at bar. The last of the treason trials before that of Casement was the trial of Ahlers, above mentioned, and he was tried at Durham Assizes, and sentenced to death there by Mr. Justice Shearman, who sat under the Commission by which the judges of assize sit. His, however, was a charge of treason committed within the realm, and it has already been shown that the Court of King's Bench itself must try treasons committed abroad. Hence a trial at bar was the proper mode of trial in the Casement case. The trial of Lynch was at bar in 1903, and there had been another famous trial at bar, that of Dr. Jameson, also arising out of South African affairs, this latter trial being for the incursion into the Transvaal in breach of the Foreign Enlistment Act. This latter trial shows that a trial at bar may take place whenever a case is of sufficient importance if the Court chooses to allow it, but it is quite at its discretion, in other cases than treason, whether it does so or not. The trial of Arthur Orton for perjury in 1873, and the action against Mr. Bradlaugh for penalties under the Parliamentary Oaths Act in 1885 were instances. The only limitation of this discretion is in cases where the Crown is interested, and the Attorney-General may then demand a trial at bar as a matter of right. The usual number of judges at such a trial is three.

The Attorney-General has also another privilege when he appears at a trial as representing the Crown. The rule in an ordinary criminal trial as to the addresses of counsel to the jury is that the prosecuting counsel addresses the jury last if counsel for the prisoner calls witnesses or puts in evidence on the prisoner's behalf; if he does not, the last word, which is considered an advantage, lies with him. This rule, however, the Attorney-General has the right of disregarding. In any event, even when no witnesses are called by the prisoner, he claims the right to say the last word to the jury. The right has frequently been criticised as a relic of ideas about State prosecutions which no longer prevail. The Crown is really not often bloodthirsty for convictions, but the right is asserted, perhaps, on the principle that one never knows what may yet turn out to be useful. Accordingly in the Casement trial, though Serjeant Sullivan did not call witnesses, nor put the prisoner in the box, the Attorney-General had "the last word."

The most important feature, however, of the Casement trial, from the point of view of procedure, was that it was the first trial for the treason of adhering to the King's enemies abroad which could be reviewed by the

Court of Criminal Appeal in case the prisoner was convicted. The Court of Criminal Appeal was not brought into existence until 1907, three years after the Lynch trial. The Court that tried Dr. Lynch at bar was the Court which had given a final decision. Serjeant Sullivan contended that this decision was wrong, and yet, in fact, that this case of *Lynch* was the only case actually decided by the Courts which was an authority against his contention that Casement could not be convicted for the treason of adhering to the King's enemies abroad. The first step in his defence had been to move, before any evidence was given by the Crown, that the indictment should be quashed on the ground that the facts charged in the indictment disclosed no offence in law; that is to say, that even though the facts were proved, or admitted by him to be true, and that they were such as would constitute the offence of adhering to the King's enemies if Casement had been present within the realm, yet that their commission having been abroad, the statute of Edward III., under which Casement was charged, did not declare that this was treason, and should be punished as such; therefore without any further proceedings Casement was entitled to acquittal. The Court intimated that this objection to the indictment ought to be made at the close of the evidence for the Crown. Accordingly Serjeant Sullivan at that point again raised his objection, and a large part of the second day and a portion of the third were occupied with a discussion of the whole question, and an attack on the authorities relied upon by the Crown. It was on the third day that Professor Morgan was heard as *amicus curiæ*, as above mentioned. At the close of these arguments the Court delivered a judgment deciding against the objection to the indictment taken by the defence. There still remained the Court of Criminal Appeal, to which these arguments might be addressed if the verdict of the jury should be against the prisoner. After the conviction there followed the appeal to that Court, and below there will be found an attempt to facilitate the understanding of those somewhat difficult arguments by a survey which is perhaps as short as the nature of the subject permits.

Very little more need be said about the trial itself. The evidence is laid before the reader in the following pages, and it seems unnecessary to attempt any summary of it. The story at length is extremely interesting, and in summary it would be but a dry skeletal outline; but there are several points relating to the trial of which something should be said. The first word spoken in the trial was the word "Oyez." Oyez was the Norman French word meaning "hear ye," and is still used in those formal proclamations made when the Courts, such as the Courts of Assize, open their sittings under the King's Commission. It is one of the few Norman French words that have survived, like the formula "*le roi le* "*veult*," used in giving the King's consent to legislation. It is said that the original pronunciation has been retained by the tradition of the Courts, and that Oh! Yes!, absurd though it seems, is quite correct.

The functions of the modern Coroner are so specific and so familiar that the reader may be somewhat surprised to find a Coroner, even though he may be the King's Coroner, taking so prominent a part in this trial of treason. It will be noticed that the officer of the Court who read the indictment, and took the prisoner's plea, and who was the only person in the Court who addressed Casement throughout the trial, is termed the King's Coroner and Master of the Crown Office, which implies that two offices are now embodied in the same holder. The King's Coroner, as all Coroners were in ancient days, was an officer exercising many wide and important functions in the service of the Crown, besides those of holding inquests; though these also often directly concerned the King, either as regarding his revenue or the State administration of police. One imagines more easily the character of the King's Coroner in early days by remembering that the Lord Chief Justice who presided at Casement's trial is, by virtue of his office, as head of the King's Bench, the Chief Coroner of the kingdom. The office of King's Coroner goes back to the ancient office of Clerk of the Crown. The King's Coroner branched off from that as a separate office, but when and how is not known. The connection between the Lord Chief Justice and the King's Coroner is indicated by the fact that the King's Coroner is appointed by the Lord Chief Justice. As to the Master of the Crown Office, his functions depend on the fact that he is the head of the administrative business of the Crown side of the Court of King's Bench. The Crown Office is coeval with the Court itself, as it was the office of the Clerk of the Crown, who has already been mentioned in connection with the King's Coroner.

The Crown Office records commence in the 3 Edward III., and therefore twenty-two years earlier in the reign of the same King who gave his name to the statute under which Casement was tried. The keeper of these records is now the King's Coroner and Master of the Crown Office, the two offices having been merged into one in 1892. In course of time the separate functions of the two offices had become indistinguishable, or rather perhaps the Master of the Crown Office had absorbed most of them. It cannot now be said that the King's Coroner has any functions distinct from those of the Master of the Crown Office. Whatever they are, the one salary of the Master of the Crown Office is the remuneration for both. Perhaps it may be desirable to add that the Coroner of the King's Household, an office still in separate existence, has no connection with the King's Coroner of whom we have been speaking.

The trial began on Monday, 26th June, and was concluded on Thursday, the 29th June. On the latter day the jury retired to consider their verdict, and returned into Court after an absence of fifty-five minutes with a verdict of guilty. The prisoner then was asked if he had anything to say why the Court should not pass sentence and judgment of death upon him; and in response he made the statement which has been previously referred to. Some controversy arose respecting it after the trial. Sir Harry Poland, K.C., whose opinion on criminal law is highly regarded by lawyers, stated that when a man who is convicted by the jury is called upon to say why judgment should not be passed upon him according to law, he is only entitled to move on some point of law in arrest of judgment. Obviously Casement did more than this; and one objection in regard to his speech was that the counsel for the Crown had no opportunity of replying to it. The case of *Wainwright*, whose trial took place in 1875, was cited by Sir Homewood Crawford, the solicitor of the City of London. When Wainwright was asked if he had anything to say, he started to deliver what would have been a long speech. He had the reputation of being an eloquent speaker, and was evidently intending to exercise his gift, but the Lord Chief Justice, Sir Alexander Cockburn, quickly stopped him, saying, "I cannot allow you to make a speech. The "only question put to you is whether you have anything to say why "sentence should not be passed upon you." The usual practice in criminal trials, especially for capital offences, is to allow the prisoner to make a verbal statement before sentence. If it is put into writing it may be read openly by the prisoner if he prefers, or by the judge privately. The statement is not interrupted, unless it attacks persons not parties to the proceedings, or otherwise contains scandalous matter. But it remains quite true that this is not a right, but a grace or judicial courtesy; and the prisoner has no legal claim to do more than take objection to the verdict and judgment. Evidently what was allowed in the *Casement* case was a matter of discretion. Was it more expedient in the circumstances that Casement should be allowed to have his say, or peremptorily to close his mouth? To stop such an appeal to political sentiment as this was not necessary for any specific public purpose; and to have appeared afraid of what Casement might say would have exaggerated his importance, and so have been neither discreet nor dignified. The Lord Chief Justice appears to have taken quite the right course in allowing Casement the liberty he actually took.

There remained to the convict the right to appeal from the sentence and judgment to the Court of Criminal Appeal, and he availed himself of it. His appeal was inconsistent with the attitude he took in his statement with regard to the jurisdiction of any English Court to determine his guilt or innocence, but to that inconsistency was due the more elaborated arguments which were laid before the Court of Criminal Appeal, though essentially they were the same previously raised, and decided against him, at the trial at bar. In the notice of appeal objections were formulated relating not only to the judgment of the Court upon the charge of the treason of adherence committed out of the realm, but also to the direction of the Lord Chief Justice to the jury as to the nature of the offence of adherence, and to the admission of certain evidence, especially the printed appeal, which was circulated amongst the prisoners in the camp at Limburg. But in the arguments before the Court no other point was, in fact, raised than that which had been before the Court of trial, namely, the question of adherence in Germany out of the realm. The Court of Criminal Appeal, presided over by Mr. Justice Darling, and consisting of five judges, took exactly the same view, we may say, of Serjeant Sullivan's new presentation of his case as the Court of trial had taken when he moved to quash the indictment. They dismissed the appeal without having called on counsel for the Crown in a judgment of the Court delivered by Mr. Justice Darling on the 18th of July, 1916, after a discussion covering two days. The account of the proceedings in the Court of Criminal Appeal follows, in the body of this book, the account of the trial. We may perhaps remark that it was an advantage to the Court of Appeal, in considering the arguments, to be relieved from the enormous strain of the trial which the Lord Chief Justice and his fellow-judges, Mr. Justice Avory and Mr. Justice Horridge, had to bear; and the reader may be indebted to that relief from strain for the apt quotation from Milton which adorned the judgment of Mr. Justice Darling. Serjeant Sullivan was not likely to be unappreciative of the humour of it, as a repartee to his own fierce attacks on the reputation of Lord Coke.

The Arguments and Judgment in the Court of Criminal Appeal.

The objection to the indictment framed under the statute of Edward III. of 1351, which was taken at the trial and argued there by Serjeant Sullivan, and also on the appeal to the Court of Criminal Appeal, was that there was no treasonable offence under this statute of Edward III. of adhering outside the realm unless the prisoner was at the time within the realm. From the year of the statute, 1351, to the year 1903, when *Rex* v. *Lynch* was tried, he contended that there had been no argument and no decision upon the statute as to adhering outside the realm, and that when the latter case was examined it would be found to be based upon misapprehensions of a case of *Rex* v. *Vaughan*, which was not really a decision upon the statute.

In this alleged absence of relevant decisions he submitted that since the prisoner was charged with adhering out of the realm, he being out of the realm, any exposition of the statute of Edward III. or comments upon it by text-writers, however great their reputation, which would fix on him the offence, were merely expressions of personal opinion which had no authority or binding force upon any judge or Court. Certain great expositors of the common law, as Lord Coke, Sir Matthew Hale, and Mr. Serjeant Hawkins, whose opinions in many matters of the common law, civil or criminal, are often taken as almost conclusive, had construed and expounded the statute in a contrary sense from that for which he was contending. The Court, however, ought not to take even their opinions as conclusive. Moreover, there was another objection to be made. These opinions had not even the value which may be attributed to the opinions of great lawyers and general professional opinion as to the meaning and construction of a statute when they are contemporaneous with the statute itself. Lord Coke, the earliest of these writers, did not comment on the Act of Edward III. until the statute of 26 Henry VIII. had come into existence and altered the whole law of treason, both as regards substantive offences and the procedure and mode of trial of offences of treason. The 26 Henry VIII. was in the year 1535, one hundred and eighty-four years after the statute of Edward III.

These being the circumstances, and the situation in which Casement was put upon his trial, Serjeant Sullivan urged upon the two Courts before which he appeared that they were untrammelled by previous authority either of decisions or opinions that had been held and expressed by eminent expounders and commentators on the law.

Addressing the Court of Criminal Appeal in two passages, one of which is at the beginning and the other at the end, he said as to the question being *de novo*, "I intend on the construction of the statute to "submit that if we had to construe this statute as though it had passed "yesterday, the first reading of it would convey a perfectly clear view of "the provisions of the statute to the mind of everybody, and that that "clear view would be inconsistent with the matter charged in the indictment "being an offence under the statute." The second passage is as follows:— "My lords, for these reasons I submit that this Court is not trammelled "by the speculative opinions of any text-writers where the statute has not "been construed by any other Court except the Court at bar in *The King* "v. *Lynch*, and accordingly that the Court should approach this statute "as if the statute had passed yesterday, and, if reading it as passing "yesterday, a clear opinion on the terms of the statute is conveyed to the "mind of the Court, that should be the reading of the statute, no matter "for how many years text-writers have expressed a different opinion."

It is obvious why Serjeant Sullivan was attacking the authority of

Lord Coke, Sir Matthew Hale, and Mr. Serjeant Hawkins, and urging the Court to approach the construction of the statute as if it were *res integra*. These writers were all against him; and it is as well to know at once that the Court declined his invitation to dismiss these writers from consideration, and construe the statute independently as if they were reading it for the first time, and it had never been commented on. Mr. Justice Darling, giving the judgment of the Court of Criminal Appeal, said, "We are "relying, confessedly relying, upon the authority of Sir Matthew Hale "and of Serjeant Hawkins in the judgment we are giving, and also upon "the opinion expressed by Lord Coke, to which I will come presently." He then quotes a passage from a judgment of Chief Justice Dallas in a case of *Butt* v. *Conant* in 1820, who said, "Now, if the authority of Lord "Hale and that of Mr. Serjeant Hawkins are to be treated lightly, we "may be without any authority whatever." Mr. Justice Darling's observation upon this is, "Here we are asked to treat them lightly; we "are asked to reject them altogether."

Mr. Justice Darling also quotes another passage which directly bears on one of the contentions of Serjeant Sullivan, that Lord Coke had not grounded his opinions upon the authority of actually decided cases. This passage, quoted by Mr. Justice Darling, is the following, and is to be found in the case of *Garland* v. *Jekyll* in 1824, "The fact is Lord Coke "had no authority for what he states, but I am afraid we should get rid of "a good deal of what is considered law in Westminster Hall if what Lord "Coke says, without authority, is not law. He was one of the most "eminent lawyers that ever presided as a judge in any Court of Justice, "and what is said by such a person is good evidence of what the law is, "particularly when it is in conformity with justice and common sense." Mr. Justice Darling's observation on this passage is, "Those are the words "of Chief Justice Best."

Though Serjeant Sullivan asked the judges to construe the statute of Edward as if it had been passed yesterday, this was really not quite what he meant. He asked that the statute should be construed freed from the accretions of text-writers of subsequent ages, and read in the light of the customs or laws of legal procedure which prevailed when the statute was passed. In this way would best be inferred what was the most probable meaning of the statute when it was passed. His position was that if this were done the statute could then be construed as hardly more than raising a question of grammatical construction, a question of the syntax of the sentence or sentences. In that case, then, he invited the judges to say that the words of the statute creating the treason of adhering to the King's enemies must be read in such a way that Casement could not have been properly convicted. The sentences plainly meant, he contended, that Casement could not have committed the treason of adhering to the King's enemies without the realm, seeing that he was not in the realm when he attempted to persuade the Irish soldiers from their allegiance. The man must be in the realm, though the acts alleged against him may have been committed outside the realm.

As a matter of common sense, and as an effective law of treason for the present day, this may appear to the reader as not at all satisfactory. But if the question is merely what is the grammatical meaning of the sentences in the Act he will, we think, consider them very puzzling, and agree that on the face of it Serjeant Sullivan's rendering is possible, or even probable. It presents a nice exercise in grammatical construction, and one arrives at a very unflattering opinion of the literary skill of the draftsmen of the Edwardian era. The ingenious renderings of the judges and Serjeant Sullivan may be read in the arguments, where is also to be found some very interesting antiquarian lore about the MSS. of the old statutes. The language, then, of the statute of treasons must be admitted to be ambiguously worded, and Serjeant Sullivan could not merely give his reading, and leave it there, without doing something more to make his reading appear to be the more probable of two or more possible ones. It was obvious that the judges could not simply be asked to read and construe the statute as if they saw it for the first time. The principle upon which Serjeant Sullivan proceeded in his argument is one expressed in a passage from Maxwell on the Interpretation of Statutes, chapter II.—"The language of a statute must be understood in the sense in which it "was understood when it was passed, and those who lived at or near the "time when it was passed may reasonably be supposed to be better "acquainted than their descendants with the circumstances to which it had "relation, as well as with the sense then attached to legislative expressions."

What Serjeant Sullivan therefore laboured to show was that the statute, at the time it was passed, must have had a different meaning from that put upon it by Lord Coke, Sir Matthew Hale, and Mr. Serjeant Hawkins, and that these "descendants" of the legislators of 1351 misunderstood what had then been done, because, in fact, they were not particularly well acquainted with the circumstances to which the statute had relation; or that they ignored them. Serjeant Sullivan's argument, put shortly, runs thus—"You say that the statute of Edward III. makes "a treasonable offence of adhering to the King's enemies abroad although "the offender was not in the realm. My answer is that at that time "a crime committed abroad could not be tried in England as, on account "of the law of judicial procedure of that period, there was no Court which "had jurisdiction to try an offence committed abroad." His inference from this was drawn as follows:—"What I submit is this, that nothing is "treason unless it can be so adjudicated treason. When you are dealing "with the Courts of law it is not a matter of morals but of law. Unless "there is some Court that can say whether a treasonable act has been com- "mitted or not, on the inquiry into the matter, it cannot be treason to "do an act which you can do without being punishable for it, or triable for "it in a Court of law. There cannot be what in law amounts to a crime "of which no Court can inform itself. You must not be presumed to have "committed a crime until you have been lawfully condemned, and if "there exists no machinery, not only for condemnation but for inquiry, "I submit that is overwhelming proof that the act cannot be a crime, when "its legal quality cannot be inquired into."

We need not consider the question whether it is theoretically true to say that an act is not a crime if no Court exists which can try it. But evidently Serjeant Sullivan's argument depends on the alleged historical fact that no Court existed in those early days of the common law, when the statute was passed, for trying an offence of adhering to the King's enemies in the realm of some other Prince. Was there any such Court? If there were not, it would be the height of absurdity to enact that adhering to the King's enemies abroad should be treason. If it were intended then that such adhering should be treason, there being no such Court, one would have to be created. The statute, however, did not create any Court or any procedure for a Court. The inference therefore drawn by Serjeant Sullivan was that it was not intended to make adhering abroad a treason unless the offender were in the realm, in which case some Court could probably be found which would have power to try that offence by the fact of the offender being in the realm.

But now suppose, in the absence of any regular Court, say, the King's ordinary Courts, which could try the offence of adhering abroad when the offender was not in the realm, that the King had the right, by the fact of his sovereignty, and without any statute conferring such a power on him, of appointing a Commission *ad hoc?* Suppose he could endow that Commission with the right to inquire into the treason according to the ordinary methods of the common law, and, on proof of guilt, with the power to impose upon the culprit the usual punishments of the common law of treason? Then it is obvious that the alleged fact of there being no Court to try the treason would be untrue, and Serjeant Sullivan's argument would collapse.

He had therefore to show that the King could not, and did not, issue such commissions unless there were statutory authority, and he contended that this statutory authority was conferred upon the King for the first time by the statute of 26 Henry VIII. in 1535.

The general rule of the common law was that crimes must be tried in the county where they were committed; the venue must be laid there, as was said. If a man were shot in one county, for example, but died in another from the wound, as he might do where the occurrence happened on the borders of counties, this raised a difficulty. In the arguments will be found much interesting information as to the dilemmas that might occur. There was a doubt whether the murderer could be tried at all until the statute of Edward I. (1272-1297). Sir James Fitzjames Stephen was of opinion that he could not; but this statute made provisions as to the venue, and laid down rules by which in one county or the other the trial might be held.

Serjeant Sullivan contended that before the statute the murderer could not have been tried, and that a statute was necessary to remove the difficulty. This being so as regards counties, he proceeded to consider what happened when such a crime as murder was committed out of the realm, in which case there would be no venue under the common law. There seems to be little doubt that this case could not have been tried at common law. But there were other Courts than the common law Courts which could have tried this offence, and others of a similar character which the common law Courts could not try. The Courts of the Marshal and Constable could have tried the offence just mentioned of murder out of the realm. The Court of the Admiral had jurisdiction to try crimes committed on the high seas, or on estuaries and rivers not in the bodies of counties. These Courts sat in virtue of Commissions issued to the Constable and Marshal and the Admiral. But if "a man be stricken upon the "high sea, and dies of the same stroke upon the land, they cannot be "inquired of by the common law"—so asserts an old writer. To remedy this difficulty, which is analogous to the case of the two counties before mentioned, a statute of 13 Richard II. (1377-1399) enabled the Constable and Marshal to hear and determine the same.

Now, in all these instances, argued Serjeant Sullivan, whether the difficulty arose out of two English counties, or the scene of action being wholly abroad, or partly abroad, or partly on the high seas and partly on the land, the common law Courts had no jurisdiction to try them, and therefore they were not common law offences. The common law was not applicable except it was made applicable by statute, and in all the above cases some statute had brought them within the sphere and jurisdiction of some Court. The Courts of the Constable and Marshal and of the Admiral indeed punished treasons, as they punished other crimes, when such crimes came within their jurisdiction; but they did not try them, nor punish them, as common law crimes. Such was the position when the statute of Edward III. was passed, laying down a law, or laws, of several kinds of treason, amongst them that of adhering to the King's enemies.

If it were intended that the offence when committed abroad out of the realm should be tried and punished here it must be punishable either in the Constable and Marshal's Court, in which case it would be triable like murder out of the realm, and not according to the common law, and with the common law punishments. If it were intended that its character should be changed, and come under the common law, then there was no Court to try it, and some procedure of Court must be provided by statute, as had always been done when the strict common law doctrine of venue had to be extended. But the statute itself was silent altogether as to procedure, and implied no other Court than the common law Court. The inference, therefore, was that it left the common law venue as it stood at that time, and did not intend to create a treason of adhering to the King out of the realm.

This argument was supported and strengthened by the fact that when the law of treason was altered, and new treasons were created by the statute 26 Henry VIII. expressly, and amongst other treasons it was enacted that adhering to the King's enemies abroad should be treason, the statute proceeded to lay down rules of procedure and to appoint a Court which should try these treasons. They were to be "inquired of and presented by the oaths of twelve good and lawful men, upon good and probable evidence and witness, in such county and shire of this realm, and before such persons as it shall please the King's Highness to appoint by commission under his great seal, in like manner and form as treasons committed within this realm have been used to be inquired of and presented, and that upon every indictment and presentment found and made of any such treasons, and certified into the King's Bench, like process and other circumstances shall be there had and made against the offenders as if the same treasons so presented had been lawfully found to be done and committed within the limits of this realm."

This tribunal was a statutory tribunal, a special Commission to be appointed by the King by statutory power, and was not a common law tribunal. By the 35 Henry VIII., according to Serjeant Sullivan, the common law came in for the first time in the case of treasons committed abroad. This statute enacted that all treasonable offences already declared such, or that should thereafter be declared to be such, to be done or committed out of the realm, "shall be from henceforth inquired of, heard, and determined before the King's justices of his bench for pleas to be holden before himself by good and lawful men of the same shire where the said bench shall sit and be kept, or else be before such Commissioners, and in such shire of the realm as shall be assigned by the King's Majesty's Commission, and by good and lawful men of the same shire in like manner" as if they had been done "within the

" same shire whereof they shall be so inquired of, heard, and determined " as is aforesaid."

The argument of Serjeant Sullivan drawn from these two statutes of Henry VIII. was that the acts committed outside the realm must previously have not been punishable, therefore not crimes, and if they had not been new offences there would have been no necessity for the first statute, " with its clumsy procedure "; and that the second statute was passed to reform this procedure, which was done by bringing the acts within the common law procedure.

In its judgment the Court did not decide on this antiquarian argument, as it may be termed, because, on their construction of the statute of Edward III., they held that the statute itself, on its own wording, made adhering outside the realm an offence of treason; and that there was a great deal of authority for this proposition. But we find in the argument Mr. Justice Darling saying that Serjeant Sullivan left out, as it seemed to him, the power of the Crown to issue Commissions for the trial of treasons committed out of the realm. To this Serjeant Sullivan replied that if there were such commissions they would have been found, and that they had not been found. In every case, so far as he knew, he said, they had been issued under statutory power. When he was asked by Mr. Justice Darling where he found a commission which was issued by statutory authority—which was the first of them?—he answered, " I cannot tell " you." Again, Mr. Justice Darling said, " When you find what " Hale, Coke, and Hawkins thought about this matter it really will not " do. The War of the Roses took place in England, and this statute of " Henry VIII. was passed when England was only just settling down from " a long period of devastating war."

The statute of 26 Henry VIII. making new treasons was repealed by the Act of Mary I. (1553-1558), which restored the law of treason as it stood in the statute of Edward III. of 1351. Other treasonable offences were created by subsequent statutes down to the reign of Queen Anne, but these were all repealed between 1860 and 1870. Serjeant Sullivan discussed these statutes for the purpose of pointing out that, even so late as the eighteenth century, they dealt carefully with the question of venue when a crime outside the realm was created; and therefore, *a fortiori*, the question of venue must have been in the minds of the legislators in the time of Edward III.

Serjeant Sullivan had now reached the stage in his argument when he might consider the interpretation of the statute of Edward III., there being against him the authority of the text-writers, Coke, Hale, and Hawkins, and the cases which they had quoted and relied on for their opinions, that the adherence to the King's enemies outside the realm was treason under the statute of Edward III. The view he presented was that none of these writers produced any valid authority, and that their opinions *per se* were not authoritative. He maintained that there was no decided case on the statute until that of *Rex* v. *Lynch* in 1903, where the indictment was for the offence of adhering abroad, and he submitted that this case had been wrongly decided.

We may observe that in the judgment the Court stated that they purposely did not rely upon this case, simply for the reason that they were of opinion that there was ample authority for the conclusion to which the Court indubitably came in that case, to be found in the decisions, and in the opinions of great lawyers, to which reference was made in the judgment in the present case.

Serjeant Sullivan did not, and could not, deny that the opinions of these writers were utterly opposed to his contention. Would he have been in a better position if he could have shown that the cases they actually cited as their authorities were irrelevant or could be explained, as he attempted to do, on the ground that these cases were of offences triable by the special Courts of the Constable and Marshal or Admiral, and not by the common law Courts? It is hardly likely that he would, considering the attitude in which the Court approached these authorities. Mr. Justice Darling, both in the arguments and in the judgment of the Court, as we have seen, read from judgments of Chief Justice Dallas and Chief Justice Best certain passages in which they had said that the Courts would have to get rid of a good deal of what was considered law if what Lord Coke said without authority was not law.

Whether Serjeant Sullivan did, as a matter of fact, prove that Lord Coke's authorities would not stand examination we shall not attempt to decide, as the Court neither affirmed nor denied; but we may refer to an observation of Mr. Justice Scrutton (which appears on page 264) at the close of a discussion on some of the cases Lord Coke had cited as authorities. This was after, it may be noted, Serjeant Sullivan had admitted that there were places in the King's Dominions, but out of the realm, in the strict sense of the region of the common law of England, where offences having been committed there could be a trial in England. Upon this Mr. Justice Scrutton remarked, "Perhaps there is a little more to be said for Lord "Coke than you thought. You will not be quite so severe on him when "you next come to address us about him, will you?"

But although the Court frankly adopted the opinions of Lord Coke, Sir Matthew Hale, and Mr. Serjeant Hawkins as the main ground of their decision, they also, by an independent reading of the statute, rejected the interpretation which Serjeant Sullivan put upon it. He had asked them to interpret it as if they were reading it for the first time. They accepted his invitation, and arrived at a conclusion which had the merit of supporting the authority of the impeached text-writers.

Serjeant Sullivan's criticism, or accusation, of Lord Coke was that he had left out the essential and governing words of the whole section relating to adhering. The offence is described in the statute as a man being "adherent to the King's enemies in his realm, giving to them aid "and comfort in the realm, or elsewhere, and thereof be probably attainted "of open deed." Lord Coke had set out the statute correctly, and had translated it correctly, but when he came to the detailed commentary he leaves out the words "in his realm," as they first occur, and makes his comment as if the whole sentence ran "adherent to the King's enemies, "giving to them aid and comfort in the realm or elsewhere." This, said Serjeant Sullivan, altered the whole meaning of the statute.

Coke's commentary was only justifiable, Serjeant Sullivan contended, on the supposition that these words "in his realm" might be omitted; and it was the commentary so made, he urged, which became the foundation of what was the plain error of the writer. This commentary runs thus— "This is here explained, viz., in giving aid and comfort to the King's "enemies within the realm or without; delivery or surrender of the "King's castles or forts by the King's captaine thereof to the King's "enemie within or without for reward, &c., is an adhering to the King's "enemie, and consequently treason declared by this Act."

Serjeant Sullivan submitted, as has already been pointed out, that these cases of delivering of castles were not at common law at all, but were within the jurisdiction of the Constable and Marshal; therefore it was not a crime to which the statute refers, because it could not be tried by the King's Courts at common law.

The reading of the statute which Serjeant Sullivan put before the Court, and the meaning he put on the statute when the limitation of the words "in his realm" was given its proper effect, as well as the opinion of the Court as to the meaning of the statute, may be best given by a quotation from the judgment.

Mr. Justice Darling said, "Taking the words of the statute them- "selves, it appears to us that the construction for which Serjeant Sullivan "contends is not the true one. He would have it that 'be adherent to "'the King's enemies in his realm, giving to them aid and comfort in "'the realm or elsewhere,' means that the adherence, because it is the "adherence which is the offence, really must be by a person who, being "in this country, gives the aid and comfort, it may be in this country, it "may be outside of it. We agree that if a person, being within this "country, gives aid and comfort to the King's enemies in this country, "he is adherent to the King's enemies; we agree (and Serjeant Sullivan "admits this) that if he is in this country, and he gives aid and comfort "to the King's enemies outside this country, he is adherent to the King's "enemies. But we think there is another offence, and that these words "must mean something more than that. We think that the meaning "of these words is this—'giving aid and comfort to the King's enemies,' "are words of apposition; they are words to explain what is meant by "being adherent to, and we think that if a man be adherent to the King's "enemies in his realm by giving to them aid and comfort in his realm, "or if he be adherent to the King's enemies elsewhere, that is, by giving "to them aid and comfort elsewhere, he is equally adherent to the King's "enemies, and if he is adherent to the King's enemies, then he commits "the treason which the statute of Edward III. defines. Reasons may be "given for that, but we think a very good reason is to be found in this, "that the subjects of the King owe him allegiance, and the allegiance "follows the person of the subject. He is the King's liege wherever "he may be, and he may violate his allegiance in a foreign country just "as well as he may violate it in this country."

We should like here to refer to an interesting argument of Serjeant Sullivan which he presented for the purpose of showing that the statute of Edward III. could not have meant to make adhering to the King's enemies abroad a treasonable offence. This argument will be found on page 210. Serjeant Sullivan said, "My lords, at the time of the statute there were "in England among the great landowners and nobles a number of persons "who were under two allegiances, one in England, and, in respect of "lands which they extensively owned in France, another allegiance in "France. The limitation of levying war, and I submit also the clear "limitation of adhering, arose from the fact that, being feudal subjects of "the King of France in respect of French lands, and of the King of "England in respect of English lands, the barons themselves would be "anxious to limit the decision of treason in such a way as that their "English lands should not be forfeited in respect of service and homage "rendered in respect of their possessions outside the realm rendered to "the King's enemies. At page 460 of the first volume of Pollock and "Maitland there is this passage—'The territory within which, according "'to later law, subjects would be born to the King of England was large; "'under Henry II. it became vast. It comprehended Ireland; at times "'(to say the least) it comprehended Scotland; it stretched to the "'Pyrenees. Then, again, the law, even of Bracton's day, acknow-"'ledged that a man might be a subject of the French King and hold "'land in France, and yet be a subject of the English King and hold "'land in England. It was prepared to meet the case of a war between "'the two Kings; the amphibious baron might fight in person for his "'liege lord, but he must also send his due consignment of knights to the "'opposite army. In generation after generation a Robert Bruce holds "'lands on both sides of the Scotch Border; no one cares to remember on "'which side he was born.' It was the Parliament that was seeking "to have a definition of treason, which, of course, at that time was "very largely a matter affecting titles to property, and developed, "indeed, in the early days as part of the law of real property." Then he says, "I submit that is a very plain reason why the Parliament would "be most anxious to see that the persons who very largely constituted the "Parliament should be put in a position of having to elect, with two "feudal claims upon them, which of their territories they should forfeit "in case their two feudal lords disagreed and went to war."

It may occur to the reader as strange that the question whether a man has committed treason should have to be determined on the construction of a statute written in a form of French which has long been obsolete, and of which the English translation makes necessary such an elaborate exercise in parsing or analysis of sentences. Moreover, unambiguous though the opinions of Lord Coke, Sir Matthew Hale, and Mr. Serjeant Hawkins are as to the meaning of the statute, it can still hardly be considered satisfactory that our Courts in the twentieth century should have to accept their authority, as it were, uncritically. The law upon which these text-writers were stating their opinions was the product of an age whose institutions have entirely passed away and their memory almost passed into oblivion—was rapidly passing into oblivion at the time when they wrote, four or five hundred years after the statute was passed. In the thirteenth century feudal institutions were in full vigour. Not much more than half a century after Lord Coke wrote, the last remnants of the feudal system are commonly said to have been abolished in the reign of Charles II. If our judges of to-day are not to rely on what Lord Coke lays down as the law of that far-away period of law, how can they themselves form an independent opinion of it when a case surprisingly happens involving that law? They must necessarily put themselves in the same mental or professional attitude towards Lord Coke and other ancient writers as their comparatively recent predecessors, Chief Justice Dallas and Chief Justice Best. The Courts have by a sort of compulsion conferred on these text-writers the authority of legislators, or, at least, of the Courts of law. So long as this professional tradition is followed the law as expounded by the authoritative text-writers may not be more difficult to ascertain than if it were, in fact, contained in an Act of Parliament or in the decisions of the Courts. It is therefore eminently desirable that the Courts should not depart from this tradition, and this sound rule the Court of trial and the Court of Criminal Appeal observed in the Casement trial. This, moreover, can be said for it, that legislators, presumably, are aware that the law has been so-and-so established by following the traditions of the text-writers, and if they choose not to interfere it may be urged that the law expresses the state of public opinion of the times. This has turned out to be true as regards the law of treason laid down and applied in the Casement case. Supposing that the Legislature, struck with what must be admitted to be the extraordinarily laboured process necessary to demonstrate that treason can be committed abroad, determined to pass an explicit law of treason, what else could Parliament do but embody the result of the Casement trial? They would probably state the law in some such language as that of Sir James Fitzjames Stephen in his Digest of the Criminal Law—"Every one commits "high treason who, either in the realm or without it, actively assists a "public enemy at war with the King." This is exactly the law as determined by the Court of Criminal Appeal from their reading of the statute of Edward III., and the interpretation of it by the text-writers whom they really followed. Yet how much simpler, and more adapted to ordinary comprehension, is it expressed by Sir James Fitzjames Stephen than in the statute or in the later, but still unmodern English, of those text-writers! Such simplicity of statement would have made any chance of Casement escaping the consequences of his guilt impossible. Serjeant Sullivan could not have availed himself of the ambiguities of an ancient statute, or the possible invalidity of a professional tradition. Such an opportunity, however, is not likely to occur again. The decision of the Court of Criminal Appeal is now as authoritative as to what the law of treason is as it is consonant with public opinion as to what that law ought to be; and Parliamentary remodelling of the statute of Edward III. will probably be deferred to a quite distant future.

After the judgment of the Court of Criminal Appeal an application was made to the Attorney-General for his certificate under section 1 (6) of the Criminal Appeal Act, 1907, authorising a further appeal by the defence to the House of Lords on the ground that the decision involved a point of law of exceptional public importance, and that it was desirable in the public interest that a further appeal should be brought. The Attorney-General, however, in the exercise of his discretion, refused his certificate.

Our final remarks on the Casement trial must refer to his execution, which took place in Pentonville Prison on 3rd August, 1916. The execution was within the walls of the prison; that is precisely as though Casement's offence had been murder. The Act of 1868, which enacted that the execution of the death sentence must be in prison, dealt only with executions for the crime of murder, and not for the offence of treason. In the latest edition of Stephen's Digest of the Criminal Law, it is stated that the Act for executing sentence of death within gaols does not apply to cases of treason, and indeed by sections 2 and 16 together appears to exclude its operation in such cases—"An execution for treason "would, therefore, it would seem have to be public." Statements founded apparently on this were also made in legal journals. If this had been true a special Act of Parliament would have been necessary authorising Casement's execution in private, unless the sentence were commuted, as a public execution could hardly have been tolerated. Several considerations it would seem have been overlooked in those statements. It had been said by Coke himself that the King might remit some part of the punishment of treason, *e.g.*, the quartering, so that there might be decapitation only, the usual judgment as to execution for treason in Coke's day. By the Forfeiture Act, 1870, the punishment for high treason is hanging, but the King, by warrant, countersigned by a Secretary of State, may substitute death by decapitation. The King changed the sentence on Lady Lisle, one of Jeffreys' victims, from burning, the penalty on women for treason until 1790, to execution by decapitation. There existed, therefore, a prerogative of the Crown to alter the details of the judgment of death. This prerogative was very frequently exercised in cases of treason in respect of the place of execution, so that there are examples of executions for treason both in public and in private—on Tower Hill or within the walls of the Tower, as the case might be. The Sheriffs Act, 1887, has more bearing, however, on the mode of executing Casement than the King's prerogative. This Act provides that where judgment of death has been passed upon a convict the Sheriff of the county shall be charged with the execution of such judgment, and may carry such judgment into execution in any prison which is the common gaol of his county.

After the execution of Casement the following statement was issued by the Government:—

Statement issued by the Government on 4th August, 1916, after Casement's Execution.

All the circumstances in the case of Roger Casement were carefully and repeatedly considered by the Government before the decision was reached not to interfere with the sentence of the law. He was convicted and punished for treachery of the worst kind to the Empire he had served, and as a willing agent of Germany.

The Irish rebellion resulted in much loss of life, both among soldiers and civilians. Casement invoked and organised German assistance to the insurrection. In addition, though himself for many years a British official, he undertook the task of trying to induce soldiers of the British Army, prisoners in the hands of Germany, to forswear their oath of allegiance and join their country's enemies. Conclusive evidence has come into the hands of the Government since the trial that he had entered into an agreement with the German Government, which explicitly provided that the brigade which he was trying to raise from among the Irish soldier prisoners might be employed in Egypt against the British Crown. Those among the Irish soldier prisoners in Germany who resisted Casement's solicitations of disloyalty were subjected to treatment of exceptional severity by the Germans; some of them have since been exchanged as invalids, and have died in this country, regarding Casement as their murderer.

The suggestion that Casement left Germany for the purpose of trying to stop the Irish rising was not raised at the trial, and is conclusively disproved, not only by the facts there disclosed, but by further evidence which has since become available.

Another suggestion, that Casement was out of his mind, is equally without foundation. Materials bearing on his mental condition were placed at the disposal of his counsel, who did not raise the plea of insanity. Casement's demeanour since his arrest, and throughout and since the trial, gave no ground for any such defence, and indeed was sufficient to disprove it.

De-Knighting of Casement.

On 30th June it was announced that the King had been pleased to direct the issue of Letters Patent under the Great Seal of the United Kingdom degrading Sir Roger Casement, C.M.G., from the degree of Knight Bachelor.

The announcement was also made on the same date that the King has been pleased to direct that Sir Roger Casement, Knight, shall cease to be a member of the most Distinguished Order of Saint Michael and Saint George, of which Order he was appointed a Companion in 1905, and that his name shall be erased from the Register of the Order.

Chronological Table.

1864, 1st September.	Roger Casement born in County Dublin.
1892, 31st July.	Enters service of Niger Coast (Oil Rivers) Protectorate.
1895, 27th June.	Appointed H.M. Consul at Lourenço Marques.
1898, 29th July.	Appointed H.M. Consul for Portuguese Possessions in West Africa.
1899-1900.	Employed on special service at Cape Town and receives the Queen's South African Medal.
1900, 20th August.	Transferred to Kinchassa in the Congo State.
1901, 6th August.	Appointed Consul for part of the French Congo Colony.
1905, 30th June.	Made a C.M.G.
1906, 13th August.	Appointed Consul for State of San Paulo and Panama.
1907, 2nd December.	Transferred to Para.
1908, 1st December.	Appointed Consul-General at Rio de Janeiro.
1911, 20th June.	Made a knight.
1911.	Receives the Coronation Medal.
1909-1912.	Employed while Consul-General at Rio de Janeiro making inquiries relative to the Putumayo rubber industry.
1913, 1st August.	Retires on a pension.
1914, 4th August.	Declaration of War between the United Kingdom and Germany.
1914, 7th October.	Makes the last demand for his pension.
1914, December.	Irish prisoners of war collected into a German camp at Limburg Lahn.
	At this time Casement is in Germany moving with freedom about the country.
	From this time until 19th February Casement addressed meetings of Irish prisoners urging them to join the Irish Brigade.
1915, 19th February.	Casement reported to have made a speech in which he said, "Now is the time for Irishmen to fight against England."
1916, 12th April.	Railway ticket taken from Berlin to Wilhelmshaven. (Found at Tralee on 21st April.)
1916, 20th April.	Red light seen flashing about a mile away at sea off Curraghane at 9.50 p.m.
1916, 21st April (Friday).	H.M.S. "Bluebell" meets the "Aud" in the neighbourhood of Tralee.
1916, 22nd April.	"Aud" blown up and sinks near the Daunt Rock Lightship.
1916, 21st April.	Casement, Bailey, and Monteith land near Tralee. Casement seen on road to Ardfert at 5.15 a.m. Casement discovered by police in M'Kenna's Fort and taken to Ardfert Barracks.
1916, 22nd April.	Casement taken to England in custody and handed over to the Metropolitan Police. Afterwards, until 15th May, kept in military custody in the Tower of London.
1916, 15th, 16th and 17th May.	Magisterial Inquiry at Bow Street Police Court and committal for trial.
1916, 26-29th June.	Trial in the High Court of Justice, London. Verdict of guilty and sentence of death.
1916, 30th June.	Casement de-knighted.
1916, 17-18th July.	Proceedings in the Court of Criminal Appeal. Appeal dismissed.
1916, 3rd August.	Casement executed in Pentonville Prison.
1916, 4th August.	Statement issued by the Government after Casement's execution.

I.—THE TRIAL.

IN THE HIGH COURT OF JUSTICE, LONDON,
MONDAY, 26TH JUNE, 1916,

BEFORE

THE LORD CHIEF JUSTICE OF ENGLAND (VISCOUNT READING),
MR. JUSTICE AVORY,
MR. JUSTICE HORRIDGE,
AND A JURY.

KING'S CORONER (Mr. Leonard W. Kershaw).

Counsel for the Crown—

THE ATTORNEY-GENERAL (The Right Hon. Sir Frederick Smith, K.C., M.P.),

THE SOLICITOR-GENERAL (The Right Hon. Sir George Cave, K.C., M.P.),

MR. A. H. BODKIN,

MR. TRAVERS HUMPHREYS,

MR. G. A. H. BRANSON,

Instructed by SIR CHARLES W. MATHEWS, K.C.B., Director of Public Prosecutions.

Counsel for the Prisoner—

MR. A. M. SULLIVAN (K.C. and Second Serjeant of the Irish Bar),

MR. T. ARTEMUS JONES,

MR. J. H. MORGAN,

Instructed by MR. G. GAVAN DUFFY, assisted by MR. MICHAEL FRANCIS DOYLE, of the American Bar.

THE TRIAL.

First Day—Monday, 26th June, 1916.

An Usher of the Court—Oyez. My lords the King's Justices do strictly charge and command all manner of persons to keep silence, for they will now proceed to the pleas of the Crown and arraignment of prisoners upon their lives and deaths, and all those that are bound by recognisance to give evidence against any of the prisoners which shall be at the bar, let them come forth and give their evidence, or they will forfeit their recognisance. God save the King.

The King's Coroner—Sir Roger Casement, you stand indicted and charged on the presentment of the grand jury with the following offence:—High treason, by adhering to the King's enemies elsewhere than in the King's realm—to wit, in the Empire of Germany—contrary to the Treason Act, 1351, 25 Edward III., statute 5, chapter 2. The particulars of offence alleged in the indictment are that you, Sir Roger David Casement, otherwise known as Sir Roger Casement, knight, on the 1st day of December, 1914, and on divers other days thereafter, and between that day and the 21st April, 1916, being then—to wit, on the said several days—a British subject, and whilst on the said several days an open and public war was being prosecuted and carried on by the German Emperor and his subjects against our Lord the King and his subjects, then and on the said several days traitorously contriving and intending to aid and assist the said enemies of our Lord the King against our Lord the King and his subjects, did traitorously adhere to and aid and comfort the said enemies in parts beyond the seas without this realm of England—to wit, in the Empire of Germany.

The overt acts of the said treason are as follows:—

(1) On or about the 31st December, 1914, soliciting and inciting and endeavouring to persuade certain persons, being British subjects and members of the military forces of our Lord the King, and being prisoners of war then imprisoned at Limburg Lahn Camp, in the Empire of Germany—to wit, Michael O'Connor and others whose names are unknown—to forsake their duty and allegiance to our Lord the King, and to join the armed forces of his said enemies, and to fight against our Lord the King and his subjects in the said war.

(2) On or about the 6th day of January, 1915, soliciting and inciting and endeavouring to persuade certain persons, being British subjects and members of the military forces of our Lord the King, and being prisoners of war then imprisoned at Limburg Lahn Camp, in the Empire of Germany—to wit, John Robinson and John Cronin and others whose names are unknown—to forsake their duty and allegiance to our Lord the King,

The Right Hon. Viscount Reading,

Lord Chief Justice of England.

and to join the armed forces of his said enemies and to fight against our Lord the King and his subjects in the said war.

(3) On or about the 19th February, 1915, soliciting and inciting and endeavouring to persuade certain persons, being British subjects and members of the military forces of our Lord the King, and being prisoners of war then imprisoned at Limburg Lahn Camp, in the Empire of Germany—to wit, John Robinson, William Egan, Daniel O'Brien, and James Wilson, and others whose names are unknown—to forsake their duty and allegiance to our Lord the King, and to join the armed forces of his said enemies and to fight against our Lord the King and his subjects in the said war.

(4) In or about the months of January and February, 1915, at Limburg Lahn Camp, in the Empire of Germany, circulating and distributing and causing and procuring to be circulated and distributed to and amongst certain persons, being British subjects and members of the military forces of our Lord the King, and being prisoners of war imprisoned at Limburg Lahn Camp aforesaid—to wit, Michael O'Connor, John Robinson, John Cronin, William Egan, Daniel O'Brien, James Wilson, and divers others whose names are unknown—a certain leaflet to the tenor and effect following, that is to say:—"Irishmen, here is a chance for you to fight for Ireland. "You have fought for England, your country's hereditary enemy. You "have fought for Belgium in England's interest, though it was no more to "you than the Fiji Islands. Are you willing to fight for your own country "with a view to securing the national freedom of Ireland? With the "moral and material assistance of the German Government an Irish Brigade "is being formed. The object of the Irish Brigade shall be to fight solely "the cause of Ireland, and under no circumstances shall it be directed to "any German end. The Irish Brigade shall be formed, and shall fight "under the Irish flag alone; the men shall wear a special distinctively "Irish uniform and have Irish officers. The Irish Brigade shall be "clothed, fed, and efficiently equipped with arms and ammunition by the "German Government. It will be stationed near Berlin, and be treated "as guests of the German Government. At the end of the war the "German Government undertakes to send each member of the brigade who "may so desire it to the United States of America with necessary means "to land. The Irishmen in America are collecting money for the brigade. "Those men who do not join the Irish Brigade will be removed from "Limburg and distributed among other camps. If interested, see your "company commanders. Join the Irish Brigade and win Ireland's "independence! Remember Bachelor's Walk! God save Ireland!"—with intent to solicit, incite, and persuade the said last-mentioned British subjects, being Irishmen, to forsake their duty and allegiance to our Lord the King, and to aid and assist his enemies in the prosecution of the said war against our Lord the King and his subjects.

(5) On or about the 31st December, 1914, and on divers days thereafter in the months of January and February, 1915, persuading and procuring certain persons being members of the military forces of our Lord the King—to wit, Daniel Julian Bailey, one Quinless, one O'Callaghan, one Keogh, one Cavanagh, one Greer, and one Scanlan, and divers others whose names are unknown—to the number of about fifty, the said persons being prisoners of war then imprisoned in Limburg Lahn Camp, in the

Empire of Germany, to forsake their allegiance to our Lord the King, and to join the armed forces of his said enemies with a view to fight against our Lord the King and his subjects in the said war.

(6) On or about the 12th day of April, 1916, setting forth from the Empire of Germany as a member of a warlike and hostile expedition undertaken and equipped by the said enemies of our Lord the King, having for its object the introduction into and landing on the coast of Ireland of arms and ammunition intended for use in the prosecution of the said war by the said enemies against our Lord the King and his subjects.

Sir Roger David Casement, how saith you, do you plead guilty or not guilty to the charge of high treason?

Mr. Sullivan—Before the prisoner pleads I, on his behalf, move to quash the indictment on the ground that no offence known to the law is disclosed by the indictment as framed. I would not take this course, in view of the decision in *The King* v. *Lynch*, had I not grounds upon which I can point out to your lordships that at the present time the prisoner stands in a totally different position from the position of the prisoner at the time of *The King* v. *Lynch*, and that the reasons why a motion to quash the indictment would not have been heard in *The King* v. *Lynch* have to-day been altered both by statute, by circumstances, and by the nature of the present indictment, which is not the same as that in *The King* v. *Lynch*. At the time of *The King* v. *Lynch* motion in arrest of judgment might have been an opportunity upon which the indictment could be objected to—writ of error lay, for the indictment being part of the record there was the error on the face of the record. Both those remedies for the prisoner have, at all events, been altered, and so far as they then existed are no longer available to him. Furthermore, my lords, the indictment in the present case differs from *The King* v. *Lynch* in this most material particular. Taking the indictment as a whole, both the offences charged, the particulars, and the overt acts alleged, there is not anywhere in the indictment an allegation of any act done anywhere within the King's dominions—I am not speaking merely of within the realm, but within any territory in which His Majesty claims dominion of any kind—and both the overt acts and the offences here charged are entirely laid——

[Their lordships conferred.]

The Lord Chief Justice—Mr. Sullivan, I have no doubt you have considered the authorities which were cited both in *The King* v. *Lynch* and in a number of earlier cases in which it is said by great judges that a motion to quash ought not to be made at this period, at any rate, in cases of treason, cases of great magnitude as they are called; you obviously had those in mind because of what you said just now. The same observations would apply in the present case as in *The King* v. *Lynch*, although I agree the procedure would be different because of the Criminal Appeal Act of 1907.

Mr. Sullivan—I quite appreciate what your lordship means.

The Lord Chief Justice—That you had in mind when you made the observation you did. It is equally open to you, and you are not prejudiced in any way by raising this point at the end of the case for the prosecution, on which you may have other points to submit; then one can see whether upon your submission any case has been made out in law against the prisoner upon this indictment, which will enable you to argue this point.

The Court thinks that that is the more convenient way of dealing with it. Of course it is open to the Attorney-General to raise the objection at once, that he objects to the motion to quash at the moment, and that it should be done later; but although that has not been done, we think it is a more convenient course that it should be taken at the end of the case for the prosecution unless you, Mr. Attorney, say anything to the contrary.

The ATTORNEY-GENERAL—No, I respectfully assent to what your lordship says.

The LORD CHIEF JUSTICE—You shall not be prejudiced in any way, Mr. Sullivan.

Mr. SULLIVAN—I thank you, my lord.

The KING'S CORONER—Sir Roger David Casement, how say you, do you plead guilty or not guilty to the high treason alleged in the indictment?

Sir ROGER CASEMENT—Not guilty.

The KING'S CORONER—Sir Roger Casement, have you been served ten days at least since with a copy of the indictment, a list of the witnesses, and copies of the panel of the jury?

Sir ROGER CASEMENT—I have.

The CHIEF CLERK OF THE CROWN OFFICE—Prisoner at the bar, these good men that you shall now hear called and personally appear are the jurors who are to pass between our Sovereign Lord the King and you upon your trial of life and death; if therefore you will challenge them or any of them you must challenge them as they come to the book to be sworn, and before they are sworn, and you shall be heard.

The following jurors, not having been challenged,

Frederick Thomas Wheeler, 18 Chambers Lane, Willesden, Shipping Clerk,
Ernest William West, 10 Balmoral Road, Willesden, Schoolmaster,
John Charles Watts, 37 Buchanan Gardens, Willesden, Warehouseman,
Albert John Abbott, 68 Caversham Avenue, Palmers Green, N., Clerk,
Herbert James Scoble, 41 Ravensdale Road, Hackney, Clerk,
Richard Charles Scantlebury, 2 Trederwen Road, Hackney, Agent,
Albert George Scopes, 261 Mare Street, Hackney, Leather Merchant,
John Burdon, 70 Drakefield Road, Balham, Wandsworth, Mechanical Engineer,
William Bowers Card, 64 Northfield Avenue, Ealing, Baker,
William Cole, 26 Coulson Street, Chelsea, Coachman,
Hyman Saunders, 68 Amhurst Road, Hackney, Tailor, and
Albert Sydney Ansley, 42 Osborne Road, Palmers Green, Bank Clerk,

were each separately sworn in the following terms:—

"You shall well and truly try and true deliverance make between "our Sovereign Lord the King and the prisoner at the bar "whom you shall have in charge, and a true verdict give "according to the evidence. So help you God."

The USHER—If any one can inform my lords the King's Justices, or the King's Attorney-General, ere this inquest be now taken between our Sovereign Lord the King and the prisoner at the bar, of any treason, murder, felony, or misdemeanour committed or done by him, let them come forth and they shall be heard; for the prisoner stands at the bar upon his deliverance; and all others that are bound by recognisances to give evidence against the prisoner at the bar, come forth and give evidence, or else you forfeit your recognisances.

The KING'S CORONER—Gentlemen of the jury, the prisoner stands indicted by the name of Sir Roger David Casement, and is charged with the following offence:—" High treason by adhering to the King's enemies "elsewhere than in the King's realm—to wit, in the Empire of Germany "—contrary to the Treason Act, 1351 (25 Edward III., stat. 5, cap. 2)." The particulars of the offence are that Sir Roger David Casement, knight, on the 1st day of December, 1914, and on divers other days thereafter, and between that day and the 21st of April, 1916, being then—to wit, on the said several days—a British subject, and whilst on the said several days an open and public war was being prosecuted and carried on by the German Emperor and his subjects against our Lord the King and his subjects, then and on the said several days traitorously contriving and intending to aid and assist the said enemies of our Lord the King against our Lord the King and his subjects, did traitorously adhere to and aid and comfort the said enemies in parts beyond the seas without this realm of England, to wit, in the Empire of Germany. The indictment sets out the overt acts that are alleged of that treason. Upon that indictment the prisoner hath been arraigned, and upon his arraignment he has pleaded that he is not guilty. Your charge therefore is to inquire whether he be guilty or not guilty upon that indictment and to hearken to the evidence.

Opening Speech for Prosecution.

The Attorney-General—May it please your lordships: gentlemen of the jury, I appear with my learned friends on behalf of the Crown to support the charge of high treason without the realm against the prisoner at the bar, who has the advantage of being defended by my learned friends, Mr. Sullivan, Mr. Artemus Jones, and Mr. Morgan.

The charge upon which the prisoner is arraigned is a very grave one. The law knows none graver. This inquiry will therefore receive, as it deserves and requires, your close and constant attention.

The law of treason, gentlemen, is principally founded upon a statute as old as the reign of King Edward III. Treason is the doing or designing anything which would lead to the death, bodily harm, or restraint of the King, levying war against him within the realm, or adhering to his enemies within or without the realm. It is alleged here by the Crown that the prisoner has been guilty of this most heinous crime, that he has adhered to the King's enemies and has attempted to seduce His Majesty's soldiers from their allegiance. It will be for you to consider, when you know all the facts, whether the Crown has proved these allegations, and whether, if they be proved, there is any circumstance of extenuation which can be urged; or whether, upon the other hand, the crimes which it is alleged the prisoner has committed are aggravated by the relationship in which he formerly stood to the Sovereign whom he has betrayed and the country at which he has struck.

It is therefore desirable that you should hear in some detail what has been the career of the prisoner. He is an able and cultivated man, versed in affairs and experienced in political matters. He was not, as you will hear, a life-long rebel against England, and all that England stood for, as others well known in Irish history have been. Let me inform you, as briefly as I can, of the principal stages in a career which has not been without public distinction, and which was directed—it may be remembered even now to his credit—not to the destruction of the power of this great Empire, but to its consolidation and development.

The prisoner was born in County Dublin on 1st September in the year 1864. He entered the service of the Niger Coast (Oil Rivers) Protectorate on 31st July, 1892, at the age of twenty-eight. He was appointed three years later, on 27th June, 1895, to be Her Majesty's Consul in the Portuguese Province of Lourenço Marques, with a residence at Lourenço Marques. He continued in this employment for three years, and on 29th July, 1898, he became Consul for the Portuguese Possessions in West Africa, south of the Gulf of Guinea. He was employed on special service at Cape Town during the war in South Africa, from 1899 to 1900; and he received, when the hostilities ended, the Queen's South African medal. He did not refuse this decoration for assistance rendered to England

Attorney-General

during this war, although it was a war of which many Irishmen profoundly disapproved, and we may perhaps therefore reasonably assume that at the age of thirty-six the crimes and delinquencies of this Empire had not engaged his attention, or at least had not conquered his intelligence. On 20th August, 1900, he was transferred to Kinchassa, in the Congo State; and he was appointed, in addition, on 6th August, 1901, to be Consul for part of the French Congo Colony. From 31st December, 1904, he was seconded for one year; and afterwards for six months from 31st December, 1905. On 30th June, 1905, he was made a C.M.G., a recognition of his public services which he did not disdain. He was appointed Consul for the States of San Paulo and Parana, with a residence at Santos, on 13th August, 1906. On 2nd December, 1907, he was transferred to Para; and on the 1st December, 1908, he was promoted to be Consul-General at Rio de Janeiro. On 20th June, 1911, he was made a knight. In 1911, the same year, he received the Coronation medal. The State of Goyaz was added to the district of the Consul-General at Rio de Janeiro; and a new commission was issued to him on 2nd December, 1912. From 1909 to 1912 he was employed, while titular Consul-General at Rio de Janeiro, in making certain inquiries relative to the rubber industry. On 1st August, 1913, after, as the facts which I have stated show, a considerable career of public usefulness, he was retired on a pension.

Gentlemen, this pension had been honourably earned, and it would therefore be neither necessary nor proper to refer to it were it not for the sinister and wicked activities of the period which I am approaching. But it is necessary now to observe what quality of conduct the prisoner judged in his conscience to be consistent with the receipt of a pension from this country. Government pensions are paid quarterly, and on each occasion must be formally claimed. The claim is made by a statutory declaration which sets out the services for which the pension was awarded and the amount claimed. The prisoner made five such declarations, the first on 2nd October, 1913, and the last on 7th October, 1914. They are in the possession of the Crown and will be produced. No payment has been made since the last date, nor would it have been made if claimed, as by that time the Treasury had directed, for reasons which you will understand, that this pension should cease to be paid.

I informed you that on 20th June, 1911, he received the honour of knighthood, and it is perhaps worth while, having regard to the singular later developments of his career, to read the letter, dated 19th June, 1911, in which he replied to the notification communicated to him by Sir Edward Grey of His Majesty's intention to bestow a knighthood upon him. He wrote, this enemy of England, this friend of Germany, this extreme and irreconcilable patriot, in the following terms:—

The Savoy, Denham, Bucks.

Dear Sir Edward Grey,

I find it very hard to choose the words in which to make acknowledgment of the honour done me by the King. I am much moved at the proof of confidence and appreciation of my service on the Putumayo conveyed to me by your letter, wherein you tell me that the King had been graciously pleased upon your recommendation to confer upon me the honour of knighthood. I am,

indeed, grateful to you for this signal assurance of your personal esteem and support. I am very deeply sensible of the honour done to me by His Majesty. I would beg that my humble duty might be presented to His Majesty when you may do me the honour to convey to him my deep appreciation of the honour he has been so graciously pleased to confer upon me.

I am, dear Sir Edward,

Yours sincerely,

ROGER CASEMENT.

Gentlemen, I read that letter because you ought to remember that those were the feelings on the 19th June, 1911, towards the country which he had served for so long, and towards the Sovereign of that country, of a man of mature years—he was, I think, forty-seven years old at the time that letter was written—a man who had had nineteen years' experience of the methods of government of this country, in which indeed he had, and not without credit, borne a part. Such a man writes in terms of gratitude, a little unusual, perhaps, in their warmth, and in the language almost of a courtier, to express his pleasure at the title with which his Sovereign had rewarded his career. And he presents his humble duty to the King, and he begs that his deep appreciation of the gracious honour may be expressed to His Majesty. And this was in 1911. The history of the relations of England and Ireland up to that date were as well known then as they are to-day. The controversies, bitter and protracted, often tragic, springing from those relations were either the commonplaces of contemporary politics, or they filled the better known pages of our elementary histories. And well understanding these controversies, fully versed in the wrongs of which Irishmen were fruitful in complaint, knowing England's ideals of government well—for at the outposts of Empire he had carried them out—he sends his humble duty to his Sovereign. What occurred between 1911 and 1914 to affect and corrupt the prisoner's mind I cannot tell you, for I do not know. I only know of one difference. The Sovereign of the country to whom his humble duty was sent in 1911 was in that year the ruler of a great and wealthy nation, unequalled in resources, living at peace, unassailed, and it almost seemed unassailable. In 1914 this same nation was struggling for its possessions, for its honour, for its very existence in the most prodigious war which has ever tested human fortitude. To the Sovereign of that country in the hour of its unchallenged greatness he sends his humble duty. It will be my task now to acquaint you with the method in which he carried out his humble duty in times dark enough to test the value of the unsolicited professions he was so forward in making.

I have informed you, gentlemen, in the most general outline of the antecedents of the prisoner, as those antecedents are known to the Crown. I cannot describe his movements after the outbreak of war until the happening of certain events to which it now becomes necessary to refer. I cannot, I say, describe his movements, but I have told you that, and you will recollect this date, the last demand for his pension was dated 7th October, 1914. Between the months of September and December, 1914, the fortunes of the struggle in France were such that a large number of British soldiers were taken captive by the enemy, and amongst those

Attorney-General

prisoners were many brave Irish soldiers. These soldiers taken, as I said, into captivity were distributed, apparently quite normally in the month of December, 1914, among various prisons in Germany, and they were treated neither worse nor better than other prisoners captured from the British Expeditionary Force. But in or about the month of December, 1914, prisoners of war belonging to various Irish regiments were removed from the different camps in which they were then imprisoned, and were collected into a large camp at Limburg Lahn. And it became evident from what followed that they were so collected for a special purpose, which had been the result of consideration and calculation on the part of the German Government.

At that time the prisoner was in Germany, moving with freedom about the country, apparently an honoured guest of the German nation. The full story of the circumstances under which he went to Germany it is not in my power to tell. But it is evident that the part he was to play was that of a man willing, and it was hoped able, to seduce from their allegiance to the King, their Sovereign and his, the Irish prisoners of war who, after fighting valiantly for the Empire, had been captured, as so many brave soldiers of all nations have been captured in this war. One can imagine the type of these private soldiers, aliens and prisoners, in an enemy country. We may perhaps surmise from the very attempt now to be described that they were simple, unlettered men, unlikely, it may have been thought, to resist a specious appeal. These men were collected by the Germans for the purpose of listening to addresses or lectures on Irish history and other matters from the prisoner, who, like themselves, had embraced the service and eaten the bread of this country. They were assembled at Limburg, on more than one occasion, and were then addressed collectively, and in some cases individually, by Casement, who moved about the camp freely, and with the full knowledge and approval of the Germans. The Germans, as you know, are very expert in this species of activity. Ireland has been disaffected. Here there was a fruitful soil for seduction. Even then it may be that the scheme of an eventual landing in Ireland had been conceived by this thoroughly resourceful and unscrupulous people. The Irish prisoners of war were there—emotional, excitable, uninformed, the easy victims, it was hoped, of seduction. Nor was the seducer lacking; the letter-writer of 1911 was to be tested.

Whether it entered his head that he was exposing poor men, his inferiors in education, age, and knowledge of the world, to the penalties of high treason I cannot tell you, for I do not know. Whether he conceived of the innocent blood which was so soon to flow in the unhappy country to which he professed devotion I cannot tell you, for I do not know. But I shall be in a position to call before you evidence which will show that between the middle of December, 1914, and 19th February, 1915, the prisoner repeatedly addressed these prisoners of war. I do not think it likely that he dwelt upon his own connection with the country which had afforded him a career, which had decorated him with a title, and from which he had accepted a pension. I suspect he did not inform them that three years before he had sent his humble duty to the Sovereign whose soldiers—while their hearts were heavy with captivity—he was attempting to seduce and to corrupt. I cannot give you a full description of his rhetoric. I can only supply such fragments of his appeals as happened to linger in the minds of those whose evidence is available for the Crown. But I pause very deliberately to say that if it be possible to give an explanation of the original journey of the prisoner to Germany, which is consistent with the duty which he owed, and which he had so recently professed to his Sovereign and his country, I hope that his explanation will be put forward by the very experienced counsel by whom he has the advantage of being defended. But whether or not his original journey to Germany is a step which can be explained, justified, or reconciled with his admitted allegiance, it must, I think, be evident that a wholly different class of considerations arises when one considers the quality of his acts in relation to these Irish prisoners.

He introduced himself to them—such was the tenor of his address on more than one occasion—as "Sir Roger Casement, the organiser of the "Irish Volunteers." He stated that he was forming an Irish Brigade, and he invited all the Irish prisoners of war to join it. He pointed out repeatedly, and with emphasis, that in his opinion everything was to be gained for Ireland by Germany winning the war; and that the Irish soldiers who were listening to his addresses had the best opportunity they had ever had of striking a blow for Ireland by entering the service of the enemies of this country. He said that those who joined the Irish Brigade would be sent to Berlin; they would become the guests of the German Government; and in the event of Germany winning a sea battle he (the speaker) would land a brigade in Ireland to defend the country against the enemy England. And that in the event of Germany losing the war either he or the Imperial German Government would give each man in the brigade a bonus of from £10 to £20, with a free passage to America.

Such were the temptations unfolded to his simple listeners by the man who reconciled it with his duty to address such persuasions to men in the straits, the bewilderment, and perhaps the despair in which these prisoners then were. Gentlemen, to the honour of Ireland, let it be recorded that the vast majority of the Irish prisoners treated the rhetoric, and the persuasions, and the corruptions of the prisoner with contempt. He was received with hisses, and was on at least one occasion driven from the camp. The Munster Fusiliers were particularly prominent in their loyal resentment of the treacherous proposals made to them. One private in that regiment actually struck, so it is recorded, the prisoner, who was saved from further violence by the intervention of an escort of Prussian Guards, who had been assigned to him for his protection by a nation which thinks of everything.

Those Irish prisoners who unfavourably received the proposals made to them by Casement were punished by a reduction in their rations. Two men, Robinson and O'Brien, who will be called before you, and who refused to join the Irish Brigade, were transferred to another camp for punishment, and were then put upon short rations. The few men who were seduced from their allegiance by the arguments addressed to them by the prisoner were rewarded by being given a green uniform with a harp and shamrock

Attorney-General

worked upon it, by unusually liberal rations, both in quality and in quantity, and by the concession of greater leisure and liberty. Amongst the Irish prisoners in Limburg at this time was a man called Bailey. Bailey, of whom you will hear more, was observed by witnesses who will be called before you to be wearing this green uniform with the harp upon the collar and upon the cap, and to be carrying side-arms after the German fashion. Evidence will be offered to you that Bailey joined the so-called Irish Brigade. He was, I think, at once promoted to the rank of sergeant in that brigade by the Germans, who were assisting and encouraging for their own purposes the formation of the brigade. The witnesses to these acts of high treason and of treachery include—Private Cronin, Royal Munster Fusiliers; William Egan, lance-corporal, Royal Irish Rifles; Corporal Michael O'Connor, Royal Irish Rifles; Private James Wilson, Dublin Fusiliers; Private William Dooley, Royal Irish Regiment; Trooper Daniel O'Brien, 19th Hussars; Corporal John Robinson, Royal Army Medical Corps; Private Michael Moore, Royal Army Medical Corps; Private John Neill, 2nd Battalion 18th Royal Irish Regiment. All these men with one exception were wounded, and have since been exchanged, and owing to the accident of their exchange they are available here at the disposal of the Crown to give evidence in order to establish the occurrences which in general outline I have indicated to you.

At this point, gentlemen, there is again a hiatus in the information which the Crown is in a position to lay before the Court. I have said enough to indicate to you that in his addresses to the prisoners Casement was in the habit of holding out, as the military adventure for which this brigade was destined, a landing in Ireland, which was described as an attempt to free Ireland from the English enemy; and it is not necessary for me to do more at this stage than to point out that the Germans were evidently not concerned to use Casement for the purpose of forming a brigade in order to add one more to the uniforms, already considerable in number, in the German Army. The inference will probably be drawn by you that it was intended then that such men as could be seduced from their allegiance should form the first fruits of a body which should be actually used for the purpose of raising armed insurrection in Ireland against the forces of the Crown, and of acting as a trained and instructed nucleus round which the disaffected section of the population might rally and grow.

The treason which is charged against the prisoner is the treason which consists of adherence to the King's enemies in the enemy country, and in relation to that treason evidence will be given to you of many overt acts; of the attempt to seduce, and in some cases of the actual seduction of His Majesty's soldiers from loyal allegiance to His Majesty; the plotting and contriving to effect a hostile landing, with stores and arms, and with armed men in His Majesty's dominions.

Gentlemen, I have said as much as is necessary at this stage to inform you of the treasonable activities of the prisoner in Germany. We must now pass to that unhappy country which has been the victim in its history of so many cruel and cynical conspiracies, but surely never of a conspiracy more cruel and more cynical than this.

Opening Speech for Prosecution.

Attorney-General

The scene of the events presently to be described was on the Kerry coast near Tralee Bay, on a lonely and wind-swept shore, the home of a scanty fisher population and of a few small farmers. On this shore, on Thursday night, 20th April, 1916, at 9.50 p.m., a labourer, called Hussey, looking oceanwards, saw a red light flashing about a mile away at sea off Curraghane—a light which it is possible was not unconnected with the happenings afterwards. And contemporaneously, or almost contemporaneously, with the landing, of which I shall say a word later, of the prisoner and his companions, a vessel, carrying arms, approached Tralee in circumstances which will satisfy you, I apprehend, that those on board that vessel carrying arms were taking part in a common adventure with the prisoner and his party, who were conveyed to this country by other means, which you will, I anticipate, conclude were also of German origin.

The enterprise of the prisoner and his friends had, happily, not eluded the vigilance of the Navy. His Majesty's vessel, the "Bluebell," had become generally aware that a hostile scheme was being attempted, and if I describe to you what was observed by those on board the sloop "Bluebell" in relation to the vessel carrying arms, you will be in a position to appreciate the general character of the plan which was formed in order to give effect to the high treason conceived and commenced on the soil of Germany. The "Bluebell," on 21st April (Good Friday), was patrolling in the neighbourhood of Tralee when she sighted a suspicious ship flying the Norwegian ensign, and with four Norwegian ensigns painted forward and aft on each side of the vessel. The captain of the "Bluebell" hoisted a signal demanding the name of the apparently Norwegian vessel, and making inquiry about her destination. The reply was given that she was the "Aud," of Bergen, bound for Genoa. The captain of the "Bluebell" informed the vessel that she must follow the "Bluebell" to harbour. The captain of the "Aud" answered—and it was noticed that he spoke in broken English—"Where are you taking me to?" The "Bluebell" thereupon intimated that she would go ahead and that the "Aud" was to follow immediately after. The "Bluebell" then proceeded to go ahead, but the "Aud" remained without moving, and a shot was accordingly fired across her bows. She then asked, "What am I to do?" and was again ordered to follow, and thereafter she did follow. She was escorted by the "Bluebell" without further trouble or incident until next morning, when they passed abreast of the lighthouse not far from Queenstown. Then the "Aud" hoisted a signal, "Where am I to anchor upon arriving in harbour?" She was informed that she was to await orders, but meanwhile to continue to follow the "Bluebell." On nearing the Daunt lightship the "Bluebell" headed for the harbour and the "Aud" stopped her engines. The "Bluebell" went back to her, and, when about a cable's length away, those on board the "Bluebell" saw a small cloud of white smoke issuing from the starboard side of her after-hold. At the same time two German ensigns were broken at her mast and two boats were lowered, one from the port side and the other from the starboard side. The "Bluebell" fired one round across the bows of the "Aud," and thereupon the boats hoisted two flags of truce, and the men put up their hands. They were then taken prisoners on board the "Bluebell," and placed under armed guard.

Attorney-General

These men were German bluejackets, doubtless a picked crew, nineteen sailors and three officers. The " Aud " sank almost immediately afterwards, about a mile and a quarter S.S.E. of the Daunt Rock lightship. Since then divers have ascertained that her cargo consisted of rifles, not German rifles, but Russian rifles of the 1905 pattern.

Gentlemen, you will not forget that, so far as it is proper in affairs of this kind to connect these matters by inference, we have established that the prisoner in Germany was attempting to seduce Irish soldiers from their allegiance with the object of forming a brigade which, or some of whose members, were to take part in an insurrection in Ireland. We shall find the prisoner Bailey a member of this brigade, and a man called Monteith, as to whom I can give little information to the Court, and who has avoided arrest—we shall find them being conveyed evidently with a definite method and purpose, but by an agency which I cannot explain to you, to Ireland. We find contemporaneously a German vessel, which has taken every means of disguising her German character, approaching the shores of Ireland with considerable quantities of rifles on board. And the association between these various events is apparent and needs no labouring.

I will continue now the local story. At about four o'clock on the morning of Good Friday, on which these men must have landed at Tralee, a boat was found a few yards from the shore by one, John M'Carthy, a farmer living at Curraghane. In the boat was a dagger, and at the same time M'Carthy found in the sand a tin box containing pistol ammunition. There were found subsequently, also buried in the sand close by or in the neighbourhood, three Mauser pistols, two handbags containing pistol ammunition, several maps of Ireland foreign in origin, a flash lamp, a large flag, two life-belts, and three coats. The number of the coats supports other evidence to the effect that the party consisted of three men. In the pocket of one of the coats there was found a railway ticket from Berlin to Wilhelmshaven, dated 12th April, 1916. M'Carthy, struck in a neighbourhood in which unusual incidents are rare by the discoveries which he had made, carried his inquiries a little further, and he then noticed the footprints of three men leading from the shore towards his house, and continuing through his yard to a stile leading in the direction of Ardfert.

At about a quarter-past five on the same morning three men, of whom one has been identified as the prisoner, were seen by Mary Gorman, a farm servant, passing along the road, also in the direction of Ardfert. The police were informed, and several officers, including Sergeant Hearne and Constable Riley, searched the neighbourhood, and in what is known locally as M'Kenna's Fort the prisoner was found to be in hiding. M'Kenna's Fort is called a fort; but I am informed by those who have seen it that it is not, as one might understand from the word " fort," so much an edifice above as an excavation below the ground, affording good cover for a man who wished to lie hid. The prisoner gave his name, on being challenged, as Richard Morton, of Denham, in Buckingham. This was the address from which the letter of gratitude to Sir Edward Grey had been written. He described himself to the police as an author. He was asked what he had written. He replied he had written " The

Preußisch-Hessische Staatseisenbahnen.

Bettkarte Nr. 0113

Fri Berlin Stadtb. —

Wilhelmshaven

Zug D 6/D 146/D 112/D 122
(ab Friedrichstr. 9$\underline{30}$ Nm.)
in der Nacht

vom .... zum ....

Wagen Nr. ....

Platz Nr. ....

Gültig für ....

I. Klasse. Preis: 10,00 M

Vormerkungsgb. 0,50 M

Zusammen: 10,50 M

Nur gültig in Verbindung mit einem Fahrausweis I. Klasse.

The Railway Ticket from Berlin
to Wilhelmshaven.

"Life of St. Brendon." He said he had come to Kerry from Dublin; had arrived at Mount Brandon on the 19th, had left there on the 20th, had slept at a farmhouse close by, and that he intended to go to Tralee. All these statements were false. He was then taken to Ardfert Barracks.

On the way to the barracks he was seen by a boy named Martin Collins to drop a paper from his coat. The paper was subsequently picked up, and it was found to be a code. It is not necessary that I should read the whole of this code—it is a lengthy document providing for many contingencies—but it is, I think, convenient that I should call attention to one or two of its terms which throw a light on the character, object, and scope of the prisoner's adventure. It contained such contemplated messages as the following:—"Await further instructions. Await "favourable opportunity. Send agent at once. Proposal accepted. "Proposal received. Please answer by cablegram. Have decided to stay. "Communication again possible. Railway communications have been "stopped. Our men are at . Further ammunition is "needed. Further rifles are needed. How many rifles will you send us? "How much ammunition will you send us? Will send plan about land- "ing on . Await details about sending on . "Send another ship to . Preparations are made about " . Send rifles and ammunition to . Cannons "and plenty of ammunition are needed. Send them to . Send "more explosives to . Send a vessel if possible."

Such, gentlemen, were the communications which it was expected by the prisoner and his German friends that the adventure in which he was engaged might require to pass between him and them. We are now in a position to connect this landing quite simply, quite clearly, and quite inevitably with the acts of seduction and the treasonable plans which were outlined in Germany. The Irish Brigade was to fight in Ireland. The prisoner attempts a landing with confederates and arms, and he carries a code which enables him to ask for another ship, for rifles and ammunition, for cannon and plenty of ammunition, and for more explosives.

At Ardfert Barracks the prisoner was charged with landing arms and ammunition in County Kerry. He replied by asking whether he might have legal assistance. On the 22nd April he was brought to England in custody and handed over to Inspector Sandercock, of the Metropolitan Police, to whom he made the statement: "I am Sir Roger "Casement, and the only person to whom I have disclosed my identity "is a priest in Tralee, Ireland."

Such, gentlemen, in a general outline, is the case which the Crown undertakes to prove and upon which the Crown relies. I have, I hope, outlined these facts without heat and without feeling. Neither in my position would be proper, and fortunately neither is required. Rhetoric would be misplaced, for the proved facts are more eloquent than words. The prisoner, blinded by a hatred to this country, as malignant in quality as it was sudden in origin, has played a desperate hazard. He has played it and he has lost it. To-day the forfeit is claimed.

Sir Roger Casement.

Evidence for the Prosecution.

John Anthony Cecil Tilley, C.B., examined by the Solicitor-General—I am a chief clerk at the Foreign Office. I produce a letter, dated 19th June, 1911, signed "Roger Casement," and addressed to Sir Edward Grey, from the Savoy, Denham, Bucks. I also produce from the records of the Foreign Office an official history of Sir Roger Casement—exhibit No. 33. That history is correct, and it describes Sir Roger Casement's career as it appears on the records of the Foreign Office. Sir Roger Casement was in receipt of a pension which was paid quarterly. The last payment was made on 30th September, 1914.

Mr. Sullivan—I have no questions.

John Richard Cole, examined by Mr. Bodkin—I am acting senior examiner in H.M. Paymaster-General's Office, Whitehall. Government pensions are payable from that office. Sir Roger Casement was in receipt of a pension payable through that office. It is the practice for the person in receipt of a pension to make a claim for the pension quarter by quarter, and to sign a receipt on its being paid. The amount of Sir Roger Casement's annual pension was £421 13s. 4d., payable quarterly, less income tax. I produce five receipts, each of which purports to be signed by Sir Roger Casement, and ranging between October, 1913, and October, 1914. The last is dated 7th October, 1914.

Cross-examined by Mr. Sullivan—I notice the date is changed on the last receipt. Did you receive it in advance of the date becoming due?—It is claimed for the September quarter, and, of course, it could not be paid till Sir Roger claimed it.

What I am aiming at is this. Would these receipts be sent out from time to time in advance of their becoming due?—They were sent out in blank except for the amount in figures.

The date?—There is no date on them.

I take it you did not receive it yourself?—No, the bank gets the money.

When did this first come into your possession?—In October, the last voucher.

By the Lord Chief Justice—Let us understand what happens. There are forms which are sent out without date?—Quite so.

Then the recipient of the pension fills in the date and pays it into his bank?—Quite so.

The bank pays it and it comes to you?—Yes.

And you get the receipt with the date?—Yes, and we keep it.

John Cronin, examined by the Solicitor-General—I live at 2 Carroll's Place, John Street, Cork. When the war broke out I was a private in the 2nd Battalion of the Royal Munster Fusiliers. I was sent to France, and I landed in that country on 13th August, 1914. On 27th August I was wounded and made prisoner at a place called Etreux. I remained there for a time, and then I was sent to Sennelager Camp in Germany. From there I was sent to Wesel Hospital, where I remained till 7th December, 1914, and then I went to the Munster Prison Camp, where there were about twenty-one Irish prisoners. The Irish prisoners were in a separate room from the other British prisoners. I was moved on 22nd December, 1914, from that camp to Limburg. The twenty-one Irish prisoners who were with me at the Munster Camp were also removed to the Limburg Camp. There were over 2000 other prisoners at Limburg when I got there—I think the total number was about 2400. They were all supposed to be Irish, and, judging from those I spoke to, they were Irish. I spoke to nearly every man in the camp.

Did you see anybody there besides the prisoners and the Germans who were in charge?—I did.

Whom did you see?—The prisoner in the dock, whom I now recognise. I first saw him in the camp about a week after I got there. He was dressed in civilian clothes, and was going round the camp with papers. One of the papers was called *The Gaelic American*, and another was called *The Continental Times*.

Did he go where he liked, or was he under restraint?—He could go where he liked.

Did he seem to be in charge of any one?—No, he had the full privilege to go where he liked. That day when I first saw him I heard him speak to seventy or eighty of us in a crowd. He came up to us and addressed us, and introduced himself to us.

By the Lord Chief Justice—He said that he was going to form an Irish Brigade, and he said, "Why live any longer in hunger and misery in "this camp when you can better yourselves by joining the Irish Brigade "which I am going to form; you will be sent to Berlin as the guests of the "German Government."

Examination continued—Did he say what this Irish Brigade was to do?—He said in the event of Germany winning a sea battle he would land them in Ireland, and Ireland would equip them.

What were they to do in Ireland?—Free Ireland.

Did he say who they were to fight against?—Against England.

Did he say what would happen to them if Germany did not win?—They would be sent to America; they would get £10 or £20 pocket money and a free passage. I have told the jury now what I remember of the speech he made on the first occasion when I saw him. He was asked who he was, and he said that he was Sir Roger Casement, the organiser of the Irish National Volunteer movement. I saw him at the camp on several occasions after, but I did not go near him, and I therefore did not hear again what he said. When I knew what he was about I avoided him.

You talked about Sir Roger Casement having those papers with him. Did any one give you these papers?—The German authorities sent them into the rooms—that is, *The Continental Times* and *The Gaelic American*, and also a little book, "Crimes Against Ireland," written by Casement. I read this literature, but I did not bring away any of these papers or the book with me as we were not allowed. We were searched when we left.

What was the book about?—(Question objected to. Objection sustained.)

Shown exhibit 4, being address headed "Irishmen"—I saw a paper like that in Limburg Camp. This document was sent down to us from those people who joined the Irish Brigade. There were four of them posted up in our barrack-room for the information of those desiring to join the brigade.

By the LORD CHIEF JUSTICE—Did you ever see Casement in your barrack-room after these were posted up?—No, I saw him in the camp after they were posted up, but not in the barrack-room.

Examination continued—I saw them posted up after Casement had been in the camp. He came again to the camp after they were posted up. When I was at Limburg, 52 out of the 2400 prisoners joined the Irish Brigade. The first to join was Quinless, who was a corporal in the Royal Irish Regiment. Others who joined were Keogh, O'Toole, Bailey, O'Callaghan, and Cavanagh.

Look at exhibit 5. Did you see that photograph, which is handed up, in *The Gaelic American*, the paper you have mentioned?—Yes. I saw a copy of the paper in the camp in July, 1915. I recognise some of the men who appear in that photograph.

[This photograph was on a leaflet and not in *The Gaelic American* itself, and Mr. Sullivan objected that the leaflet was not admissible; it was not shown to have anything to do with the prisoner, and not being admissible, a description of it could not be asked of the witness. The Court ruled that the question could be put, as the picture presented the same picture which the witness had described as being in *The Gaelic American.*]

The man on the right I recognise as Quinless, of the 11th Royal Irish Regiment; next to him, Cavanagh, of the South Irish Horse; next to him O'Callaghan, of the Munster Fusiliers; in the middle, Bailey, of the Royal Irish Rifles; the tall man next to him I do not know by name; then there is Keogh, of the Connaught Rangers. The little man on the left is a German in the Irish Brigade uniform. That uniform was silver grey. There were some that had a green shade. Quinless and Keogh had a different uniform to the remainder; they had a brighter grey. They held the rank of feldwebel in the Irish Brigade—that is the German for sergeant. There was a green shamrock on the cuff, and a green collar, and then on the cap there were a shamrock and a button. When we first went to Limburg we were fairly well treated as regards our food. After Casement had spoken to me at the camp I found a difference in my treatment. They reduced us from 750 grammes to 300 grammes of bread, and mangolds were substituted for potatoes. I do not know what happened to the men who joined the Irish Brigade.

They were sent up to a camp near Berlin, and I had nothing to do with them. I was exchanged and sent back to this country from Limburg Camp on 2nd February, 1916.

Cross-examined by Mr. SULLIVAN—Where were you when war broke out?—At home.

Were you a reservist?—Yes.

You were in civil employment at the time?—Yes.

I suppose you had been living in Cork for some years?—The latter part.

Immediately before you rejoined the colours you had been there for some years?—Six years and a half.

You told us, I think, that you had once seen Sir Roger Casement before?—Yes.

That was in Cork?—Yes.

Evidence for Prosecution.

John Cronin

In connection with the Irish Volunteer movement, was it not?—Yes.

That was a considerable time before the war, eight or nine months?—Just about that time.

Can you fix a date yourself?—I could not fix the date.

Can you fix even the period of the year at which you saw him there?—I could not say. I know it was 1913.

He was at that time organising the Irish Volunteers?—Yes.

In Ireland?—I could not be sure whether it was him or not. There was a hostile demonstration there.

You told us that you had seen, or that you thought you had seen, Sir Roger Casement before. Assuming you were right in your impression that it was Sir Roger Casement you had seen, was that nine months before the war?—Something like that.

It was in the year 1913?—Yes.

Assuming it was Sir Roger Casement, was he at the time engaged in recruiting for the Irish Volunteers?—Addressing the meeting.

Was he at a public meeting?—It was a public meeting; it was in the City Hall.

You went there yourself?—I did.

Being in the City Hall at the meeting you attended yourself, did you know that the meeting was summoned for the purpose of organising the Irish Volunteers?—Yes.

For the purpose of recruiting for them?—Yes.

And to get money to supply them with arms?—I could not tell you anything about that.

Was there not a little jingle of money about the project?—No.

Was not that one of the objects of the meeting, to raise funds?—I do not know.

As well as raising recruits?—I do not know what the object of the meeting was.

You attended it yourself?—Yes.

And you tell me that at the City Hall, although you attended the meeting yourself, you are unable to say what was the object of the meeting at which you were present?—The object of the meeting was about the Volunteers.

You told me that they were appealing for recruits?—That was their object, I suppose.

I want to know in addition to that, were they appealing for the means of getting arms for their recruits?—I could not tell you.

This was in 1913. Had you been present at any other meeting?—No.

I think you said something about there being a hostile demonstration at this meeting?—Yes.

Was the hostile demonstration caused by some expression of approval with regard to the Ulster Volunteers?—Yes.

The meeting being hostile to the Ulster Volunteers?—I do not know about that. It was broken up then as far as I know.

You were present at the meeting that was broken up, and you told me the disturbance was caused by the fact that some person made some approving allusion to the Ulster Volunteers. Was it after that that the meeting was broken up?—Yes.

John Cronin

Was it in consequence of that, as far as you could see, that the meeting was broken up?—I could not tell you.

At all events, in the City of Cork there was a feeling of very strong hostility to the Ulster Volunteers. Is not that so?—I do not know.

By the LORD CHIEF JUSTICE—It is quite possible, I suppose, it was broken up in consequence of that?—I suppose so.

By Mr. SULLIVAN—You rejoined the colours and you went out to France?—Yes.

And we have you at Limburg. You recognise Sir Roger Casement as being the person who addressed you at Limburg?—I partly knew him when I saw him.

You partly knew him from this interesting episode in Cork?—I would not be sure, but I thought I had seen him before.

At this meeting in Cork?—I do not know properly where I had seen him.

You do not like to commit yourself to that. What I want to get at is, have you a clear recollection of what he said to you when he saw you in Limburg?—Yes.

I suppose you cannot recollect everything he said?—I could not. I have not the brains of a solicitor.

Did he speak of raising the Irish Brigade in Limburg in connection with the Irish Volunteers in Ireland?—Yes.

Did he say that they would fight in Ireland?—Yes.

That they were to fight in Ireland?—Yes.

And for Ireland?—Yes.

And for nobody else?—For nobody else, only for Ireland.

Did he say they were to be landed in Ireland after the war was over?—No, in the event of Germany winning a sea battle.

In the event of Germany winning a sea battle, they might be landed before the war was over?—The war could not be over till the sea battle was won.

That is a still more remote date than the one I suggested to you. I want to know, did not he speak of Germany having won the war before the brigade was to move to Ireland?—No.

He did not speak of Germany winning the war before the brigade was to move to Ireland?—No.

But the seas were to be clear before the brigade was to go to Ireland?—Yes.

Did he state that the brigade was to be financed, the money provided for it, by Irishmen in Ireland and in America. Do you remember his saying that?—No.

But he told you that if Germany failed to win the war the members of the brigade would be sent to America?—Yes.

Instead of to Ireland?—Yes.

Were you in any way connected with any of the Volunteer movements in Ireland?—No.

Before you left Cork, in fact, was there a Volunteer force, an armed force, in the city?—There was a Volunteer force, but they were not armed.

Had they any arms?—I never saw them going out.

Was this a volunteer force organised in antagonism to the Ulster Volunteer force?—I do not know.

Evidence for Prosecution.

You do not know?—No.

Did it, at all events, purport to be? Did the people connected with it purport to be in opposition to the Ulster Volunteer force?—I was not interested in it.

You did go to the meeting?—Yes, for curiosity.

At their meeting, at all events, was it not perfectly clear that the population were organising against the Ulster Volunteers?—I did not hear it mentioned.

Reference to the Ulster Volunteers created an uproar?—It created an uproar when they said, "Three cheers for Sir Edward Carson."

And then——?—The meeting ended.

There was an uproar?—Yes.

The meeting did not seem to be in favour of Sir Edward Carson?—I do not think so.

How long did you remain in Limburg Camp?—From 23rd December, 1914, till 2nd February, 1916.

You were discharged from Limburg?—Yes, on the 2nd February this year.

You were there all the time. What was the latest date at which you saw Sir Roger Casement there? Can you fix the date?—About the middle of February.

Which year?—1915.

The speech that he made to you, the speech that you listened to, must have been some time about the beginning of January, I gather?—Yes.

His visits to the camp were between the beginning of January and the middle of February?—Yes.

Can you say how often he was there, to the best of your recollection?—I saw him on five or six occasions myself.

Five or six occasions within that six weeks?—Yes.

When was the food ration reduced in Limburg?—The end of February, 1915.

Was there any change in the food ration later?—Yes.

When was the next alteration in food ration?—Somewhere about April.

Was there any further alteration before you left?—No, no more after that.

The ration you gave in your direct examination, was that the last ration you were receiving, 300 grammes of bread and mangolds?—Yes.

That was the last ration you were receiving?—Yes.

That represents the final amount to which you were reduced at the April reduction?—Yes.

Could you tell me what was the reduction at the end of February? It was reduced from 750 grammes to 300 grammes of bread at the end of February.

Then what was the reduction of the ration that took place in April?—The reduction of rations which took place in April was they gave me no potatoes, only mangolds.

The potatoes were cut off in April?—Yes.

By the Lord Chief Justice—Do you mean it was in April that you got the mangolds instead of potatoes?—Yes.

By Mr. SULLIVAN—Was the reduction in rations universal through the whole camp?—To the British prisoners' camp?

Yes. Did the reduction of rations apply to every one who was left in the camp?—Yes, to everybody who was left, of British prisoners, but there were Russians and French.

There may be a difference; are you not an Irishman?—There were Russians and French there as well.

At all events, the rations were universal?—To the British, but the French rations were not reduced.

And the Russians?—I do not know Russian. I could not speak to them.

You had refused to join this Irish Brigade?—Certainly.

At the outset, in January?—Yes.

There was no doubt or question about that?—No, but I was marched up to the French lines every fortnight to know whether I would join.

It was clear from the start that you were not going to join?—Quite clear.

By Mr. JUSTICE HORRIDGE—I understood you to say they kept on trying at you, and marched you up to the French lines every fortnight?—Yes, till the day I left.

By Mr. SULLIVAN—Up to the day you left, in February, 1916?—Yes.

Did the men who did join leave that camp and go away?—They did, and they came back in uniform.

And went away again, I suppose?—They were there now and then in the camp.

Re-examined by the ATTORNEY-GENERAL—When you say you were marched to the French lines every fortnight to try to get you to join, who gave you the orders?—The gentleman and interpreter in charge of the three companies. There were three companies, and we were marched up, thirty at a time, in charge of those who joined the Irish Brigade, and a German officer.

When you were marched to the French lines, who asked you this question?—Quinless and Keogh.

And that, you say, lasted as long as you were there?—Yes, till I came home.

DANIEL O'BRIEN, examined by Mr. TRAVERS HUMPHREYS—I was formerly a private in the Leinster regiment. I joined that regiment in 1912, and about a month afterwards I was transferred to the 19th Hussars. I went with that regiment to France. I was wounded in the retreat from Mons, and I was taken prisoner while I was in hospital. I was first taken to a place called Doberitz, where there were about a couple of hundred prisoners from Irish regiments. From there I went to Limburg along with the other Irish prisoners that I have mentioned. We arrived at Limburg about 15th December, 1914. When we got there there were only about 50 other men in the camp, but afterwards there were about 2500 Irish prisoners of war.

Besides the prisoners of war, do you remember any one else coming there, anybody who made a speech?—Yes.

Who?—Casement. I recognise the prisoner as Casement. He spoke to all the men. I heard him make a speech for the first time about

19th February, 1915. I heard him say, "Now is the time for Irish-"men to fight against England; now is their opportunity for doing so; "join the Irish Brigade." He said he came to form an Irish Brigade, and he wanted all Irishmen to join the Irish Brigade and become guests of the German Army. He said that if they were successful in winning the war they would land the Irish Brigade along with the German Army in Ireland, and they would fight against England there. If Germany did not win the war, then they would be sent by the German Government to America with a guarantee of £5 and a situation. I do not remember anything else that he said. He said a lot—I cannot remember all of it—but what I have told is the substance of it.

How did the men who were listening behave?—They behaved all right till they began to find him out. They behaved all right for a quarter of an hour, and then they found out who he was, and they hissed him and booed him out of the camp. I saw one of the Munster Fusiliers actually push him. That Munster Fusilier got shifted out of the camp.

Did you join the Irish Brigade?—No; if I did I would not be here to-day.

Did anything happen to the men who refused to join the Irish Brigade?—Yes, we got punished; we got our rations cut down. I heard Sir Roger Casement speak only once, but I saw him in the camp several times. The time when he made the speech that I heard was the first time that I saw him. I saw him in the camp about twice after that. He was walking about on those occasions. I know about a dozen who joined the Irish Brigade; there were fifty-two all told who joined the Irish Brigade. The names of some who joined were Quinless, Royal Irish Regiment; Keogh, Royal Irish Regiment; O'Callaghan, Connaught Rangers; Bailey, Royal Irish Rifles; Cavanagh, Royal Irish Horse; O'Toole, Irish Guards. Shown exhibit No. 5—I recognise in that picture Quinless on the right; then next to him Cavanagh; then a man whose name I do not know; then Bailey, O'Toole, and Keogh. I believe that the man at the end is an interpreter. I saw the men wearing the uniform in which they appear in the picture. The men who joined the Irish Brigade were sent away to Berlin.

The Lord Chief Justice—That they were sent away is all that the witness can say.

Examination continued—When they came back in the uniform did they stay with you and the other prisoners?—No; they were kept separate by themselves. Shown exhibit No. 4, address headed "Irishmen"—I saw a document like that in the barrack-room while I was in camp at Limburg. I first noticed it after Casement came and visited us. I read it.

Whereabout in the barrack-room was it?—They were sent round to each barrack-room, brought round by a German soldier to each barrack-room. I left Limburg in February of this year; I came over here as an exchanged prisoner of war.

Cross-examined by Mr. Sullivan—Can you tell me how long after you arrived in Limburg that the speech of Sir Roger Casement took place?—About two months.

Were you moving about the Irish camp?—Yes.

Did not you hear any other speech but one?—That is all.

Did you see him speaking in the camp prior to that?—Yes.

How often?—I saw him once speaking, but I saw him in the camp afterwards.

Do I understand you to say that besides this speech you have reported to us you saw him delivering another speech?—No, I saw him in the camp. I did not pay any attention to him.

You yourself never saw him delivering any speech except the one you listened to?—That is all I saw.

I suppose you cannot recollect everything he said?—No.

Did he first of all speak about the Irish Volunteer movement?—No; he spoke about the Irish Brigade.

Did not he mention the Irish Volunteers?—He might have done. I did not hear him. I was not there at the beginning of it.

Did you only listen to a small part of his speech?—That is all, and went away.

You only heard a small part of his speech?—Yes.

But in what you did hear did he speak of the Irish Brigade fighting in Ireland?—Yes.

Did he say the Irish Brigade would be used in Ireland only?—In Ireland.

Did he say they were to be transferred to Ireland when Germany had won the war?—Yes.

And if Germany failed to win the war they should go to America?—To America, yes.

Arrangements would be made to have them go to America. Did you speak to Sir Roger Casement at all yourself?—No.

You did not say anything to him?—No.

You simply remained in the camp, I gather, and said nothing and did nothing?—No, because I could not do.

When were your rations reduced?—Just after Casement went away.

Was that the end of February?—About a week afterwards.

Was it about the end of February?—It was getting on close to the end of February.

Have you not been speaking about the 19th February?—Yes, the 19th February.

How do you fix the date of the 19th February?—Because I have good reason to.

By the LORD CHIEF JUSTICE—You are asked how you fix it?—Because my rations were cut down about a week afterwards. I shall never forget it.

By Mr. SULLIVAN—Your rations were cut down at the end of February?—Yes, about the end of February.

And you fix the 19th by reference to the date of the cutting down of your rations, which was at the end of February?—Yes.

That is why you say it was the 19th when you heard the speech. Were the rations cut down for every man in the camp?—Every man.

And was recruiting going on after Sir Roger Casement left?—Yes.

The recruiting for the Irish Brigade went on as usual?—Yes.

Although the rations had been cut down?—Yes.

For everybody?—For everybody.

Evidence for Prosecution.

In April was there a fresh cutting down of rations? Were the rations cut down further in April?—Yes.

What reduction of rations was made at the end of February?—I could not exactly tell you, but it was very small.

By Mr. JUSTICE HORRIDGE—What was it you say was very small?—The amount of bread. That is what we were living on, a piece of bread, and what we were getting.

By Mr. SULLIVAN—And in April was your ration further reduced by substituting mangolds for potatoes?—Yes.

Was that universal in the camp?—Yes.

Did recruiting for the Irish Brigade still go on?—Yes.

I think you mentioned in your evidence about 52 men?—About 52 men joined the Irish Brigade.

Is that in the whole period of recruiting?—Yes.

Up to the time you left Limburg Camp?—Yes.

Re-examined by the SOLICITOR-GENERAL—To take you back for a moment to the speech you heard Sir Roger Casement make, he said the Irish Brigade were to fight in Ireland?—Yes.

Did he say who were to take them to Ireland to fight?—The German Army.

Did he say against whom they were to fight?—To fight against England.

By the LORD CHIEF JUSTICE—There is one question I want to put. You told us there were some 2500 altogether in the Limburg Camp?—Yes, my lord.

Were any steps taken to find out whether the 2500 were Irish?—They were supposed to be Irish.

Why?—It was supposed to be an Irish camp. They all came as Irishmen to this camp.

Before they were removed to the camp was there anything done to find out whether they were Irish?—Yes.

What?—You had to put your name down, and where you were born, and your religion.

Were there any but Irish regiments there?—Yes, mixed—English, Scotch, and Irish.

At Limburg?—Oh, no, at the various camps before we went to Limburg.

There were English, Scotch, and Irish at the various camps. When you went to Limburg what regiments were there?—They were all mixed—English, Irish, and Scotch—but they were all supposed to be Irish.

They were mixed regiments, not only Irish regiments?—All regiments.

You say they were all supposed to be Irish. What do you mean by that?—It was supposed to be Irishmen who went to Limburg Camp. It was supposed to be a special camp just for Irishmen alone.

JOHN ROBINSON, examined by Mr. BRANSON—I live at 45 Ross Street, Bristol. I was a corporal in the Royal Army Medical Corps. I joined the Army in June, 1906. At the outbreak of war I was stationed at Dublin. I went to France on 19th August, 1914, attached to the 13th Field Ambulance, and on 24th August, 1914, I was taken prisoner at Thulin. I was wounded in the head, and also in the knee and in the shoulder.

Sir Roger Casement.

John Robinson

I was taken to hospital at Recklinghausen, in Germany, and from there I went to the prisoner-of-war camp at Sennelager. There were other Irish prisoners there. No difference was made at the start between the British prisoners who were Irishmen and the British prisoners who were not, but a difference was made about three months afterwards, when the Irish Brigade was formed. The Irish prisoners were all taken away and put in a hut by themselves. We Irish prisoners only had camp work to do, while the rest had to work and carry and saw wood. I left Sennelager Camp with the rest of the Irish prisoners—some 200 or 300—on 23rd December, and went to Limburg. The prisoners at Limburg were all supposed to be Irish prisoners. I remember Sir Roger Casement coming there after I had been there a little while. I recognise him as the prisoner. I saw him in the camp.

What was he doing there?—He was speaking with the Irish Brigade.

Speaking about——?—The Irish Brigade. I did not catch all he said, but I remember him saying, "Now is your chance to fight for Ireland "and free it. I am very glad to see you here. This is the only chance "you will have to fight for Ireland. Why do you not join the Irish "Brigade?" Then he spoke about the treatment of Ireland in England. That is all I remember.

What was the Irish Brigade to do?—They were supposed to land in Ireland and free Ireland.

By the LORD CHIEF JUSTICE—Tell us what you heard him say—not what they were supposed to do?—That is about all I can remember at the present time. He said he was very glad to see so many Irishmen here, that now was our time to fight for Ireland and strike a blow, and he hoped we would all join the Irish Brigade.

Examination continued—Did he say with whom the Irish Brigade were going to fight?—Fight against England. He said that if Germany had a victory on the sea they would land the Irish Brigade in Ireland, but if Germany did not win at sea then we were all to go to America. At the start there was no money mentioned, but at the end of the speech he said that we would all get £10 in money and be sent off to America. He did not say who was to give us the £10.

How many people were listening to this?—There were generally about forty or fifty, sometimes thirty. I heard him make speeches on four different occasions. About a week or so would elapse between the different occasions.

What sort of reception did he get from those who were listening?—Very poor; he did not get a good reception. On one occasion he was struck, and on another occasion I saw him get pushed. When he was struck he swung his umbrella round to keep the prisoners off him, and when he was pushed he walked out of the camp. There was no one with him at that time. A couple of German sentries came on the scene the second time I saw Casement there, and he went out of the camp with them. On that occasion the crowd that was round was getting a bit excited, and they did not want to listen to him. Shown exhibit No. 4, address headed "Irishmen"—I saw that in the Limburg Camp. It was a form very much like this; the same size, only what I saw was typewritten. It was in the centre of the camp when I saw it. A fellow had it in his hand,

and there was a crowd round reading it. There was a kind of buff form handed round with questions on.

Who gave you these forms?—The Germans. I got one, and I filled up the answers to the questions. Every man had to fill up the document and hand it back to the Germans. I handed my document back, and I have not seen it since. I stayed at Limburg for five months, and I was shifted from there to Giessen. I did not join the Irish Brigade. There were about 150 other prisoners taken to Giessen. None of them had agreed to join the Irish Brigade. As far as I can remember, between fifty and sixty at Limburg joined the Irish Brigade. I did not see any of those persons at Giessen. I remember the names of one or two of the prisoners who joined the Irish Brigade—Bailey, Keogh, Quinless, and O'Toole. I saw some of the persons who joined the Irish Brigade in uniform—a green uniform with a little harp on the collar and a harp on the cap. I had never seen the uniform before. On 8th October I was exchanged and came back to this country.

Cross-examined by Mr. SULLIVAN—How long was Sir Roger Casement speaking on the occasions that you have detailed to us, the first time you heard him speak, for instance?—About a quarter of an hour to twenty minutes.

Can you remember all he said?—No.

Or do you only remember bits?—A few words or so.

He wanted you to join an Irish Brigade?—Yes.

Did he say that the Irish Brigade was to fight for Ireland?—Yes.

Did he say it was to fight in Ireland?—Yes.

And did he address you? Did he say it was to go to Ireland when the Germans had won the war?—No, he said if Germany had a victory on sea.

Did he speak about Germany winning the war?—Yes.

What did he say about Germany winning the war?—He always said that Germany would win, but we contradicted him, and said they would not.

You have done your best to stop it, anyhow?—I have done a little bit.

I suggest to you that he represented when Germany had won the war that the Irish Brigade was to go to Ireland unless there was a victory at sea meantime. Was that what he said?—I cannot remember that. I remember him saying if Germany had a victory on sea he would land us in Ireland.

But there is no doubt it was in Ireland you were to serve?—Oh, yes, at that time.

Did he speak of the sources of payment?—Yes, there was £10 mentioned.

Was the £10 mentioned owing to somebody asking what was to happen if Germany never won the war?—Of course, I could not say that. I was not there always.

What had happened immediately before the £10 was mentioned?—He was just speaking about the Irish Brigade, and somebody asked him about money, and he said we would get £10.

Were they to get £10 in any event, or were they to get £10 to go to America with if Germany failed to win?—£10 if they joined the Irish Brigade.

In any event?—Yes.

John Robinson

Are you sure of that?—Yes.

Is it true that he always spoke on the assumption that Germany was going to win the war?—Yes.

And his idea was, in that event he wanted to free Ireland. Did he say that?—Yes.

Did one or two men ask him what would happen supposing Germany did not win the war?—Yes.

Was it then that the statement was made about the £10?—In or about that time.

And about sending them to America?—Yes. The £10 was to join the brigade.

Was not the date of this speech about a fortnight after you got there?—Yes, about a fortnight.

Did not you get there about the 23rd December?—Yes.

A number of Irishmen reached the place at the same time, about the 23rd December?—Yes.

In the commencement of his speech did he say there was no money in it?—Yes, at the start.

At the start he said there was no money in it, and you tell me that although he told you there was no money in it he also told you in the same speech you would get £10 merely for joining?—Yes. That was the second time I heard him speaking.

Was it the second time that the £10 came in?—Yes.

Are you sure of that?—Yes.

Was not the £10 to take you to America?—I never heard about that.

You are a native of Belfast, I think?—Yes.

How long have you been with the colours?—About ten years.

I suppose from time to time you have been back in Belfast?—Yes.

Have you spent any time in Belfast during the last five years?—Yes.

Any long period of time? Have you been there for any considerable time?—Yes.

During the last five years?—Yes.

You have spent long periods of time there. Did you hear Sir Roger Casement in his speech refer to the formation of the Irish Volunteers in Ireland?—I never heard him speak about it.

At any time?—I never heard him speak about it.

You never heard him at any time describe himself as the organiser of the Irish Volunteers in Ireland?—No, I do not think I ever heard that.

Are you sure about that, or is it that your memory fails you?—No, I never heard him speaking about that.

During the time you were in Belfast during the last five years had you seen bodies of armed Volunteers going about Belfast?—Yes.

Nobody interfering with them?—No.

When first did you notice these armed Volunteers in Belfast?—Do you mean the National Volunteers or the Ulster Volunteers?

Were not there both sets?—Yes.

The Ulster Volunteers were formed first, were they not?—Yes.

And the National Volunteers were formed later?—Yes.

To resist the Ulster Volunteers?—Yes.

Evidence for Prosecution.

John Robinson

Did you attend any of the meetings that were held in Belfast in connection with the armed Volunteer movement on either side?—No.

Was there great excitement in Belfast about the meetings that were held?—Not very often.

Did you read any of the reports that were circulated about the formation of those bodies?—No.

You read none?—No.

When did you leave Belfast prior to the war?—The 5th August, 1914.

You practically joined from Belfast?—Yes.

Had you been in civil employment?—Yes.

I did not appreciate that, I beg your pardon. Up to the moment you left Belfast were there bodies openly parading Belfast without objection from anybody?—I could not tell; I do not know much about the Volunteers.

You could see armed men marching about, not soldiers or policemen?—I have seen armed men.

Marching about?—Yes.

Re-examined by the SOLICITOR-GENERAL—You told the jury that you heard Sir Roger Casement say that if Germany won a victory at sea the Irish Brigade would be landed in Ireland?—Yes.

Did he say who would send the Irish Brigade to Ireland?—Germany would send us to Ireland.

Did he say what they were to do when they got there?—Free Ireland.

Did he say whether they would have any fighting to do?—He did not go into that; he said it was to free Ireland when they got there.

Did he say from whom they were to free Ireland?—From England.

By the LORD CHIEF JUSTICE—Have you got exhibit No. 4 before you?—Yes.

Can you tell us did you ever see that document in the camp when Sir Roger Casement was there?—Yes.

Was he actually in the camp?—Yes.

Do you remember when that was?—In or about May.

What was being done with it?—There were about a dozen copies of it issued round to the men; there were two or three posted on the doors of the barrack-room.

When you say twelve were issued to the men can you tell us were the men reading them?—Yes.

Several of them?—Yes; it was issued round to groups; several would get in groups, and one man would read it.

You said in answer to the Solicitor-General Germany would send the Irish Brigade to free Ireland from England when they got there?—Yes.

Who do you mean by "they," when "they" got there?—The Irish Brigade.

WILLIAM EGAN, examined by the SOLICITOR-GENERAL—I live at 14 Barrett Street, Dublin. I was born in Kingstown, and I went to school in Dublin. I joined the Royal Irish Rifles in September, 1904. There was a man named Bailey in the same regiment whom I knew; I had gone to school with him. When the war broke out I went with my regiment to France in August, 1914. I was wounded at Neuve Chapelle in October,

1914, and I was taken prisoner by the Germans. I was taken to Cologne, where I was put into the hospital, Lazarette, No. 6. I remained in Cologne close on three months, and then I was sent to Limburg. I got there about 3rd February, 1915. I saw Bailey there.

Did you recognise him at once and speak to him?—Yes, he spoke to me. On 19th February I was passing the camp—at the time I was in a delicate state of health—and I saw a man speaking to three prisoners. He was a tall man, dressed in dark clothing, with a long coat, a soft hat, and he carried an umbrella on the left arm. I passed on and did not take any further notice. I am doubtful whether I should know the man again. After that I had two pamphlets given to me. One of them was given me by a German officer. I think it was called "How to Free Ireland," but I am not sure. I also received a book along with the pamphlet. It was given to us by a German sergeant. I only read a small part of the book; it was concerning '98. The title was "Crimes Against Ireland "and How to Free It," and it was edited by Sir Roger Casement. I did not bring it away with me from the camp as I was forbidden. Shown exhibit No. 4—that is what I have called the pamphlet. It was given to me by a German officer; I tore it up. Besides that document I was given another form by a German sergeant. I left it on the table. There were many of them in the room at the time, but I was not allowed to bring one away.

What were you to do with that form?—We were to answer the questions that were on it. I filled in the answers and gave the form back to the sergeant. While I was there a number of the prisoners joined the Irish Brigade, among them being Bailey, Scanlan, and Greer, all from my regiment, the Royal Irish Rifles. Being shown the photograph, exhibit 5—I recognise five out of the six men in that photograph. The first man on the right is Quinless, the third man is O'Callaghan, the centre man is Bailey, the sixth man is Keogh, and the seventh man is a German interpreter of the name of Metz. I saw some of the men who joined the brigade after they joined it. Their uniform appeared to me to be of a silver-grey with green facings, and there was, I am not sure, whether it was a harp or a shamrock on the collar, but a crown without the harp in the cap. I had not seen this uniform before till I saw it on the Irish Brigade. I only saw two men wearing a belt—Bailey and Quinless. I saw them coming from the town of Limburg; they passed me on the road; they both had belts and side-arms of a German pattern on. I did not join the Irish Brigade. About fifty-two men joined the brigade. After this we seemed to get treated worse because we would not join the brigade. The food was cut; they made our allowance in the food less than it really was. I arrived in England on 7th February this year; I was exchanged. When I left Germany Bailey was at Zossen. He used to come to Limburg for recruiting purposes. I did not speak to Bailey after he joined the brigade. I saw him at the Castle at Dublin on 6th May, 1916. I recognised him there, and he seemed to know me.

Cross-examined by Mr. SULLIVAN—You lived in Dublin when the war broke out?—Yes.

Were you in civil employment?—I was.

Living there in Dublin?—Yes.

Evidence for Prosecution.

William Egan

Where were you engaged; what business were you in?—I was a porter in the City of Dublin Steam Packet Company.

Were you in Dublin on the Sunday before the war broke out?—I was.

Could you remember where you were on that Sunday?—I was at Kingstown.

Were you in the city at all during the afternoon?—Not to my knowledge.

You were out at Kingstown?—Yes.

The Sunday I am referring to is the Sunday of the Hogue affair; do you remember the Sunday that the goods were landed at Hogue?—I do not remember.

Were you not in the city that day?—No.

The war broke out a few days afterwards?—Yes.

Even prior to that incident, did you see Volunteers armed and drilling in Dublin?—No.

Did you see them drilling?—No.

You never saw the Volunteers drilling in Dublin?—No.

Or marching through the city?—No.

Did you ever see them at all until you left Dublin?—I was not interested in them.

Without being interested in them, if a body of armed men, who were neither policemen nor soldiers, passed you in the street would you notice them?—I would.

Did such bodies pass you in the streets in Dublin?—No.

Are you sure of that?—Yes.

You never saw them?—No.

With regard to the recruiting that you say was going on in Limburg, when were your rations reduced?—They were reduced in February.

At the end of February?—About the middle of February.

Some time in February at all events?—Yes.

What rations were reduced?—The bread rations.

Was it reduced for every one in the camp?—It was.

Was there a further reduction of rations in April?—Yes.

For every one in the camp?—Yes.

There was no more reduction of rations after April?—No, not that I know of.

Was not recruiting going on for the Irish Brigade after that?—It was going on all through my time there.

So that it was not only the men who did not join, but every one in the camp had their rations reduced, had not they?—The men who joined the brigade, their rations were not reduced.

Were not they removed from the camp?—They were, to the top of the camp.

They were removed to a camp of their own?—Yes.

Was it within the same lines?—Yes.

But they were removed to the top of the camp?—Yes.

They had privileges that no one else had, you say?—Yes.

Better food?—Yes

And given new uniforms, apparently?—Yes.

Sir Roger Casement.

Michael O'Connor

Michael O'Connor, examined by Mr. Bodkin—I am a corporal in the Royal Irish Regiment. My home is in Wexford. I went with the British Expeditionary Force in August, 1914, and I was wounded and taken prisoner by the Germans on 20th October. After a little while I was taken to Darmstadt, and then about the middle of December I went to Limburg. When I first got to Limburg there were about 300 Irish prisoners of war there. Shortly after they were joined by other 1600, who came from Hamlin, Sennelager, and Munster, so that there would be about 2000 British prisoners who were Irishmen. I remember seeing Sir Roger Casement at Limburg about the end of December, 1914. I heard him addressing some men. He said, "Now is the time for to fight or strike "a blow for Ireland," and that England was nearly beaten. I should think there were about seventy men listening to him. I was on the outskirts of the crowd. I have told all that I heard him say. I saw him on that later occasion, but I did not hear what he said. The people were hissing and booing him down the lines that day. He said that those who hissed him were followers of Johnnie Redmond, the recruiting sergeant of the British Army. A sergeant-major of the 4th Dragoon Guards called Casement a traitor. That sergeant-major was sent to Giessen or some other camp for punishment along with Corporal Robinson. These are the only occasions on which I saw Sir Roger Casement at the camp. I left the camp in the next autumn, in October. I saw two books at the camp. One was entitled "Crimes Against Ireland," by Sir Roger Casement, and the other was entitled "The King, the Kaiser, and Ireland." I could not see any author's name to that last production. Shown exhibit No. 4, address headed "Irishmen"—I saw that in printed form in the camp. It was not in typewritten form. I could not tell how it came to be amongst the men in the camp, but I know the books and the papers, *The Continental Times* and *The Gaelic American*, were distributed. I saw the document which is similar to exhibit No. 4 shortly after getting to the camp. I could not tell the exact date, but it was long after Sir Roger Casement addressed the first meeting. I could not say whether it was before or after he addressed the second meeting. I left Limburg in October, 1915, and I came home as an exchanged prisoner of war. I saw Bailey in Limburg Camp on a couple of occasions, and I also saw him in Dublin when I got back.

Cross-examined by Mr. Sullivan—You fixed the date of the first time you heard Sir Roger speak at the end of December?—Yes.

The next time about the 3rd of January?—Yes, the next time about the 3rd of January.

Have you a pretty clear recollection of how the dates stand?—Yes, in January.

January was the second occasion?—Yes.

The other may have been earlier?—It was close at the end of December, about the 22nd.

What was the last time you saw him in camp?—The 3rd of January.

You never saw Sir Roger Casement in the camp afterwards?—No, but I heard he was there on the 19th.

Do you remember ever hearing of his being there afterwards?—No.

The 19th of February was the last day upon which you ever heard he was there, but you did not see him on that occasion?—No, I did not.

Evidence for Prosecution.

In that first speech how much did you hear, two or three minutes, or ten minutes?—I was just on the outskirts of the crowd; I heard them passing remarks.

Did you remain on the outskirts of the crowd only a few minutes?—Yes.

You stayed there as long as there was anything going on, I suppose?—No.

Did you go away after a few minutes?—Yes.

You heard him say that England was nearly beaten; did you hear him suggest the war was nearly over then?—No, I did not.

England was nearly beaten?—He could have said it, but I did not know.

If England was nearly beaten, was not it in the context that the war was nearly over?—It might have been.

Then whatever he was talking about, he spoke of it in the context that the war, at all events, was nearly over?—Yes.

Do you assent to that?—I assent to that.

The war being nearly over, he was recruiting an Irish Brigade?—Yes.

MICHAEL MOORE, examined by Mr. BODKIN—I am No. 3457, Royal Army Medical Corps, serving on H.M.S. "Cambria" at Dover. My home is in Kilkenny. On 9th August, 1904, I joined the South Lancashire Regiment, and then I was transferred to the Royal Army Medical Corps. I went with that arm to France in August, 1914. There I was taken prisoner, and sent to Sennelager Camp. I stayed at Sennelager from 1st September till 22nd December, when I went to Limburg Camp. There were others with me, all Irishmen, and they came from different regiments. They numbered about 2000, and they came from Sennelager. At Limburg, when I got there, I found other regiments there from other camps. I remember Sir Roger Casement coming to Limburg Camp. I had been there for about a week before I first saw him. I saw him passing through the lines, and at the end of the lines I saw him speaking to some men. I could hear what he said. The first occasion on which I heard him address any men was on or about 3rd or 4th January, 1915. He told them he came there for the purpose of forming an Irish Brigade, and wanted the men to join it. That is all I heard him say on that occasion. About the end of February, very nearly two months later, I heard him again address other men in the Russian Camp at Limburg. When any Irishmen joined the Irish Brigade they were sent up to the Russian Camp. I saw, roughly, about fifty there; they were dressed in khaki, except one or two who were in Irish Brigade uniform. I know the names of those one or two. Keogh was one, and Dowling was another. Quinless was also there. Keogh and Dowling were the only two in that new uniform. The others who had joined the camp were in khaki, and some in civilians' clothes. Those who had joined the Irish Brigade stayed in the Russian Camp; the Russian lines are in the same camp. The other Irish prisoners who were in the Russian part of the camp had been marched up under an escort. That was only on one occasion; I was only taken up on one occasion. On that occasion I was marched up by a German escort. We were marched up a section each time; that would be about forty-five or fifty men. When I got there on the occasion on which I was one of the section I saw Keogh and Dowling there and Sir Roger Casement. Sir Roger Casement asked those men to join the Irish Brigade, I being among the men, and he said any man that

Michael Moore

would join the Irish Brigade he would give him uniform, better food, and better housing. He also said in case of the Germans losing the war he would send those men to America, give them a free passage, and £10 or £20 pocket money, and guarantee employment in America. The Irish Brigade was to be sent from Limburg to a camp outside Berlin; he said they were to be the guests of the German Government. He also said the first German victory on the water he would land the brigade in Ireland.

Did he say what kind of victory?—Naval victory. The Irish Brigade were to be landed in Ireland. I expect they were to be landed in Ireland from German vessels. I did not hear him say how the Irish Brigade were going to get to Ireland, but he said he would land them in Ireland. There is nothing more I can tell that I heard Sir Roger Casement say that day. I came back to the camp. I never heard him on any other occasion—only on two occasions. As to how what he was saying on this day that I listened to him was received by the men, some hissed and booed him. Nobody agreed to join on that occasion. After that we were marched back down to our own camp. Our rations were cut down about February or shortly after February, about a week or fourteen days after this speech I heard. I saw a book entitled "Crimes Against Ireland" in the camp. That book was printed in English. There were three or four copies between every room. They were distributed by the Germans. (Shown exhibit No. 4.) I have seen a paper similar to that in camp. I have seen more than one. They were distributed to the men by the Germans. They were distributed amongst the men some time about the month of February. I could not exactly say whether it was before or after this speech of Sir Roger Casement which I have been telling about, but it was about that time. Papers were also distributed, *The Continental Times* and *The Gaelic American*. I left Limburg in October of last year as an exchanged prisoner. After a little while I rejoined the Royal Army Medical Corps at Aldershot. The uniform in which those two men were was a light green uniform with dark green facings; it was a German pattern tunic. They wore German side-arms, a brown belt, and a German bayonet.

Cross-examined by Mr. SULLIVAN—Apparently Sir Roger Casement discussed what was to happen to the Irish Brigade if Germany lost the war, did not he?—Yes.

In that event the Irish Brigade would go to America?—Yes.

If Germany lost the war. I suggest to you that he said that he would land them in Ireland if Germany won the war?—If there was a sea battle, and if Germany came out victorious in the first sea battle, he would land the Irish Brigade in Ireland.

Did he speak of the Irish Volunteer movement?—Not to my knowledge.

Or did he speak of the Home Rule movement in Ireland or getting Home Rule for Ireland?—I have never heard him.

Was there no reference to Home Rule in the event of Germany winning the war? Was there no reference to Home Rule?—There was one, that Germany would give Ireland Home Rule.

If she won the war?—If she won the war.

But do you tell me that there was no reference to Home Rule to be won by the Irish Brigade?—No.

Are you sure of that?—I have never heard him say it.

Evidence for Prosecution.

JOHN NEILL, examined by the SOLICITOR-GENERAL—I live at Borris, Balnagree, County Carlow. I am No. 4231, 2nd Battalion, 18th Royal Irish. I was wounded and taken prisoner at La Bassee. I was taken to Hanover, where there were other Irish prisoners.

What happened just before you left Hanover?—There was a German general came there and he inquired for all Irishmen——

Mr. SULLIVAN—This is something which took place at Hanover with which the prisoner is in no way connected.

The WITNESS—He inquired for all Irishmen.

The LORD CHIEF JUSTICE—Wait a moment; it is not necessary to have that.

The SOLICITOR-GENERAL—The charge is that the prisoner aided and supported the German Government. Helped them in what? In seducing British soldiers to join the German Army or fight for the Germans. That means they were all engaged in one common object for one common purpose. I submit we have a right to prove what the Germans were trying to do when we are proving that the prisoner helped to do it. May I read one passage from Archbold, where the cases are summed up at page 400: "In cases of conspiracy, and of high treason encompassing "the King's death, &c., or in which the case for the Crown is that the "crime was the result of a conspiracy, anything said or written by one of "the accomplices, not as a confession simply, but for the purpose of "furthering the common design, is admissible evidence against the "others"; and there are other passages of the same kind.

Mr. SULLIVAN—I will call attention to the fact that there is no charge of conspiracy here at all. I quite agree that in a case like *Mulcahy* you may possibly have charges against a man of being engaged in conspiracy by way of treason with a number of individuals. Having charged that, you may first prove the conspiracy and then prove any acts of Mulcahy—where the act of each conspirator is held to be the act of every member of the body, but where it starts with no conspiracy, to assume that a conspiracy has been not only charged, but proved, is the first step in what is now sought to be done, namely, the admission of this evidence. But there is no charge against Sir Roger Casement of conspiring with any person or persons in Germany. There is no allegation that he confederated with any member of the German Army in doing this; the charge before you, my lord, is a charge simply of doing an act which is the personal act of the man himself, and in the absence of some connection, even in that case, the acts of his agents for the furtherance of his purposes, if you prove them to be his agents, are to be admissible, but the statements and acts of persons whom, as far as the evidence goes, he has never seen in his life cannot be introduced, I submit.

The LORD CHIEF JUSTICE—May it not be a step in proving he was adhering to the King's enemies in Germany?

Mr. SULLIVAN—I submit not. What is proposed to be put in evidence, as I understand from the notice furnished, is, first of all, a speech, or observations, made by a German general at a place where Sir Roger Casement is never alleged to have been; it is in some strange camp. Assume the charge is that he adhered to the King's enemies, the statement of one of the King's enemies is not the evidence of that charge, I most respectfully submit.

The Lord Chief Justice—Not the mere proof of the statement made by one of the King's enemies, but I understand the way it is put by the Crown is that he was working in assisting the King's enemies, and in that sense was adhering to them by a number of acts which are then given as the overt acts.

Mr. Sullivan—That is the charge.

The Lord Chief Justice—This evidence is said to be given as a step in proving he adhered to the King's enemies, the fact that the man went from Hanover to Limburg, of course, is clearly admissible; that you would not object to.

Mr. Sullivan—Your lordship will take my submission.

The Lord Chief Justice—The only other point is whether the general's observations are admissible.

[Their lordships conferred.]

The Lord Chief Justice—I understand you to press the point. You want us to rule upon it, Mr. Solicitor-General? We shall have no hesitation in ruling if you desire it; the only question is whether you think it is sufficiently important.

The Solicitor-General—I strongly submit I am entitled to put it, but I do not press it strongly at all, that I should ask what was said. I did want to ask whether a speech was made; I do not care very much whether he tells the jury or not what was said.

The Lord Chief Justice—That is the only point upon which there can be any discussion. I do not think there is any doubt what the ruling should be, but what is the value of it if you get it? I suggest it is hardly worth pressing if you get the fact of the speech.

The Solicitor-General—Then I will not press it. I recognise the objection, but not any argument in favour of it.

Examination continued—About three days before I left Hanover a German general came there and he called all the Irishmen together. Then he made a very small speech to us. He told us how the English behaved very badly.

The Lord Chief Justice—We must not have that.

Examination continued—After that small speech he never called us together any more. Nothing else happened before I left Hanover. When I left Hanover I went to Limburg. A draft of 150 Irishmen came with me from Hanover to Limburg. There were quite a few soldiers with me who were not Irishmen. When we got to Limburg some of those who were not Irishmen were found out and sent away to some other place; where we never knew. When I got to Limburg I saw Sir Roger Casement there. I saw him on the evening when we got to Limburg. That evening he said how all the Irishmen looked very smart and very soldier-like men, and that after a short time at Limburg he would bring all the Irishmen back again and make them as smart as ever. Casement did not say that to me; he said it out to the crowd. When we got to Limburg we were all together, the whole draft of 150 who had come from Hanover. Casement made a speech to all of us. On that evening he never mentioned anything about the Irish Brigade, but he told us in his speech that on the following Sunday we were all to go to church service. He said that all the Irishmen there at present should have clothes, and footwear given to them; we were to get wooden shoes on the following morning, and were to be well fed, and well looked after by the Germans. That is what he said to us on the evening we got there. Personally I did not know who he was: he never told us his name on that evening—not for a couple of evenings afterwards. That is nearly all he said that evening as well as I can remember. Next morning we got the wooden clogs, and Sir Roger was in the camp on the following morning again. He did not say anything to us then about joining the Irish Brigade: he never mentioned anything about the Irish Brigade at that time. He came into all the barrack-rooms. He never told us who he was. As near as I can remember that was on a Friday, and it was on Thursday we arrived. On the Friday he came again to the camp, and then something happened on the following Sunday.

On the Sunday we went down to church service, and we went into a barrack-room where church service was supposed to be going on. When the crowd of us went into the barrack-room we saw Sir Roger on a table; he was getting ready to give a speech in the barrack-room. He had an Irish Brigade book in his hand. He said he was going away for the space of a fortnight, and when he came back he wanted to see fifty names in this book, and with the fifty names which were to be in this book for men to join the Irish Brigade he was going to form an Irish Brigade. He also said the German Government would equip the brigade with arms and ammunition and uniforms. He also mentioned something about pay; that the Irish Brigade would get something about from £10 to £20. He did not say where they would get that from. He also told the Irishmen on that Sunday that they were all to join this brigade, and that if Germany ever gained a naval victory they would land the Irish Brigade in Ireland, and to strike a blow for old Ireland once again and to gain Home Rule. He also said how the Germans were very much like the Irish and the Irish very much like the Germans. Personally I did not believe that. He also said that Ireland had the strongest power now in the world at her back. That is all I remember. He also said he would leave the Irish Brigade book with some sergeant over some section, and whoever wanted to join this brigade was to sign his name to this book, and when they joined the Brigade they were free men, and they would be sent to Berlin and well looked after. He also wanted to know if all the men there at the meeting were all true-bred Irishmen. No one signed the book on that day. The book was left with some sergeant—I forget the name of the sergeant whom it was left with. Casement then went away. I think he came back on the following day. He did not do anything on that day so far as I recollect. He gave no speech or anything like that, but he visited both barrack-rooms again. Then he left us, and it was a fortnight before he came back again. I did not see anything of the book after he left or before he came back again—I never saw anything of the book. He said he was going to Berlin for that. As to the date when he came back, to the best of my memory it was either at the latter end of December or early in January.

When he came back on that occasion he said something to the men.

Sir Roger Casement.

John Neill

He told the Irishmen then, when he came back, that he was very disappointed to see that there were no names entered in his book for this Irish Brigade, and he also wanted to know what were the Irishmen thinking of if they said they would not go and fight for their country now at this time, and that England was completely beat, and that there was no danger of their not being landed in Ireland, and that he was the head man over the Irish Volunteers in Ireland, and that he was very proud to see how smart-looking they looked, and he also hoped to see the Irish Brigade would soon be formed, and to go and fight for Ireland. No one signed the book that day. I never saw any one sign the book at all. When Casement went away I cannot say whether anybody went with him. When he came back the second time a corporal of the name of Corporal Quinless joined the Irish Brigade. That was on his second visit to Limburg—the one I have been speaking of at the end of December or early in January. On that occasion Corporal Quinless joined. Corporal Keogh also joined. After they had joined they left the camp. I saw them afterwards, and when I saw them again they were dressed in a uniform. It was a greenish-coloured uniform, something like the German uniform, and there was a harp and a shamrock on it. I cannot say whether they had any arms. They had no arms with them in the barrack-room that I was in when we were brought up to visit them in this barrack-room or this Irish Brigade office. When they came back to Limburg Casement was there, but he was not with them in the barrack-room. When these two men came back they stayed in one of the barrack-rooms down at the top end of this camp, and all the sections of the remaining Irishmen were marched up in sections to this Irish Brigade office, and brought before these three men, and asked different questions about their country and what they thought of the Irish Brigade, and now was the time to fight for old Ireland and gain Home Rule once more. There were three men—Quinless, and I think the other two men were two namesakes, two Keoghs. It happened more than once that we were marched up before these men. Some of the men enlisted in the Irish Brigade. When the men had joined the Irish Brigade they were sent to Berlin.

Casement then went away for a month. He said he was going away for a month, but he never said where he was going to, and he wished to see this brigade very strong when he came back. He came back in about a month after, and a clergyman, Father Nicholson, came there next. When Casement came back he just told these people that joined the Irish Brigade when this Irish Brigade was formed they were first to go to help the Turks against the Russians. After he came back Sir Roger Casement spoke to the men in my hearing. He spoke to them in the camp in No. 1 Lines, No. 1 Company, No. 2 Battalion. He used to come into the barrack-rooms. He made a speech in several places—outside and inside in the barrack-rooms he made these speeches. Those are the words that passed from Casement on this occasion—first of all, the Irish Brigade were to go and help the Turks against the Russians, and, secondly, they were to go and help the Germans against the British, and, thirdly, they were to go and shed blood for their own native country. I heard him say those things. I never saw Casement after that. There were fifty men joined the Irish Brigade up to the time when I came away from Limburg.

The treatment and food got very bad. We noticed there was a great difference in it from the first time we went to Limburg. We were well treated for about a fortnight, or near that; then the food commenced to be reduced. The bread was reduced, the meat was reduced, and potatoes were reduced. I came away from Limburg on the 20th May, 1915.

Cross-examined by Mr. SULLIVAN—You have told us that you heard Sir Roger Casement speak about the Irish Brigade fighting for the Turks against the Russians; is that true?—Yes, that is true.

Did you tell anybody that it was Quinless had stated that to you?—Quinless also stated that.

At the same time or at a different time?—At a different time.

Who was present when Sir Roger Casement stated it?—There were about fifty present or more.

Do you know Michael Moore, of the Royal Army Medical Corps? Was he in the camp with you?—You see I forget them all. I could not recognise every man in the camp.

(At this stage Michael Moore came into Court.)

Did you see this man in the camp?—I might have seen him, but I forget him.

I will have to have Robinson and Cronin in. Did you know Daniel O'Brien in the camp?—No.

Did you know Michael O'Connor in the camp?—Yes.

Was he present there?—Yes, he was in the camp.

On this occasion?—I cannot say on this occasion, but he was in the hospital some time in Limburg.

What date do you fix for the speech about the Turks?—I disremember the dates. I cannot think of all, you know.

As near as you can go?—I cannot think of any dates.

Can you fix the date you arrived at Limburg?—As far as I can go, we arrived at Limburg early in December, 1914. That is as near as I can go.

How long after that did you hear this talk about the Turks?—I have heard the talk about the Turks several times.

How long after that did you hear the talk about the Turks by Sir Roger Casement?—He just mentioned about the Turks once.

How long was that after you had arrived in Limburg? Listen, is this true, "Casement came back about the 1st of February, 1915." Is that true?—Yes.

"And Father Nicholson came at the same time." Is that true?—Yes, that is true. Father Nicholson came there about that time.

Then that is true. Would this be true, that you saw Casement in the camp at this time, but he did not speak to you, and you never saw him again? Is that true?—At the time I never saw him. He went away. I have seen him several times in Limburg.

On this occasion, will you fix the date of the occasion, the only occasion, so it should be rooted in your mind, that you heard him speak of the Turks?—I cannot speak to the date I heard him speak of the Turks because I disremember.

You disremember the dates?—Yes.

You cannot say was it early or late?—I cannot say.

Was it the time he came with Father Nicholson?—Yes.

It was the time he came with Father Nicholson?—Yes, it was on his third visit.

Did he come with Father Nicholson more than once?—No.

Did you yourself fix the date of Father Nicholson and Sir Roger Casement coming back to the camp as the 1st February, 1915?—I did not.

Do you remember making the statement of the evidence that you were to give?—Yes.

To whom did you make the statement?—To some one at the War Office.

How long ago?—On 27th May last.

Was it taken down in writing in your presence?—Yes.

And you signed it?—Yes.

Was it true?—Well, there was a lot of it; very nearly it all was true.

Am I to understand there was a lot of it that was not true?—You are not to understand there was a lot of it that was not true.

Was it all true?—Yes, it was all true. My statement I gave there, yes, it was all true, only I did not give them all my statement; I forgot something, but brought a lot of it back to my memory since then.

Listen to the statement that was all true at the time: "Casement "came back about the 1st February, 1915, and Father Nicholson came at "the same time." Was that true?—Yes, that was true.

About the 1st February, 1915?—I cannot fix the date, you know.

Did you fix the date?—To the best of my opinion it was about that time he came there.

"When Casement came back we were marched up to Barrack No. 41 by "sections, as usual, and Quinless told us that Casement had told him to tell "us that the Irish Brigade was to fight on the Western Front with the "Germans against the English, and next to help the Turks against the "Russians, and the next was to shed blood for our native country." Did you say that?—Yes.

Was that true?—Yes.

"I saw Casement in the camp at this time, but he did not speak to "me. I never saw him again." Was that true?—On that previous evening I did not see him.

Let me give it you again: "I saw Casement in the camp at this "time"—this was about the 1st February, 1915, when he came back with Father Nicholson—"but he did not speak to me. I never saw him "again." Is that true?—He did not speak to me on that evening. I did not see him; he went away out of that camp on that evening, but I saw him afterwards. I did not see him again on that evening.

"I never saw him again"?—On that evening.

Was it true? I will go further. "I heard that he gave an address "to the Munsters in their barracks, and that they shouted him down. I "could hear the shouting going on." Do you not see you are pointing the fact that you never saw him again, although you heard he was in a different part of the camp?—On that evening he did address the Munster Fusiliers in the barracks.

But you were not there?—I was not in the lines.

You could only hear shouting?—He was a free man in Germany, and could go about where he liked.

Follow me again; I will give you every opportunity of understanding.

Evidence for Prosecution.

Was it true, of the 1st February occasion, that he came to the camp with Father Nicholson, you saw him in the camp, but he did not speak to you, and you never saw him again?—On that evening I never saw him again; but he was in the camp several times afterwards, and I saw him in the camp; I never saw him again on that evening.

You heard he gave an address to the Munsters, and could hear the shouting?—Yes.

But you never saw him?—On that evening after.

Will you give me the date you next saw him?—He was in the camp every day, I might say.

But only once with Father Nicholson?—Only once with Father Nicholson.

That was about the 1st February?—Yes.

Therefore, assuming you put in the words "You never saw him "again that evening," do not you see that you signed a solemn statement of your evidence against a man to be tried for his life, that so far as that day was concerned he did not speak?—He did not speak to me on that day.

And that was the only day he was there with Father Nicholson?—In the camp himself and Father Nicholson separated, going through the camp.

I am talking about days?—Yes.

If he did not speak to you that day, he could not have said anything about the Turks or Russians or anything else?—He spoke about the Turks and Russians, and also left orders with this man that joined the Irish Brigade to tell the Irishmen that joined the Brigade——

Are you telling us what you heard him say, or repeating what somebody else told you; what is it?—I am telling you now about him, what he said.

By the LORD CHIEF JUSTICE—Who is "he"?—Sir Roger Casement.

By Mr. SULLIVAN—Was it what he said in your presence?—In my presence and in the presence of about fifty more of our men—that when they joined this Irish Brigade they were to go and help the Turks against the Russians on the Turkish frontier, then after that they were to go and help the Germans against the British, and then after that they were to go and shed blood for their own native country.

And after that?—He said no more then. He said that in the presence of my comrades and myself.

Did you tell us in your direct examination that was the day he was in camp with Father Nicholson; did you tell us that?—There was so much uproar in this camp at Limburg, it was very hard to remember all that was said in it.

Did you tell us that that happened on the day he came back to the camp with Father Nicholson?—Yes.

Then why did you tell the gentleman at the War Office that on that day, though you saw him in the camp, he did not speak?—It is very hard to remember everything; there were a lot of things.

You told the gentleman at the War Office that though Sir Roger Casement did not speak, Quinless did say things on that day?—It is very hard to remember a lot of things, you know.

John Neill

May you be wrong in your recollection?—No; I do not think I am wrong in my recollection.

At any time?—Yes.

Now, let us see what happened, and the assurances given you in his speech that you did hear. You heard him say he was the organiser of the Irish Volunteers, did not you?—Yes.

That he was raising an Irish Brigade?—Yes.

Was it in connection with the Irish Volunteers?—Yes.

Did you hear him say that it had been subscribed for by Irish Americans in America?—Yes.

And that they were to fight in Ireland?—Yes.

To win Home Rule?—Yes.

Did he say fight in Ireland only?—At that time only to fight in Ireland.

That was the basis upon which they were being recruited?—Yes.

Did he say that the war was nearly over?—No; he never mentioned anything about the war being nearly over.

Did he speak of what might happen when the war was over?—Yes.

When the war was over, if Germany won, did he say that the Irish Brigade could easily be landed in Ireland?—Yes.

Did he say, if Germany lost the war, on the other hand, they should go to America?—Yes.

So if Germany won, they were to go to Ireland?—Yes.

And if they lost, they were to go to America?—Yes.

Was there any mention of helping them in America, whether they could get any money to help along in America?—Yes.

How much?—From £10 to £20.

If they landed in America?—Yes.

Was that speech made more than once in your presence?—Only once in my presence.

Can you remember the names of the men who were present and heard it?—I do not remember the names of all the men who were present, but all the men came from Hanover; the majority of the men who came from Hanover were present at that meeting.

Cronin is in Court now. I ask that he should stand up. (Cronin stood up.)

Cronin—I did not come from Hanover.

Mr. Sullivan—I am not accusing you of that. Will you face the witness-box for the purpose of the question?

(To witness)—Do you know John Cronin here; did you see him in the camp?—No, I disremember entirely.

I have given you the names of a number of others. You did know Michael O'Connor?—Yes, Corporal O'Connor.

He has been examined. Did you know John Robinson?—I disremember Robinson.

Did you know a man named James Wilson?—I disremember him too.

I want you to give me the name of a human being who was present and heard this speech of Sir Roger Casement on the day that Father

Nicholson was there?—There was another one there, but they are prisoners there now.

Re-examined by the ATTORNEY-GENERAL—How many times do you think you saw Casement altogether?—I have seen him a lot of times.

About how many?—I disremember how many times; he was there so often in that camp.

How long were you there?—I was there for seven months.

Was he there at intervals?—He was there the first time I landed at Limburg.

How many times—not exactly, but roughly—do you think you heard him speak?—I have heard him speak several times, for every time he was in the camp he was all the time talking.

Three, four, or six times, or how many?—Nearer forty-six times.

I do not know, but you can tell us, was it your habit to take notes of what he said, and the dates he said the various things?—I cannot speak of the dates he said these things, but every time I saw him in Limburg he was always talking to the prisoners a lot, and when I passed quite close to him I always heard him speaking of the Irish Brigade.

Were you badly wounded there?—Yes, pretty bad.

Were you able to get about a little?—Yes, I was able to walk about.

When were you first asked about the dates on which he had said anything? Who first asked you to say the day or date on which he said any particular thing?—This gentleman that came from the War Office and took my statement about Sir Roger Casement.

That was the 27th May, was it not?—Yes.

MICHAEL HUSSEY, examined by the ATTORNEY-GENERAL—I am a labourer living at Curraghane. I remember the night of the Thursday before Good Friday. That night I had been seeing a friend, and I was coming home about half-past nine o'clock. When I came home about half-past nine I noticed a light out at sea. It was a red light, and it lasted for a few seconds; about two seconds. I stood for a while looking out at sea at the light. Next morning I went down to the strand to the same place where I was that night and where I had seen the light. I went there for seaweed. On going there I saw a boat up on the sand-banks, above high water. It was at the same place where I had seen the light. I have seen that boat since; I have seen it in Court here, but not in this Court. I have not seen the boat itself, but I have seen a picture of it. I have never seen the boat itself again. I remember going to the police barracks at Ardfert. There I saw the boat. With regard to the red light I saw out at sea, I think it would be about half a mile out at sea at the time I saw it.

Mr. SULLIVAN—I have no question.

The Court adjourned.

Sir Roger Casement.

Second Day—Tuesday, 27th June, 1916.

Evidence for the Prosecution—continued.

John M'Carthy, examined by the Attorney-General—I am a farmer at Curraghane, Curragh Head, about a quarter of a mile from the sea. At the shore there is a wild and rough sea. I remember Good Friday morning, 21st April, 1916. I left my house about two o'clock in the morning. It was dark then. When I left my house I went along the shore towards a well which is over a mile from my house. I did not see anybody or anything on my way, nor did I hear anything. I came the same way back about four o'clock. The tide was coming in then. I noticed the boat that I found; it was coming before the tide, and about 20 or 30 yards from high-water mark on the shore. (Shown exhibit No. 7.) That is a photograph of the boat. There were four oars floating in the water, and I took them up. I could not do anything with the boat; I could not move it as it was too heavy, and I had to leave it there. I stayed there myself about three-quarters of an hour, and then I went to the house and sent my little boy to get a neighbour, Pat Driscoll, to help me with the boat. He and I shifted the boat up a small bit, but we could not do much as it was too weighty. We got the boat only a little bit out of the water. She was full of water, and we had to wait till the tide went down. I found a dagger in the boat. (Shown exhibit No. 8.) That is the dagger I found. There was nothing else in the boat. I found a tin box on the sand. (Shown exhibit No. 9.) That is the tin box I found. It was up on the bank, covered with earth. It was barely covered over. There was a little hole made in the earth and a little wash of earth over it. Some of the earth had been washed away. The box was hitched up with strand cords, and I did not open it. I noticed three footprints on the sand. I did not notice anything more. I did not see anybody at the time.

By Mr. Justice Avory—The three footprints that I saw were the prints of three men.

Examination continued—These prints were going in the direction of my house from the boat. I did not notice whether or not there were any marks of nails in the boots. I could see the footmarks for parts of the way, but in other parts of the way I could not see them. I traced them for about 20 or 30 yards in the direction of my house. I could not see whether they ended at my house or not; I could not find them near my house at all. When I was coming back with Driscoll, after he had helped me with the boat, I met my little girl, who is about eight years of age. She was playing with these revolvers that I now see in exhibit No. 10. Two of them were out of the cases, and I took them to the house with me. Along with the revolvers there was a sort of bag, which is exhibit No. 11. I found it where I got the revolvers. I took them to the house with me, and I sent Pat Driscoll to

The Boat found by M'Carthy, of Curraghane.

the barracks at Ardfert. The police came then, and I gave these things up to them. They also saw the boat, but I was at the boat before them when they came back to me. Coming back from the shore, when I had seen the boat, I did not see anything else, but the police got two bags. I was there when they found them. (Shown exhibits Nos. 12 and 13.) These are the bags they found. The boat, the oars, the bags, the tin box, the dagger, and the pistols were carried to the barracks; I had to carry them up in my cart with a horse. I think the police also got some life-jackets. (Shown exhibit No. 14.) I was there when these were found, and they were all carried to the barracks. The sea was very rough that morning. I did not notice any footprints in my own yard.

Cross-examined by Mr. SULLIVAN—Do you usually get up at two o'clock in the morning?—No.

Or had you been to bed at all?—Yes.

Then you got up this morning at two o'clock in the morning?—Yes.

What got you up so early?—I went to a well.

Thirsty?—No.

What brought you to the well?—Saying a few prayers.

The ATTORNEY-GENERAL—It was Good Friday morning, it being a holy well.

By Mr. SULLIVAN—Being Good Friday morning, did you say it was a holy well?—I heard the old people keep saying it was.

Were you ever saying your prayers at the well before?—No.

It is a long way from your house?—Over a mile.

A dark night; a pretty dark night, was it not?—It was when I was leaving.

You left in the dark, having got up at two o'clock in the morning to say prayers at a well you had never been to before?—Yes.

What made you do it on this particular morning? All your life you had been living at Curraghane, had you not?—Yes.

What urged you, was it your conscience, to get up at two o'clock in the morning?—It was to say a few prayers.

Whereabouts is the well? Would you describe where in the country it is—in what direction?—It was to the north of my house where I live.

What is the name of the well?—It is an Irish well; I could not think of it.

If it is an Irish name you ought to think of it all the sooner, though we are in a strange country?—I have not the Irish.

You have not the Irish of it, but whereabouts is it? Would you describe it to me? What is the name of the place it is at?—Ballyprior.

You did not meet anybody at this well at two o'clock in the morning?—No.

Nobody else was out on Good Friday morning at two o'clock saying prayers at the holy well; is not that so?—That is so.

Nobody else was there?—I saw nobody.

It was dark, and it would be very hard to see anybody, would it not?—It was clearing for day at that time.

You prayed at the well; was it at the well you said your prayers?—Yes.

For how long?—About half an hour.

John M'Carthy

What time was it then when you were thinking of going home to breakfast? What time was it?—I could not exactly tell you; I had no time on me.

You do not wear a watch?—No.

You could not tell what time it was?—No.

Was it daylight now?—Yes, it was dawn.

You did not get home until pretty late that morning?—I did not.

What time was it by the time you got home?—It would be between seven and eight o'clock, I should think.

I mean when you got home the first time; what time was it when you got home the first time?—I would get home, I suppose, about six.

The first time you went home to send the boy?—I would get home before six o'clock or about six

You had then spent the whole of that morning on the strand?—Yes.

Did any neighbours come around the boat?—Yes, they did.

How many of them?—That I could not tell you; I did not count them.

There are not very many neighbours in that part of the country?—They were a deal together when they heard about the boat.

A number of them assembled when they heard about the boat; what number of them assembled?—I should think it would be about fifteen to twenty of them there.

They were tramping up and down all over the place?—Yes.

And of course by the time the police arrived there were the footprints of about fifteen or twenty neighbours and many footprints, there were your two trips; what about the little boy and the little girl; did they go down near the boat?—Yes.

And Driscoll, he came down near the boat?—Yes.

So there were too many footprints to be of any use to the police by the time the police arrived, is not that so?—These footprints were there before anybody came.

Owing to your piety on that morning you were able to see the footprints at the first daylight that came before anybody else was there; is not that so?—Yes.

Mary Gorman, examined by the Attorney-General—I am a servant at the house of John Allman, Rathoneen. I remember the morning of Good Friday last, 21st April. I was about that morning at 4.30, and I saw three strange men passing the gate. The gate is in the yard. They were coming from the sea and going towards Ardfert. I was about two yards from them. The light was bright, and I could see what they were like then. One was a tall man, another nearly as tall, and the third was a small man. The tall man was carrying a knapsack across his shoulders and a walking cane and overcoat. The other two wore dark clothes too, and carried overcoats. They were walking quickly. I saw the face of the tall man. I saw Constable Riley later in the same day, and the tall man that I had seen in the morning was with him. I recognised him. He is in the Court just now, and I now point out the prisoner. The yard in which I was when I saw this man was about two miles from the sea. Our house is a mile from the old castle called Rathoneen.

Evidence for Prosecution.

Cross-examined by Mr. SULLIVAN—At what time was it you saw the three men passing the gate?—4.30.

Half-past four?—Yes.

Are you usually out and about at that time of the morning?—My usual hour is four o'clock.

THOMAS JOHN HEARN, examined by the SOLICITOR-GENERAL—I am a sergeant in the Royal Irish Constabulary, stationed at Ardfert. I remember the morning of 21st April last. I got a report that day from John M'Carthy. A man named Driscoll brought the report to me from John M'Carthy. I went with another constable to Curraghane, and I went down to the strand. I saw John M'Carthy and a number of men there. I also saw a boat on the strand, and I examined it. I got the assistance of the men, and we pulled it on to the sandbanks. (Shown exhibit No. 7.) That is a photograph of the boat. After we had pulled the boat up to the sandbanks I went with M'Carthy to his house, and he handed me a dagger and three pistols. (Shown exhibits Nos. 8 and 10.) These are the dagger and pistols. The boat was a flat-bottomed, four-oared boat, having hoods at the stem and stern about 11 inches high. It was a flat-bottomed boat with a tank on each side—air tanks about 11 feet long. The sides were made of timber. There is a part at the bow, and that was made of canvas. That is what I mean by the word "hood." There was a small hood at the stern also of canvas. When M'Carthy handed me the pistols and the dagger, he also handed me a small black satchel, which is exhibit No. 11—the one nearest to me on the table.

I went down with M'Carthy to make a further search for pistols where the others were found. I examined the satchel, and I found in it a flash lamp, portion of a map, and twenty rounds of pistol ammunition. I identify the flash lamp, the map, and the twenty rounds of ammunition. The map seems to be one of a portion of the coast round Bray. The kind of country that we were searching was a flat, deserted country covered with sand piles or sandbanks. I made a further search, and I found a brown leather hand-bag and three life-belts buried in the sand. (Shown exhibits Nos. 13 and 14.) These are the brown handbag and the life-belts. The constable who was with me found a large black bag, which I now identify as exhibit No. 12. I brought the bags into M'Carthy's house and searched them. In the brown leather bag I found a flash lamp and twenty rounds of ammunition, and there were also some maps, but I am not able to say exactly which maps they were. They are some of the maps which are in my hand just now. There are no maps in the bag now. I sent M'Carthy to the strand, and he brought back a tin box with him (exhibit No. 9). I examined the contents of the tin box, and I found 900 rounds of pistol ammunition in it. I examined the three pistols, and they were loaded. I got M'Carthy's horse and cart, and put all these things on the cart, and then I went to the strand and put the boat on the cart there, and it was taken off to the police station.

On the way to the police station I met Constable Macklin, and I had a conversation with him. I left him with the horse and cart, and I cycled back to the barracks myself. I took Constable Riley along with me. Riley and I took our carbines with us, loaded them, and went and searched the

Thomas J. Hearn

country. We found a man at a place called M'Kenna's Fort. It is a circular Irish ruin, with a trench all round it varying from 9 to 14 feet deep. It is all covered with brushwood. In the fort I saw the prisoner who is now in the dock. I found him at 1.20 in the afternoon. I spoke to him and asked him what he was doing there. He replied, "By what authority do you "ask me the question, and am I bound to answer you?" I then said that I would ask him any question I wished, and he was bound to answer me, and, if he did not, I would arrest him under the Defence of the Realm Regulations. I asked him his name, and he replied "Richard Morton, Denham, Bucks." I asked him what was his occupation, and he said he was an author. I asked him to give me the name of some book he had written, and he said he had written a book on the life of St. Brendon. I asked him what port he arrived at in Ireland, and he said Dublin. He also said that he came to County Kerry and went to Mount Brandon, and had come from Mount Brandon to the fort where I had found him. He said he arrived there at 8 o'clock in the morning—Good Friday morning, 21st April. I asked him if he had any passport or papers about him, and he said he had none. I asked him where he was going to, and he said he intended to go to Tralee. I have told the Court the whole of the conversation that passed at that time. I noticed that the lower portion of his pants was wet, and that there was sea sand on his boots. I took him away then to bring him to the police station on to the public road, and as I came to the public road I met a little boy named Martin Collins. He had a pony and trap. I got him into the trap with Constable Riley, and I sent Riley with him to the house of Mary Gorman, and I followed on foot. I was not with them when they saw Mary Gorman. I remained on the road till Riley returned with the prisoner, and when he came back I took him to the police station. From the police station he was taken to Tralee. After bringing him to the police station I searched him and charged him with being concerned with the landing of arms on the coast of Ireland. I cautioned him, and he replied, "Can I "see a lawyer?"

On searching him I found five sovereigns and eleven shillings. Constable Riley helped me to search him. I did not see Riley taking anything from his pockets; I was not present on the occasion. In the black bag I found a large flag, a green and yellow flag, with a representation of a castle in the centre and some foreign language underneath. I now identify the flag that I found in the black bag. In the black bag I also found a pair of field glasses, a flash lamp, 40 rounds of ammunition, and some wearing apparel. I found a number of maps also in the black bag. These were the remainder of the maps I had in my hands just now. I found a piece of paper attached to one of the maps. (Shown exhibit No. 17.) That is the piece of paper that was found attached to the maps. The paper found in the black bag seems to be a kind of diary, and it begins, "February 16, left Cork, arrived Dublin 12 p.m., February 19, Mary Mac. F. left Dublin, February 23 she went "to Cork, February 23, Murray to Castle, referred H.J.S. 26th, ill in "bed; 26th, left Dublin; 27th, ill there," and a number of further entries, ending up with entries on April 7th, "agreed at last, 7 p.m.; 8th again." Then it looks like Hevesham, I think, and then "11th April, left Dublin "for Wicklow; 12th April, left Wicklow in Willie's yacht." I found that

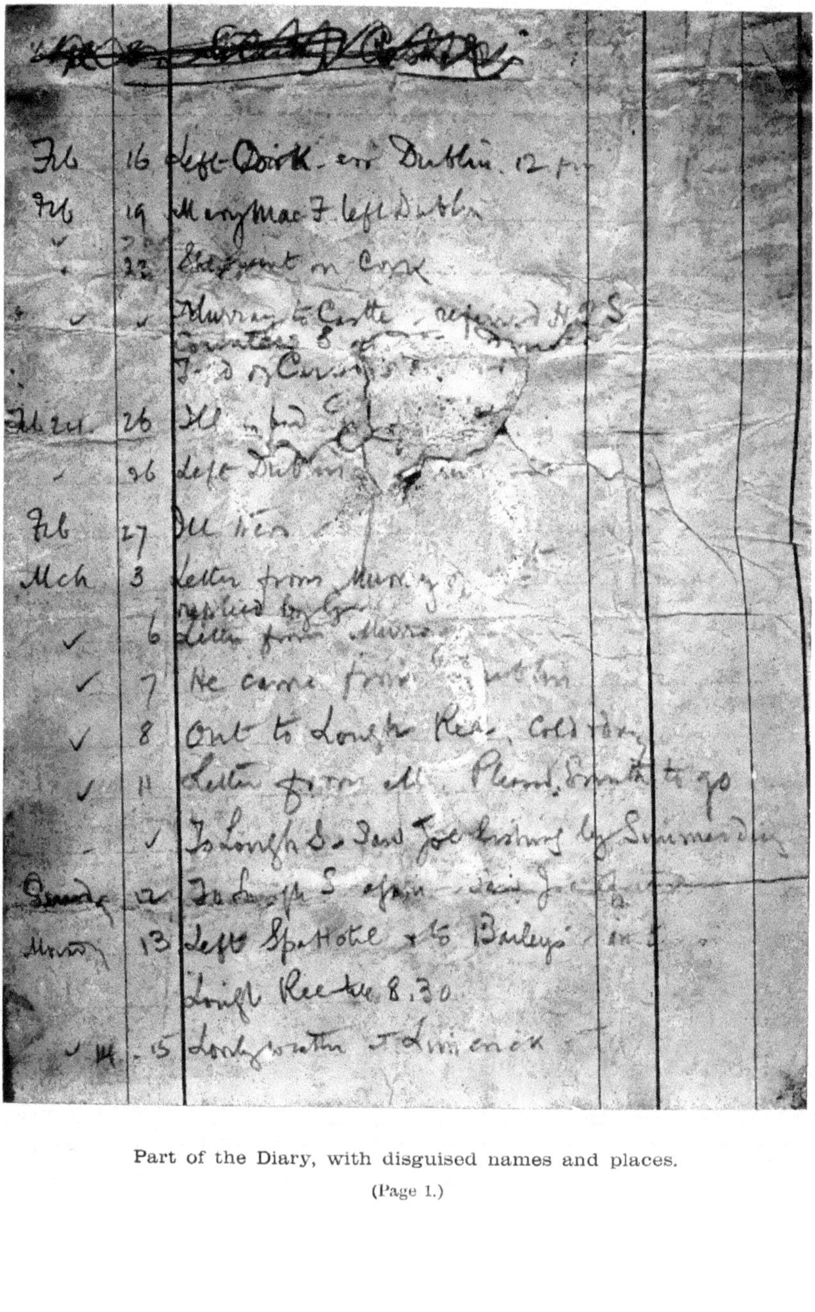

Part of the Diary, with disguised names and places.

(Page 1.)

in the bag. I have looked through those maps which were found in the black bag, and the remainder in the brown bag. I afterwards made a further search at the fort, and I found a portion of a lunch similar to what was found in the black bag. The lunch was rolled up in paper. (Shown exhibit No. 5.) I cannot say whether that was the paper in which the lunch was wrapped; it was not I who found that paper.

Cross-examined by Mr. SULLIVAN—How long were you stationed at Ardfert?—Seven years.

That is from 1909?—Yes.

With regard to this place that you found Sir Roger Casement, it is spoken of as a fort?—Yes.

It is not a fort as we understand it in the present day?—No.

It is one of those old ruins?—An old Danish ruin.

Perhaps a couple of thousand years old?—Yes.

Sir Roger was unarmed?—Yes, he was.

He had no offensive weapons of any kind?—No.

Or defensive weapons?—No.

At all events, he was not in the fort for any martial purpose as far as you could see; is not that clear?—I cannot say that.

When you arrested him did he ask you, or when you cautioned him did he ask you, whether he could have the services of a lawyer?—He did.

And did you answer him that he would enjoy all the privileges of the British Constitution?—No.

What did you say to him?—I said, of course, he could have a lawyer.

You did not refer to the British Constitution?—No.

You have suggested, I think, that Sir Roger Casement was hiding in the fort; in what portion of the fort was he?—He was at the furthest end of the fort from the main road; the fort is 98 yards off the public road, and he was at the further end of it.

Could not you see him?—No, I could not see him, not till we got into the fort.

That is to say, he was in the centre of the circle?—No, he was outside, sitting in the trench, outside the ring of the fort.

Outside the ring of the fort?—Yes.

You eventually arrested him, and charged him, you say, with landing arms?—Yes.

Do you remember, in 1914, before the war, the Arms Proclamation?—Yes.

As an officer of the constabulary, were you concerned in acting under it for a while?—Yes.

Prior to that had there been considerable importation of arms?—Yes.

As a matter of common knowledge in the country, was there, prior to that, a very large importation of arms in the north of Ireland?—Yes.

Was it in consequence of what happened in the north of Ireland that the people were arming so far south as Tralee?—I could not say that.

Did they, at all events, purport to be arming?—They did.

As against the armed person in the north of Ireland?—Yes.

Were they bearing arms openly?—They were.

Without interference by the public authorities?—Yes.

Thomas J. Hearn

And actually on the outbreak of war was the proclamation against the importation of arms withdrawn on the 16th August?—Yes, that is so.

And your directions, even so far as they went to interfere with the importation of arms, ceased on the 16th August on the withdrawal of the proclamation for the time being?—Yes.

And the arming of the population went on then unrestricted for a while?—Yes.

And the parade of arms uninterfered with by any authority?—Yes.

People drilling?—Yes.

Marching?—Yes.

Skirmishing through the country?—Yes.

Without any action taken on behalf of the police. This arming, of course, commenced before the war, did it not?—Yes, it did.

It commenced some time in 1913 in the south, did it not?—Yes.

It had commenced earlier in the north?—Yes.

Was there a great deal of excitement in the south with regard to the reports of what was going on in the north of Ireland?—There was.

I suppose at the police barracks even in Ardfert they read the papers?—Yes.

What papers did you take in the barracks at Ardfert?—The *Cork Examiner* and the *Independent*.

I suppose you read the speeches that were being circulated through your district by the *Cork Examiner* and the *Independent*?—Yes.

And you took no steps to prevent the circulation of the speeches that appeared in those journals?—No.

They reported speeches urging armament on both sides, the *Independent*, at all events; they reported the speeches up in the north as well as the speeches in the south, did not they?—Yes.

The LORD CHIEF JUSTICE—Are you speaking of before or after the war?

Mr. SULLIVAN—Before the war.

(*To witness*)—And their circulation with these speeches you have told me was in no wise hampered by the police authorities?—No.

Did you notice in the speeches reported with regard to the arming in the north of Ireland that the justification for the arming in the north of Ireland purported to be that the majority of members of Parliament for English constituencies objected to the Home Rule Bill; was that put forward in the Ulster speeches?—Yes.

And that although there was a majority in the House of Commons in favour of the bill, that its opponents in the north were justified in arming to resist it because the English members disapproved of it?—Yes.

And were speeches reported to that effect, not only by Irishmen in the north of Ireland, but were there speeches to the same effect reported as having been delivered by distinguished Englishmen from English constituencies who attended these great meetings?—Yes.

And did those speeches in your district greatly affect and agitate the minds of the people?—Well, not in the locality where I am stationed.

Not in Ardfert?—No.

But in the south generally?—Yes.

Evidence for Prosecution.

Thomas J. Hearn

Do you remember shortly before the war broke out the excitement in the south being accentuated by what was known as the Curragh incident?—Yes.

By that time the arming of Ireland, north and south, had gone entirely beyond the control of the police, had it not?—Yes.

If there was to be any protection for the peaceable population from that armed on either side it would lie with the military?—Yes.

After the Curragh incident was not there very grave unrest amongst the people of the country as to whether they could trust that the military would protect them against the Ulster armed Volunteers?—It was believed there was not enough military in the country for their protection at the time.

And the Curragh incident had thrown some doubt on their willingness to act, had it not?—Yes.

In that state of affairs, having neither police nor military competent to protect one, it was left to people in Ireland to protect themselves, is not that the truth of it?—Generally speaking, it is.

Generally speaking that was the truth of it. Now, as you say, when the war broke out the Arms Proclamation was withdrawn and the arming went on as before?—Yes.

And continued right up to last month?—Yes.

Except so far as hampered by the Defence of the Realm Regulations? —Yes.

Your charge against Sir Roger Casement was a charge made under the Defence of the Realm Regulations?—Yes.

Although the Defence of the Realm Regulations may have hampered the importation of arms, was the drilling of armed men still permitted to take place without interference by the civil authorities?—Yes.

They continued as before?—They did.

Marching, counter-marching, and getting up skirmishing and sham battles all over the country?—Yes.

Were there frequent complaints from the civil population of this matter being tolerated?—Yes.

And the police were powerless to protect them from it? Is not that so?—Yes, powerless.

The LORD CHIEF JUSTICE—To protect them against what? I do not quite follow.

By Mr. SULLIVAN—These armed people were tramping all over the country?—Yes.

They marched on every man's property as they wished?—Yes.

They fought their sham battles in any part of the land they chose for themselves, is not that so?—That is right.

And the police were powerless to interfere with them?—Yes.

Do you remember after the war broke out that the Home Rule Bill passed as we know; it is in the statutes?—Yes.

But that an Act of Parliament was passed suspending its coming into operation?—Yes.

That is also in the statutes. Did that greatly accentuate the feeling of unrest in the country?—Yes.

Thomas J. Hearn

Re-examined by the SOLICITOR-GENERAL—I am not going through all this with you, but is the result of what you said that the country where you were stationed was at the time seething with unrest?—Yes.

And that some of the people had arms?—Yes.

The landing of arms and ammunition from abroad in that country, what kind of effect would that have had?

Mr. SULLIVAN—I object to any speculative question; there were some arms landed, three pistols and 900 rounds of ammunition.

The LORD CHIEF JUSTICE—You took up the subject which Mr. Solicitor is entitled to explain.

By the SOLICITOR-GENERAL—What effect would the landing of a cargo, I do not say three pistols, but a cargo of arms and ammunition in that country have had upon the population?—It would have had a very grave effect.

It has been put to you that the people were arming only against the Ulstermen from the north; is that so?—Partly against Ulster and partly against conscription.

By Mr. JUSTICE HORRIDGE—You know the place where the boat was found?—Yes.

You know the place where you say you found Sir Roger Casement?—Yes.

Is the house at which the woman Mary Gorman was a servant, John Allman's house, on the way from where the boat was to where you found him in the fort?—Oh, no.

How far out of the way?—From where I found the boat to where I found him in the fort would be about two English miles across country.

How far out of the route was the house of this man at which Mary Gorman says she saw him about?—That would be within 480 yards of this fort.

The house where she lived?—Yes.

BERNARD RILEY, examined by Mr. BODKIN—I am a constable in the Royal Irish Constabulary, stationed at Ardfert. I was with Sergeant Hearn on the morning of 21st April. I remember going with him towards Rathoneen in the direction of Curraghane. We searched about in that direction, and we came to a place which is called M'Kenna's Fort, where we saw a man. I now identify that man as the prisoner. When I first saw him his head and shoulders were appearing over some shrubbery in the fort. He had not seen me; he was looking in a different direction. I had my rifle with me. I went in his direction, and immediately he turned towards me I put up my carbine and covered him. I told him to stand where he was, quite close to me; that my rifle was loaded, and if he moved a foot I should shoot him. He said that was a nice way to treat an English traveller. I cautioned him, and he said, "I am not "armed; I will not do you any harm." I called for Sergeant Hearn, and he came up after a few minutes. There was a conversation between the sergeant and the prisoner, and after that the prisoner was taken into custody. I took him back to Allman's house, where Mary Gorman was employed as a servant. The little boy Collins was driving a vehicle towards Allman's house, and the prisoner and I had a lift in his cart. I saw Mary Gorman and she saw the prisoner. We went back again from Mary Gorman's on foot. When we got some way I saw Martin Collins again. Sergeant Hearn and the prisoner remained on the public road, and I went inside to search the fort for the other two men believed to be there.

Returning to the public road, Martin Collins was there; he had followed us up. Martin Collins spoke to me on the way to Ardfert, and he gave me two pieces of paper. I put my initials on them to identify them. (Shown exhibit No. 18.) These are the two pieces of paper which Martin Collins gave me. They appear to be typewritten or partly typewritten, and against each sentence in typewriting there is a number put. On the back of the paper there is some writing in pencil in the English language. The numbers are nearly consecutive—00611, 00621, 00631, 00632, and so on, all of them beginning with 00, and the remainder of the figures are nearly consecutive, though not quite. There is one number against each sentence. It begins with sentences. The first is: "Cease communications with." Then they go on: "Await "further instructions"; "Await favourable opportunity"; "Agent has "started for"; "Agent will start for"; "Agent is underways for"; "Send agent at once"; "Keep agent back"; "Call agent back"; "Proposal accepted"; "Proposal refused"; "Proposal must be recon- "sidered"; "Proposal not plainly enough explained"; "Please answer "by letter"; "Answer follows by letter"; "It is impossible to stay at"; "Have moved on for"; "Have decided to stay," and then "Direct your "attention on." In the photograph it looks to be in ink so as to make "j" into "y" by having a little loop in front. Then "Take up "communication with"; "Nothing further is known"; "Nothing "further has been heard from"; "We have our positions at"; "Letter "received"; "Letter not received"; "A letter will follow"; "Letters "are not sure"; "Do not send further letters"; "Communi- "cation again possible"; "Our chiffre is compromised"; "Railway com- "munications have been stopped"; "Enquiries must be made about"; "Our men are at"; "Further ammunition is needed"; "Further rifles "are needed"; "How many rifles will you send us?" "How much "ammunition will you send us?" "Will send plan about landing on"; "Await details about sending on"; "Preparations are made about"; "We have heard from"; "More detailed information is not to be got"; "My cable adress is"; "My adress for letters is"; "Send communi- "cations to the adress of"; "Give me new adress for"; "Last wire "has not been understood"; "Send another ship to"; "Send rifles "and ammunition to"; "Cannons with plenty of ammunition are "needed"; "Send them to"; "Send more explosives" "Send vessel "if possible." I have seen the figure "7" on the paper, and I see a little mark across each down stroke of the "7." That is not an Irish way of writing the figure "7," but it is an Irish way of making a capital "F." The Irish way of writing the figure "7" is the same as the English way of writing the figure "7." I do not write Irish myself. The pencil writing reads: "If any message sent, use 'Clifton wire';

"friends ready to receive our messages at 2 a.m. middle Greenwich "time. Begin always 'Sectpol' and rest in our cipher. This holds "good from 22nd April till 20th May. If by then no news, the friend's "station will be closed for good; after that only by cable to Mr. Hehlin, "Davos Village, Switzerland." Signed "James Kingsley." I see some letters below the words "James Kingsley," but I do not know whose handwriting these letters are in. They are not mine. The last one looks like "e" or "c," and the first looks like "n." There is no place named Clifton in that part of Ireland that I know of.

The prisoner was taken to the police station and was searched. I took part in that. In his waistcoat pocket there was exhibit No. 16. That was in the inside pocket of the vest he was wearing. I looked at it, and I remarked to him, "This is not Irish," meaning what was written on it in pencil. He said, "I do not know, I have never seen it before." What appears to be written on it is "Moller, Hensingfors, Kroner 34."

That day I went back to M'Kenna's Fort, and I found three topcoats (exhibits Nos. 19, 20, and 21). I remember seeing No. 19 looked at and searched through. There was nothing found on it in my presence. I first saw exhibit No. 31, with the district inspector at Tralee, Mr. Britten. On 27th April I went back again to the fort, and on that occasion I found a piece of paper in the fort. (Shown exhibit No. 15.) That is the piece of paper I found. It has some pencil writing on it, but I cannot read it; it appears to be in a foreign language. When I arrested Casement I noticed that there was some sand on the green woollen muffler he was wearing, and that the ends of the muffler were slightly damp and wet. His boots also had sand in them, and all the coats were quite wet—sodden.

Cross-examined by Mr. SULLIVAN—You say there is no such place as Clifton in that immediate neighbourhood?—Not to my knowledge.

How long are you stationed in Ardfert?—About six years.

Are you a native of the district?—No.

What part of the country do you come from?—I come from Ulster.

This place that you searched, how long after the arrest was it that you searched it for the overcoats?—I should say about an hour afterwards, say, between one and two hours.

Between one and two hours afterwards you found the overcoats there. Had you made any search originally?—Through the fort?

Yes?—Yes, I had, for men.

You apparently had not noticed the overcoats?—They passed my notice. They were covered by the shrubbery. They were folded up and hidden in the shrubbery.

And they escaped your notice in that way?—Yes.

With regard to this paper (exhibit No. 15), you have that paper before you, and you cannot find any English word or words that you can recognise on it, can you?—Except my own initials.

By the LORD CHIEF JUSTICE—There are your initials; it was merely for identification that you put them on?—Yes, my lord.

MARTIN COLLINS, examined by the SOLICITOR-GENERAL—I live at Ardfert. My father is a farmer. I am twelve and a half years old. I remember last Good Friday morning. I was going back to my uncle's

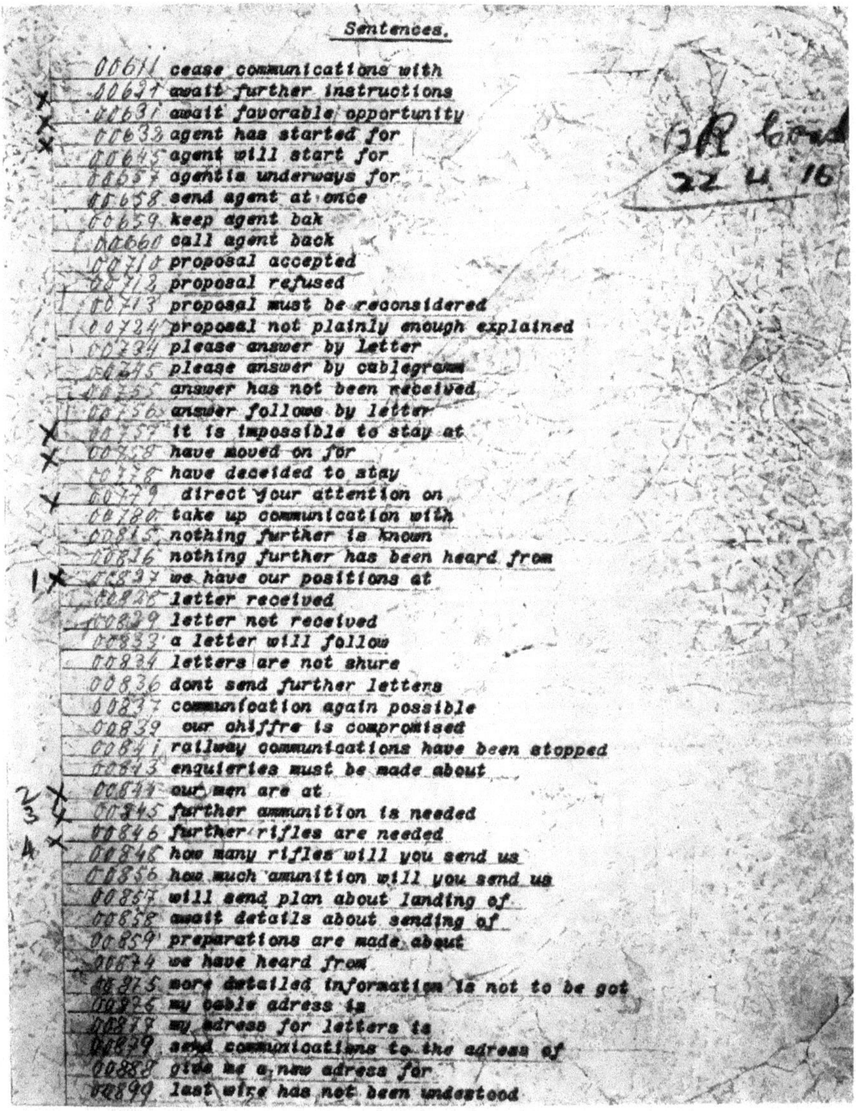
Sentences.

00611 cease communications with
00627 await further instructions
00631 await favorable opportunity
00633 agent has started for
00645 agent will start for
00657 agent is underways for
00658 send agent at once
00659 keep agent bak
00660 call agent back
00710 proposal accepted
00712 proposal refused
00713 proposal must be reconsidered
00724 proposal not plainly enough explained
00734 please answer by letter
00745 please answer by cablegramm
00755 answer has not been received
00756 answer follows by letter
00757 it is impossible to stay at
00758 have moved on for
00778 have deceided to stay
00779 direct your attention on
00780 take up communication with
00815 nothing further is known
00816 nothing further has been heard from
00827 we have our positions at
00828 letter received
00829 letter not received
00833 a letter will follow
00834 letters are not shure
00836 dont send further letters
00837 communication again possible
00839 our chiffre is compromised
00841 railway communications have been stopped
00843 enquieries must be made about
00844 our men are at
00845 further ammunition is needed
00846 further rifles are needed
00848 how many rifles will you send us
00856 how much ammunition will you send us
00857 will send plan about landing of
00858 await details about sending of
00859 preparations are made about
00874 we have heard from
00875 more detailed information is not to be got
00876 my cable adress is
00878 my adress for letters is
00879 send communications to the adress of
00888 give me a new adress for
00899 last wire has not been understood

Part of the Secret Code picked up by the boy, Martin Collins.

place in a pony and trap. I came near a place called M'Kenna's Fort, which I know. I saw some people there—Constable Riley, Sergeant Hearn, and a strange man. I have seen the strange man since. Looking round the Court I see him there; he is the prisoner. I stopped. The police were coming out from the fort at the time with the strange man. As the strange man was crossing the fence he dropped some papers from behind his back. Constable Riley asked me to give him a drive back as far as John Allman's, my uncle's, and I did that. Constable Riley and the strange man got into my cart, and I drove them back to John Allman's. I heard Constable Riley ask for Mary Gorman, and then he asked her if the strange man was the man she had seen in the morning, and Mary Gorman said "yes." I stayed at Allman's for half an hour. I was going to Tralee, and I stopped at the fort again, and Tom Doone went in and picked up the papers and gave them to me, and I gave them to Constable Riley. Tom Doone is a boy who is younger than I am. He found the papers at the place where I saw the strange man brought out. (Shown exhibit No. 18.) That is the piece of paper I saw the prisoner drop. It was torn like that when I got it. I looked at it, and then I gave it to Constable Riley.

Cross-examined by Mr. SULLIVAN—Did you see this boy, Tom Doone, actually pick up the paper?—Yes.

Was the paper lying there on the ground in your view?—Yes.

As you drove along the road?—Yes.

You could see the paper from the trap as you drove along the road, could you?—I saw the strange man drop the paper.

Did you see the paper on the ground after he had dropped it?—Yes.

It was visible from the road, was it?—Yes.

Had you your dinner at Allman's?—I had.

How long did you remain there?—Half an hour.

You drove up and saw Mary Gorman?—Yes.

And heard this conversation?—Yes.

And had your dinner?—Yes.

And got back in half an hour?—Yes.

FREDERICK AMBROSE BRITTEN, examined by Mr. TRAVERS HUMPHREYS—I am district inspector in the Royal Irish Constabulary. On 21st April I saw three overcoats in the custody of the police. One of these is exhibit No. 19, and I took a piece of paper from the pocket of that coat. Exhibit No. 31 is the document that I took from the pocket. It is a first-class sleeping railway ticket from Berlin to Wilhelmshaven, dated 12th April, 1916. I know a little German. I see a number of figures down the left-hand side of exhibit No. 18. I notice the way in which the figure 7 is made. I should say that it is very like a German 7. Exhibit No. 15 is written in German and in German characters.

Cross-examined by Mr. SULLIVAN—What is your headquarters?—Tralee.

How long are you stationed in Tralee?—Five years.

I suppose you read the papers?—Sometimes.

What paper do you read?—Anything I can get hold of—the *Irish Times*, the *Independent*——

The *Irish Times* is the one that you take for preference, I think?—Yes.

Sir Roger Casement.

Frederick A. Britten

I want to know whether you read the *Irish Times* of 14th July, 1913. I can give you a copy to look at (newspaper handed to witness)?—I could not tell you.

Will you turn to page 8. Did you read the account of those speeches of the July anniversary celebration of the 12th July?—No, I should think not. I do not remember reading it.

Will you just glance through it. There are some striking matters in it. Will you look at the bottom of the second column on that page, about 30 lines up, the passage beginning—"I hope it will never be forgotten in that context, as regards the second reading of this bill the other day——"

By the LORD CHIEF JUSTICE—The difficulty of it is, so far the witness has said he has not read it.

By Mr. SULLIVAN—Will you look at the passage commencing with those words, and see whether you have not read that before?—I am sure I read something like it.

Will you read it through again and make sure whether that is not what you did read before?—I could not possibly make sure whether I read it before or not.

That is the paper you usually read, and it is circulated in the town of which you are the district inspector?—Yes.

It was something to this effect, at all events:—"I hope it will not be "forgotten in that context, as regards the second reading of this bill the "other day, there was as regards England, the predominant partner, a "majority upon the division of over 30 against the bill?"—Yes.

That is against the Home Rule Bill?—Yes.

Now, will you look higher up in that column, three lines before the cross-heading, and see if you do not remember reading that before, circulating in your district?—I do not quite know where you mean.

You see "Confidence in" as a sub-heading?—Yes.

Just above that you see a passage commencing "We can rely." Do you remember reading something to that effect?—I remember reading that sort of talk.

"We can rely not only on thousands but tens of thousands of people "in England who are prepared to assist us." There was any amount of that sort of speaking going on?—In the papers.

Some of them were perhaps more definite. Then in the very last paragraph of the meeting that is reported there, do you see a passage beginning "In England they were prepared to stand"?—Who is speaking, whose speech is it?

I will give you the name if you wish, but I am a little diffident about it. It is the very last paragraph of the eloquent speech that closed the meeting except the vote of thanks?—There are so many meetings in different parts of Ireland, and they are mixed up together.

I will mark the passage for you if you wish it. That is the passage I want you to look at. Did you read passages of this kind circulating in your district—"They would be right in resisting it by force, and in their "determination to resist it they would have the sympathy and support of "thousands of people in England, and amongst those thousands he had "the greatest pleasure in reckoning himself." You remember speeches to that effect, at all events?—Either speeches or comment to that effect.

They were circulated broadcast through the country?—No doubt.

(*Irish Times* of 14th July, 1913, marked exhibit No. 37.) Now I will turn to the issue of 18th September, 1913. I have marked two passages in that issue. Have you read that passage between the parallel ink columns, "Sir Edward Carson in Ulster." Have you read that or speeches to that effect about that time circulating?—Yes, it is always the same.

"He could add this as a word of partial assurance, that they had many "powerful friends in England who thought as he did. It was all very well "to talk of the great forces which were marshalled behind the Government "and which could be used in the event of extreme necessity in Ulster. The "reply to that was that the forces of the Crown were the servants of the "nation, and at least one-half of the nation believed that the employ-"ment of this force would be a monstrous crime"?—Yes.

Now, will you turn to the next page. I have marked for you, "If the "resolution of Ulster were put to the test, they would find those in England "who had felt it their duty to encourage the men of Ulster in their attitude, "and who would be prepared to prove by their deeds that when they said "that Ulster was right they meant Ulster was right, and who would be "prepared to share the risk"?—Yes.

Then there is one other eloquent passage I want to deal with.

The Lord Chief Justice—Have we not gone far enough into this?

Mr. Sullivan—Very well, my lord, I at once accept the suggestion.

Re-examined by the Solicitor-General—Were those speeches made before the war?—Yes.

There is nothing about entering the service of Germany?—No.

Or helping the Germans to invade Ireland?—No. (*Irish Times* of 18th September, 1913, marked exhibit No. 38.)

Robert William Larke, examined by Mr. Bodkin—I am a constable in the Royal Irish Constabulary stationed at Ardfert. On Good Friday, 21st April, I went to the sand at Curraghane, and I found a black bag. It was buried in the sand. There were some things in it when I found it. These were placed in M'Carthy's cart and taken to the barracks.

Mr. Sullivan—I have no question.

James Butler, examined by Mr. Branson—I am a sergeant in the Royal Irish Constabulary, and on 22nd April last I conveyed the prisoner, Sir Roger Casement, from Tralee to Dublin by train. As the train was approaching Killarney Station the prisoner asked whether he could have a newspaper, and I said "yes." The train stopped at the station. The head constable of Killarney was at the station, and he came to the carriage door where we were. He said something to me, and the prisoner heard what he said. The head constable said, "Did you hear what happened to "the two lads at Puck"? I said "No." The head constable replied, "They ran into the tide and were drowned." Puck is about 20 miles from Tralee. Its proper name is Killorglin. On the train leaving the station the prisoner commenced to sob and cry, and remained so for some time. He then turned round to me and asked me where was Puck; was it near Castlemaine Bay, and I said it was. Then after a while he said, "I am "very sorry for those two men; they were good Irishmen; it was on my "account they came over here." I had also some conversation with the prisoner at Mallow Station. When the train arrived at Mallow Station we had to change and get into another train, and during the interval we were waiting for it I asked him had he ever been to Mallow before, and he replied and said he knew the Blackwater well. The town of Mallow is built on the Blackwater. On arriving at King's Bridge Station, Dublin, on the way to Harbour Hill Barracks, we both left in a cab, and while in the cab he asked me, did I think he would be able to get a bed when he arrived at the destination, and I said I thought he would. Then he said he felt very tired, that he had been up twelve nights.

Cross-examined by Mr. SULLIVAN—The place called Puck is in fact the town of Killorglin?—Yes.

The natives pronounce it in one syllable?—Quite so.

As a matter of fact, this accident you are speaking about at Killorglin had happened some days before, had it not?—On the day before, I think.

But it had happened at a distance of, I suppose, 30 miles, at all events, from Curraghane?—Yes, about that, 30 miles.

The two men in question who were drowned are not men whose names we have heard mentioned in this case. Is not that so?—That is so, but it was not known at the time who they were.

There is a slip at Killorglin where the road runs down, and a motor car had run off the slip into the tide, and the two men had got drowned?—Yes.

It is not the first time that a motor car has run off that slip into the water, but at that time it was not known who the two men were?—It was not known at that time.

But, as it afterwards transpired, they were not men that we are dealing with in the present case?—No, I do not think so.

FREDERICK WHITTAKER, examined by Mr. TRAVERS HUMPHREYS—I am a sergeant-major of the Military Provost Staff Corps. I was on duty on Saturday, 22nd April, at the Harbour Hill Barracks, Dublin, when I received the prisoner Casement into my custody from Sergeant Butler. I received at the same time three bags (exhibits Nos. 11, 12, and 13) and the tin box (exhibit No. 9), and also three overcoats, which were then in a brown paper parcel. I handed over my prisoner to the custody of Sergeant Bracken, and the property to Sergeant O'Donnell, of New Scotland Yard.

Mr. SULLIVAN—No question.

THOMAS BRACKEN, examined by the SOLICITOR-GENERAL—I am a sergeant of the Military Foot Police, stationed at Ship Street Barracks, Dublin. On 22nd April I went to the Military Detention Barracks with an escort, and I received from the sergeant-major in charge of the barracks the prisoner, Sir Roger Casement. I took him *via* Holyhead to Euston Station, London, arriving there on the morning of the 23rd April. I there handed him over to the custody of the Metropolitan Police. I brought over some property at the same time. I did not bring three bags, but I brought some money and a penknife. I handed the property to the police there.

Mr. SULLIVAN—No question.

Evidence for Prosecution.

Joseph Sandercock

JOSEPH SANDERCOCK, examined by Mr. BODKIN—I am an inspector of the Criminal Investigation Department, New Scotland Yard. I went on the early morning of 23rd April to Euston Station and met the prisoner on his arrival by the Irish mail. I received him into my custody from Sergeant Bracken. On arriving at New Scotland Yard I told the accused that I was an inspector of police, and that he would be detained pending inquiries as to a charge that would be preferred against him later. He said, "Do "you know who I am"? I replied, "Yes." He added, "I am Sir Roger "Casement, and the only person to whom I have disclosed my identity is a "priest at Tralee in Ireland." The accused was about to make a statement when I cautioned him, and told him that anything he said would be taken down and used in evidence for or against him at his trial. I informed him that he would be seen by responsible officials at 10 o'clock that day, to which he replied, "I have nothing further to say now." Later on he was taken to Brixton Prison, and, later on again, on 25th April, to the Tower of London.

Mr. SULLIVAN—No question.

SYDNEY RAY WAGHORN, examined by the SOLICITOR-GENERAL—I am leading seaman on H.M.S. "Bluebell." On 21st April last I was leading signalman. I remember last Good Friday, 21st April. I was on board the "Bluebell" on that day, off the south-west coast of Ireland. I remember on the evening of that day sighting another ship. When I sighted this other ship we were about 90 miles off the south-west coast of Ireland. I cannot give the position more closely than that. This other ship was about 15 miles from us when I first saw her. We got nearer to her. She was flying Norwegian colours. They were painted on each side—two forward and two aft. I was ordered to signal to her. I signalled her, asking her name and where she was bound, and she replied "'Aud,' bound for Genoa." I gave her some orders; I told her we were taking her to Queenstown, and I told her that she was to follow us. She did not follow us—not at once—and my vessel fired a round across her bows. I knew that Queenstown was, roughly, 138 miles from us to the eastward. After we fired the shot she then followed us. We got within 3½ miles of Queenstown. There is a lightship there called Daunt's light-vessel. When we got near that light-vessel something happened; the "Aud" stopped her engines. The "Bluebell" was a cable's length from the "Aud" when the "Aud" stopped her engines. After she stopped her engines I noticed a cloud of white smoke issuing from the after-hold on the starboard side. She then showed two German naval ensigns at the masthead. She lowered two boats, and men got into them and pulled towards the "Bluebell." The "Bluebell" fired a round across the bows again. The boats then put up a flag of truce, and the men in the boats put up their hands. They were taken on board the "Bluebell." There were twenty-three altogether. Twenty of them were German bluejackets, and three were officers. Two of them were German naval officers; I could not say for certain what officer the third one was. When the men were taken on board the "Bluebell" they were placed under an armed guard. After that the "Aud" sank. The smoke issuing from her side and the sinking of the "Aud" all happened in about ten minutes. She sank about a mile and a quarter south-south-east from the Daunt light-vessel.

Sydney R. Waghorn

Cross-examined by Mr. SULLIVAN—You were about 90 miles from land when you first saw this ship?—Yes.

You were 138 miles from Queenstown?—Yes.

I suggest you had the mizzen bearing about north, distance about 80 miles?—I do not know anything about navigation.

We want to find the spot on the ocean which is 90 miles from land and 138 miles from Queenstown. We ought to be able to find that, ought we not? It was, at all events, out in the Atlantic Ocean?—Yes.

Did you tell my lord just now that you steered a course east to the Daunt Rock lightship?—No.

I thought you said so?

Mr. JUSTICE HORRIDGE—He said Queenstown was east.

By Mr. SULLIVAN—Do you mean the bearing of Queenstown was due east?—No.

Queenstown was to the east, but obviously very far to the north of you?—No.

What was the bearing of Queenstown?—Queenstown lay, roughly, eastward.

Have you any idea of the lie of the south coast of Ireland?—Yes.

Are you aware that you cannot steer due east to Queenstown, or, rather, to the Daunt Rock; you have to go round the Daunt Rock before you can turn into Queenstown with a ship drawing any water?—Yes.

When you say Queenstown lay to the east of you, do you suggest that the bearing of Queenstown was east?—I do not suggest anything about the bearing. I do not know anything about navigation at all.

What hour of the day was it that you saw this vessel?—About 6 o'clock in the evening.

At 6 o'clock in the evening on the day in question you could form a very fair opinion as to what your course was, could you not?—No.

Can a leading signalman of H.M.S. "Bluebell" not assist me in telling me even approximately what course was made for Queenstown after you took this ship the "Aud" in charge?—I cannot tell you the course that was made approximately.

But when you say it was to the east you mean as regards the northern star it would lie to the east of it?—Queenstown would lie to the eastward of where we first picked up the vessel.

But you do not know what the bearing of Queenstown was?—No.

You do not know whether you went to the north or to north-east?—I do not know any course.

By the LORD CHIEF JUSTICE—You have nothing to do with the course?—No, my lord.

You have not to read the course?—No.

By Mr. SULLIVAN—But you do know that you were 90 miles from land?—Roughly, 90 miles from land.

And 138 miles, roughly, from the Daunt Rock lightship?—Yes.

JOHN DEMPSEY, examined by Mr. TRAVERS HUMPHREYS—I am a diver employed by the Admiralty, and I live in County Cork. On 10th May last I received instructions to go from Queenstown to the wreck of a ship. The position of the ship was marked by a buoy. The ship was lying about a mile and a quarter south-south-east of the Daunt lightship. I was lowered down to the wreck of the ship, and when I got to the bottom of the sea I found the ship there. There were some flags painted on the ship; there was a Norwegian flag painted on the hull. I saw only one side of the vessel at that time. I afterwards saw the other side of the ship. I could not tell whether there was a Norwegian flag painted on that side, as she was lying right over on that side. I examined the ship, and found a hole in her on the starboard quarter. That hole was between 12 and 14 feet in diameter. On the bottom of the sea, abreast of the hull, I saw a lot of rifles and ammunition strewn along the bottom. I brought up with me one of the complete rifles. (Shown exhibit No. 25.) That is the rifle I brought up; the others were the same as that. I saw a number of others, but the others were older patterns. I also brought up some broken rifle butts. Exhibit No. 26 is one of them. I also found and brought up a bayonet case, exhibit No. 27. There were plenty down there. I also brought up a cartridge clip and a cartridge. I got the cartridge from the bed of the sea, lying by itself. The cartridges were scattered about the bottom loose on the bed of the sea. When I found the cartridge it was in the clip. There were thousands of other cartridges there. That would be about eleven o'clock on Wednesday forenoon. I went down later in the day, but the weather started to get very rough, and I had to give up my diving operations.

Mr. SULLIVAN—No question.

Colonel NICHOLAS T. BELAIEW, examined by the SOLICITOR-GENERAL—I am a member of the Imperial Russian Guard. I am a representative of the Russian War Office, and I am on the Russian Government Supply Committee at India House. I have examined the rifle, exhibit No. 25. That particular rifle is a Russian army service rifle, manufactured by the Imperial Russian Tould in 1905. The number of it is 80908. Exhibit No. 27 is not a Russian scabbard. I have never seen such a scabbard in the Russian service.

By the LORD CHIEF JUSTICE—I am not quite certain, but I think I have seen something like this coming from South America.

Examination continued—The clip exhibited is a Russian clip. The cartridge case is like the Russian cartridge case, but there are some small differences; for instance, in this cartridge I do not see at the bottom of the cartridge any regular marking. At the bottom of the cartridge case we used to have some markings, the date of manufacture, and the name of the plant or works. I do not see any marking here. Then there is also some slight difference in the shape of the cartridge, and also some difference in the size of the powder grains and the charge of the cartridge case. That being so I do not think that the cartridge was made at the Russian Government works. I am quite familiar with the cartridges which are made at the Russian Government works, and so I can state that this cartridge has not been manufactured at the Russian Government works. It is difficult to state definitely whether the cartridge would fit the rifle which is exhibited, because that rifle is in a very bad state, but, as far as I can judge from the dimensions of the cartridge case and of the rifle, I think that this cartridge can fit.

Mr. SULLIVAN—I have no question.

Sir Roger Casement.

Lieut.-Col. P. J. Gordon

Lieutenant-Colonel Philip James Gordon, examined by Mr. Bodkin—I am a lieutenant-colonel attached to the Directorate of Military Intelligence at the War Office, Whitehall. I am familiar with the military maps which are in use in the British Army. I have seen maps, exhibits 23 and 35. They are portions of the map of Ireland. Putting the portions together in their proper order I think one would get a complete map of Ireland, but I have not actually put them together; they are cut into pieces of different sizes. I should say that there is enough material to construct from them two complete maps of Ireland. I have examined the maps carefully. These maps are a reproduction by some process, probably heliotypography, of a photographic production of a quarter-inch Ordnance Survey map of Ireland. I do not know of any map prepared or published in this country which resembles it in general appearance. It very closely resembles the map of middle Europe, prepared by the German Government, in general appearance. It is on the same scale, $\frac{1}{300,000}$, and the meridians are numbered as from Ferro instead of from Greenwich. That is also done in the German map of middle Europe on a $\frac{1}{300,000}$ scale, and is never done in English maps. There are some signs for indicating roads which differ from the Ordnance methods. In the coloured portions of the maps the main roads are the same as on the Ordnance Survey maps, but there are additional roads with a special conventional sign which do not appear on the Ordnance Survey maps. It has been added. I am acquainted with maps which use that conventional sign; it is a fairly common conventional sign for a road which is not of the best class, but better than an ordinary cart track. It is not used on Ordnance Survey maps. I notice certain colouring on that map. The green patches on the map, indicating woods, are not exactly the same as on the Ordnance Survey map; they appear to have been put in from some special information. On several of the sheets, on which garrison towns appear, there are certain conventional signs which do not appear on our maps. I do not know exactly what they are, but they apparently refer to the defences of these garrisons. There are some patches of colour used in connection with such towns. They are the conventional signs to which I refer, and they only appear at the garrisons.

By the Lord Chief Justice—There are patches of colour which indicate the land near towns. Every symbol on a map is what we call a conventional sign or symbol. The green patches are only shown on towns where there are garrisons. The other towns have no special conventional sign.

Cross-examined by Mr. Sullivan—Do I understand you to say that these green patches are anything special? They do not represent towns, do they?—They do not represent towns; they represent certain areas about towns.

All these green patches?—Not all the green ones, the ones in vivid green, emerald green; and those in duller green represent woods.

What?—The patches of bright emerald green are the ones near defended towns, garrisons; the small, dull, olive green patches represent woods.

Look at Sligo. (Map handed to witness.) You will not tell me that Collooney is a garrison town. Could you get a more brilliant green than decorates Collooney?—The only patches on this map in green indicate woods.

What I wish to point out to you is that Collooney has got the bright green you have just been speaking of. That you say represents a wood around Collooney?—It is not exactly the same.

Is Limerick a garrison town?—No, not a defended port. It is not what we understand by a garrison town.

Limerick is not a garrison town in what sense? It is a town with a garrison, is it not?—It is a garrison town, but by garrison we understand a defended port.

Is not the term "garrison town" usually applied to a town that is well equipped with barracks, and at which large bodies of soldiers are stationed?—Yes, a town in which there are barracks and bodies of soldiers.

Do you know the town of Limerick?—I have never been there. I have never been in Ireland.

Will you take that bit of the map which represents Lough Swilly? There are not five garrison towns on Lough Swilly, are there?—Certainly not.

Are there five of your green patches marked all along Lough Swilly?—Those green patches do not represent garrison towns. As I say, it is only conjecture on my part.

If they represent garrison towns, does not that represent that Lough Swilly has at least five of them dotted all along it?—They do not represent garrison towns.

Then may I take it that it is pure speculation on your part as to what these green circles do represent?—It is. I have said that already.

Do you see by that map that on Lough Swilly where there are no towns at all, in a lonely country, there are five circles?—Seven altogether.

There are seven circles dotted all along Lough Swilly where there are no towns of any kind, sort, or description?—I am merely suggesting that they represent certain defended areas in the neighbourhood of garrisons.

Will you tell me, looking at these seven patches on Lough Swilly—you see where Lough Swilly runs?—Yes.

If you are not giving away any secret, will you tell me what is the nearest garrison town of any kind to Lough Swilly? Would it not be 'Derry?—I would not be referring to garrison towns at all, only to garrisons.

Do you suggest to my lords that there are seven stations on Lough Swilly with garrisons in them?—This map has not been prepared in this country.

Is not your answer, that you do not know what those seven patches on Lough Swilly represent?—I have already said several times it is conjecture.

Re-examined by the Solicitor-General—To make it quite clear, what do you mean by the word "garrison"?—Probably "defended port" would be a better word to use.

Have you looked at the places where these bright green patches are on the maps?—Yes.

Are there at or near those places garrisons in the sense in which you use the word?—That does not come into my department.

Sir Roger Casement.

Maurice Moriarty

MAURICE MORIARTY, examined by Mr. TRAVERS HUMPHREYS—I live at Tralee, and I drive a motor car for Mr. Nolan. I remember last Good Friday. I drove Mr. Nolan's motor on that day. I started about eleven o'clock, and I got one passenger at Rock Street and two at Balloonough. Rock Street is a street in Tralee, and I picked up one passenger there. I took up the two others in Tralee. Ballyheige is ten miles from Tralee. That road takes us through Ardfert. I drove through Ardfert. I gave some evidence at Bow Street Police Court in London. I saw at Bow Street Police Court one of the persons who had been in my car on that day. He gave his name to the police as Mulcahy, but his right name is Bailey.* He was in the dock when I saw him at Bow Street. I drove these persons to Ballyheige. After we drive through Ardfert the road takes one near to the sea, to a place called Banner Strand. Banner Strand is near Curraghane. I got about 300 yards from the sea when the tyre burst. A police sergeant came up to see the car then. After that I drove those three persons on to Ballyheige, and then to Causeway, about six miles from Ballyheige. I then took them through Abbeydorney back to Tralee.

Mr. SULLIVAN—No question.

GEORGE CARTER, examined by Mr. BODKIN—I am a constable in the Royal Irish Constabulary. On Saturday, 22nd April, I was in the neighbourhood of Curraghane, near Abbeydorney. That is not very far from Ardfert—three or four miles. I saw there a man, whom I afterwards took into custody. I afterwards saw that same man at Bow Street Police Court in London. He was then in the dock standing beside the prisoner, Sir Roger Casement. His name was Bailey.

Mr. SULLIVAN—No question.

DANIEL O'DONNELL, examined by Mr. TRAVERS HUMPHREYS—I am a detective-inspector at New Scotland Yard. On 28th April I went over to Dublin, and on 6th May I went to the Royal Irish Constabulary Depôt at Phœnix Park. A man, whose name was afterwards given as Bailey, was handed over to my custody, and I brought that man over to London. While he was in Dublin that man was seen by some of the soldiers who have given evidence in this case. He is the same person.

Mr. SULLIVAN—No question.

EDWARD PARKER, examined by the SOLICITOR-GENERAL—I am an inspector of the Metropolitan Police on duty at New Scotland Yard. On the morning of 15th May I went with other officers to the Tower of London, where I saw the accused, Sir Roger Casement. I spoke to him, and said, "I am a police officer, and have a warrant for the arrest of Sir Roger "Casement; are you Sir Roger Casement?" He replied "Yes." I then read through a copy of a birth certificate I had in my hand, and asked him if he was born on 1st September, 1864, in the district of Kingstown, County Dublin, and he replied, "Yes." I said, "Was your "father Roger Casement and your mother Annie Casement? Was your "father a captain in the Antrim Militia?" and he replied, "Yes." I

* *See* Appendix for the very interesting statement made by Bailey, taken by Inspector Britten at Abbeydorney on 23rd April, 1916.

then read the warrant to him, and he made no reply. Exhibit 1 is the warrant that I read to him. I took Casement to Bow Street Police Station, where he was subsequently charged. After he was charged he said, "Am I allowed to say anything now?" He was cautioned that if he did it would be taken down and used in evidence, and he then said, pointing to Bailey, who was charged with him, "Well, that man is innocent. I "think the indictment is wrongly drawn up against him. If it is within "my power to provide defence for the man I wish him to be in every "way as well defended as myself, and if he has no means to obtain his "defence, I am prepared to obtain them for him." I produce the *London Gazette* of 5th August, 1914, exhibit 3. That is the *Gazette* containing the official announcement of the declaration of war with Germany.

Mr. SULLIVAN—No question.

WILLIAM EGAN, recalled, further examined by Mr. BODKIN—I spoke of having been at school with a man named Bailey. That man Bailey was in the camp at Limburg as a British prisoner of war. I saw that same man in Dublin on 6th May under a military escort. I saw that same man at Bow Street Police Court standing in the dock beside the prisoner, Sir Roger Casement.

Further cross-examined by Mr. SULLIVAN—In the camp at Limburg were there French, Russian, and Irish all in the same camp?—No.

Did not they mix by day?—They did in working parties, when they were going to work.

What I want to know is, when you went to the camp at first, were the French cooking for the Irish prisoners?—Yes.

Do you remember that the cooking for the camp was done in the French camp?—No, it was done in our camp.

You say they were not moving about the camp freely. Could not you visit the French camp?—No, unless we had a pass.

Were passes common?—No, it was only a privilege.

The SOLICITOR-GENERAL—I now ask your lordships to rule with regard to the admissibility of that document, exhibit No. 4, the address to the Irish soldiers which was circulated throughout the camp by German soldiers or officers. I put it in this way. This document being so circulated, it is plain that the Germans, our enemies, were using means to persuade Irish prisoners of war to join the Irish Brigade, the Irish Brigade being formed by the German Government, and provided by that Government with arms and ammunition, and so on. At the same time it is proved that the prisoner does the same thing, and so he was in that enterprise adhering to and aiding and supporting the German authorities. That is, of course, one of the points which we have to prove. I submit to that end this document is admissible in evidence as showing what the Germans were doing and what Casement was helping them to do.

The LORD CHIEF JUSTICE—What do you say, Mr. Sullivan?

Mr. SULLIVAN—I submit that the argument addressed to your lordships, and the observations of the Solicitor-General, show that he is not relying upon this document having been brought to the knowledge or attention of Sir Roger Casement in the course of his visits to Limburg. Therefore it is a document that is not brought into contact with the prisoner or under his observation; and it is not sought to be admitted on that ground. The ground upon which it is sought to be admitted is that you find other people doing something similar to what he was doing. On the charge here, which is not a conspiracy in any shape or form, I respectfully submit that whatever other people may have been doing, or whatever view they may have been taking as to what benefit or not they might derive from what he was doing, unless it is alleged and proved that it was a conspiracy between two people to do an act, which has not been alleged, and I submit is not proved, the concurrent similar acts of two different people are not in themselves evidence of conspiracy to do the same act. In the course of life many people seek to attain the same end possibly for very different reasons. The fact that you find people seeking to attain the same end is no evidence, I submit—the mere concurrence of events—that they are seeking in confederacy, one with the other, to do the same thing, which is the essential component of the admissibility of a document on the ground that it is uttered by the agent.

[Their lordships conferred.]

The Lord Chief Justice—We are of opinion that this document is admissible. It is clear upon the evidence as it stands, and we have to deal with the case at present upon the evidence as it stands, that the German officers and authorities were attempting to seduce the British soldiers who were prisoners of war in this camp from their allegiance. This leaflet was circulated and distributed amongst these prisoners—that is, the British prisoners of war—who were all said to be Irish in this camp. The prisoner Casement had been to the camp and had made a speech or speeches, and was attempting to get men to join the Irish Brigade, according to the evidence as given at the moment, and he is charged with adhering to the King's enemies by giving them aid and comfort. The means by which they, the German authorities, were seeking to assist themselves was by getting these Irish prisoners of war to join this Irish Brigade for the purpose stated, and the prisoner was doing the same thing according to the evidence as at present given. In these circumstances it seems to us quite clear that this document, having been distributed after he (Casement) had come upon the scene, and, according to the evidence, seeking to bring about the same operation and the same result, the evidence of this document, exhibit No. 4, must be admissible in evidence against him on this charge. Therefore we admit it.

The Solicitor-General—My lord, the document has not yet been read to the jury. Perhaps I had better now read it.

The Lord Chief Justice—Yes.

The Solicitor-General—It is in these terms—"Irishmen! Here is "a chance for you to fight for Ireland! You have fought for England, "your country's hereditary enemy. You have fought for Belgium in "England's interest, though it was no more to you than the Fiji Islands. "Are you willing to fight for your own country? With a view to securing "the national freedom of Ireland, with the moral and material assistance "of the German Government, an Irish Brigade is being formed. The "object of the Irish Brigade shall be to fight solely the cause of Ireland, "and under no circumstances shall it be directed to any German end. "The Irish Brigade shall be formed and shall fight under the Irish flag

Michael Francis Doyle,
of the American Bar,
who assisted the defence in Court throughout the trial.

"alone; the men shall wear a special, distinctly Irish uniform, and have "Irish officers. The Irish Brigade shall be clothed, fed, and efficiently "equipped with arms and ammunition by the German Government. It "will be stationed near Berlin, and be treated as guests of the German "Government. At the end of the war the German Government under- "takes to send each member of the brigade who may so desire it to the "United States of America, with necessary means to land. The Irishmen "in America are collecting money for the brigade. Those men who do not "join the Irish Brigade will be removed from Limberg and distributed "among other camps. If interested, see your company commanders. "Join the Irish Brigade and win Ireland's independence! Remember "Bachelor's Walk! God Save Ireland!"

The ATTORNEY-GENERAL—That, my lords, is the case for the prosecution. There is no statement.

Motion to Quash Indictment.

Mr. SULLIVAN—My lords, I intimated at another stage of the case that I had considerations to address to the Court on the question of whether the indictment to which the prisoner has since pleaded disclosed an offence known to the law and triable before your lordships. I fear I shall have to trespass on the time of the Court for some little period.

The LORD CHIEF JUSTICE—Whatever time you may require is at your disposal. It is essential that you should have all the time you wish. Please do not hurry.

Mr. SULLIVAN—What I was going to say was a matter for the guidance of the Court, that I should probably occupy, in the debate of this matter at any rate, such a period of the afternoon that I would ask for personal indulgence that I might not be called upon to speak further to the evidence, if your lordships would kindly allow that.

The LORD CHIEF JUSTICE—Certainly.

Mr. SULLIVAN—The indictment which your lordships have before you under the new statute sets out the charge as being "High Treason "by adhering to the King's enemies elsewhere than in the King's realm, "to wit, in the Empire of Germany, contrary to the Treason Act, 1351." Now, my lords, we are all aware that that statement, in the description of the offence as far as I have gone, is certainly not taken from the words of the statute, 25 Edward III. On the contrary, the words "elsewhere "than in the King's realm," so far from following the charge of adhering to the King's enemies in the statute, are followed by directly contrary words, "adhering to the King's enemies within his realm," and, as we all know, are followed by the further words, "giving them aid or "comfort within the realm or elsewhere," as it has been translated.

My lords, the matter is not agitated for the first time, but there is no case as far as I know, and my colleagues, Mr. Artemus Jones, and Mr. Morgan especially, have assisted me in my search, and have gone through a great number of cases—there is, as far as I know, no case in which it has ever been submitted to any Court, argued, and decided, that a statute which in terms commences by a declaration that the offence shall be committed within the realm has ever after argument been adjudged to extend to an offence outside the realm; no reported case, at all events. One case was cited in a previous argument thirteen years ago on behalf of the Crown as being an authority that way which I shall have to deal with at some length, and I think I shall prove to almost mathematical demonstration that, so far from establishing the proposition for which it was cited, it, in fact, was a case of adhering to the King's enemies in the realm in the plainest of plain terms, not charged in the indictment, but the place lay within the realm of England; and from the nature of the trial and tribunal, I hope to point out to your lordships that that view must inevitably be taken.

The LORD CHIEF JUSTICE—Are you referring to *Vaughan's* case?

Mr. SULLIVAN—*The King* v. *Vaughan.* I hope to establish that in *The King* v. *Vaughan.* The offence charged was actually committed within the realm, and was tried as such. But, my lords, before I come to that, may I be permitted to develop on an interior line? Treason was a generic term applied to a great number of offences, all savouring of breach of allegiance to His Majesty the King. The subject of all allegiance itself falls under two totally distinct heads, allegiance of the person and allegiance of the occupier of a locality, because, as your lordships are well aware, the occupier, even though he be an alien enemy, a resident within the realm, owes a local allegiance, if I may use the term in that context, to His Majesty the King so long as he resides within the King's peace and has his protection. Such a local allegiance is it that he, although by birth and personality an alien enemy, may be indicted and convicted of treason to our Lord the King. That is perfectly clear. May I refer your lordships to the first volume of Hale, page 92: "If an alien army"—it is printed "army," it is obvious it must be "amy," an alien friend—"if an alien amy comes into England, "and here compass the death of the King, Queen, or Prince, this is a "man compassing within this law; for, though he be the natural subject "of another Prince, yet during his residence here he owes a local allegiance "to the King of England, and though the indictment shall not style him," a natural born subject. It then proceeds to deal with the form in which he may be indicted: "If an alien amy subject of another Prince "comes into this Kingdom and here settles his abode, and afterwards war "is proclaimed between the two Kings, and yet the alien continues here "and takes the benefit of the King's laws and protection, and yet com- "passes the death of the King, this is a man compassing within this law; "for, though he be the natural subject of another Prince, he shall be "dealt with as an English subject in this case, unless he first openly "remove himself from the King's protection by passing to the other Prince, "or by a public renunciation of the King of England's protection." We are not dealing with that. Then further he deals with a merchant coming into the realm and a foreigner residing and trading here under the King's protection. I do not think on behalf of the Crown it will be for one moment contended that a resident within the kingdom, although the subject of a foreign prince, is not bound by the local allegiance of which I speak. The importance of that in considering the point to which I am approaching is that a man may in truth be the subject of two allegiances so long as he is on land, for he is subject to the allegiance of his natural prince and he is subject to the allegiance of the prince in whose dominion he may be. When we come to consider what the statute of Edward III. dealt with, it will be of importance, I submit, to bear in mind that one of the reasons why Parliament, or the declaration submitted to Parliament, contains the words "within the realm" was consciousness of the fact that once you went without the realm, in the sense of going into the realm of another prince, you were there dealing with a man who might be in a difficult position, and who was not in the free untrammelled allegiance to a single prince that His Majesty's subjects within His Majesty's own realm might be. That will at once distinguish the position of one who, going outside the realm, namely, outside the four seas, nevertheless does not pass into the realm or under the allegiance of another Sovereign. This case is that of a man upon the high seas, the natural born subject on the high seas, outside the four seas, which I will show to your lordships are unquestionably, for the purposes of the construction of the statute, within the realm of England, with reference to the cases—the man who passes on to the high seas, it is true that he may be without the realm—but I think I will show your lordships authority that he is still within the King's dominions, and under the sole duty of allegiance to his one Sovereign, and under allegiance to nobody else, while he is upon the high seas.

The LORD CHIEF JUSTICE—Speaking generally, with reference to the particular words of the statute for the moment, you are leaving the words of the statute and dealing with the common law.

Mr. SULLIVAN—For the purposes of approaching the wording of the statute.

The LORD CHIEF JUSTICE—Is not there authority for this proposition that a man without the realm may be excused for what would otherwise be an act of treason if he commits it under terror of death? I thought the law had always drawn that distinction.

Mr. SULLIVAN—I think the authority goes even further, because the man who within the realm joins in the levying of war upon His Majesty is excused under the doctrine your lordship mentions.

The LORD CHIEF JUSTICE—If it is right to say there is authority for the doctrine that I put forward to you, it would seem to indicate there is the offence of treason apart altogether from whether it is within this statute if it is a breach of duty or of allegiance committed without the realm.

Mr. SULLIVAN—For the purpose of argument I may be permitted to concede that, but it would not be treason within the statute.

The LORD CHIEF JUSTICE—That is another point.

Mr. SULLIVAN—Nor would it have been charged if sought to allege it against a person in old times under adhering, but of compassing the death of the King within the earlier decisions, that everything must be reduced down to that basis of inference, that once you do any act of treason it could be said to be evidence of the primary act of treason which was the compassing and imagining of the King's death. I deal with this as an approach to the words of the statute and with reference to the cases cited purporting to be binding with reference to this matter. Under the statute your lordships will note as an argument that the words of the statute "within the realm" meant within the realm; there is no procedure. Procedure was the very essence of common law in those days. You could not find a venue for the offence committed outside the realm till a period that I will come to when venue was provided by statute. Your lordships will find in the 2 Dyer, in the Third Philip and Mary, case 131b, the opinion of the judges there delivered was that there was no venue for various treasons until, my lords, it was provided by the statute of Henry VIII. Accordingly it is, I submit, abhorrent to the ideas of jurisprudence that a statute should create an offence that could be only, so to speak, in the air, that a man could be a criminal by statute, and yet there would be no means, on the construction of the statute which made him criminal, of determining what should be done with him for the crime that he had committed; and if as late as the reign of Philip and Mary the opinion of the judges was to this effect, and it was only cured in the reign of Henry VIII., your lordships will have all that long period of time between the passing of the Act of Edward and the passing of the statute of Henry VIII., in which on the construction sought by the Crown there were crimes of which there was no Court to take cognisance. The mistake with regard to this matter, for I submit there has been a mistake, originates with the writings of Coke. So far as the research of my colleagues can go, they can find no earlier authorities; but when you come to deal with Lord Coke's writings your lordships will find that this part of the Third Institute dealing with the subject, in which the statement is made in plain terms, does not purport to be a portion of his speculative writings, on which Stephen comments so bitterly, but purports to be an exposition of the result of the investigation of the authorities which he cites as supporting him in his contentions. At the bottom of page 10 of the Third Institute your lordships will find in the marginal note at the bottom "Adherent." This is here explained, viz., "in giving aid and comfort "to the King's enemies within the realm or without, delivery or surrender "of the King's castles or forts by the King's captain thereof to the King's "enemies within the realm or without for reward, &c., is adhering to the "King's enemy, and consequently treason declared by this Act." His references are interesting because they have nothing whatever to say to the proposition which he so boldly states, and, as far as we can discover, states for the first time, that adhering within the realm means adhering within the realm or without. The first reference is to the Book of Assize and Pleas of the Crown. His other references are to the Rolls of Parliament. He gives four references, the 7 Richard II., items 15, 17, and 24, and the 7 Henry IV., item 47. Now, none of those cases have anything to do with the statute that I ask your lordships to construe. If your lordships take the 7 Richard II., item 15, one of the matters cited for the justification of this proposition, it is a case of the surrender of the King's castle; that is an act of adhering abroad.

The Lord Chief Justice—That is given afterwards by Hale, Foster, and a number of authorities.

Mr. Sullivan—And Hallam's comments on Hale's timid acceptance of doctrines he would not himself have enunciated is borne out if we find the foundation of them repeated and obviously copied; the foundation does not, in fact, exist. When I come, as I will be able to come, of course, to deal with the statement in Hale, I will again have to point out that Hale does not purport to be dealing in speculation as to what construction the statute ought to have; he only repeats all these authorities as being passages from Lord Coke as being the foundation of the doctrine which he again quotes from Lord Coke.

The Lord Chief Justice—What I am not quite clear about in following your argument is this. Do you say it is not a crime at common law for a British subject to adhere to the King's enemies without the realm?

Mr. Sullivan—For the moment the argument is not addressed to the common law at all.

The Lord Chief Justice—I tell you why I am putting that to you; we cannot lose sight of it, I think. You are quite justified in saying, if you think it right, that it does not affect your argument; but if we have to construe the statute of 1351 we have also to bear in mind what has been said by other great judicial authorities as to the statute, particularly Lord Blackburn, who said it was declaratory of the common law. You are thrown back to the common law of the realm in order to understand the statute. I quite agree we still have to construe the language of the statute and are bound by it, but it is important to see what the common law of the realm is.

Mr. Sullivan—I submit by the common law of the realm at the time of that statute it was perfectly clear that the common law could not deal with treasons abroad, for the reason that they would not be triable at common law.

The Lord Chief Justice—Because you say there was no venue?

Mr. Sullivan—Because I say there was no venue. That is a very strong argument. Again Lord Coke I will have to cite. He purports to give authority to show that venue could be found; and that again, on being searched, does not bear out the proposition for which it is cited.

The Lord Chief Justice—Are you going to come to the 2 Dyer, to which you made reference?

Mr. Sullivan—Yes. On the question both as to the common law and the statute the opinion of the judges is that the cases of treason without the realm were not triable before, at the earliest, the 28 Henry VIII. The first item upon which Lord Coke passes his opinion is the 7 Richard II., item 15 on the rolls. That is not a case of treason; it is an impeachment of the Bishop of Norwich for peculation and breach of contract with the Crown. An investigation of the case shows that it was in his capacity as Army contractor that the Bishop was impeached, having apparently contracted with the Crown to furnish forthwith an army of certain dimensions and maintainment, and having failed to do so, and having also dealt with supplies in a manner which apparently did not commend itself to the Court. It was not dealing with treason at all. So far as can be discovered it was not a case of treason; at all events it is charged in that very general way, and on investigation it is very hard to say, even if you had got behind the statute of the old days of accroachment of the Royal prerogative, how that breach of contract to supply the King with the men he undertook to enlist could possibly have been treated as treason. At all events, it was not treated as treason.

Item 17 is a case of two persons named Cressyngham and Spykesworth, custodians of the castle in Flanders, who were put in arrest, and put to their answer in Parliament for surrendering the castle. There is no mention of treason in the Act. One of the persons was released, and the other, his answers not being considered satisfactory, was committed during the pleasure of His Majesty; it does not purport to be treason, nor is any word savouring of treason alleged in the Act.

Mr. Justice Avory—What else does it purport to be?

Mr. Sullivan—It was probably a case just as the court-martial on a naval officer for losing his ship, and investigation of the loss; it was an investigation of the circumstances under which the castle was captured. When I come to these cases in Hale I find that I am, in fact, giving Hale's own answer to this particular case, because the case of the castle is dealt with in Hale, and when I come to deal with Hale your lordship will see that he is not satisfied that this is treason, saving that, of course, it might be treason if he traitorously surrendered the castle, but the case itself does not show that any such charge was ever involved.

Then item 24 is another case of surrendering a castle, and taking money as part of the terms. It is not charged, my lord, either under the statute or as treason, nor is the word "adhering" mentioned. The defendant is reproved by the Chancellor for treating with the enemy without the King's authority. One of the knights who were defendants (they were all put to their answer in Parliament) is accused of accroaching the Royal power by issuing letters of safe conduct without the Royal authority, and apparently taking money for doing it. That was the charge in that case. There is no conviction for treason; they were committed to prison till they paid a ransom, and the charge, which was very loose, was not under the statute or in respect of treason at all; it seems to have been some charge of corruption of some sort; but it is impossible to spell into that any conviction under the statute of Edward. Furthermore, these cases cited are all cases of military commanders in the service of the King. The military commander in the service of the King was always within the jurisdiction of the King's Marshal, whoever he was. The military servants of the Crown have, so far as I know, always been on a different footing to the ordinary civil subject of His Majesty with regard to their obligations, and with regard to the means by which they may have been dealt with for military offences coming within the cognisance of the marshal or constable. At all events, none of these cases cited for the bold statement in Lord Coke's text have the slightest bearing to justify Lord Coke in making the statement. It is interesting to note with regard to these military offences that in the reign of Queen Anne a statute was passed, the Mutiny Act of the 7 Anne, which I will refer to afterwards, and in the Mutiny Act of the 7 Anne there is an express section dealing with what would be adhering to the King's enemies in respect of persons in military service of Her Majesty abroad. It is then declared to be high treason, and apparently created high treason, and it certainly would be a strange comment on the statutory authority, if in truth it has been high treason for hundreds of years, that, nevertheless, a section should be introduced into a Mutiny Act as late as the 7 Anne declaring it to be high treason if it clearly had been within the statute that we are dealing with, the 25 Edward III. Military persons have always been outside the ordinary jurisdiction, and for that reason, as I think Sir Matthew Hale agrees, these cases are of little use, and certainly are little justification for reading the statute in the way in which it was sought to be read.

The Lord Chief Justice—The reference to Hale in dealing with this is pages 168 and 169.

The Attorney-General—I was asking my friend for the reference with regard to the criticism of Coke.

Mr. Sullivan—It is the criticism of cases.

The Lord Chief Justice—I thought Hale was more emphatic about it; he took the same view.

Mr. Sullivan—I must have misconveyed myself if I suggested to your lordship that I was going to quote any passages of Hale criticising Lord Coke; the criticism of Lord Coke was my reference to Stephen's criticism of Coke.

Mr. Justice Horridge—I understood you to say that Hale had dealt with the case, and had said that if it had been sought to be done traitorously it might be high treason.

Mr. Sullivan—I will read it; it is at the bottom of page 168, the last page.

The Attorney-General—Will not you read page 167 first, at the beginning of the second paragraph?

Mr. Sullivan—If you please. "If an Englishman during war "between the King of England and France be taken by the French and "there swear fealty to the King of France, if it be done voluntarily, it is "adhering to the King's enemy; but if it be done for fear of his life, and "then he returns, as soon as he might, to the allegiance of the Crown of "England, this is not adherence to the King's enemies within this Act."

Mr. Justice Horridge—This is the Act of Edward?

Mr. Sullivan—Yes, the Act we are dealing with.

The Lord Chief Justice—That was the kind of authority that I had in mind when putting the proposition of the common law to you. If that is right it establishes it at common law against you.

Mr. Sullivan—If it is right it is put not as a statement of the common law but as a statement on the statute.

The Lord Chief Justice—That may be only arguing in a circle; there you, at any rate, have authority for saying the statute of Edward in 1351 was merely to declare the common law, because there was some doubt about it.

Mr. Sullivan—It is a circle.

The Lord Chief Justice—I have come across somewhere in the reading for the purpose of this case, I think it is Sir John Campbell, when Attorney-General, said the statute was passed to get rid of that miserable state of things, and that is why the statute of Edward III. was passed.

Mr. Sullivan—Though in a circle, I submit, so far from weakening my argument, that strengthens my argument. If you find cited, whether you call it under the statute or by common law, authorities for a proposition applying to the statute, that is strong evidence that if the authorities are, in fact, mistaken as to the basis of decision, and there never has been a decision upon it, that then your lordships will have to construe not the common law but the statute in the terms of the declaration as representing whatever the true meaning of those terms may be, the common law anterior to it. Now, my lords, I was passing to the bottom of page 168, unless the Attorney-General wishes me to read any more.

The Attorney-General—No, I wanted that paragraph which suggested what my lord said. I think at the top of page 168 you have Weston's case.

Mr. Sullivan—Yes. "This was the case of William Weston for "delivering up the estate of Oughtrewicke, and John de Gomenys for "delivering up the Castle of Ardes, in France, both of which were im- "peached by the Commons, and had judgment of the Lords in Parlia- "ment."

Mr. Justice Horridge—Are these the cases you gave under the items?

Mr. Sullivan—No; this is a new case cited by him, the 1 Richard II., No. 40. William de Weston was to be drawn and hanged, but execution was respited; and execution was respited in the second case. Then: "And note, though the charge were treason, and possibly "the proofs might probably amount to it, and Walsingham, *sub anno* 1 "Richard II., tells us it was done by treason; yet the reason expressed in "the judgment against Weston is only"—then he quotes the judgment, and he says, passing on to the passage I wished to approach, "The "truth is, if it were delivered up by bribery or treachery, it might be "treason, but if delivered up upon cowardice or imprudence without "treachery"—purely upon the suggestion I made, it was an inquiry into the method of the delivery of the castle—"though it were an offence "against the laws of war, and the party subject to a sentence of death by "martial law, as it once happened in a case of the like nature in the late "times of trouble, yet it is not treason by the common law, unless it was "done by treachery; but though this sentence was given *in terrorem*, "yet it was not executed: it seems to be a kind of military sentence, though "given in Parliament." That is the passage I wished to refer to.

Mr. Justice Horridge—That is a very strong line, that it would not be "unless it was done by treachery." That is not a mere "might"; it is defining the law.

Mr. Sullivan—"The truth is, if it were delivered up by bribery or "treachery, it might be treason."

Mr. Justice Horridge—The last sentence you read is what I was referring to: "Unless it was done by treachery."

Mr. Sullivan—"Yet it is not treason by the common law, unless "it was done by treachery; but though this sentence was given *in* "*terrorem*, yet it was not executed; it seems to be a kind of military "sentence, though given in Parliament."

The Lord Chief Justice—That means if it was surrendered by reason of cowardice or imprudence, then it would not be treason at common law, or might not be, whichever phrase you choose to adopt; but if, on the other hand, it was surrendered by reason of bribery or treachery, that would be treason. Is not that the effect of it?

Mr. SULLIVAN—I submit not. I submit, when you read the whole passage, he really is not dealing with the question of adhering outside the realm at all, and is simply dealing with these two cases, and establishing nothing with regard to the statute or the common law, and he simply passes from them dismissing them as military sentences, throwing no light one way or the other.

The LORD CHIEF JUSTICE—That is an observation which is justified, I think, in my opinion, so far as it relates to surrendering the castle of the King by reason of cowardice or imprudence; but it is not justified if it relates to the surrender of the castle by reason of bribery or treachery; he seems to draw that very distinction. He says cowardice and imprudence is not treachery, but military law.

Mr. SULLIVAN—The opening statement, where one expects to find the most definite opinion, if definite opinion exists, is "The truth is, if it "was delivered up by bribery or treachery." That is the extreme case; it might be treason.

Mr. JUSTICE HORRIDGE—Supposing treason was not known outside the realm, it seems a funny sort of dissertation; he is dealing with giving up a castle outside the realm, and it seems, to my mind, a very large order to have this alternative put if the law was that there was no such thing as treason outside the realm.

Mr. SULLIVAN—What I am dealing with is, you will always have to come back to Lord Coke's authority to find the substance of the doctrine of treason outside the realm. Apparently Lord Coke thought it required authority to support it, and, my lord, I cite page 168 of Hale to the effect that these cases of the delivery of castles by their military custodians are not cases on the statute, and therefore are not authorities. The cases at all events are not authorities on the matter that I am dealing with.

Mr. JUSTICE HORRIDGE—Had not you better read the next passage; that is one of the difficulties I feel in your way; the statute of Henry "touching the trial of foreign treason, viz., adhering to the King's "enemies, as also for compassing the King's death without the kingdom, "at this day the statutes of 35 Henry VIII., chapter 2, hath sufficiently "provided for it."

The LORD CHIEF JUSTICE—It is under the statute this jurisdiction arises.

Mr. SULLIVAN—I have not come to the statute of Henry VIII., but on the passage I cite in my submission, until you have the statute of Henry VIII. the matter would be pure speculation only, because there could not be crimes for which the man could not be tried. If the authority in Dyer is correct, which apparently he suggests, the statute of Henry VIII. provides for the trial.

Mr. JUSTICE AVORY—Was not an English subject who committed murder abroad triable in this country if he came back?

Mr. SULLIVAN—I think not, my lord, at common law; I think the old difficulty of venue existed; that is my impression reading it, though at the moment I cannot give the answer on the book.

Mr. Justice Avory—I think you will find authority for the proposition he can be tried, and if he can be tried the Court probably found some way out of the difficulty about venue.

Mr. Sullivan—At the moment I am under the impression that, until some statutory provision was made, the common law took no cognisance of what a man did on territory that did not belong to the common law. I will have to cite, when I come to deal with *The King* v. *Vaughan*, and other cases of that type, authorities that the common law had no cognisance even of crimes committed within the realm, where the portion of the realm within which they were committed was outside the common law jurisdiction; it was to remedy that that one of the statutes was passed; there are two statutes of Henry VIII., the 28 Henry VIII. is one and the 35 Henry VIII. is the other.

The Lord Chief Justice—The 35 Henry VIII. we shall have to look at. Before you leave Hale there is a passage which seems to have a very direct bearing upon the point we are discussing at page 169; I do not think it has been read: "Touching the trial of high treason."

Mr. Sullivan—Mr. Justice Horridge read that just now.

The Lord Chief Justice—But I want the last part of it: "Touching "the trial of foreign treason, viz., adhering to the King's enemies, as "also for compassing the King's death without the kingdom, at this day "the statutes of 35 Henry VIII., chapter 2, hath sufficiently provided for "it." This passage I want to call your attention to: "But at common "law he might have been indicted in any county of England, and especially "where the offender's lands lie, if he have any." The authority for that is the 5 Richard II. If that is right, it gives authority for the trial for foreign treason in any county, particularly in a county where offender's lands lie.

Mr. Sullivan—If, in truth, that was supported by the authority given, that would get over the difficulty I allege.

Mr. Justice Horridge—And it would be inconsistent with what you tell us is the result of the case in the 2 Dyer.

Mr. Sullivan—An investigation of the case cited shows it to be as follows——

The Lord Chief Justice—You have considered it.

Mr. Sullivan—Yes. It was the case of a riot at Cambridge in which the burgesses rioted, and in the course of the riot apparently made some attack on the colleges, and some attempt to burn their charters. The case in question is that the burgesses were summoned to Parliament in respect of the riot occurring in their town, and their townsmen attempting to burn the records of the University; the burgesses were summoned to Parliament to show cause why their charter should not be forfeited.

The Lord Chief Justice—Are you suggesting that is the authority for this proposition in Hale? What has that to do with foreign treason?

Mr. Sullivan—My colleague, Professor Morgan, has investigated every one of these more ancient cases, and he returns me this extract of the case cited, and if there is some other case, I can only say it is not this one.

The LORD CHIEF JUSTICE—It seems to me miles away from the point; it is not like Sir Matthew Hale.

Mr. SULLIVAN—Is not this a justification for Stephen's Commentary on Coke, at page 57, that passages in the Third Institute are often entirely unwarranted by the authorities which he quotes for them?

The LORD CHIEF JUSTICE—It is a novel proposition to say that because Stephen commented severely on Coke, that therefore we are to take the same comment as made on Sir Matthew Hale.

Mr. JUSTICE HORRIDGE—That cannot be the case; there must be some mistake about that.

Mr. SULLIVAN—I agree; it does seem to me a transference to an object that was not within the original ambit of the statute. I quite forgot it was Hale I had open before me.

The ATTORNEY-GENERAL—I have sent for that particular case. My learned friend will allow me to point out it may or may not be the ground of the comment made by the learned author, Hale, but the advocate who appeared for the Crown said, in *Gallon's* case, "If a "man be adherent to the King's enemies in France, his land is forfeitable, "and his treason shall be tried where his land is, as has been oftentimes "done in respect of the adherence to the King's enemies in Scotland." That was said in the course of the argument.

The LORD CHIEF JUSTICE—What do you mean by *Gallon's* case?

The ATTORNEY-GENERAL—That is the case referred to.

Mr. SULLIVAN—It was the case of the burgesses of Cambridge.

The ATTORNEY-GENERAL—I have sent for it.

The LORD CHIEF JUSTICE—It does seem so strange, though it may be so, that in those days when there was so much happening abroad in which the Kings of England were interested, that it should not have been treason to commit the act in France, but treason if committed in England.

Mr. SULLIVAN—Is the reference right, the 5 Richard II., trial 54?

The ATTORNEY-GENERAL—That is *Peter Gallon's* case.

Mr. SULLIVAN—How there came to be discussion on the law of treason in the case I referred to I do not know. The case was looked up on the Roll of Parliament.

The ATTORNEY-GENERAL—I understand it is reported in Fitzherbert's Abridgment. I only happen to know of the case because I have the reference in the passage to the argument of the representative of the Crown.

The LORD CHIEF JUSTICE—I know there is a reference to it in Fitzherbert's Abridgment. We will see what the case is.

Mr. SULLIVAN—We may perhaps have looked at the wrong case. Sir Matthew Hale is more likely to be right than we are. My friends got it from the Rolls of Parliament, and apparently the reference is at all events consistent with the Rolls of Parliament. There may be a misapprehension about it. Hale introduces some new cases. Stephen's Commentary on Hale at page 62 is that he is too fond of repeating Coke literally and ignoring his mistakes. That is what Stephen says about Hale. Hale quotes three cases from the Close Roll, namely, 6 John, membrane 19; 7 Edward III., part 1, membrane 15 and membrane 9.

They are all prior to the statute. The first is apparently throwing little light on the subject, because it deals with the confiscation of the lands of the barons who renounced their allegiance to King John in Normandy. We are all familiar with the disputes that were going on in Normandy as to who was the King of Normandy; the position of a baron in those days must have been a somewhat difficult one, not from the dual alliance but the dual claims of his alliance, and they fought out their battles over his body. The barons in Normandy who acknowledged fealty to the wrong lord had their lands forfeited in the reign of John. This is before the Act, and it does not throw much light on the subject we are discussing here, and would, perhaps, involve considerable investigation on feudal law.

The LORD CHIEF JUSTICE—I am very loath to interrupt or to interfere with your argument, because it is obviously based upon a very complete research, but the difficulty is we must at some time come to more modern times, and the law laid down there. You see these matters have been discussed, and although it may be true that Lord Coke went further than he was justified in going, still if you find that later authorities have adopted that view, and that there is a judicial authority for it, even though it does not actually decide the case, it is asking much of us to ask us to decide that Lord Coke was wrong.

Mr. SULLIVAN—If I submit there has been no case decided on it——

The LORD CHIEF JUSTICE—Not on the express point.

Mr. SULLIVAN—If, as I submit, this is a case of first impression, so far as the decisions upon it go, by any Court of justice affecting either person or property——

The LORD CHIEF JUSTICE—Is that quite right?

Mr. SULLIVAN—I say if it is.

The LORD CHIEF JUSTICE—I do not follow. You will tell me directly when you come to it how there could be a conviction in *Lynch's* case if the present argument is right. Lynch was indicted for treason in South Africa.

Mr. SULLIVAN—I am going to deal with *Lynch's* case, in which the case was allowed to go to the jury, but I preferred to deal with the authorities there cited.

The LORD CHIEF JUSTICE—I do not want to take you to *Lynch's* case at once unless it is convenient. I doubt whether we serve any useful purpose by looking too much into these earlier authorities when we have to deal with modern times and the law that binds us now.

Mr. SULLIVAN—I am sorry your lordship did not express any desire beforehand that it might be most necessary to deal with *The King* v. *Lynch.* That is reported in 1903 King's Bench at page 444. In the Law Reports, report of *The King* v. *Lynch*, this point is not reported.

The ATTORNEY-GENERAL—Yes, at page 446.

Mr. SULLIVAN—There was a motion to quash the indictment.

The ATTORNEY-GENERAL—On this ground?

Mr. SULLIVAN—On this ground, but your lordship sees that there is simply a very short argument given, and the only decision of the Court is upon a matter of procedure; that is why I originally called attention to it; the only judgment of the Court is not upon the point we are considering, but solely on the question of procedure whether the indictment should be quashed.

The LORD CHIEF JUSTICE—I do not know whether you have had the opportunity of reading the long argument upon it.

Mr. SULLIVAN—Yes, I have, from the shorthand notes.

Mr. JUSTICE AVORY—The point was repeated on the conclusion of the case for the prosecution.

Mr. SULLIVAN—I shall have to trespass again and borrow the shorthand notes of *The King* v. *Lynch*.

Mr. JUSTICE AVORY—You will find on the conclusion of the case for the prosecution the argument was really put before the Court; it was quite shortly put at the earlier stage.

Mr. SULLIVAN—So I noticed. The argument comes at page 107 of the shorthand notes, and is continued on page 108. There is an authority cited—*Maclane's* case and *Smith O'Brien's* case—and the observation of Mr. Justice Finucane is stated later on, namely, that the adherence is imputed to the person charged, not to the place of the offence. The important matter to show what was in the mind of the Court is the manner in which Lord Alverstone dealt with *The King* v. *Vaughan* at page 109—"It seems to me that *The King* v. *Vaughan* is a direct authority against "you; it is in the 13 State Trials, and the passage is at page 525 and page "526. I have no doubt you have looked at this most carefully. There "are passages in Hale and others that are against this contention. They "may be the relics of a barbaric age, but you have to deal with them."

There is an observation further up on the same page by the Lord Chief Justice—"I have no doubt you have considered it, but it seems to "me that *The King* v. *Vaughan* is a direct authority. The charge against "the prisoner is left to the jury upon the count only of adhering to the "King's enemies, that being done upon the high seas, and the point is then "attempted to be taken that he was not a British subject at all." The Attorney-General calls attention to the fact that there is no count for compassing, as the counsel for the defendant had suggested, and then the Lord Chief Justice says, "It seems to me *The King* v. *Vaughan* is a "direct authority against you." Then he says, "I have no doubt you have "looked at it most carefully; there are passages in Hale and others that are "against this contention. They may be the relics of a barbaric age, but "you have to deal with them."

Then there is a quotation from Hale. The argument of the Attorney-General commences at the bottom of page 111. And he says, "I men-"tioned a statute which was passed in the eighteenth year of George II. "which related to the case of a certain number of English subjects who had, "while this country was engaged in war with Spain, taken commissions from "the Spanish Government and been guilty of buccaneering and piracy in "the West Indies. The statute was passed to remove any doubt that these "persons might be tried for piracy although the act that they had com-"mitted was also one of high treason. I shall just read the words of the "statute." I will deal with the statute in one moment. He cites the dictum, because he admits it is no more, of Mr. Justice Willes, in advising the Lords in *Mulcahy's* case; that is clearly a dictum, and no more.

The LORD CHIEF JUSTICE—I think that is quite right; it was not necessary for the decision, but that was the opinion of all the judges. It was the opinion of the judges delivered to the House of Lords in *Mulcahy's* case, and they construed the language of the statute of 1351 contrary to your present argument.

Mr. SULLIVAN—In the summary of the argument in the House of Lords it would appear he said at the bottom of page 317—" By the statute of " 25 Edward III., statute 5, chapter 2 (extended to Ireland by Poyning's " Act, see *O'Brien* v. *The Queen*), it was declared to be treason." Then he purports to quote the words of the statute—" When a man doth compass or " imagine the death of our Lord the King," &c., " or if a man do levy war " against our Lord the King in his realm or by adhering to the King's " enemies in his realm or elsewhere and thereof he probably attainted of " open deed." He purports to quote the words of the statute because it is in inverted commas. It was a dictum pure and simple; the case of *The Queen* v. *Mulcahy* had nothing to say to treason without the realm at all; the point that went to the House of Lords did not involve that question.

The LORD CHIEF JUSTICE—I think you are quite justified in saying that.

Mr. SULLIVAN—The case is reported in 3 English and Irish appeal cases at common law, and the decision in the Court below, apart from this question of the jury, and the only matter of argument in the Court below, was whether a man could commit an act in Dublin when not in Dublin himself to commit it, it being proved it was done by a member of the Corporation of which he was proved to be one.

Mr. JUSTICE HORRIDGE—I have not the copy of Lynch's trial in the shorthand notes, but I have *The Times* Law Reports, and it seems that the point was not only taken, in the first instance, before plea, but was taken afterwards at the close of the case.

Mr. SULLIVAN—At that time the argument was developed.

Mr. JUSTICE HORRIDGE—Whether rightly or wrongly, the Lord Chief Justice must have decided the point by leaving the issue to the jury.

Mr. SULLIVAN—He did, on the authority of *The King* v. *Vaughan*, which the Lord Chief Justice more than once repeats is conclusive and decisive on the subject; and if he was right in that, and if *The King* v. *Vaughan* that he purports to follow is conclusive on the subject, I could not hope to convince your lordships after this lapse of time, and your lordships, in this Court at all events, would follow the same precedent. Now let me take *The King* v. *Vaughan*, which is reported in the 13 State Trials.

Mr. JUSTICE AVORY—It is also reported in 2 Salkeld.

Mr. SULLIVAN—I am reading at column 487; that will give your lordship the indictment for the trial of Captain Thomas Vaughan. It was an indictment tried before Sir Charles Hedges, judge of the High Court of Admiralty, the Lord Chief Justice Holt, the Lord Chief Justice Treby, the Lord Chief Baron Ward, Mr. Justice Turton, and others of His Majesty's Commissioners. It was tried before the Lord High Admiral and the other persons that were mentioned in the statute that I will have to open to your lordships, as showing conclusively that it was tried in respect of acts done within the realm of England, though not within the jurisdiction of the common law.

Mr. JUSTICE AVORY—Surely that was a trial under a special Commission.

Mr. SULLIVAN—It was presided over by the judge of the High Court of Admiralty.

The LORD CHIEF JUSTICE—And Lord Chief Justice Holt.

Mr. SULLIVAN—Yes. I suggest that since the President of the Court was the Admiralty judge, that shows it was tried under a statute which I will pass to, and I will show that the judge of Admiralty and divers other weighty persons, that were construed to mean Her Majesty's judges, sat with him under the statute of 28 Henry VIII.

The LORD CHIEF JUSTICE—There is no doubt whatever it was an indictment for high treason on the high seas.

Mr. SULLIVAN—It was an indictment for high treason within the realm, as I will show your lordship; it was on the narrow seas. I will show that at that date there was no doubt or question that the place where the acts were committed was within the realm of England. The date of the trial is in 1696, and in 1696 to doubt the realm of England extended to the narrow seas would itself be such an act as might have been extremely dangerous to a century earlier. I am reading two-thirds down column 488. The prisoner was indicted for "being then on the "high seas, within the jurisdiction of the Admiralty of England, about "14 leagues from Deal, did then and there by force and arms falsely, "maliciously, and traitorously aid and help and assist the enemies of our "said Lord the King." That is the first count. The second is of great importance: "As a false traitor against our said Lord the King further "designing, practising, and with his whole strength intending the common "peace of tranquility of this kingdom of England to disturb," an offence, observe, against the common peace of the kingdom, "and a war and "rebellion against the said King upon the high seas within the juris- "diction of the Admiralty of England to move, stir up, and procure; "and the said Lord the King, from the title, honour, royal name, and "imperial crown of his kingdom of England, and dominions upon the "high seas, to depose and deprive; and miserable slaughter of the sub- "jects of the said Lord the King, and this kingdom of England, upon "the high seas, and within the jurisdiction aforesaid, to cause and pro- "cure; on the said 8th day of July, in the said seventh year of the King, "upon the high seas, about 14 leagues from Deal, and within the "dominion of the Crown of England, and within the jurisdiction of the "Admiralty of England aforesaid"; then with other traitors war against the King he levied and waged; he levied and waged war.

Mr. JUSTICE HORRIDGE—It was not upon a British vessel, was it? I do not gather that; it was on a French vessel; it was not within the theory that an English ship is a portion of the Dominions?

Mr. SULLIVAN—No.

Mr. JUSTICE HORRIDGE—It is laid as within the Admiralty jurisdiction. The "Franconia" showed us that the ordinary Admiralty jurisdiction was not, at any rate, beyond the three-mile limit, and this was 14 leagues from Deal; the facts were that it was not on a British ship, and it was levied outside the Admiralty jurisdiction.

Mr. SULLIVAN—Outside the common law jurisdiction and within the Admiralty jurisdiction, and not being a British ship, it being a French ship, shows that he must have been within the realm. I will show you by overwhelming authority that he was within the realm.

Mr. Justice Horridge—The indictment alleges it as such.

Mr. Sullivan—The indictment alleges it as being within the realm, and it further provides: "And the said Thomas Vaughan then and there "being aboard the said ship of war called the 'Loyal Clencarty,' assembled "with other false rebels and traitors as aforesaid." That is a word applicable only within the realm. "Assembled with the other false "rebels and traitors as aforesaid, maliciously, wickedly, and traitorously "sailed a cruising to several maritime places, with the aforesaid ship "of war called the 'Loyal Clencarty,' with an intent to take, spoil, and "carry away the ships, goods, and money of our said Lord the King, "and his subjects, by force and arms, upon the high and open seas, "within the jurisdiction aforesaid; against the duty of his allegiance, the "peace of our Lord the King, his crown and dignities; and likewise "against the form of a statute in this case made and provided."

Now that, I do submit, is the clearest indictment of a man doing something within the realm, and I will show you that he was within the realm. I will suggest to you that when you look at the President of the Court in his relation to the other members of the Court assisting him, the President was the judge of the Admiralty Court, and that shows he was tried under the 28 Henry, and not the 35 Henry. Had he been tried under the 35 Henry for a foreign treason, the Admiralty judge would not have sat as the President of it. Now, the question arises whether the piracy which was the offence alleged to have been committed was within the realm of England. My lords, on that there are any number of cases. In *The King* v. *Heyn*, in the Law Reports 2, Exchequer Division, I wish to cite from page 178. The Chief Justice says at the bottom: "Even to our times the doctrine of the three-mile "zone has never been adopted by the writers on English law. To Black- "stone, who in his Commentaries treats of the sea with reference to the "prerogative, as also to his modern editor, Mr. Stephen, it is unknown, "equally so to Mr. Chitty, whose work on the prerogative is of the "present century. It was not till the beginning of this century that any "mention of such a doctrine occurs in the Courts of this country. But "to the Continental jurists the suggestion of Bynkershovk seemed a "happy solution of the great controversy as to the freedom of the sea." In Coke upon Littleton, section 432, it is said: "For if a man be upon "the sea of England, he is within the kingdom or realm of England and "within the ligeance of the King of England and of his Crown of Eng- "land. And yet the high sea is out of the jurisdiction of the common "law and within the jurisdiction of the Lord Admiral." Selden defines the boundary of the kingdom of England—"Within the kingdom is taken "for that which is within the four seas," at page 387, and at page 399 he says "within the four seas and within the realm signifies one and "the same thing." He says the realm means more than the land of England, and he shows the Admiralty Commissioners' jurisdiction extends far beyond it. In Hale *De Jure Maris* it is said, "The narrow sea "adjoining to the coast of England is part of the waste and demesnes "and dominions of the King of England whether it lie within the body "of any country or not. This is abundantly proved by Master Selden." Then he goes on to distinguish between the wide sea, as he calls it, as out of the precincts of the seas belonging to the realm of England, and he speaks of the narrow seas at 11 and 14. Selden cites the Admiralty Commission to show that the territorial waters of the British Channel terminated only with the coast of France. As late as the seventeenth century, I think you will find, my recollection is this, cases in which complaint was actually made by a certain king, the Spanish or the Dutch, that the King of England had failed in his duty of neutrality of keeping the King's peace up to the French shore.

The LORD CHIEF JUSTICE—You need not labour that point, at any rate, as we are at present advised that *The King* v. *Vaughan* does not bind us.

Mr. SULLIVAN—Very well, my lord. Now if *The King* v. *Vaughan* does not deal with the matter, the next argument of the Attorney-General in *The King* v. *Lynch* was the statute of the 18 of George II. That is set out *in extenso* in the shorthand notes, if I may quote from them, at page 112. *The King* v. *Vaughan*, the Attorney-General said, was the chief authority upon which he relied, and I think he puts it forward as being a matter of considerable importance. The chief difficulty I feel is that there are so many authorities. He puts it in the forefront of his argument. Now I will come to deal with the statute.

Mr. JUSTICE AVORY—It is the 18 George II.?

Mr. SULLIVAN—Yes; chapter 30. Now I will cite the statute, and I would ask your lordships to bear in mind this: there were two statutes of Henry VIII. dealing with all sorts of offences. As regards the first one, the recital sets out that there are treasons, felonies, murders, robberies, and so forth, which escaped unpunished, which are committed on the King's dominions on the high seas, because they have to be tried under the civil law. They are all civil law offences, and have to be tried by the civil law of the Admiralty. They removed that, and the statute of 28 Henry VIII. provided a tribunal, or, rather, provided a procedure to enable the tribunal to try them according to the course of the common law. Now, the statute of 28 Henry VIII. dealt with all sorts of offences committed within what was called the King's dominions on the high seas, and I will have to comment on that, that if there was a foreign law of treason it must have been noted at the time. At all events that was only with regard to the argument of *The King* v. *Vaughan* which I have disposed of, and I will not refer to it. But under the statute of Henry VIII., at the time of the Act of 1745 which I shall read to your lordship, the following difficulty had arisen. Indicted under the statute of Henry for piracy committed in the King's jurisdiction of the high seas outside of the four seas, the pirates produced letters of commission of alien enemies accordingly justifying themselves by the fact that they were not pirates *hostes humani generis*, but only persons committing piracy within the 28 Henry VIII. by breach of allegiance and making war upon the King's ships, which were so many castles of the King. It stands in this way, that it does seem somewhat amusing that a man for being a pirate should be anxious to prove that he was something worse; but, in fact, that course was being taken, and doubts had arisen whether the production of the commission of the alien persons at war with the Crown removed that offence against the King's ships from the category mentioned, namely, the treasons that were cognisable by the Court of Admiralty according to the civil law.

There being that distinction to draw I rely on my argument before I approach the case that the civil law recognised the breach of the personal allegiance on the high seas without the realm of England, but still within the King's dominion of the high seas, and within the jurisdiction of the Admiralty, which was a civil law as recited in the statute. It was to remove those doubts that this Act was passed in 1745, and what did it provide? It provided, first, that notwithstanding that he had an alien commission, and thereby adhering to the King's enemies on the high seas without the realm he would have committed the civil law offence of one of the treasons mentioned in 28 Henry VIII., that though he should prove that, he might be nevertheless tried for piracy as originally indicted on his commission of the alien enemy which was to save him from being tried as a pirate. It had two other provisions. It provided that if he was convicted or acquitted as a pirate he should not be tried again for high treason, and it winds up by a proviso, that where he is not proceeded against as a pirate he is not to be free—the statute did not interfere with the right to indict him as a person committing a treason on the high seas; under what statute? Under the statute of 28 Henry VIII., and the misapprehension of that reading in *The King* v. *Vaughan* was that if you read it as making a person liable to be charged with high treason without the realm, as Lord Alverstone did, as being applicable to solid ground outside the realm, it would be an authority against me, but he is not to be tried for high treason on solid ground. The only statute that would refer to that is not the statute of 28 Henry VIII., which you are at liberty to proceed under by the saving clause of the Act of 1745; it is the statute with regard to the foreign treasons passed in 35 Henry VIII., and passed, I submit, to deal, not with the statute of Edward, but to deal with the infinite multitude of what I may term fancy treasons that had grown up by special statutes in the reign of Henry VIII. which rendered it extremely difficult to say from day to day whether one's opinions were loyal or treasonable. Owing to the number of statutes in the reign of Henry VIII. creating special offences for treason, that was followed in 35 Henry VIII. by a statute of foreign treasons enabling for the first time foreign treasons abroad, of which I think at the time there were a multitude, to be tried within the realm of England.

Now I will refer to the statute of 1745, and I think it bears out exactly what I said.

The Lord Chief Justice—It seems extraordinary to contemplate that according to the common law of this country if a person committed this offence abroad, and he could be got within the realm, you could not prosecute him as a traitor.

Mr. Sullivan—According to the case in Dyer, if that be an authority, until the statute was passed enabling you to do so, you could not do it.

The LORD CHIEF JUSTICE—I wanted to look at that case, but I have not looked at it, because you said you would refer to it later.

Mr. SULLIVAN—I am sure that Lord Coke in dealing in the Third Institutes with piracy says practically the same thing, if I may turn to the Third Institute again. I am not quite sure Lord Coke does not say the same thing under the head of "Piracy" in chapter 49. He says on page 113 (this is *apropos* of piracy), "Treason done out of the realm "is declared to be treason by the statute of 25 Edward III."—that is the one we are construing here—"and yet at the making of this Act of 28 "Henry VIII. it wanted trial at common law." So, according to Lord Coke, he points out at page 113 that until 28 Henry VIII. these acts were not triable at common law.

The LORD CHIEF JUSTICE—It is a very strong statement of the law against you by Lord Coke.

Mr. JUSTICE HORRIDGE—It begins by the assumption that treason outside the realm was triable.

Mr. SULLIVAN—No, but treason done out of the realm is declared to be treason.

The LORD CHIEF JUSTICE—By the statute.

Mr. SULLIVAN—By the statute that we are discussing. I have Lord Coke's authority against me, and I have sought to face that candidly.

Mr. JUSTICE HORRIDGE—You have Sir Matthew Hale and the *obiter dictum* in the House of Lords against you.

Mr. SULLIVAN—The *obiter dictum* is not the expression of an opinion, but purports to be the quotation from something.

The LORD CHIEF JUSTICE—Mr. Justice Willes is delivering the judgment of all the judges in the House of Lords, and if you look at the judgment of the House of Lords, Lord Cairns agrees with every word, with all the opinions and views expressed.

Mr. SULLIVAN—If that establishes that the quotation is correct I certainly would have no case, but it is a quotation. He purports to quote the statute, and if that was the statute I should not have to trouble your lordships.

Mr. JUSTICE HORRIDGE—What do you mean by "purported to quote the statute?"

Mr. SULLIVAN—It is in inverted commas.

Mr. JUSTICE HORRIDGE—He is saying what he thinks the Act enacts; it is almost incredible that he made the mistake of omitting words from the statute when he purported to quote it correctly just before. If he purported to say what the statute really enacted and put it in inverted commas, then it would be against you.

Mr. SULLIVAN—It would. He quotes the words accurately in the immediately preceding passage. In the case of *The Queen* v. *Mulcahy* that observation had nothing to do with the case. It points to the fact that at common law there surely could not be known an offence for which a man could not be tried, and Lord Coke himself states that although treason done out of the realm is declared to be treason by statute, a statute can create any offence, but common law was certainly not cognisant of offences that it could not try itself, and yet at the making of this Act of 28 Henry VIII. it wanted trial at common law.

Mr. Justice Avory—Does not the statute of 35 Henry VIII. assume that certain treasons at all events committed abroad were triable here?

Mr. Sullivan—Certainly.

Mr. Justice Avory—What are they, do you say; what treasons do you say are triable here?

Mr. Sullivan—To go through the various statutes of Henry VIII. would wander, to some extent, when one recollects that within a very short period it was enacted by statute to be treason anywhere at any time or at any place so far as I read the statute, first to believe that Elizabeth was legitimate, and you are given every permutation and combination of the King's views on subjects such as that, also views on ecclesiastical subjects, and views on theology. Offences of all sorts were created and made treason under the statute of Henry VIII. The history of treason in that reign is the most interesting thing, and I should have thought that 38 Henry VIII. was a climax to enable a great number of these offences to be tried which had been created in his reign, and had not been tried because the common law had no cognisance of them if they were out of the realm, and they certainly could not be done out of the realm, according to the terms of a great number of statutes. The 35 Henry VIII. was passed with reference to treason as a very large code—or not a code—because he is substituting one for another, but, at all events, combining a large number of statutes creating offences which could be punished as treason, though committed out of the realm, and would enable them to be dealt with, provision for which did not exist if Lord Coke is right in his appreciation of it, and if the opinions of the judges were right as late as Philip and Mary.

Mr. Justice Avory—That is what I was putting to you, that the only object of the Act of 35 Henry VIII. is, as the words say, "Forasmuch "as some doubts and questions have been moved, that certain kinds "of treasons" can be tried here. It was for the purpose of making those, if I may adopt the phrase you used, eccentric forms of treasons which you have just been referring to.

Mr. Sullivan—When committed out of the realm.

Mr. Justice Avory—For the purpose of making them triable. Does not that enactment assume that that which had always been triable at common law was already triable.

Mr. Sullivan—The recital of the statute, I submit, shows that the cases could not have been tried, because the recitals show it; it deals with all matters declared to be treason.

Mr. Justice Avory—It begins by saying that "Doubts and questions "have been moved, that certain kinds of treasons, misprisions, and con-"cealments of treasons done, perpetrated, or committed out of the King's "Majesty's realm of England," might by the common law be inquired into within the realm; that is the only doubt that has arisen. I should rather assume that when no doubt has ever arisen what was known to be treason by the common law was already triable.

Mr. Sullivan—"That all manner of offences being already made and "declared——"

Mr. Justice Avory—I think you must begin earlier.

Mr. Sullivan—"Forasmuch as some doubts and questions have been "moved, that certain kinds of treasons, misprisions, and concealments of "treasons done, perpetrated, or committed out of the King's Majesty's "common laws of this realm cannot be inquired of, heard, and determined "within this his said realm of England."

Mr. Justice Avory—That is only the certain kinds of treason there referred to.

Mr. Sullivan—Might I submit the certain kinds of treasons are to be found reading on, "For a plain remedy order and declaration therein "to be had and made"—that is with reference to those matters—"be "it enacted by authority of this present Parliament, that all manner "of offences, being already made and declared, or hereafter to be made "or declared by any of the laws and statutes of this realm, to be treasons, "misprisions of treasons, or concealments of treasons, and done, per- "petrated, or committed, or hereafter to be done, perpetrated, or com- "mitted by any persons out of this realm of England, shall be from "henceforth inquired of, heard, and determined before the King's justices "of his Bench, for pleas to be holden before himself." That shows it was all triable by the King's Bench.

Mr. Justice Avory—That only sweeps them all into that statute.

Mr. Sullivan—Yes, it does.

The Lord Chief Justice—It is from that statute that the King's Bench derives the authority for trying all treasons committed abroad.

Mr. Sullivan—If such there be.

The Lord Chief Justice—It is for that reason that this case is being tried here.

Mr. Sullivan—If such there be; anything that is treason; it creates no new treason; it is mere procedure. The importance is that the necessity for the statute was that the King's Bench, which was the representative of the common law, had no jurisdiction till it got the statute, so says Dyer, and if, therefore, you have no jurisdiction till you get a statute, I submit that that is conclusive that the offence did not exist at common law.

Mr. Justice Horridge—Just follow the argument you put with the point that Mr. Justice Avory puts to you. Your argument is that it could not be treason outside the realm, because it was not triable by the King's Bench. That is as I understand your argument. Is that right?

Mr. Sullivan—At common law.

Mr. Justice Horridge—That statute says expressly that there are treasons abroad which cannot be tried here, and which therefore the statute enacts shall be tried here, and therefore if your argument is correct there would be no treason abroad at that time, because the very ones they are dealing with here and saying are treasons are things which they say cannot be triable at law.

Mr. Sullivan—At the time of 35 Henry VIII. I stated there were a great number of treasons.

Mr. Justice Horridge—If they could not be treasons when committed abroad because the King's Bench could not try them the whole principle of the Act is wrong.

Mr. Sullivan—I did not say that, for, as I stated, the common law could have no knowledge of crimes that it could not investigate, but the statute could create a crime in any part of the world, and the statute might provide for this trial if it provides that anything already made and declared by any law or statute of this realm to be treason may be tried. It is not that the statute would not make it a treason because it could not be tried, but I suggest common law knew no treason that it, at all events, could not try. That is my argument which I submit to your lordships. The importance of that with regard to the argument on the Act of 1745 is that the proviso at the end is not a proviso as read by the Court in *The King* v. *Lynch*.

Mr. JUSTICE HORRIDGE—In Archbold, at the foot of that statute, it goes on as to the mode of trial of treasons committed without the realm before the passing of this statute, see 2 Hawkins, chapter 25, section 48, and they refer to *Platt's* case, 1 Leach, page 168. You seem to have Hawkins against you.

Mr. SULLIVAN—The last part of the statement on that page is in my favour. To enforce my argument as to the common law I will refer to the section relied upon by the Crown in the Act of 1745—"Provided that "nothing in this Act contained shall be construed to extend to prevent "any persons guilty of any of the said crimes, who shall not be tried "according to this Act, from being tried for high treason within this "realm, according to the aforesaid act of the twenty-eighth year of King "Henry the Eighth."

Mr. JUSTICE HORRIDGE—Are you reading the statute of 5 and 6 Edward?

Mr. SULLIVAN—No, the Act of 18 George II.

The LORD CHIEF JUSTICE—The 1745 Act.

Mr. SULLIVAN—Yes, in the shorthand notes that is being cited.

Mr. JUSTICE AVORY—Have you looked at *Platt's* case in 1 Leach?

Mr. SULLIVAN—I have. I am going to refer to it. *The King* v. *Platt* was an application for *habeas corpus*.

Mr. JUSTICE AVORY—That is quite consistent with good law being laid down.

Mr. SULLIVAN—The best of law is consistent with *habeas corpus*. In that case it does not appear what the matter charged was. It was high treason. Now within the words of the statute of Edward that we are discussing the first section might be construed in terms to extend to compassing the King's death anywhere in the world, and the terms are wide enough to cover it. All that I am arguing is that where the terms of the statute are not wide enough to cover it, it could not be extended, and accordingly we do not know what the charge against Platt was except that it was high treason. The decision arose on warrant, and warrant only.

Mr. JUSTICE AVORY—Listen to this passage from the report. "This "warrant therefore contains sufficient certainty to show that the high "treason which it charges the prisoner with having committed was, in fact, "committed out of the realm of England. It was the ancient opinion, "that the species of treason which consists, by 25 Edward III., chapter 2, "in adhering to the King's enemies, might be tried, before the statute "35 Henry VIII., chapter 2, within the kingdom, by the rules of the "common law, though the aid and comfort was afforded without the "realm." That is a direct authority that that particular treason can be tried within the realm, although the aid and comfort to the enemy is given without the realm.

Mr. Sullivan—There are a number of cases in which it has been done in this sense when the offender is within the realm. That was the case of *The King* v. *Wheldon;* where the offender is within the realm, he may aid and comfort the enemy outside the realm, and be guilty of the offence charged; that is the opinion of Mr. Justice Finucane.

The Lord Chief Justice—He may be within the realm, although giving the aid and comfort without the realm.

Mr. Sullivan—Yes, the offence may be committed within the realm, he being there, the offender.

The Lord Chief Justice—He may send information.

Mr. Sullivan—He may.

Mr. Justice Avory—That was *Platt's* case.

Mr. Sullivan—*Platt's* case does not show what he is charged with at all. He was charged with treason at Savannah. The question for decision in *Platt's* case was, could the Court deal with him, and they held they could not, because they were not the Court to try him. They held they were not the Court under 35 Henry VIII., and therefore application for *habeas corpus* should be made to the Court that could try him; that contention did prevail, so that was the net decision of *Platt's* case.

Mr. Justice Avory—The decision was they refused the *habeas corpus.*

Mr. Sullivan—They did; they said they had no jurisdiction to enter into the matter at all; they were not the right Court to have cognisance of the matter, because they were not the Court within 35 Henry VIII. Now, it is a most significant fact that, whatever observations you may find, you cannot find in any reported cases a prosecution under the statute in which the point is decided other than *The King* v. *Lynch.* *The King* v. *Lynch* proceeds on *The King* v. *Vaughan* expressly; your lordships are satisfied that that supposed view of the judgment disappears, and with the foundation the edifice goes too.

The Lord Chief Justice—Supposing you put your pen through *The King* v. *Lynch*, assume that you are entitled to do that, at any rate, in this Court, which is a doubtful proposition, considering that we are a Court of co-ordinate jurisdiction, but assuming you could get back to the words of the statute, everything must turn upon the words of the statute.

Mr. Sullivan—That is all I am arguing.

The Lord Chief Justice—The whole point is whether the word "else-"where" governs "aid and comfort" or governs "adhering to the "King's enemies."

Mr. Sullivan—I should not have kept your lordships for the length of time I have done were not it that I thought that there stood in my way of coming down to the words of the statute what appeared to be the authorities which required to be analysed as giving the words of the statute a meaning different to what they should ordinarily bear. That has been the point of my argument, and is my apology for taking up so much time.

The Lord Chief Justice—I do not think you have occupied too much time. Supposing you have done what you set out to do—this is what I mean—you still get back to the statute.

Mr. SULLIVAN—I submit the words of the statute themselves, unless you are driven by authority to give them some different meaning, and I submit you are not, are reasonably plain and absolutely clear with regard to the offence charged, otherwise may I point out this, that if the words of the statute mean the charge that I have read out in this indictment, why is it that they are not set out as being the charge? The fact that the statute is not quoted, and the fact that something is alleged that is not in terms within the statute, is the foundation of my argument, that that which is alleged here, not being the wording of the statute, is, in fact, a contortion of the statute.

The LORD CHIEF JUSTICE—I follow.

Mr. SULLIVAN—The words are, "If a man do levy war against our "Lord the King in his realm, or be adherent to the King's enemies in "his realm giving them aid and comfort in the realm or elsewhere." Have not the words "in the realm" the same significance in both contexts? The word "or" occurs before the words "be adherent"; there is no suggestion of the word "or" before the words "giving aid and "comfort." Levying war and adhering are two offences, not three. The construction sought to be placed on the statute by the Crown provides three offences out of these two clauses I have read, because a man may be charged with either being adherent to the King's enemies in his realm, or on the construction of the statute contended for, charged with giving them aid and comfort in the realm or elsewhere.

Mr. JUSTICE HORRIDGE—That does not necessarily follow; it may be that there are two offences; the first one, if a man do levy war against our Lord the King in his realm or elsewhere, and the second offence, the word "elsewhere" governing both, adhering to the King's enemies in his realm, giving them aid and comfort in his realm or elsewhere.

Mr. SULLIVAN—The statute has been in consideration for a very long time, and I am not aware that that construction of "elsewhere" applied to "within the realm" in regard to levying war has ever before been suggested in any case.

Mr. JUSTICE HORRIDGE—It may not be necessary to do it, but it does not follow that it makes three offences.

Mr. SULLIVAN—I agree. My only apology for not at the moment answering your lordship's observation is that, so far as I had been able to investigate the statute and read it, at the moment I do not remember having that opinion suggested to me before, or have I noticed it.

Mr. JUSTICE HORRIDGE—It may be it only makes two, if you are correct, one levying war against the King in his realm, and the other by adhering to the King's enemies in his realm or elsewhere. The definition of adhering is giving them aid and comfort in the realm or elsewhere.

The LORD CHIEF JUSTICE—The whole question really is whether you read the words "aiding and comforting" as if they were in a bracket. If you do that, Coke, Hale, Hawkins, and Fitzherbert are all of them right; if you do not do that then there is a considerable foundation for your argument that you must read the words "or elsewhere," as if they were the alternative of giving aid and comfort within the realm. If you do read them, on the other hand, as laying down that the offence is adhering to the King's enemies within his realm or elsewhere, you give full meaning to the words "giving aid and comfort" as words which are describing and manifesting the intent with which the statute is there dealing. Giving aid and comfort as manifesting the intent would apply both to adherence to the King's enemies within the realm, and to adherence to the King's enemies without the realm.

Mr. Sullivan—I agree, if you deal with it on the basis of being adherent to the King's enemies in his realm, and they were simply defined as being giving to them aid and comfort in the realm or elsewhere; that is one construction, but it is a totally different construction; we are not dealing with brackets.

The Lord Chief Justice—There is authority for saying we have no right to look at brackets. We decided that in this Court, or at least expressed an opinion after hearing the authorities in this Court quite recently, and there is the authority of Lord Esher in the Court of Appeal for saying you must disregard brackets.

Mr. Sullivan—The construction must be on the express terms of the statute as they stand. You do not attribute to a statute words that are repugnant unless you are driven to it; you do not attribute to a statute that it is tautological; you merely read it and give effect to the statute as being couched in the necessary terms to expound its own meaning. If therefore you have to expound the statute by its own terms, I submit that it is clear from the Norman French that the giving them aid and comfort refers solely to the man, the person named in the prior part of the statute, and the person who at the date of the statute had to be within the realm, and therefore to be tried. Looking at the Norman French, according to the grammatical construction, it is the person who shall be adherent, giving them aid and comfort, wherever they may be, adherent to the King's enemies in his realm.

The Lord Chief Justice—The Norman French does not help you; it brings you back to the same point. I have looked at it, and it leaves you just where you were.

Mr. Sullivan—It is perfectly clear, I submit, on the grammatical construction, within his realm must be given effect to in that context there, and "donnant" is not a description of the offence committed, it is only a description of the overt acts by which it may be proved.

The Lord Chief Justice—The difficulty which I always feel is that you are arguing it before us as if it was a case of first impression. We have to deal with it with the authority of all these great authorities of the common law, who all say the law of treason is applicable outside the King's realm.

Mr. Sullivan—I quite recognise it.

The Lord Chief Justice—So far as I know—I have no doubt you have had the opportunity of far greater search than I have been able to make—I know of no authority in any text-book in your favour.

Mr. Sullivan—Nor do I.

The Lord Chief Justice—It is a strong construction when we are dealing with authorities such as Coke, Hale, Hawkins, and Fitzherbert.

Mr. Sullivan—What I submit is a matter of great importance is this, that a text-book is an excellent exposition of the common law, when you require what was the common law received prior to the law regulating the affairs of man and man at a distant date, for that is the common law, but text-books are no authority on the construction of a statute unless they are vouched by judicial decisions that that construction is right. The statute is the primary expounder of its own meaning; the text-book is an excellent exposition of what was the received opinion of lawyers after the statute.

The LORD CHIEF JUSTICE—I do not want to interrupt you—I am afraid we have been doing so a good deal lately for the purpose of elucidating the point—but you must not take me as assenting to that proposition. I cannot myself assent to the position that when you find all the great authorities on the law of England for three or four centuries stating that the law of England is laid down in a particular statute, and is so and so, that we shall pay no attention to those words, and disregard them, unless you can find something which shows that those opinions are entirely wrong. I think we are bound to pay great attention to them myself.

Mr. SULLIVAN—I quite appreciate that view. What I wanted to convey was, if these authorities are to be regarded, or if the terms of the statute are to be regarded, we have to go back to the terms of the statute to get the construction, and if the proper construction of the statute is what I suggest, then it is the words of the statute you must pay attention to. I put it no more than that.

The LORD CHIEF JUSTICE—I quite agree with that.

Mr. SULLIVAN—There are nine cases on this section that we have been discussing, I hope not at too great a length, and in every case the distinction has been, if he could be said within the jurisdiction to aid the enemy without.

The LORD CHIEF JUSTICE—May not the reason be that you do not get cases of treason or adhering to the enemy without the realm reported in our text-books, because when a person commits treason without the realm he takes care to stay there?

Mr. SULLIVAN—Yes.

The LORD CHIEF JUSTICE—Unless you get them within the realm you cannot get them.

Mr. SULLIVAN—I must apologise for occupying so long.

Mr. JUSTICE HORRIDGE—You have not given us the 2 Dyer yet.

The LORD CHIEF JUSTICE—We will have that to-morrow.

Mr. SULLIVAN—I have been applying for the 2 Dyer but I have not had it yet.

The LORD CHIEF JUSTICE—Anyhow we will deal with that to-morrow.

Adjourned till to-morrow morning at 10.15 o'clock.

Motion to Quash Indictment.

Third Day—Wednesday, 28th June, 1916.

Mr. Sullivan—My lords, I had concluded my observations when the Court rose.

The Lord Chief Justice—You were going to call attention to the case in the 2 Dyer.

Mr. Sullivan—Yes, but will your lordship allow one of my friends to go on?

The Lord Chief Justice—Certainly.

Mr. Morgan—May it please your lordships; in this case I should like to add a few words.

The Lord Chief Justice—There is a difficulty about this; by the statute there are two counsel assigned; if it is merely to call attention to that part of the argument which had already been dealt with by you, merely to the case in 2 Dyer we will hear Mr. Morgan as *amicus curiæ* in the matter.

Mr. Sullivan—Might I suggest the true reading of the statute is really to provide for the defence of prisoners in certain trials, and one of them is a trial for treason. There are provisions in the statute enabling counsel to be assigned to the defence of those charged for capital offences unable to defend themselves. Those who do defend themselves, I submit, are in no worse position by the statute in not taking the counsel assigned to them, in the sense of assigned counsel only, than one unable to assign his own counsel; he should not be in a worse position on the reading of the statute, and I would ask your lordships to adopt that view of the statute.

The Lord Chief Justice—Whatever the view may be as to that, it is unnecessary to determine it, because we will hear Mr. Morgan, reserving that point, and treat him as *amicus curiæ* in the matter.

Mr. Sullivan—I am very much indebted to your lordships.

Mr. Morgan—May it please your lordships, my learned friend, Mr. Sullivan, drew attention yesterday to the opinion of the judges recorded in 2 Dyer, 131b, in the 2 Philip and Mary. I submit the language of the charge in that case is most emphatic and does not admit of any ambiguity. It says, "No offence of treason committed out of the "realm was triable here by the course of the common law." I submit that no lawyer at that time could possibly have come to any other conclusion. I think your lordship put the question yesterday as to whether or not we held that adhering to the King's enemy without the realm was not an offence at common law. I submit certainly until the statute of 35 Henry VIII., and as we contend after it, it was not an offence at common law. The authorities on the point that an offence committed outside the King's realm and dominions is not an offence at common law, and if it is an offence is not triable here, are overwhelming, and no mediæval lawyer would come to any other conclusion.

The LORD CHIEF JUSTICE—You say they are overwhelming, but where are they? According to the statute of Henry VIII., it seems to me plain that there were certain forms of treason which undoubtedly then existed, and which were offences of treason committed without the realm; that is clear from the statute.

Mr. MORGAN—And triable here?

The LORD CHIEF JUSTICE—No; there are two separate points. What I am putting to you is that there were offences of treason committed without the realm; the statute of Henry VIII. says so. I have not the exact language before me, but it says there are some offences already declared and those which may be declared in the future.

Mr. MORGAN—But they must have been statutory offences declared by statute.

The LORD CHIEF JUSTICE—What I want to know is, have you considered what those are?

Mr. MORGAN—Yes, I have; one will be compassing the King's death.

The LORD CHIEF JUSTICE—That is by statute?

Mr. MORGAN—Yes.

The LORD CHIEF JUSTICE—Under which statute is that?

Mr. MORGAN—The 25 Edward III., which contains no words of limitation about "within the realm" as regards the particular kind of treason.

The LORD CHIEF JUSTICE—What do you say would be the effect? According to that reading of the statute of 1351, the words "within the "realm" are not there to qualify in any way the effect of the words "compassing the King's death." Then do I understand your view to be that, notwithstanding that, the offence would be triable and punishable if committed without the realm?

Mr. MORGAN—Would be or would not be?

The LORD CHIEF JUSTICE—Would be.

Mr. MORGAN—Before the 35 Henry VIII.?

The LORD CHIEF JUSTICE—Yes.

Mr. MORGAN—No; certainly not.

The LORD CHIEF JUSTICE—Was the offence created?

Mr. MORGAN—That is open to argument. I think it may have been. There were no words of limitation as regards "within the realm" in connection with the definition of compassing, and therefore it was open to hold that Parliament had declared that as regards the offence of compassing the King's death the treason might be committed out of the realm; but in the absence of that declaration I do not think the common law would have ever held that it was a crime.

The LORD CHIEF JUSTICE—I am not satisfied about that.

Mr. MORGAN—The authorities on that point, Stephen and Archbold, and the case of *The King* v. *M'Leod*, are absolutely clear, that according to English common law all crime is local.

The LORD CHIEF JUSTICE—The question is whether this is not the one exception; murder was made an exception.

Mr. Morgan—Yes, by statute; but it was expressly said murder wherever committed. I do not know, having regard to the view of trial by jury taken by mediæval lawyers, how they could have come to any other conclusion. All offences by common law must be tried by a jury of neighbours; that is the whole point of the venue.

The Lord Chief Justice—You must not be under the impression, speaking for myself, that that satisfies me, because I called attention yesterday to the passage in Hale which is important upon the point to the contrary.

Mr. Morgan—May I ask that passage?

The Lord Chief Justice—My impression is it is page 169 of the first volume of Hale's Pleas of the Crown. It is the reference to the case in the 5 Richard II. This is what Sir Matthew Hale says: "But at "common law he might have been indicted in any county of England, "and especially where the offender's lands lie if he have any." That is dealing with the trial of foreign treason; that is adhering to the King's enemy and also for compassing the King's death without the kingdom. It begins: "Touching the trial of high treason." That is the passage I read yesterday.

Mr. Morgan—I think that authority is in the hands of my learned friends, the counsel for the Crown; I do not know what they make of the passage; it is in Norman French in Fitzherbert.

The Lord Chief Justice—I wish to bring to your attention that there is very distinct authority in the plainest language to the contrary of what you were asserting.

Mr. Morgan—There seems very considerable doubt upon it. Hawkins, in his Pleas of the Crown, refers to it at page 306.

Mr. Justice Horridge—The Attorney-General referred to it.

Mr. Morgan—It is Hawkins' Pleas of the Crown, volume 2, page 306, chapter 25, section 48: "It seems to have been a great doubt "before the making of the statute of 35 Henry VIII., chapter 2, in what "manner and in what place high treason done out of the realm was to "be tried."

The Lord Chief Justice—It assumes the offence; the only question is how the offence was to be tried.

Mr. Justice Avory—Would you go on with the passage?

Mr. Morgan—It does not say adhering to the King's enemies; compassing would be high treason done out of the realm.

Mr. Justice Horridge—I understood you to say that the words of the statute of Edward had made it clear that compassing the King's death outside the realm was brought within the law of treason, because there were no words "in the realm" following; but before that there was no power to try any treason.

Mr. Morgan—I said before the 35 Henry VIII.

Mr. Justice Horridge—That is later still.

Mr. Morgan—I said that by the statute of 25 Edward III. compassing might be held to be an offence anywhere; it does not say whether within or without the kingdom.

Mr. Justice Horridge—Therefore there was no treason at that

time, according to you, before the statute of Edward III., committed outside the realm?

Mr. MORGAN—I very much doubt whether there was.

Mr. JUSTICE HORRIDGE—What the Lord Chief Justice pointed out was that that passage from Hawkins assumed that there are such things as treasons committed outside the realm.

Mr. MORGAN—Certainly, it comes between the 25 Edward III. and the 35 Henry VIII. There may have been certain treasons which, though not triable owing to defects of jurisdiction, were none the less treasons when committed out of the realm; but it does not refer to adhering to the King's enemies; that must refer to compassing. It proceeds: "For some seem to have holden, that it was triable only upon an appeal "before the constable and marshal." That is the whole of our case. All the cases quoted by Coke and Hale before 1535, with perhaps this one exception, were cases either of military sentence, as Hale puts it, in the High Court of Parliament, as he says at volume 1, page 238: "I "know no authority on the question of treasons for other sentences "than the High Court of Parliament or the Constable and Marshal." The only jurisdiction to be exercised over treasons done without the realm before the 35 Henry VIII. must have been either that jurisdiction or the jurisdiction of the Admiralty.

Mr. JUSTICE AVORY—That is what some people thought. Read also what other people thought.

Mr. MORGAN—"Others, that it might be tried upon an indictment, "laying the offence in any county where the King pleased." I do not observe any authority for that.

Mr. JUSTICE AVORY—Except Hawkins is an authority.

The LORD CHIEF JUSTICE—And Lord Coke, the authority of the Institutes.

Mr. MORGAN—Coke, in the Institutes, does not give any authority except the single case that Hale refers to. Lord Coke's authorities for trial for adhering to the King's enemy without the realm are cases in Parliament which, as my learned friend pointed out yesterday, do not recite the word "treason" in the statute at all, and they are not cases of treason: "And others, that it was triable by way of indictment in "that county only wherein the offender had lands." I have not had time to look up the authority cited, and I do not know what it is: "But "surely it cannot reasonably be doubted"—then he quotes Dyer 131b, which is dead against him—"but that it was triable some way or other; "for it cannot be imagined that an offence of such dangerous conse-"quence, and expressly within the purview of 25 Edward III., should "be wholly dispunishable, as it must have been, if it were no way "triable." That is simply an idle speculation. He throws up his hands and says he cannot understand how it could have been otherwise.

The LORD CHIEF JUSTICE—Hawkins was rather an authority.

Mr. MORGAN—That is a purely speculative passage.

Mr. JUSTICE AVORY—It is not an uncommon way of expressing a judgment.

Mr. MORGAN—Can that get over the plain words of the statute?

The LORD CHIEF JUSTICE—You can hardly say that the great masters of the common law in past times simply threw up their hands and speculated upon what was the law; they are laying down the law; at least they are stating what they, great exponents of the law, thought was the law in those days.

Mr. MORGAN—Can that do away with the plain words of the statute? We are dealing with the construction of the statute.

The LORD CHIEF JUSTICE—I agree that it cannot.

Mr. MORGAN—Nearly all these authorities are based upon Coke, regarding whom Stephen says that his authority on matters of legal history is absolutely worthless. He speaks of his extraordinarily disordered mind, and the way in which whenever he comes across two words which mean the same thing he thinks they mean different things, which is obviously what he has done with regard to this clause of the statute.

Attention was drawn to the case in Leach of *The King* v. *Platt*. I admit that those words of *obiter dictum* there used would seem at first sight to tell against us. The words are—"It was the ancient custom"—I do not think any authorities are given—"that the species of treason which "consists by 25 Edward III., chapter 2, in adhering to the King's enemies, "might be tried, before the statute 35 Henry VIII., chapter 2, within the "kingdom, by the rules of the common law, though the aid and comfort "was afforded without the realm, but that every other species of treason "committed out of the realm must be tried in the place where it was "committed, or under the provisions of that Act of Parliament." Well, all I can say is, in the first place, that passage is directly contradicted by the authority in 131b of Dyer.

Mr. JUSTICE AVORY—The case in Dyer is not a judgment delivered in open Court after argument; it is an opinion expressed by some judges who met together at Serjeants' Inn.

Mr. MORGAN—Quite so. I should have thought the opinion of the judges who met together in Serjeants' Inn would outweigh the opinion, for instance, of Sir Edward Coke writing in his library and quoting authorities which it is evident he had never read.

Mr. JUSTICE AVORY—You are assuming two facts of which there is no proof, either that he wrote them in his library or that he did not know what he was talking about.

Mr. MORGAN—My learned friend, I think, proved that yesterday by his quotation from the Rolls of Parliament which Coke cites and which do not bear him out. I think that passage in *The King* v. *Platt* is capable of an interpretation which is not inconsistent either with Dyer or with the statute of the 35 Henry VIII.

The LORD CHIEF JUSTICE—In the case in Dyer what was being discussed was how the case was to be tried, not whether the offence had been committed.

Mr. MORGAN—Yes.

Mr. JUSTICE HORRIDGE—The point for discussion there was whether or not the statute of Philip and Mary had repealed the provisions for trial under the statutes of Henry. That was the direct question for consideration. I have not had the report before me till now, and I may be wrong with regard to it. That does not lay down what you read shortly to us—" And "it seems that notwithstanding this, the statute 35 Henry VIII., chapter "2, is in force, because no offence of treason committed out of the realm "was triable here by the course of the common law, therefore this statute "enlarges the power and authority of the trials of the realm in this point." That is the passage you rely upon. It goes on—" But for treason committed "in a foreign country, and triable in the British realm"—that is the King's Bench—" or in any county at the pleasure of the King, by statute "33 Henry VIII., chapter 23, it seems otherwise."

Mr. MORGAN—Yes, since the statute; that is my whole point.

The LORD CHIEF JUSTICE—The statute of 33 Henry VIII.?

Mr. MORGAN—No, the statute of 35 Henry VIII.

The LORD CHIEF JUSTICE—No, it is 33 Henry VIII., chapter 23, apparently.

Mr. MORGAN—The point is, the authority is purely statutory.

Mr. JUSTICE HORRIDGE—The real point they were discussing was whether the statute of Philip and Mary had repealed the provisions of 35 Henry VIII.

Mr. MORGAN—Yes, but none the less the statement is perfectly clear and emphatic.

The LORD CHIEF JUSTICE—The difficulty is if you look for authority there seems none. The references are to Coke's Institutes and to Hawkins' Pleas of the Crown, the two authorities to which we have been referring.

Mr. MORGAN—No, this opinion was delivered before Coke lived. It is in the reign of Philip and Mary. These annotations are added by the author of the reports.

The LORD CHIEF JUSTICE—They are annotations with reference to it.

Mr. MORGAN—Yes, but one had no right to import them.

The LORD CHIEF JUSTICE—The reason I was referring to it is that, apart from that, I do not know what authority there is for the proposition.

Mr. MORGAN—What proposition?

The LORD CHIEF JUSTICE—The one mentioned by the judges.

Mr. MORGAN—There is the whole authority of the doctrine of venue in the common law.

Mr. JUSTICE HORRIDGE—The extraordinary thing is what was endeavoured to be deduced from that by Mr. Sullivan was if it could not be tried in this country it could not exist, and the other sense in which you are quoting it is, supposing the offence exists, you say it cannot be tried.

Mr. MORGAN—That is not the point I am addressing myself to. I am dealing with the point that it could be and was tried before the 35 Henry VIII. As to the point put by Hale, I say that this statement in Dyer, whatever it may say about the existence in the air, so to speak, of treason committed abroad, is quite emphatic as against Hale and Coke, that treason committed abroad could not be, and never had been, tried here by common law. Surely the passage is decisive on that.

Now, may I turn to the passage in *The King* v. *Platt*, and show how it supports my argument, although at first it appears to admit of quite a different construction? "It was the ancient opinion that the species of "treason which consists by 25 Edward III., chapter 2, in adhering to the "King's enemies, might be tried before the statute 35 Henry VIII., chapter

"2, within the kingdom by the rules of the common law, although the aid "and comfort was afforded without the realm." It does not say without the King's dominions; the Act of Henry VIII. does. The very title of the statute says that. I do not know whether you see my point, my lord. I am trying to contend that the remarks in *The King* v. *Platt* are not in the least inconsistent with our position. What they say is this, that treason without the realm, not without the King's dominions, may have been tried before the statute of 35 Henry VIII., but they do not say that treason without the King's dominions might have been tried here. My whole point is the common law extends all over the King's dominions except where they were under their own local law, and therefore the cases that the Court may have had in mind are cases where the person within England adhered to the King's enemies, and gave them aid and comfort in some other portions of His Majesty's dominions.

Mr. Justice Horridge—If it is right that the statute was declaratory of the common law, the statute of Edward III. uses the word realm, and your contention must be, before the statute of Henry VIII., treason committed outside the realm, not the King's dominions.

Mr. Morgan—I am coming to that. The kind of case of adhering that he might have had in mind is where the person is within the realm, *ex hypothesi* it might be that he sends letters or intelligence or aid to some other portion of His Majesty's dominions. The act may then be an act to be partly committed in this country and partly without this country. Nearly all the cases of adhering are cases of that character. Therefore I submit that that case bears out my contention.

Mr. Justice Horridge—That is the answer Mr. Sullivan gave yesterday; it is not turning on the difference between the King's dominions and the realm.

The Lord Chief Justice—That is quite a different point, and it seemed a good distinction; that was what Mr. Sullivan pointed out yesterday; you may have adhering to the King's enemy by giving aid and comfort without the realm, and, nevertheless, the adhering to the King's enemy might be an act committed within the realm; that may be quite correct.

Mr. Justice Horridge—I am afraid I have not followed the other point you are trying to make—the distinction between the King's dominions and the realm in the statute of Henry VIII. I tell you candidly I have not followed it, and I do not know now what it is.

Mr. Morgan—The distinction is not of so much importance as the point made by my learned friend yesterday.

The Lord Chief Justice—That we accepted yesterday as being a perfectly sound distinction.

Mr. Morgan—Does not that contention dispose, or I will not say dispose of it, but harmonise *The King* v. *Platt* with the case of Dyer.

The Lord Chief Justice—Speaking for myself, I think if all you had to meet was that sentence in the 1 Leach, *The King* v. *Platt*, I do not think it is against you. I thought that Mr. Sullivan had established that on that sentence.

Mr. Morgan—Then I need not labour that point.

Mr. Justice Horridge—Assume that to be so, you must assume as regards giving aid and comfort it existed before the statute outside the realm.

Mr. Morgan—I think that the main point there is, this means treason by adhering to the King's enemies without the realm and without the dominions; the point is important because the statute of 25 Edward III., as things were then, could not before the 35 Henry VIII. have supported an indictment for treason outside the dominions; it could have supported an indictment for treason within the realm, and it could have supported an indictment for treason within the dominions, but it could not have supported an indictment for compassing outside the dominions till the 35 Henry VIII.

The Lord Chief Justice—That assumes the point.

Mr. Morgan—Does it, my lord?

The Lord Chief Justice—The question is, what is the meaning to be attributed to the words in the statute?

Mr. Morgan—May I put it this way, is the point that we have to meet this, that by common law, before 35 Henry VIII. treason was an offence of such a character that, even though committed abroad without the dominions, quite independent of the statute 25 Edward III., it was an offence at common law? I will address myself to that point.

The Lord Chief Justice—As I understand the passage, particularly with reference to that passage in Hale and some others, it seems to have been regarded as a case of such exceptional gravity, and a crime of such exceptional gravity and magnitude, as to form an exception to the general rule of the English criminal law that all crime is local; that is the point.

Mr. Morgan—Quite.

Mr. Justice Horridge—I understood Mr. Sullivan yesterday to be giving a reason why it was not, from the fact that there could be no local venue of it. The statute of Henry VIII. and the case in Dyer both assume that the offence can exist although there is no venue for it. That would answer his argument as to the reason why these were not triable, because there was no venue; they both say where certain treasons exist as to which it is very doubtful whether there is power to try—they recognise the existence of that in each case.

Mr. Morgan—They do not say they exist at common law; I contend that all the authorities laid down emphatically that no offence at common law in the absence of statute can be committed abroad. I merely draw attention to a book like Archbold where he says, in speaking of a venue, at page 33, "The natural jurisdiction of the Courts of common law is "territorial, and no person can be tried for an offence committed on "land abroad except under the authority of the statute." Stephen says the same thing: "As a general rule, offences committed by British "subjects out of England are not punishable by the criminal law of "England." The only exceptions to that were the jurisdiction of the constable and marshal, and the statutory exceptions. "All cases in "which crimes committed abroad can now be tried in England are cases "in which statutory provisions have been made to that effect." If you look at *M'Leod* v. *The Attorney-General of New South Wales*, it is there laid down most emphatically that all crimes are local, and not a single exception is made to that statement.

The LORD CHIEF JUSTICE—That was a question as to the extent of the jurisdiction of the dominion or of the State.

Mr. MORGAN—The New South Wales Legislature had passed an Act making it bigamy for a New South Wales citizen to marry elsewhere, being already married in that State.

The LORD CHIEF JUSTICE—There seems no doubt, you certainly need not labour the proposition before us, which we think is elementary and is quite clear, that the general law is that all crime is local. There is no doubt about that. There are certain exceptions created by statute, and the question is in this particular case whether treason was not an exception; but I would also remind you that whatever the view may be as to that, it still will not alter the interpretation of the words which we have to give to the statute of 1351, which is the point that we must always come to, although here we may get some light by investigating the common law before the statute came into existence.

Mr. MORGAN—Quite; I am addressing myself for the moment to that question of common law jurisdiction. If one has to confine oneself to the words of the statute, I submit you cannot get away from that. I think it is not without significance that Coke, in quoting the statute, it is true, sets out the whole statute in detail in the exact words, but when he comes to comment on each particular head of treason, though he still quotes the Norman French, he deliberately leaves out the words "within his realm" in their first position. I think, to begin with, that is a quite indefensible thing to do in commenting upon a statute. There is a case of *The King* v. *Wheldon*, in which this point was raised. At page 11 he leaves out altogether the first words, "within the realm." My learned friend remarks if he leaves them out, they are out, which is a very easy way of disposing of the passage. That is really all I have to say. I presume, after what your lordship said yesterday about *The King* v. *Vaughan*, that we need not deal with the question of Admiralty jurisdiction for the reasons which your lordships gave.

Then I only conclude by drawing your lordships' attention to a remark made by Mr. Justice Finucane in *The King* v. *Wheldon*. It is quoted in *The King* v. *Lynch*, and it is in the 26 State Trials, at page 293. In commenting on these words, "Be adherent to the King's "enemies in his realm," he makes this remark, "The locality is annexed "to the person adhering, not to the enemy to whom he adhered." Accordingly, that is the correct interpretation, and, at any rate, the words must be understood to come to this, the defendant must have been within the realm, or the King's enemies must have been; if it never was within the realm it seems to me to be quite impossible to bring the facts alleged in the indictment within the statute. That is our case. I thank you, my lord, for listening to me so patiently and giving me such indulgence.

The LORD CHIEF JUSTICE—Before you sit down, if you attribute importance to *The King* v. *Wheldon* you must make your point a little clearer to me. I have not followed your last point.

Mr. MORGAN—I use it simply by way of illustration; it did not directly decide the point. I do not quote that case as an authority;

in fact, the other learned judge sitting, as I frankly admit, judging by his remarks, was rather against me; I merely quoted Mr. Justice Finucane's remarks, which are in the nature of *obiter dictum*, as illustrating the point at issue that the words "within the realm" must be annexed to somebody; they cannot be absolutely meaningless; they occur in the first part of the clause, and presumably govern the rest of the clause according to the ordinary rules of construction.

The Lord Chief Justice—Nobody suggests they are meaningless.

Mr. Morgan—Then I shall leave it for the counsel for the Crown to suggest what they do mean.

Mr. Justice Avory—This judgment may be important in *Wheldon*, the judgment of Mr. Justice Chamberlain.

Mr. Morgan—Yes, although it is true on that point, it may tell against me.

Mr. Justice Avory—"We are also of opinion that the essence of the "offence is adhering to the King's enemies, and it is immaterial where "they are. It is an offence not constituted by statute, but an offence at "common law, and the statute only says that no man shall be indicted "but for treason, as there specified it is not created by the Act. And "indeed, if it were necessary, it does substantially appear, because two "overt acts state that an open and public war is carried on by the French, "and that the prisoner was adhering to the persons exercising the Govern- "ment of France. So that if it were necessary it is substantially charged "that he was adhering to the enemies without the realm."

Mr. Morgan—Quite; I am quite prepared to meet that.

Mr. Justice Horridge—That part must be against you.

Mr. Morgan—No, I contend it is not, but it is rather in my favour.

The Lord Chief Justice—That is the way to deal with the point, but you must now prove that it is so.

Mr. Morgan—Yes, I will try to do so.

Mr. Justice Avory—That was not written in the library.

Mr. Morgan—No; but I contend that that passage is in my favour, while at the same time I freely admit it may be open to another construction. May I draw attention to the language used by the learned judge: "We are of opinion that the essence of the offence is adhering "to the King's enemies, and it is immaterial where they are," that is the enemies; that is quite consistent with our view in this case, that the person was within the realm; he was charged with consulting in Ireland the State of France in case they should invade; he was within the realm and the enemies were without. That is the whole point.

The Lord Chief Justice—The last words are important: "So that "if it were necessary it is substantially charged that he was adhering "to the enemies without the realm."

Mr. Morgan—To the enemies without the realm, but he himself was within the realm. My point is that is the proper construction of the statute, that the defendants must be within the realm at the time; that is obvious if the overt acts are within the realm.

The Lord Chief Justice—Yes.

Mr. Morgan—And the defence was that the enemy was without the realm. I think if that case is carefully studied it will appear to support our position as regards the latter portion of that passage to which my attention was drawn just now. Mr. Justice Chamberlain goes on to say it is an offence not constituted by statute, but an offence at common law. As regards that point he does not say that it was an offence at common law to adhere to the King's enemies if the defendant as well as the enemies were without the realm, and that is the whole of our position. It was no doubt always an offence at common law to adhere to the King's enemies within the realm. The statute is absolutely declaratory on that point. The word "adhering" occurs in some of the old authorities before 1351; it was always an offence at common law to adhere to the King's enemies within the realm, probably within the dominions, certainly within those dominions which were Ireland—they had the common law imported into them. That is quite a different proposition to saying that the common law took notice of offences committed outside the King's dominions altogether, or even that they were offences at common law in the absence of statutory authority. I respectfully submit that the considerations advanced yesterday by my learned friend, and those which, to the best of my poor ability, I have tried to advance this morning, are absolutely conclusive against this indictment.

The Lord Chief Justice—Do you remember one of the cases in which a person was indicted and convicted of treason without the realm, that is, in Ireland? I do not remember where it is, but I have seen it.

The Attorney-General—*O'Rouke's* case and *Perrot's* case.

The Lord Chief Justice—That is the case.

Mr. Morgan—I have looked up the case, but it is very badly reported in the State Trials, and I have not been able to find any authority on adhering to the King's enemies. The person, I believe, was charged for compassing and not adhering to the King's enemies within the realm. It has been held since Poyning's Act, since Henry VIII., that Ireland was part of the realm.

The Lord Chief Justice—It depends on a different statute; it was held that was within the realm since Poyning's law.

Mr. Morgan—If *Perrot's* case occurred, as I think it did, since Poyning's law, Ireland was part of the realm; if Perrot was charged with adhering to the King's enemy it is not inconsistent with our argument.

The Attorney-General—May it please your lordship. It must, I think, be long since the great sages of the common law have been treated in such large numbers with so much disrespect in any Court of justice in this country, and certainly the assault which my two learned friends have directed at these great masters of the common law was by no means, as it seems to me, the fruit of caprice; it was necessary to the bold contention which they proposed to lay before your lordship; it was necessary that they should discover one method or other of criticising all these great authorities, household names in the history of our jurisprudence, because, by a singular accident, all of them were unanimously opposed for a long period of years to the contentions which my learned friends have been driven to put before your lordship in this matter. I do not think that my learned friends will dispute that they owed the inception of this contention and many of the arguments by which they have sought to support it, to the advocate who made the same submissions in the case to which your lordships' attention has already been directed, *The King* v. *Lynch*. I propose, if I may, to devote the few observations with which I shall think it necessary to trouble your lordships, first to the law as I conceive it to have been at common law and before the statute of Edward III., and afterwards to the state of the law as that statute left the law, and then to consider shortly the effect of the statute of Henry VIII. upon the statute of Edward III.; and to inform your lordships of some of the decisions which, contrary to the statement inadvertently made by my learned friend, Mr. Sullivan, have held that treason without the realm can be tried in this country. I may have imperfectly apprehended what my learned friend said, but I understood my learned friend to say yesterday that he knew of no case in which a person charged with treason without the realm had been made justiciable in this country. I think I shall be in a position to direct my learned friend's attention, and also your lordships' attention, to many such cases.

The Lord Chief Justice—I did not understand Mr. Sullivan to contend that; I thought he said there were no cases which had in terms decided that these words in the statute 1351 were to be interpreted as they were being interpreted by the Crown in this indictment, that is, that adherence to the King's enemies without the realm was an offence.

The Attorney-General—If that was all that my learned friend said I should not quarrel with it. It is quite true that if you take the long list of cases in which this matter has been considered there has been no advocate, so far as I know, in the whole history of those cases who has ever been bold enough to put forward this contention as to the meaning of the statute, though decisions of the Courts have, as I will show your lordships, proceeded many times upon the opposite view; in no case since the statute has that contention ever been put forward by any advocate.

Mr. Justice Horridge—Till the case of *The King* v. *Lynch*.

The Attorney-General—Till the case of *The King* v. *Lynch*. If I may make an observation as to the common law it is necessary, as my learned friend pointed out, that it should be borne in mind in considering these matters that the statute of Edward III. has been repeatedly and authoritatively stated to be declaratory of the common law of this country. Now, it is put in argument that the theory of the criminal law in this country is, and has always been, that crime is local in its character, and that conclusion is well founded; but it has always, as I hope to satisfy your lordships, been either stated or assumed when these matters have been carefully considered that the offence of treason was an exception to this general rule, and if one examines for a moment the conception upon which the law of treason depends, one sees at once the grounds upon which this inception has been admitted. The view taken by the law has always been that allegiance, that impalpable and almost indefinable idea which connects the subjects with the Sovereign, is carried by the subject wherever that subject goes and wherever the subject sojourns. It is a personal tie binding the subject to the Sovereign and providing certain legal consequences wherever the subject goes, and a moment's reflection will, I think, make it clear when one is dealing with matters of the gravity that are raised by the doctrine of high treason that it must have been impossible that the common law of this country could have excluded the conception that treason or acts of treason, whether compassing or adherence, which were committed without the realm—I said, a moment's observation must make that plain when one is dealing with the affairs of a country, particularly of an insular Power, such as this country is. It is, I should have thought evident that, except in the case of actual invasion, traitorous acts, acts of treason, certainly acts of adherence to the King's enemies, were far more likely in the ordinary course to be committed without the realm than within the realm; in other words, the King's enemies in the more common and obvious cases of adherence, except in the cases of invasion, very rare as they are in history, are likely to be found not within the realm, but without the realm. It would indeed have been strange if the common law of this country had permitted a subject of this country, bound to the Sovereign by the personal tie of allegiance, to go to the country which for so many centuries was an enemy of this country, France, at the door of this realm adhering to the King's enemies, and then concede that although the personal tie of allegiance had subsisted during the periods during which these acts of adherence were committed, yet in the view of the criminal law of this country no violation had taken place of the law of treason as that law was understood at the time. It would, I submit, have been inconceivable had such a doctrine ever been held. I will show your lordships in a moment that not only has no high authority ever said that this offence was not recognised as an offence at common law, but that the whole trend of authority is in the opposite direction.

Now, I come to make an observation upon the statute of Edward III., a statute as we have seen declaratory of the common law. My learned friends dealt with the statute of Edward III., if they will allow me to say so, in a manner which was, I think, a little perfunctory, especially having regard to the elaboration of some other branches of their arguments. They assumed rather than argued that the statute of Edward III. had the meaning which they attempted to put upon it. I submit, on the other hand, to your lordships that the views which have been unanimously held by the great writers upon our criminal law as to the effect of the statute of Edward III. are not only well founded, but they are the only views which can reasonably, if one considers the wording of the statute, be admitted or accepted.

Will your lordships be so good as to look at the words which your lordships recollect are at page 1031 of Archbold? I ought perhaps to make this preliminary observation, that in dealing with a statute so ancient as this, couched in the language which is before your lordships, one does not always adopt all the same standards of grammatical construction which one applies to statutes of King George V. These are the words, "If a man do levy war against our Lord the King in his realm or be "adherent to the King's enemies in his realm, giving to them aid and "comfort in the realm or elsewhere, and therefore be probably attainted "of open deed by the people of their condition." Those are the material words. The submission which I make is that the views of those who have always held that these words contemplated and covered the offence of adherence without the realm are well founded, and, as I have said, are not only reasonable, but are almost the necessary construction of the words. How, then, ought the words to be read? They ought, in the submission of the Crown, to be read exactly as if before the word "giving" and after the word "realm," in the phrase "giving to them "aid and comfort in the realm," there were brackets, that those words, in other words, were in brackets. Let it be so read, "If a man do levy "war against our Lord the King in his realm or be adherent to the King's "enemies in his realm (giving to them aid and comfort in the realm) or "elsewhere." With submission, that is not only a probable construction, but it is by far the most reasonable construction that can be put upon those words. You have here the use of the phrase, "be adherent to the "King's enemies in his realm," and then the need is felt by the draughtsman, such is the suggestion I make, to give some explanation or some enlargement of the phrase which is being used, the phrase "be adherent "to the King's enemies," and he interpolates the phrase "giving to them "aid and comfort in the realm," making the words "or elsewhere" an addition to the phrase "be adherent to the King's enemies in his realm." I have ventured to submit to your lordships that was not only a reasonable construction, it is really, if one construes the statute as a whole in the light of the general consideration which I venture to lay before your lordships on the common law before the statute, a necessary construction.

The Lord Chief Justice—Mr. Attorney, would you assent to this view of the construction, taking the words "or elsewhere," may they not govern both the adhering to the King's enemies within the realm or elsewhere, and also giving to them aid and comfort in the realm or elsewhere?

The Attorney-General—There are two possible views; that is one of them, and the one I have indicated to your lordships is the other. The conclusion which follows from either of those views has been variously supported, one or the other, by various writers.

The Lord Chief Justice—It seems a little difficult to understand why one should limit giving aid and comfort to the King's enemies in the realm. I do not know why it should not be equally an offence without the realm when in an island in all probability the King's enemies will mostly be found without the realm.

Mr. Justice Horridge—That is what I was going to ask. Assuming that, "elsewhere" might govern both.

The Attorney-General—Your lordship suggested that yesterday.

Mr. Justice Horridge—I do not see why the statute should limit the giving of aid and comfort in the realm when it may extend, according to your submission, to adhesion outside the realm.

The Lord Chief Justice—That seems to me to get added force if one bears in mind and recollect that the words "giving to them aid and "comfort" are really a parenthesis, and describing what is meant by adhering to the King's enemies. If you read it in that way it would seem to me that the words must necessarily govern both adherence and the descriptive words; you are dealing with the same offence.

The Attorney-General—Quite. It may be from that point of view it covers the whole phrase, including the levying of war.

The Lord Chief Justice—That is also possible.

The ATTORNEY-GENERAL—I do not mind which of those views is taken.

Mr. JUSTICE HORRIDGE—The quotation from Mr. Justice Willes merely leaves that out, and makes it govern the adherence.

The ATTORNEY-GENERAL—Yes. As to the position in law which followed upon the passing of the statute of Edward III., it seems to me the passage quoted from Hawkins—I apologise to my learned friend for mentioning such as authority—is very apposite. He says on page 306, under "Indictment," "It seems to have been a great doubt before the "making of the statute of 35 Henry VIII., chapter 2, in what manner and "in what place high treason done out of the realm was to be tried. For "some seem to have holden that it was triable only upon an appeal before "the constable and marshal; others that it might be tried upon an indict-"ment, laying the offence in any county where the King pleased; and "others that it was triable by way of indictment in that county only "wherein the offender had lands; but surely it cannot reasonably be "doubted but that it was triable some way or other." I think my learned friend called this the cry of despair, "for it cannot be imagined "that an offence of such dangerous consequence, and expressly within the "purview of 25 Edward III., should be wholly dispunishable, as it must "have been if it were no way triable."

As I understand the significance of this passage, it is very great, because between the statute of Edward III. and the statute of Henry VIII. the learned author, who had been giving great attention to these matters, says that there were great doubts. But what did the doubts relate to? Did the doubts relate to the question whether high treason done out of the realm was an offence? He does not enumerate that as among the many grounds of doubts he thinks it worth while to call attention to. The doubts were as to in what manner and detail high treason done out of the realm was to be tried. He gives various views that had been held by various authorities. "For some seem to have holden that it was triable "only upon an appeal before the constable and marshal; others that it "might be tried upon an indictment, laying the offence in any county "where the King pleased"—that is, leaving the King to choose the venue where the offender had lands. He states in weighty language his conclusion, "That it was triable some way or other; for it cannot be "imagined that an offence of such dangerous consequence, and expressly "within the purview of 25 Edward III., should be wholly dispunishable." So that the high authority of Hawkins says again, in the plainest possible way, in this statement, which is not in the least an answer, but a positive conclusion, that high treason done out of the realm is expressly within the purview of 25 Edward III.

The LORD CHIEF JUSTICE—Is there any authority of which you have cognisance which says that if high treason is committed without the realm it is not an offence at common law?

The ATTORNEY-GENERAL—No, and I may boldly say there is none.

The LORD CHIEF JUSTICE—I know of none. Even in the case in 2 Dyer, to which reference is made, it was assumed that the doing of the act is an offence. All that it does is to say it is not triable by the course of the common law.

The ATTORNEY-GENERAL—Yes. The emphasis is on the word "triable" in that connection. I will come to the case in Dyer later.

Mr. JUSTICE HORRIDGE—Before you leave that, it may be the statute does not deal with specific treason by adherence, there may be treason outside the particular one which was an offence, although there was no means of trying it; he is not dealing with the particular case of adherence there.

The ATTORNEY-GENERAL—That is perfectly true. It might have been expected, I submit, that if in making this grave statement that the offence was expressly within the purview of 25 Edward III., he wanted to put forward the view that there was a distinction to be drawn between certain treasons under the Act, he would have done so.

Mr. JUSTICE HORRIDGE—I think that is quite a fair comment.

The ATTORNEY-GENERAL—And such being the case, namely, that doubts had arisen in the language of Hawkins as to what the proper method of trying these admitted offences was, the statute of Henry VIII. was passed; and I may remind your lordships, as possibly an additional reason why that statute should have been thought necessary, that there had been a great increase in the number of constructive treasons in the reign of King Henry VIII., all kinds of dynastic considerations intervened, and doubt was felt as to the proper method of dealing with them. That is at page 1032 of Archbold. The note is, "Venue for treasons committed "abroad."

The LORD CHIEF JUSTICE—The title is not in Archbold, but it is "An "Act concerning the trial of treasons committed out of the King's "Majesty's dominions."

The ATTORNEY-GENERAL—Yes, it is purely machinery. "Forasmuch "as some doubts and questions have been moved, that certain kinds "of treasons, misprisions, and concealments of treason done, perpetrated, "or committed out of the King's Majesty's realm of England cannot, "by the common laws of this realm be inquired of, heard, and deter- "mined within this his said realm of England; for a plain remedy, "order, and declaration therein to be had and made, be it enacted by "authority of this present Parliament that all manner of offences being "already made, declared, or hereafter to be made or declared, by any "of the laws and statutes of this realm, to be treasons, misprisions of "treasons, or concealments of treasons, and done, perpetrated, or com- "mitted, or hereafter to be done, perpetrated, or committed, by any "person or persons out of this realm of England, shall be from henceforth "inquired of, heard, and determined before the King's justices of his "Bench for pleas to be holden before himself, by good and lawful men "of the same shire where the said Bench shall sit and be kept, or else "before such commissioners and in such shire of the realm as shall be "assigned by the King's Majesty's commission, and by good and lawful "men of the same shire, in like manner and form to all intents and "purposes as if any such treasons, misprisions of treasons, or concealments "of treasons had been done, perpetrated, and committed within the same "shire where they shall be so inquired of, heard, and determined as is "aforesaid." It is worthy of notice, perhaps, that the form of the statute supports the view which, as I have said, all the great authorities over so long a period of time have taken, as to its content and scope, because it purposes to be a declaration for the purpose of relieving doubts as to the precise method in which these crimes universally conceded to be triable somehow ought to be dealt with.

The LORD CHIEF JUSTICE—So far as one can follow from the reference to the cases cited yesterday and to-day the doubts that have arisen were all as to the mode of the trial and the venue.

The ATTORNEY-GENERAL—Quite.

The LORD CHIEF JUSTICE—No doubt, so far as I can follow, is anywhere expressed as to the act being an offence, and an offence punishable according to the law of England; the only question was, if you had got the person, where were you to try him?

The ATTORNEY-GENERAL—I have given some attention to this matter, and I have had the assistance of my learned friends, who are both industrious and persevering in these matters, and I think I may say there is no past case that any of us know in the books in which any doubt whatever has been thrown upon the view that it was an offence; I know of none, and I do not think my learned friends are in a position to call attention to any.

The LORD CHIEF JUSTICE—The words in Dyer, the only words that are relied upon, seem to point just the other way. These are the words relied upon, "Because no offence of treason committed out of the realm "was triable here by the course of the common law, therefore this statute "enlarges the power and authority of the trials of the realm in this "point." It seems that it is an offence to commit treason without the realm, but it says the difficulty is, according to the course of common law, where is the offence to be tried.

The ATTORNEY-GENERAL—That is the same view that Hawkins takes. It is worth noticing about the case in Dyer, the charge in question, as I understand the very short report, is contained in a memorandum which is not, I think, the conclusion of the judges, because the conclusion is given below. The conclusion, I think, begins about seven lines from the bottom of the page, "And for the cause above, the judges, Sir John "Baker and Hare, Master of the Rolls, were assembled, and they thought "as above, and by the words above, according to the order and course "of the common law, it shall be intended that the trial shall be in the "county where the indictment is"—I rather think the earlier part is the case put before them, and the conclusion arrived at is set out in the last six lines.

The LORD CHIEF JUSTICE—It is not unimportant to observe how it came before them. There was the statute of 35 Henry VIII., then came the statute of 1 and 2 Philip and Mary, and Philip and Mary having said a certain thing, "that all trials hereafter to be had, awarded, or made "for any treason shall be had and used only according to the due order "and course of the common laws of this realm, and not otherwise," had that statute of Philip and Mary in any way repealed or modified the effect of 35 Henry VIII.

The ATTORNEY-GENERAL—That was the whole point.

The LORD CHIEF JUSTICE—That was the whole point they were discussing?

The ATTORNEY-GENERAL—Yes.

MR. JUSTICE AVORY—The resolution was that trial should be in the county where the indictment was; that was the only resolution that was come to.

The ATTORNEY-GENERAL—That is quite true. I do not propose to say anything more about that now. It might be useful to call your lordships' attention to the various cases—I think I can do it compendiously—some of them of considerable antiquity, some more recent, in which the view of the statute which I am endeavouring to press upon your lordships has been accepted and acted upon in one way or other. There was a case of *William de Weston*, which is reported in 1 Richard II., Roll of Parliament, volume iii., pages 10 to 12. In that case it was found by Parliament, as recorded on the roll, that William, having undertaken to keep safely the Castle of Outkrewyk, in Flanders, without any duress or lack of victuals, wickedly delivered and surrendered it to the King's enemies by his own default alone, against all right and reason, and against his allegiance and undertaking. There is the resolution of Parliament that he was sentenced to be drawn and hanged.

Then there is the case of *John de Gomenys*, who was sentenced for delivering up the Castle of Ardes. Now, it was held, a little strange to say, that as he was a gentleman, and had served Edward III., he was not a liege man of Richard II., he was only to be beheaded. Now the question arose, in reference to both those matters, whether the charge was treason. Both the acts, and they would have been acts of adherence in surrendering the castles if they were treason at all, were committed in Flanders. Now, Hale has considered his case in his Pleas of the Crown at pages 167 and 168, and in the second paragraph of 167 he says, "If an Englishman "during war between the Kings of England and France be taken by the "French, and there swear fealty to the King of France, if it be done "voluntarily, it is an adhering to the King's enemies; but if it be done "for fear of his life, and that he returns, as soon as he might, to the "allegiance of the Crown of England, this is not an adherence to the "King's enemies within this Act." Then in the next paragraph, "If "a captain or other officer, that hath the custody of any of the King's "castles or garrisons, shall treacherously, by combination with the King's "enemies or by bribery or for reward, deliver them up, this is adherence "to the King's enemies. This was the case of William Weston for "delivering up the Castle of Oughtrewicke and John de Gomenys for "delivering up the Castle of Ardes, in France, both which were impeached "by the Commons, and had judgment of the Lords in Parliament, "Rot. Par. 1 R. 2, p. 40, namely, William Weston to be drawn "and hanged, but execution was respited." Then it gives *Gomenys*' judgment, and says, "The execution was respited." Then the learned author adds this note, which is very much in point, "And note, though "the charge was treason, and possibly the proofs might probably amount to "it, and Walsingham, *sub anno*, 1 R. 2, tell us it was done by treason; "yet the reason expressed in the judgment against Weston is only"—then he puts it in Norman French, on the ground of surrender.

Then it goes on. "The truth is if it were delivered up by bribery "or treachery it might be treason, but if delivered up upon cowardice or "imprudence without any treachery, though it were an offence against the "laws of war, and the party subject to a sentence of death by martial law, "as it once happened in a case of the like nature in the late times of "trouble, yet it is not treason by the common law, unless it was done "by treachery." The learned author took those two cases on the whole as conclusive that the matter was dealt with under the head of treason, and is of opinion that if it was delivered up not by cowardice but from treachery it might properly be dealt with as treason.

Mr. JUSTICE HORRIDGE—And that is, at the earlier portion of the passage, specially stated to be adhering to the King's enemies.

The ATTORNEY-GENERAL—I am indebted to your lordship; in terms it is so stated. I have other cases, but the most useful to refer to now is *Lord Wentworth's* case, a case reported in the 4 State Trials at page 314. In this case the indictment has been found, and is available for the purpose of consideration. The indictment charges and sets forth that Lord Wentworth, Edward Grimston, and Ralph Chamberlain were indicted jointly with others for that occupying and exercising their aforesaid several offices at Calais in parts beyond the seas, on 20th December they traitorously were adhering, aiding, and comforting, and procuring to Henry, King of the French, the public enemy of the said King and Queen and of this realm of England, in order to traitorously deprive the said King and Queen from their possession of the said town of Calais and the castle of the same, and deliver the same into the hands and possession of the said Henry, now King of the French. As regards Lord Wentworth the indictment was removed into the House of Lords, where he was found not guilty. Grimston was tried before Commissioners, which, as your lordships will recollect, is another alternative method of trial, and found not guilty. Chamberlain was tried before the same Commission, found guilty, and executed. That was a case of treason without the realm, in Calais.

The LORD CHIEF JUSTICE—What was the date of that?

The ATTORNEY-GENERAL—1558.

Mr. JUSTICE HORRIDGE—That was when Calais was a portion of the King's dominions, but it was not within the realm. Calais was ceded in the time of Queen Mary.

Mr. SULLIVAN—Calais was represented in Parliament as late as James I. Parliament purported to legislate with regard to a place outside of the realm, up to the time of James I.

The LORD CHIEF JUSTICE—There was a conviction only in one case, the case of *Ralph Chamberlain.*

The ATTORNEY-GENERAL—Yes.

The LORD CHIEF JUSTICE—That could be explained, could it not, without praying in aid the doctrine required for this case. The conviction on that indictment may have been perfectly right because, if the offence was committed at Calais in the circumstances, it was not necessarily the special treason of adhering to the King's enemies without the realm.

The ATTORNEY-GENERAL—It was not necessarily, but the facts, so far as they are set out, I should have thought rendered the conclusion a probable one that it was that part of the statute that was considered. They were "Aiding and comforting and procuring," so the indictment says, "to Henry, King of the French . . . in order to traitorously "deprive the said King and Queen from their possession of the said "town of Calais." I observe from the full indictment that it does treat Calais in that case as part of the King's dominions; but there are so many other authorities in which it does not arise that I will not trouble your lordships further with that case.

The LORD CHIEF JUSTICE—It is not worth pursuing.

The ATTORNEY-GENERAL—No. Your lordship asked some questions about some cases which dealt with the case of Ireland. My learned friend, Mr. Sullivan, informed your lordship of the case of *O'Rurke*, which was tried in 1591, reported in 4 State Trials at page 708. The indictment charges *O'Rurke* "as a false traitor against the Lady Elizabeth, Queen "of England, France, and Ireland, at Dromhere, in the realm of the said "Lady, the Queen of Ireland, in parts beyond the sea, traitorously con-"spired and compassed the death of the Queen," and then it sets out various overt acts and charges, "adherence to the Queen's enemies in "the realm of Ireland in parts beyond the seas." Then in another part it charges "That the Bishop of Rome and Philip, King of Spain, had "prepared a great army hostilely to invade this realm of England," and that "O'Rurke traitorously received, fed, and comforted, and aided "very many of the aforesaid Spaniards, enemies of our said Lady the "Queen, arriving in certain ships in the said realm of Ireland." In the third place it charged "That O'Rurke, in the realm of Ireland in parts "beyond the seas, traitorously aided and comforted certain rebels and "traitors of the realm of Ireland." The other counts in the indictment I do not think are very material to the matters under consideration here. There the judgment of the Court was that he had been guilty of treason.

Mr. JUSTICE HORRIDGE—Did not the indictment lay the act done in Ireland as being in the realm of the Queen?

The ATTORNEY-GENERAL—It was charged as being outside the realm of England; it was charged as being within the realm of Ireland.

Mr. JUSTICE HORRIDGE—It says "Our Lady the Queen."

The ATTORNEY-GENERAL—"Lady the Queen of Ireland"; but it was treated as being outside the realm of England. Then, my lords, the next is *Perrot's* case, tried in 1592, reported in 4 State Trials at page 708. In that case we also have the indictment. The indictment charged "That Perrot, late Deputy of the Lady the Queen, in her realm of Ireland "in parts beyond seas, as a false traitor against the Queen at Dublin, in "the said realm of the said Lady the Queen of Ireland, compassed the "Queen's death, and to bring about the overthrow of the Commonwealth "of the realms of England and Ireland," and "That the Pope and the "King of Spain had prepared an army to invade the realm of England, "and that Perrot, in the realm of Ireland, wrote traitorous letters inciting "the King of Spain to perform his malicious purpose." That was similarly dealt with. Those cases are open to the comment which Mr. Justice Horridge has made.

The LORD CHIEF JUSTICE—What is your reference to those cases in 1591 and 1592; is it Hargreaves?

The ATTORNEY-GENERAL—I think it is Hargreaves.

Then, my lords, the next case I ask attention to is that of *Lords Middleton and Castlemaine, John Stafford, and Others*, tried in the year 1695. In that case we have the indictment. That is a very clear case.

It charges that they were indicted as false traitors, for "That they, "without this realm of England, in France, in parts beyond sea, "traitorously adhered to the King's enemies in the same war, and "traitorously assembled and united themselves to and amongst the said "enemies carrying on war against the King, and comforted, aided, and "supported the said enemies contrary to their allegiance." Most of the persons indicted were outlawed, including Stafford. He subsequently surrendered, and pleaded in bar some technical point and produced letters of pardon, but that does not affect the case. It was a clear case of a charge of adhering to the King's enemies without the realm, in France. It was a charge of treason, and there was a conviction.

The Lord Chief Justice—Where is that reported?

The Attorney-General—It is not reported.

The Lord Chief Justice—You have only got the indictment?

The Attorney-General—I have the indictment from the Records.

Mr. Justice Horridge—Do you know by whom it was tried?

Mr. Sullivan—They did not come within the realm to stand their trial, and that is why they were outlawed, as your lordships might presume.

The Lord Chief Justice—It looks rather like it.

The Attorney-General—That, again, throws a light on the question of whether they committed an offence.

The Lord Chief Justice—Yes, the point is whether it was an offence.

Mr. Justice Avory—How could they be outlawed unless they had committed an offence?

Mr. Sullivan—That is not the point. My lord, Mr. Justice Horridge asked where the trial took place, and what happened at the trial. I was answering him that there was no trial because they did not appear to stand their trial.

Mr. Justice Horridge—That was in answer to me, but you have not given an answer to my brother Avory. You have not answered whether or not that does not involve a crime.

Mr. Sullivan—Of course, they purported to be outlawed for a crime, but what I am pointing out is that there was no trial.

The Lord Chief Justice—You can say it is not to be taken as a judgment, because they were not heard.

Mr. Sullivan—That is all.

The Lord Chief Justice—They did not come here and submit themselves to the jurisdiction?

Mr. Sullivan—No.

The Lord Chief Justice—Still it shows that there was a conviction.

Mr. Justice Horridge—And it shows what the view of the law then was in 1695.

The Attorney-General—Then, my lord, the next case I desire to call attention to is the *Duke of Wharton's* case in 1729.

The Lord Chief Justice—Is that the Spanish case?

The Attorney-General—Yes, my lord, in Spain. In that case, too, we have the indictment. The indictment charged "That a war was "being carried on between Philip and George I., the former being an "enemy of the said King," and "The Duke of Wharton adhered to the "King's enemies in foreign parts, and beyond the sea without this realm "of Great Britain, to wit, in the realm of Spain, alleging as an overt act "that he joined and united himself to the army of Philip, prosecuting the "war against King George and attacking Gibraltar." Your lordships will notice in this case that both the overt act and the enemies were without the realm. In this case also the sentence was one of outlawry, and here, again, the Duke of Wharton did not enter an appearance.

I have the indictment here if I might read two passages from it. It charges that "Philip, Duke of Wharton, late of Westminster, in the "county of Middlesex, being a subject of the said Lord the late King, "well knowing the premises, not having the fear of God in his heart, nor "pondering the duty of his allegiance, but moved and seduced by "instigation of the devil as a false traitor against the said Lord, the "late King, his Sovereign, true natural and undoubted Lord, utterly "withdrawing the hearty love and due obedience, fidelity, and allegiance "which true and faithful subjects of the said Lord, the late King, were of "right bound to bear towards the said Lord, the late King, on the first "day of May, in the thirteenth year of the reign of the said Lord, the "late King, and at divers other days and times, as well before as "afterwards, in foreign parts and beyond sea without his realm of Great "Britain, to wit, in the realm of Spain, by force of arms, &c., falsely, "maliciously, knowingly, devilishly and treasonably was adherent, "aiding, and assistant to the same Philip, King of Spain." Then near the end of the indictment there come the following words:—"At which "same Wednesday next after the Quinzaine of Easter, before the said "Lord the King, that now is at Westminster, the Sheriff of the county of "Middlesex aforesaid, returned the aforesaid writ of causing to put in "exigent to him directed thus endorsed—By virtue of this writ to me "directed at my county (Court) of Middlesex, holden for the county of "Middlesex aforesaid, at the parish of St. Andrewes Holborne, in that "county aforesaid, on Thursday, to wit, the twelfth day of December, "in the same year, within written, the within named Philip, Duke of "Wharton, was first put in exigent, and did not appear." So that under the King's writ pursuant to the statute the trial was ordered at the Court as specified in the way I have just read.

The Lord Chief Justice—He did not appear.

The Attorney-General—He did not appear, and was thereupon outlawed.

The Lord Chief Justice—That seems to have happened in many of these cases.

The Attorney-General—Yes, naturally, unless they happen to be caught here.

The Lord Chief Justice—Do you notice in that case whether the overt acts were without the realm?

The Attorney-General—Yes, I think they were all. I will ask one of my learned friends to look it up.

The Lord Chief Justice—The conviction would have been quite good if there was only one overt act within the realm.

The Attorney-General—Yes, I think all the overt acts and all the enemies were without the realm.

The Lord Chief Justice—Perhaps Mr. Bodkin will look and tell us.

Motion to Quash Indictment.

The ATTORNEY-GENERAL—If your lordship pleases. I am told that all the acts were outside the realm, as my recollection was, and that they were all concerned with a projected attack on Gibraltar.

The LORD CHIEF JUSTICE—All the acts done by Philip, Duke of Wharton, were done without the realm.

The ATTORNEY-GENERAL—Yes.

Then, my lords, the next case is one of some interest and importance, the case of *William Cundell*. The only report I have of that case is in 4 Newgate Calendar. We have the indictment, but there is a report. William Cundell was indicted for adhering to the King's enemies in the Isle of France, and, as I have said, the Crown has a record of the case and a copy of the indictment.

Mr. JUSTICE HORRIDGE—What is the date?

The ATTORNEY-GENERAL—1812. It is reported in volume iv., Newgate Calendar, at page 62. I will read the short facts. "In 1808 "a number of British sailors and mariners were confined as prisoners of "war in the Isle of France. The prison being much crowded, was "greatly incommoded with dirt and vermin, and there being no way of "escaping from such inconvenience but that of desertion, every art was "practised by their keepers to induce the unhappy prisoners to enter "the French service. Fifty men, among whom were Cundell and Smith, "had not virtue enough to resist the temptations on one hand, and the "hope of escaping from distress and filth on the other. They forgot "their country and allegiance, and put on the enemy's uniform, acting "as sentinels over those who were so recently their companions in "captivity. These traitors continued to do duty with the French until "the surrender of the island to the British forces, when Cundell and Smith "with ten others positively refused to accompany the enemy, and threw "themselves upon the mercy of their country, having immediately "surrendered to the English, while the thirty-eight others marched off to "old France. These culprits were now transmitted to England, and a "special commission was issued for their trial, which took place at the "Surrey Court-house, February 6th, 1812. Cundell, Smith, and five "others were found guilty of adhering to His Majesty's enemies, when the "Attorney-General stated that he thought the ends of justice obtained, "and that he would not press the conviction of the remaining five, who "were discharged, not for any want of proof of their guilt, but through "the clemency of the Government."

Then there is the speech of the Attorney-General, which I do not think I need read. The Lord Chief Baron then proceeded to pass sentence, and there was sentence in the ordinary way, which your lordships are familiar with. Then—"The prisoners were then reconducted to their cells. Almost "every individual in Court was dissolved in tears during the melancholy "scene. On Monday morning, the 16th March, 1812, William Cundell "and John Smith, pursuant to their sentence, were hung." That is a very clear case. The indictment, as I have said, and the record show that the adherence to the King's enemies was without the realm. There was a formal trial, and in their presence they were convicted, and executed. All the overt acts there were in the Isle of France.

Mr. JUSTICE HORRIDGE—I do not know where the Isle of France was.

The ATTORNEY-GENERAL—I think it was in Mauritius.

Mr. JUSTICE HORRIDGE—And it was owned by France.

The ATTORNEY-GENERAL—Yes, a French colony. The war, of course, was between the French Government and ourselves.

Mr. JUSTICE HORRIDGE—It obviously was in their possession by the statement of the facts.

The ATTORNEY-GENERAL—Quite.

The LORD CHIEF JUSTICE—It is given as an authority in Archbold, at page 1050, not exactly on this point, but as an illustration of an overt act.

The ATTORNEY-GENERAL—Yes.

Mr. JUSTICE HORRIDGE—I do not see why it is not an authority. It is given in fact on this point, because it says, "The words of the Treason "Act, 1351, are 'or be adherent to the enemies of our Lord the King in "'his realm, giving to them aid or comfort in the realm or elsewhere.' The "offence defined by these words is 'adhering to the King's enemies within "'the land or without, and declaring the same by some overt act.'" The three cases which are nearest are *Lord Middleton and Others*, *The Duke of Wharton*, and *Cundell*.

The ATTORNEY-GENERAL—Yes, those, it is submitted, are exactly in point, and, of course, the earlier cases also.

The LORD CHIEF JUSTICE—The advantage of *Cundell* is that not only is it reported on the facts, so that one can see it in the Calendar, but also there was a trial.

The ATTORNEY-GENERAL—Yes.

The LORD CHIEF JUSTICE—The other cases are cases of outlawry.

The ATTORNEY-GENERAL—Yes. My lords, the fact that there are not a larger number of authorities in which the matter has been specially dealt with is, of course, due to the obvious consideration that if people have committed acts of this kind without the realm, they are not in the habit of returning to the realm if they can help it so long as the Power against which they conspire is ruling there.

The LORD CHIEF JUSTICE—Have you looked at all at paragraph 13 of the case of *Mulcahy* in the House of Lords?

The ATTORNEY-GENERAL—I have sent for that particular volume.

The LORD CHIEF JUSTICE—What puzzles one is that Mr. Justice Willes, in giving the opinion of the judges, certainly uses language which, if correctly reported in inverted commas, seems to be citing with approval the judgment in *O'Brien's* case.

The ATTORNEY-GENERAL—Your lordship means the passage in which he says it is treason if the man is adhering to the King's enemies in his realm or elsewhere?

The LORD CHIEF JUSTICE—Yes. The importance of it is that for the purpose of declaring the law he leaves out the words which have given rise to so much discussion here, "giving them aid and comfort."

The ATTORNEY-GENERAL—Yes, just as Lord Hale did.

The LORD CHIEF JUSTICE—If that is right, it brings down to the year 1868 the opinion of the judges of the King's Bench delivered by Mr. Justice Willes to the House of Lords in answer to the summons, and that opinion was approved by the House of Lords, Lord Cairns as Chancellor.

The ATTORNEY-GENERAL—Yes.

Motion to Quash Indictment.

The Lord Chief Justice—Although it was not necessary for the decision—Mr. Sullivan was quite right in saying it is *obiter*—it is a very high expression of judicial authority which we cannot brush aside as mere speculation.

The Attorney-General—My learned friend dwelt rather more on the fact that this view was *obiter* than on the fact that the case in Dyer was *obiter*.

My lords, if I may I will now shortly direct attention to the dicta of some of the great authorities upon our common law. Some have already been mentioned. I will do it with as much economy of time as I can. In Coke's Third Institute, page 63, the enumeration of treason by the learned author contains the following dictum:—"The fourth is adhering "to the King's enemies within the realm or without, and declaring the "same by some overt act."

The Lord Chief Justice—The reference given in Archbold to that passage is pages 10 and 11.

The Attorney-General—I have the book before me. "Adhering is "here explained, viz., in giving aid and comfort to the King's enemies "within the realm or without; delivery or surrender of the King's castles "or forts by the King's captain thereof to the King's enemies within the "realm or without for reward, &c., is adhering to the King's enemies, "and consequently treason declared by this Act."

The Lord Chief Justice—If it is not inconvenient to you, Mr. Attorney, would you refer us to Fitzherbert's Abridgment I think it is 5 Richard II. There is a report there of a trial which we have not got. I interpose because we do not think it necessary to trouble you to read again what is said in Coke's Institute unless there are other passages you wish to refer to. We got it all before us yesterday.

The Attorney-General—If your lordship pleases. I find it a little difficult to translate the report of the case, and for some reason which I need not trouble to state it was not found possible last night to get a translator, but I think I understand enough of it to show that there must have been some misapprehension in the mind of my learned friend in the account he gave your lordships of it.

The Lord Chief Justice—I forget what particular case it is cited in. It is cited in one of the passages read to us yesterday.

Mr. Justice Horridge—I think it is Hale.

The Attorney-General—There is a reference in a side note in Hale at page 169.

The Lord Chief Justice—That is the particular passage to which attention was called which I think is the strongest, and which says that at common law the offender might have been indicted in any county of England if he committed treason abroad.

The Attorney-General—Yes. I did not select it as among the number of authorities which I cited to the Court.

The Lord Chief Justice—It is rather difficult to understand.

The Attorney-General—It is difficult to understand. Not only that, but the dictum in question which is quoted is a dictum not proceeding from the Court, but from the representative of the Crown; and without wishing to underrate the authority of such a statement it did not seem to me to be of the same authority as a decision of the judges.

The LORD CHIEF JUSTICE—No, except that the representative of the Crown, the King's Attorney, who was arguing, treated it as a matter beyond all question.

The ATTORNEY-GENERAL—He did.

The LORD CHIEF JUSTICE—That was the only point.

The ATTORNEY-GENERAL—That is quite true.

The LORD CHIEF JUSTICE—You read a few lines of it to us yesterday.

The ATTORNEY-GENERAL—Yes. I am reading from the translation, but I can refer your lordships to the passage.

The LORD CHIEF JUSTICE—Is it under "Trial" in Fitzherbert?

The ATTORNEY-GENERAL—Yes. What he says is this, according to the translation we have had prepared, "If a man be adherent to the King's "enemies in France his land is forfeitable and his adherence shall be tried "where his land is, as has been oftentimes done in respect of the adherence "to the King's enemies in Scotland."

The LORD CHIEF JUSTICE—That is the passage I have before me. I follow the translation much better since you have read it to me in English, but I can make out that that is what it is.

The ATTORNEY-GENERAL—I rather understood my learned friend, Mr. Sullivan, who has evidently paid great attention and research to these matters, to suggest that this case——

Mr. SULLIVAN—I did not cite the case at all. By mistake I went to the Parliamentary Rules. It is given in Coke under "Catalogue of Par-"liamentary Rules," and I went to the Rules and forgot Fitzherbert.

The LORD CHIEF JUSTICE—It is a wrong reference. We did not understand about Cambridge being without the realm. It seems clear now that this is the authority of the King's Attorney. It is not a judgment.

The ATTORNEY-GENERAL—No, that is quite true.

Mr. JUSTICE HORRIDGE—That was cited in support of the proposition that at common law the offender might have been indicted in any county of England, especially where his lands lie.

The ATTORNEY-GENERAL—Yes. That is what the Attorney said for what it was worth. The case itself refers to the Cardinal of Rome as far as I understand it.

The LORD CHIEF JUSTICE—It seems to me to treat the law as beyond question. That is the point of it.

The ATTORNEY-GENERAL—Quite.

The LORD CHIEF JUSTICE—There is a very learned argument to be found in one of these cases by Sir John Campbell when he was Attorney-General of the Crown, in which he went through a number of authorities with reference to treason; not the particular case we have before us to-day about adhering to the King's enemies. You do find, and no doubt you will continue to find, particularly with the advantage the Attorney-General has in reference to the records and Crown documents, statements as to what happened which are of great use.

The ATTORNEY-GENERAL—Quite.

The LORD CHIEF JUSTICE—The only other authority I know—you will give us any additional ones if you think there are any—is East's Pleas of the Crown. There is a short reference to it there.

The ATTORNEY-GENERAL—Yes.

Motion to Quash Indictment.

The LORD CHIEF JUSTICE—The reference I have found is in volume 1 at page 80. "Englishmen living in a foreign country at the time of a rupture "with us, and continuing there afterwards, are not on that account "adherents to the King's enemies unless they voluntarily swear fealty to "them or actually assist them in the war; or, at least, unless they refuse "to return home," and then it goes on to deal with something else. He treats that as being an offence of adherence to the King's enemies.

The ATTORNEY-GENERAL—Quite. At page 78 your lordships will find this passage—"In considering what shall be deemed an adherence to the "King's enemies, much of what has been already said under the head of "levying war is equally applicable. Those other species of aid or comfort, "in the words of the statute, which, when given to a rebel within the "realm, would make the subject guilty of levying war; if given to an "enemy, whether within or without the realm, will make the party guilty of "adhering to the King's enemies, though in the case of giving aid to "enemies within the realm a subject might, in some instances, be brought "within both branches of the Act." "Whether within or without the "realm" is very positive language.

The LORD CHIEF JUSTICE—The only comment to be made upon that is this. I had noticed it, but I thought it did not advance us in the argument, because the aid may be given to the enemy without the realm, the actual adherence being within the realm. That is the point Mr. Sullivan made yesterday. It is possible.

The ATTORNEY-GENERAL—It is a possible construction. I should have thought when it spoke of aid and comfort being given to an enemy within or without the realm it was thinking of aid or comfort which makes up adherence.

The LORD CHIEF JUSTICE—The passage to which I called attention, which follows upon that, seems to make the meaning clear, and I think does give effect to your construction of those words.

The ATTORNEY-GENERAL—I think it does.

The LORD CHIEF JUSTICE—And he gives the instance: supposing an Englishman abroad, when we go to war with France, voluntarily swears fealty to the French King, that becomes adhering to the King's enemies without the realm and is the offence of treason. There is no doubt the whole of the act is done outside the realm.

The ATTORNEY-GENERAL—Quite.

The LORD CHIEF JUSTICE—It makes it quite plain.

The ATTORNEY-GENERAL—The two passages taken together no doubt do.

The LORD CHIEF JUSTICE—I do not think there is anything in Foster's Discourses of the Law of Treason on this point. I have looked at it with some care.

The ATTORNEY-GENERAL—No, I do not think there is. Now, my lords, there are one or two other references I might give to make the matter quite plain. The first is Alexander Luders on High Treason. At page 12 the learned author says: "The meaning of the words 'to levy "'war against the King in his realm, to adhere to his enemies, and "'assist them within the realm or elsewhere,' must necessarily be the "same in this Act that is in other contemporary instruments or writings."

Then at page 13 he says: "It is reasonable to infer that the war forbidden to be levied within the realm was the same kind of war as might have been levied without the realm, and that the enemies not to be adhered to were such enemies as were capable of levying such war, and of being assisted out of the realm as well as within it."

Then another work of authority is Holbourne's Readings, 1681, at pages 12 and 13. He is dealing with the various heads of treason, and he says: "The fourth part is to adhere to the King's enemies. Aiding the enemies within or without, is an aiding of those that come into the land or of those who are without. Aiding is by sending them aid, as of victuals or of weapons and the like, by giving them counsel, or by other ways, whereby they may receive strength or comfort from him."

The LORD CHIEF JUSTICE—Yes. The same observation applies to that as to several of them. You may aid and comfort the King's enemies without the realm by an act which you do within the realm, and in order to come within the proposition we are now discussing, you must get both the act of adherence by the person and also the aid to the enemy without the realm, must you not?

The ATTORNEY-GENERAL—I think that is so.

The LORD CHIEF JUSTICE—That is the difficulty of some of these passages. For example, sending a letter giving information to the enemy would be to aid the enemy without the realm, but the act is done within the realm.

The ATTORNEY-GENERAL—Yes. It may be that in some of these *dicta* the language might cover one or the other.

I think I have now referred your lordships to the authorities as far as they are known to me. My submission is that the doctrine of the common law has treated acts of adherence without the realm as being treason; that the meaning of the statute of King Edward III. is not ambiguous, but that it also treats adherence without the realm as falling under one of the heads of treason; that no controversy has ever been raised which would tend to show—whether such an act, that is to say, adherence without the realm, was triable in this country or not—that it was not an offence; that it has never been contended in any textbook or in any Court of law from the time when the statute of King Edward III. was passed to the present day, as far as I am aware, with one possible exception, that whether triable or not, adherence without the realm was an offence, and the offence of treason; that the statute of Henry VIII. which dealt with procedure defined clearly the circumstances under which such treason should be justiciable in this country; and that the whole current of opinion amongst those who have been treated as authorities upon these matters is in one direction when they construe the statute of King Edward III. and the common law before it; and whether one takes the great authorities who have written upon the common law of England, or whether one takes the opinion of all the judges carrying on a long and most impressive weight of judicial and other opinion from the earliest times till the year 1868, it is impossible to resist the conclusion that an act of adherence to the King's enemies without the realm was and is justiciable in the Courts of this country.

My lords, I have one observation to make in conclusion. I have indicated that the matter was much discussed in *The King* v. *Lynch*. The official report in the Law Reports hardly illustrates the extent to which the matter was discussed, but it was presented with some considerable weight of argument to the Court, and an answer not without elaboration was made by the then Attorney-General, and it was dealt with, or pronounced upon by the Court; and it is certainly a circumstance which ought to be borne in mind that the conviction itself in *The King* v. *Lynch*, had this doctrine been well founded, would have been wrong. It is an extremely recent authority, establishing, as I have said, that the whole trend and weight of judicial and other authority has been in the same direction.

The Lord Chief Justice—The only difficulty is that in *Lynch's* case, notwithstanding that there was a learned and somewhat elaborate argument, the Court pronounced no judgment upon it, but proceeded to deal with the case as if the argument advanced on behalf of the defence was ill founded, otherwise the summing up of the learned Chief Justice and the conviction must have been wrong.

The Attorney-General—I think one cannot resist the conclusion, when one notices in what a cavalier manner, if I may use the expression, the learned judge dealt with the argument, that it had not made a very deep impression upon his mind. We must draw that inference. The fact is that the conviction took place, and it could not have taken place had this contention been well founded. So that your lordships have the earliest authorities and the most recent authority, and my submission to the Court is that this objection is ill founded and cannot be supported.

Mr. Artemus Jones—My lords, I do not propose to follow my learned friend over the authorities which have been quoted. I desire to deal first of all with the case of *The King* v. *Lynch*, which is the only authority we have to get over as regards the wording of the statute. It is perfectly true, as your lordships have pointed out, that a judgment in *The King* v. *Lynch* was not delivered, but it is clear from the shorthand notes of the proceedings what the view was that the then Lord Chief Justice took. His view was that *The King* v. *Vaughan* was an authority which expressly overruled the view which was then put forward on behalf of Lynch. Why it was that the facts of *The King* v. *Vaughan* were not gone into I do not know, but it is clear from the indictment in *The King* v. *Vaughan* that it lends no authority to the view which the Lord Chief Justice then took. The first count alleged acts committed within the jurisdiction of the Admiralty, and, I think, in the second count hostile acts were alleged within the dominion of the King.

The Lord Chief Justice—We have already expressed our view upon that. You are quite justified in referring to it, and there has been no argument to the contrary. *The King* v. *Vaughan* is no authority against you.

Mr. Artemus Jones—If your lordship pleases. With regard to the ancient writers which have been quoted, I propose humbly to follow my learned friend, the Attorney-General, subject only to this observation.

The question which your lordships have to determine is the construction of the words of an Act of Parliament, and the primary duty in the construction of a statute is to take the language of the statute itself, provided it is free from ambiguity. My submission is that if you look at the words of the statute no ambiguity can arise from them. I notice that your lordship was reading the words of the statute from Archbold——

The LORD CHIEF JUSTICE—No, I was not. I read them from the revised statutes with the Norman French on the other side.

Mr. ARTEMUS JONES—I have looked at the actual statute itself, and I have something to say about that, because a good deal depends upon the grammatical construction of these words. I suggest that the punctuation marks and other things set out in Chitty and Archbold do not actually appear upon the document itself.

The LORD CHIEF JUSTICE—I have looked at a number of copies, reproductions of this Act, in the revised statutes and elsewhere, containing Luder's translation, and I have found that the commas vary in almost every case; and apparently, according to the interpretation that the author wished to give, he has inserted the commas. You can take up some authors and you will find the commas that make it so plain that you wonder that there can be any dispute about it; you can take up another which makes "aiding and comforting" run on to the "else-"where" without a comma. So I think we have to start with this, that commas have no place in the discussion before this Court.

Mr. ARTEMUS JONES—Might I supplement that by pointing out that Coke, who is treated with so much veneration, actually misspells the word. It is clear, if he had taken the trouble to go to the statute itself, he would not have made that mistake. Might I refer your lordships to what is known as the Record Office version of the statute. Your lordships will remember that a Commission was appointed somewhere in the reign of George III. to get the statutes together, and an official version was published in the year 1810, which sets out on one side the actual Norman-French words printed in the characters, with the contracted forms and abbreviations that were current at that time, and on the other side you have the translation. My submission to your lordships is that the construction which the learned Attorney-General seeks to put upon these words cannot be maintained, because that construction is repugnant to the express terms of the statute itself. That is my proposition. The recital begins in these words: "Whereas divers opinions have been before "this time in what case treason shall be said and in what not; The King "at the request of his Lords and of the Commons hath made a declara-"tion in the manner as hereinafter followeth: That is to say, when a "man doth compass or imagine the death of our Lord the King, or of "our Lady his Queen," and so on, "or if a man do levy war against "our Lord the King in his realm"—those are the words of limitation which must refer either to the enemy or to the person charged—"or be "adherent to the King's enemies in his realm"—exactly the same words of limitation which must apply either to the enemy or to the person charged, and which I suggest are words of limitation defining the limits within which the act of adherence must be committed. Then it goes on:

"Giving to them aid and comfort in the realm or elsewhere." It is a little difficult to understand how the Attorney-General can say that those words "or elsewhere" should be in fact transferred from where they are put into another part, added to the preceding words. If the learned Attorney-General is right in his construction, Parliament could have meant nothing when it put in these words, "in his realm." Supposing you strike out the words "in his realm" in both offences, this is how the sentence would read: "If a man do levy war against our "Lord the King, or be adherent to the King's enemies, giving to them "aid and comfort in his realm or elsewhere." Then the construction which the learned Attorney-General puts upon it would no doubt be sound, but he cannot put that construction forward, because Parliament must not be presumed to have meant nothing when it used these words of limitation. If I may borrow the language of the advocate who argued the case of *The King* v. *Lynch*, such a construction as this gives the go-by altogether to these words of limitation. I submit that what the statute of Edward III. had in mind when it used these words, "giving "to them aid and comfort in the realm," was the particular form which adhering to the King's enemies might assume, and against which they were legislating.

I submit to your lordships, with the greatest respect not only to the ancient writers but also to His Majesty's judges, that in the construction of an Act of Parliament the supreme authority is the language of the Act itself, and the function of your lordships is simply to give to them, to quote the words of Chief Justice Jarvis, the elementary rule of interpretation, giving to ordinary and plain words their plain and ordinary meaning. If the wording of the statute admitted of any other meaning, I agree that the interpretation put forward by the learned Attorney-General might be upheld.

There is one point, and that is with reference to the Indictment Act of last year. The Lord Chief Justice yesterday went to the heart of the whole controversy when he said the question was whether the words "or elsewhere" governed the words immediately preceding them, or governed the rest.

The Lord Chief Justice—Or governed both.

Mr. Artemus Jones—Or governed both. On the other hand, they may be purely descriptive words. If they are words of description and not words of definition, then I submit the construction put forward by the learned Attorney-General cannot be upheld. The view which the learned counsel took who framed this indictment is exactly the same view as that which I am putting before this Court. May I refer your lordships to section 3 of the Indictment Act of last year.

Mr. Justice Horridge—Supposing it is, is he a greater authority than Hale or anybody else? How can it help us that somebody who framed the indictment before us took a particular view?

Mr. Artemus Jones—I may be wrong, but I was under the impression that I was discussing the indictment in this case.

Mr. Justice Horridge—How can it help us if the indictment covers the offence? We can draw the inference as well as the man who drew it.

Mr. ARTEMUS JONES—Put in that form I agree, but I think your lordship will see the point of my argument when I have developed it. Section 3 of the Indictment Act says: "Every indictment shall contain "and shall be sufficient if it contains a statement of the specific offence "or offences with which the accused person is charged, together with "such particulars as may be necessary for giving reasonable information as to the nature of the charge." Under the rules, I think it is Rule 4, sub-section 3, "The statement of offence shall describe the "offence shortly in ordinary language, avoiding as far as possible the "use of technical terms, and without necessarily stating all the essential "elements of the offence, and if the offence charged is one created by "statute, shall contain a reference to the section of the statute creating "the offence."

Now, if your lordships turn to the indictment here, the statement of the offence and the reference to the statute creating it is set out in a sentence: "High treason by adhering to the King's enemies elsewhere "than in the King's realm, to wit, in the Empire of Germany, contrary "to the Treason Act, 1351." Then particulars follow, and in the particulars the Crown allege that "On the said several days traitorously con-"triving and intending to aid and assist the said enemies of our Lord "the King against our Lord the King and his subjects, did traitorously "adhere to and aid and comfort the said enemies," showing clearly that the learned counsel who framed this indictment treated those words, "aiding and comforting," merely as words of description; and they appear in the particulars under the statute which says you must give particulars which may not give all the necessary ingredients of the offence, but shall at least give information as to the nature of the offence. The submission I make to the Court is that if the view of the Crown is that those words "aiding and comforting" are words of definition and not words of description, it was not the view of the learned counsel who framed the indictment, because he treats them as descriptive words and descriptive words alone. To go back to the statute once more, I have only put very shortly the point that I make, namely, that the construction which the Crown is putting upon these words is actually repugnant to the words of the statute itself. You must wipe out altogether those words "within "his realm," which appear in both offences, before you can put this construction upon the statute; and that being so I submit with deference to your lordships that the argument put forward on behalf of the defendant is a valid and substantial one.

[Their lordships conferred.]

Judgment on Motion to Quash Indictment.

The LORD CHIEF JUSTICE—A submission has been made to the Court by the defence that this indictment should be quashed on the ground that it discloses no offence known to the English law. Another way of putting the same proposition is that the Court should rule, according to the contention of the defence, that the Crown has failed to prove an offence in law. The prisoner is charged with that species of treason which is known as adhering to the King's enemies. The charge in the indictment is the offence of "high treason by adhering to the King's "enemies elsewhere than in the King's realm, to wit, in the Empire of "Germany, contrary to the Treason Act, 1351." The argument advanced and supported by careful, well-reasoned, and able arguments of Mr. Sullivan and those who supported his contention is to the effect that adherence to the King's enemies without the realm is not an offence against the statute of Edward III., that is to say, the statute of 1351. We have had the advantage of elaborate argumeuts, by no means too elaborate on behalf of the defence, and also on behalf of the Crown by the Attorney-General; and although this point has been discussed many times in the books, and decided, according to our view, in the most recent case of treason, *Lynch's* case, yet it merits careful examination by this Court. The argument is that this Court must construe the words of the statute of 1351 and must pay no regard to any commentary that may have been made by learned authors, however distinguished, when arriving at the meaning of the words. That we must interpret the words of the statute is beyond question. That we should not be entitled to do violence to the words of the statute may, I think, also be assumed.

But if the words of the statute are not clear, and if it be possible to construe the statute in two different ways, then the comments of great lawyers, masters of the common law, during the last three or four centuries, cannot be allowed to pass by this Court without the greatest regard and consideration. The words in question, in the statute 25 Edward III. are these—paraphrasing them—"It shall be treason if "a man do levy war against our Lord the King in his realm or be "adherent to the King's enemies in his realm, giving to them aid and "comfort in the realm or elsewhere." The contention is that those words "or elsewhere" govern only the words "aid and comfort in the "realm," and have no application to the words "be adherent to the "King's enemies." As the offence is of adhering to the King's enemies, if the words "or elsewhere" do not apply to the adhering, then the contention of the defence would be right. If, on the other hand, the Crown's contention is correct that those words "or elsewhere" do govern the adhering to the King's enemies, then it is plain that it is an offence to adhere to the King's enemies by an act committed without the realm. In order to avoid ambiguity I would add also this, that to constitute the offence for this purpose it is not sufficient to show that the aid and comfort has been given to enemies without the realm. The act of adherence which constitutes the charge also must have been committed without the realm for this purpose, because the whole of this indictment is based upon the offence of adhering to the King's enemies without the realm.

Now, I repeat what I said during the course of the argument, that we must construe these words of this statute, now some 560 years old, without reference to commas or brackets, but merely looking to the language. The history of the law of treason of this country is certainly of importance in considering the statute of 1351. It is unnecessary at this time, and having regard to the authorities to which I shall call attention in a moment, to refer in great detail to the early law; but I have no hesitation myself in stating that if a man adhere to the King's enemies without the realm he is committing the offence of treason; that he was committing the offence of treason at common law, notwithstanding that the offence was committed without the realm. We have heard considerable argument to establish that the common law of England never knew a crime which was not committed within the territory of England, that is to say, in ancient times, of course; and it is said the common law of England still obtains except in so far as it has been altered by statute. There is some authority for the proposition which I have stated to which I mean to refer, which is in Sir Matthew Hale's Pleas of the Crown, vol. 1, page 169, in which he says: "Touching the trial of foreign "treason, viz., adhering to the King's enemies without the kingdom at "this day the statute of 35 Henry VIII. hath sufficiently provided for "it"; and this is the passage upon which I lay special stress: "But "at common law he might have been indicted in any county of England, "and especially where the offender's lands lie, if he have any."

The reference is given for that to a case in the fifth year of the reign of Richard II., which is to be found in Fitzherbert's Abridgment, under the heading of "Trial," section 54. The substance of it—I am not quoting the exact words—is that the then King's Attorney stated to the Court, and apparently, so far as one can judge from the report, without any contradiction by the Court, and, so far as I know, without any contradiction to be found in any book up to this very day, that that was the law, and it was adopted as the law by Sir Matthew Hale in the passage which I have read. I will make this observation with reference to the common law, that it is quite right to say—it might be said—that whatever may have been the common law ought not to affect our decision in determining the interpretation of the statute. I will accept that and say we must construe the language of the statute even though that statute is declaratory of the common law; but it is a matter not lightly to be passed by that the common law before the statute was, in my opinion, as I have stated it. It has been said more than once, certainly by Lord Blackburn and others, that this statute of 1351 was declaratory of the common law. There is no doubt that at that time there was great agitation amongst the subjects of the King because of the fear of the consequence of being charged with treason, which was a crime at that time so vague, or thought to be so vague, that those who might be charged with it were apprehensive of the consequences; and the result was that on petition to Parliament the statute then became law and received the assent of the King in the words to which I have referred.

Now from the year 1351 until the thirty-fifth year of the reign of Henry VIII., there is little to assist us; but in the reign of Henry VIII. a statute was passed which in my view is of importance in this connection. The statute is entitled "An Acte concerninge the triall of Treasons "comytted out of the King's Majesties domynions." It recites—again I am paraphrasing the language—that doubts and questions had arisen as to the trial of treasons and misprisions of treasons committed abroad.

It is worth noting that the doubts had not arisen as to whether the act, if committed abroad, would amount to treason, but only as to the trial. Then the statute proceeds: "Be it enacted by authority of this "present Parliament that all manner of offences being already made or "declared or hereafter to be made or declared by any of the laws and "statutes of this realm to be treasons," then "shall be tried by the "King's Justices"—that is the King's Bench, and also as an alternative by Commissioners where a Commission is appointed. Now, that statute assumes that the offence of treason can be committed without the realm; and it prescribes in respect of all such offences as have already been declared the mode of procedure, or, rather, the venue of the trial. The statute shows plainly that the offence existed. From that time the statute has regulated the trial of offences committed without the realm.

It is by virtue of that statute and subsequent statutes, which have really done nothing more than provide that the counties of London and Middlesex shall be one county for this purpose, that the jurisdiction of this Court is derived. It is because we are sitting as judges of the King's Bench that we become the judges to try this case, for the reason that if it is a treason committed without the realm, the venue is prescribed by this statute of Henry VIII. as of the King's justices where they sit and be kept. That statute of Henry VIII. is, to my mind, authority for this proposition, at least it shows clearly what the law was at the time it was passed. That there was the offence of treason without the realm; and further, quite consistent with the reading which the Crown wishes to give to the statute of 1351, it would apply to the offence of adhering to the King's enemies without the realm. The doubts that have arisen from beginning to end, so far as we have been able to trace in looking through the various books to which we have had access, and to which our attention has been called, are never as to the offence, but only as to the venue; and the whole difficulty which arose was, as was pointed out by learned authors, and more especially in Hawkins' Pleas of the Crown, book 2, chapter 25, section 48, where this matter is dealt with in passages that have been read, and of which I will only read one short passage now, as to the venue. There the learned author says: "It seems to have been a great doubt before the making of the "statute of 35 Henry VIII. in what manner and in what place high treason "done out of the realm was to be tried"—there is not the faintest suggestion that the offence did not exist, but only a doubt as to the manner and place of trial—"for some seem to have holden that it was triable "only by an appeal before the constable and marshal; others, that it "might be tried upon an indictment, laying the offence in any county "where the King pleased; and others, that it was triable by way of "indictment in that county only wherein the offender had lands; but "surely it cannot reasonably be doubted but that it was triable some "way or other; for it cannot be imagined that an offence of such "dangerous consequence, and expressly within the purview of 25 "Edward III., should be wholly dispunishable, as it must have been "if it were no way triable." I am content to adopt every word of that language of that great master of the law, and also of Sir Matthew Hale, whom I have just quoted. The only observation I wish to make upon it is that the defence would say, as Mr. Sullivan pointed out, and I think rightly, that upon this section 48 it does not follow that the meaning must be given to the words now under discussion, because it is said there were other offences of treason without the realm. But equally it must be observed that there is no exception drawn for this statement, and there is nothing which would support the exception being made save the interpretation of the statute contended for by the defence. I can find no justification for doubting that these learned authors meant their language to apply equally to a case of adhering to the King's enemies without the realm as to any other kind of offence of treason without the realm.

I will not read again the passage in Coke's Institutes, but in volume 3 there is a statement of the law which is plain in its terms, and which Mr. Sullivan quite frankly stated was an authority against him if the Court accepted it as an authority. The passages have been read so often that I do not propose to read them again. They are to be found in chapter 1 of the Third Institute of Coke, on pages 10 and 11.

Then, coming to the later days, there are passages in a case in 1868, *Mulcahy* v. *The Queen*, reported in Law Reports, 3 English and Irish Appeal Cases, at page 306, in which Mr. Justice Willes, in giving his opinion of the law relating to treason to the House of Lords —not only his opinion but the opinion of all the judges—adopted the construction of the words of the statute of 1351, that the offence was committed if a person be adherent to the King's enemies in his realm or elsewhere. He leaves out the words which have given rise to this discussion, that is, "giving them aid and comfort." The views were adopted by the House of Lords. It is right here again to say that Mr. Sullivan pointed out, and again I say in my judgment accurately, that these observations of Mr. Justice Willes were by the way; they were *obiter*; but nevertheless they were the considered opinion of the judges to the House of Lords, and the House of Lords did not dissent from any one of the views expressed.

Then at last we come to the decision of *The King* v. *Lynch*, decided in 1903. There the same argument was advanced by the defence that has been put forward before us, and it was persisted in and elaborately argued. The Court there came to the conclusion that the defendant's contention was wrong, and, although it gave no judgment, the then Lord Chief Justice proceeded to sum up and directed the jury as if it was an offence. Lynch was convicted by the jury, and if the argument of the defence is right in this case, Lynch never should have been convicted, and the Court ought to have ruled that no offence had been disclosed either by the evidence or in the indictment. The Court did not so rule, but on the contrary directed the jury upon the assumption that the offence was disclosed if the jury took a particular view of the facts.

Now, that is a current of authority which is strong. I will not pass over the case in Dyer to which our attention was called, and upon which much reliance was placed by Mr. Sullivan. His argument was that when you look at that case you will find that there it was asserted that there was no such offence known to the common law as treason committed out of the realm; and, indeed, he went further, that no such offence was known to the law at all, because no means had been found of trying the offence until the statute of 35 Henry VIII. But on examination of the case in Dyer—2 Dyer, page 131 (*b*)—it is clear it is not a judgment at all; it is a memorandum of the judges and the King's serjeants, some doubt having arisen as to whether a statute of 1 & 2 Philip and Mary had overruled the statute 35 Henry VIII. in so far as that statute declared that treasons without the realm should be tried by the judges of the King's Bench. The result was that they came to the conclusion that the statute of Henry VIII. was not overruled, and reliance was placed before us upon these words, "because no offence of treason committed out of the realm "was triable here by the course of the common law." The first comment upon that is this. It assumes that there was an offence of treason committed out of the realm, but the difficulty was that it was not known how it was triable by the course of the common law, and all that the learned judges did—the judges and the Master of the Rolls there assembled—was to declare what they thought was the effect of this statute 1 & 2 Philip and Mary. It does not touch the question which is now being argued before us. It does not assume that at common law there was no offence of treason without the realm. It is the opposite. The only difficulty again, such as one finds running through centuries of our law, is as to the procedure when there was treason without the realm; that is, as to the venue of the trial.

Now, our attention was called by the learned Attorney-General to a series of cases of which I only propose to refer to three, and in truth to rely only upon one. First of all there was the case of *Lord Wentworth, Grimston, and Chamberlain.* The indictment there, we were told by the learned Attorney-General, was for an offence committed in Calais. Lord Wentworth apparently was sent to the House of Lords to be tried, Grimston was acquitted, and Chamberlain was convicted. I find it difficult to take that case as an authority; indeed I do not think we can regard it as one, because it was tried in the year 1558, and according to the indictment it seems clear that the offence was laid treating Calais as within the King's dominions. Consequently, in my judgment, that case cited to us by the Attorney-General does not help us. The next case he cited was the *Duke of Wharton* case, which was tried in the year 1729. There, according to the statement made from investigation of the indictment and the records, the offence was of adhering to the King's enemies in Spain. There, according to the overt acts to which our attention was directed, the offence of adhering was committed in Spain, and the aid and comfort were given in Spain. So that the complete offence of treason without the realm was there charged. As a result the Duke of Wharton did not appear, and he was outlawed; but it assumes again that according to the law of England he had committed the offence. The observation to be made upon it is that the defence did not appear to put forward its view, and therefore it might not have the full authority which would be given to a case in which the argument was put before the Court on behalf of the defence.

The third case was that of *William Cundell*, tried in the year 1812, of which the records are extant, and of which there is no report except in the 4th volume of the Newgate Calendar, page 62. That was a case of adhering without the realm to the King's enemies, and giving them aid and comfort there. The case was tried. The persons were within the jurisdiction of this Court, and sentence was pronounced. According to that it seems clear that in 1812 there is distinct authority for the proposition that it is an offence to adhere without the realm to the King's enemies. It was the case of persons who were confined in the Isle of France, and who had then forsaken their allegiance to the King and taken it to the French. I think, in view of that judgment to which our attention has been called, it cannot be said that there is no authority to be found in our books for the proposition advanced by the Crown until the authority of *The King* v. *Lynch*.

I do not propose to go further through the various authorities. I have called attention to the most important of them. I come to the conclusion that the offence, if proved in fact, has been committed in law. We are merely considering now the case upon the assumption that the facts prove it. The argument of the defence is put forward on that basis, that no offence is made out in law. Of course, it must not for one moment be thought, and is not thought by those who understand our procedure, that that in any way admits the offence. It is merely a legal argument. The result of it is that in my judgment the words "giving to them aid and comfort" may be read as in a parenthesis; but I do not exclude the application of the words "or "elsewhere" to that parenthesis; I think it applies just as much to the parenthesis as it does to the preceding words. I am of opinion, although it is not necessary to state it for the purposes of this case, that the words "or elsewhere" govern both limbs of the sentence—both the adhering to the King's enemies and the aid and comfort to the King's enemies, and that it is an offence to adhere within the realm or without the realm to the King's enemies, and it is equally an offence to adhere within the realm to the King's enemies by giving them aid and comfort without the realm.

For these reasons I am of opinion, notwithstanding the learned and able arguments that have been addressed to us, that the point fails and that the motion to quash the indictment must be refused.

Mr. Justice Avory—I agree that this objection fails whether it be regarded as an objection to the indictment that it discloses no offence upon the face of it or whether it be regarded as an objection that there is no evidence to go to the jury of an offence committed within the meaning of the statute of Edward III. It would, in my opinion, be sufficient in this Court to say that the point which has been argued so strenuously and with so much learning before us has been already decided by this Court in the case of *The King* v. *Lynch;* but, having regard to the criticisms which have been passed upon that case, I think it right to add my own reasons for coming to the same conclusion as that which has been expressed by my lord the Chief Justice.

First of all, it is not right to say that the point was not in fact decided in *The King* v. *Lynch.* While it is true that no formal judgment was pronounced on the objection, it will be found by reference to the report of the case in 19 Times Law Reports that the Lord Chief Justice stopped the Attorney-General in his reply to the argument and said that they were satisfied on the point, and unless he wanted to cite any further authorities, they did not wish to hear him further. That was in fact a decision that the point taken was a bad one. But further, and beyond the fact to which allusion has been made, that the prisoner in that case could not have been convicted unless the point was decided against him, it will also be found in the same report of the summing up of the learned Lord Chief Justice that he, towards the close of his summing up, used these words. He reminded the jury "that the "charge against the prisoner was that of aiding the King's enemies; "and he had already told them that the facts which had been laid before "them amounted to aiding the King's enemies, and that wherever it "was done this was an offence in respect of which, if proved, the "prisoner ought to be found guilty upon this indictment." So that there was an express direction in terms in that case to the jury that wherever the acts were done of adherence to the King's enemies that was an offence within the meaning of the statute.

Now, it is, I think, also clear that in interpreting this statute of Edward III. the Court must do it in the light of the fact that it has been decided to be an Act of Parliament declaratory of the common law. I cannot doubt that before this statute of Edward III. it was treason in a British subject to join the forces of an enemy abroad, and that if a British subject had joined the forces of an enemy abroad at war with this country, and he afterwards returned or was brought back to this country, he could be tried here for that offence. When one has regard to the nature of this offence of high treason, I think it is obvious that it must have been so. Foster in his Crown Law thus describes the offence of high treason: "High treason being an offence committed against the "duty of allegiance, it may be proper to consider from whom and to "whom allegiance is due. With regard to natural-born subjects there "can be no doubt. They owe allegiance to the Crown at all times and "in all places. This is what we call natural allegiance in contradistinc- "tion to that which is local. Natural allegiance is founded in the "relation every man standeth in to the Crown, considered as the head "of that society whereof he is born a member; and on the peculiar "privileges he deriveth from that relation which are, with great "propriety, called his birthright. This birthright nothing but his "own demerit can deprive him of. It is indefeasible and perpetual; "and consequently the duty of allegiance which ariseth out of it, and is "inseparably connected with it, is, in consideration of law, likewise "unalienable and perpetual."

In view of that definition of the offence of high treason, I think it cannot be doubted, as I have said, that such an offence committed by a British subject abroad was triable, justiciable, in this country; and the only doubts which had arisen before the statute of Henry VIII. were as expressed by Hawkins in his Pleas of the Crown in the passage which my lord the Chief Justice has already read; not a doubt whether it was triable here; not a doubt whether it was an offence committed by a British subject; but a doubt only as to the proper place and the proper manner in which it should be tried. He points out that some have held that it should be tried in one county; others have held that it should be tried in another county; others have held that it should be tried upon an indictment laying the offence in any county where the King pleased. That, no doubt, had reference to a special Commission issued by the King for the trial of a particular treason, and which special Commission would, in my opinion, get rid of all difficulty about local venue.

Now, that being so, if this was an offence triable in this country before the statute of Edward III., that is to say, if the offence of treason committed abroad was triable in this country before the statute of Edward III., and the statute of Edward III. is declaratory only of the common law, it would be a strange conclusion that the statute has limited the offence to treasons committed or to overt acts which have been committed within the realm. As the Attorney-General has pointed out, the offence of adhering to the King's enemies, giving aid and comfort to them, is an offence which is more likely, *prima facie* at all events, to be committed out of the realm than within it, and it would be a strange enactment to provide if the common law was, as I have said, that after this date the offence could only be committed by a person who was within the realm at the time when he committed it.

With reference to the construction of the actual words, again it would be sufficient, as my lord has pointed out, to say that the great authorities have uniformly put upon these words the construction which the Crown invite us to put, namely, that the statute does not limit this kind of treason to treason committed by a subject within the realm. But there appear to be two constructions of it which have been adopted, either of which will satisfy and answer this objection. It may be that the words "or elsewhere" are to be read as applying to the words "be adherent "to the King's enemies," that is to say, if he be adherent to the King's enemies in his realm or elsewhere; or it may be, as Serjeant Hawkins seemed to think. In book 1, chapter 17, of his Treatise, he says, "As to the "second point, namely, what shall be said to be an adherence to the King's "enemies, this is explained by the words subsequent 'giving aid and "'comfort to them'"; and it may be therefore that the proper construction of this section is that the words "giving aid and comfort in the "realm or elsewhere" are an explanation or an exposition of the kind of adherence to the King's enemies which is aimed at by the statute. Nobody questions that the words "or elsewhere" apply to the giving of aid and comfort to the enemy, and it may be therefore that the proper construction is that if a person gives aid and comfort to the King's enemies either in the realm or elsewhere he is committing the offence of adhering to the King's enemies within the meaning of this statute. Whichever view be taken, as I have said, it is sufficient to say that all the authorities agree that it is not limited in the manner in which the learned counsel for the prisoner have invited us to confine it.

It only remains to consider in one word the statute of Henry VIII., which provides for the trial in this country of treasons committed abroad.

In my view there is nothing in this statute which assists the argument for the prisoner. The recital of it is, "Forasmuch as some doubts and "questions have been moved that certain kinds of treasons, misprisions, "and concealment of treasons done or committed out of the King's realm "cannot by the common law be inquired of." In my opinion that recital or preamble of the statute rather assumes that there are already certain kinds of treason committed out of the realm which may be tried within the realm, and the probability is that it was only for removing doubts as to the other kinds of treason, many of which had been enacted either in the reign of Henry VIII., or shortly before. At all events, it makes it clear that after that date any treason committed out of the realm may be tried, as this one is being tried, by His Majesty's judges in the King's Bench.

For these reasons I agree that this objection must be overruled.

Mr. Justice Horridge—After the very careful consideration by the Lord Chief Justice of the law before the statute, of the statute, of the cases in which the decision involved construction of the statute, and of the writings of learned authors, I do not think I should usefully occupy the time of the Court by again reviewing those matters. All I wish to say is this. My view is that the true construction of the statute is the one which is to be found in the opinion of the judges in the case of *Mulcahy* v. *The Queen*. In the words of Mr. Justice Willes, "If a man be adherent "to the King's enemies in this realm or elsewhere," and that there ought only to be added to those words the direction as to the use of the words "or elsewhere" contained in the judgment of the Lord Chief Justice. I agree with every word of the judgment, and I also agree that this objection fails.

The Lord Chief Justice—Mr. Sullivan, are you in a position to tell us now as to the course you propose to take? Do not do so if it is inconvenient.

Mr. Sullivan—The prisoner desires to make a statement, and then I shall address the jury.

The Lord Chief Justice—Very well. (*To the jury*)—You must understand, gentlemen, that the statement which the prisoner wishes to make to you is not made upon oath, and he cannot be cross-examined upon it.

The Prisoner—May I have permission to read the statement which I desire to make?

The Lord Chief Justice—Yes.

Statement by the Prisoner.

The Prisoner—My lords and gentlemen of the jury, I desire to say a few words only with reference to some of the statements made by the prosecution. As to my pension and the honour of knighthood conferred upon me I will say one word only. The pension I had earned by services rendered, and it was assigned by law. The knighthood it was not in my power to refuse.

But, gentlemen, there are especially four misstatements given in the evidence against me which I wish to refute. First, I never at any time advised Irishmen to fight with Turks against Russians, nor to fight with Germans on the Western Front. Secondly, I never asked an Irishman to fight for Germany. I have always claimed that he has no right to fight for any land but Ireland. Thirdly, the horrible insinuation that I got my own people's rations reduced to starvation point because they did not join the Irish Brigade is an abominable falsehood. The rations were necessarily reduced throughout Germany owing to the blockade, and they were reduced for Irish prisoners at exactly the same time and to the same extent as for the German soldiers and the entire population of Germany. The other suggestion that men were sent to punishment camps at my instance for not joining the Irish Brigade is one that I need hardly pause to refute. It is devoid of all foundation. Fourthly, there is a widespread imputation of German gold. I owe it to those in Ireland who are assailed with me on this very ground to nail the lie once and for all. It was published by newspapers in America, and originally, I think, in this country; and I cabled to America and instructed my American lawyer, Mr. Councillor Doyle, to proceed against those newspapers for libel. Those who know me know the incredibility of this malicious invention, for they know from all my past record that I have never sold myself to any man or to any Government, and have never allowed any Government to use me. From the first moment I landed on the Continent until I came home again to Ireland I never asked for nor accepted a single penny of foreign money, neither for myself nor for any Irish cause nor for any purpose whatsoever, but only the money of Irishmen. I refute so obvious a slander, because it was so often made until I came back. Money was offered to me in Germany more than once, and offered liberally and unconditionally, but I rejected every suggestion of the kind, and I left Germany a poorer man than I entered it. Money I could always obtain from my own countrymen, and I am not ashamed here to acknowledge the debt of gratitude I owe to many Irish friends and sympathisers who did freely and gladly help me when I was on the Continent; and I take the opportunity here of stating how deeply I have been touched by the generosity and loyalty of those English friends of mine who have given me proof of their abiding friendship during these last dark weeks of strain and trial.

I trust, gentlemen of the jury, I have made that statement clearly and emphatically enough for all men, even my most bitter enemies, to comprehend that a man who, in the newspapers is said to be just another Irish traitor, may be a gentleman.

There is another matter I wish to touch upon. The Attorney-General of England thought it consistent with tradition of which he is the public representative to make a veiled allusion in his opening address to the rising in Ireland, of which he has brought forward no evidence in this case from first to last, and to which, therefore, you and I, gentlemen, as laymen, would have supposed that he would have scrupulously refrained from referring to. Since the rising has been mentioned, however, I must state categorically that the rebellion was not made in Germany, and that not one penny of German gold went to finance it.

Gentlemen of the jury, I have touched on these personal matters alone because, intended as they were to reflect on my honour, they were calculated to tarnish the cause that I hold dear. That is all, my lords.

Serjeant Sullivan's Speech for the Prisoner.

Mr. Sullivan—If your lordships please, gentlemen of the jury, it is indeed a matter of congratulation that such a trial as this at such a time is taking place here in the capital city of your nation in open Court according to the ordinary process of law regulating the lives of the civil subjects of His Majesty. That is a great tribute to the confidence and courage of your race, but its lesson would be worse than lost if in the trial your verdict should be to the smallest degree coloured by passion, prejudice, or preconception arising from matters outside this Court. The trial is a trial for the life of a man. It is more than that. You represent your country. The old form of giving in charge, prevalent elsewhere in His Majesty's dominions, proclaimed that the prisoner threw himself upon his God and upon his country for his deliverance. The prisoner is not a countryman of yours. He is a stranger within your gates. He comes from another country where people, though they use the same words, perhaps, speak differently; they think differently; they act differently. It is your duty to demonstrate in the face of the world, whose attention is challenged, and most properly challenged, by this brave proceeding of open trial in such a case, that old virtue for which you have achieved a reputation the world over, the virtue of the accordance of fair play between man and man. That you will endeavour to do so, I know well, for I am deeply and sincerely and gratefully cognisant from my experience in this Court of the kind of spirit of fair play that is accorded to any stranger who ventures within your precincts.

But, gentlemen, your task is not an easy one. We do not in a moment throw off the atmosphere in which we have always lived, and we cannot in a day shake from our minds that which has lingered there and has become almost a form of faith by being pondered on and thought of from day to day. Your task is a difficult one and a serious one. I can well judge of the burden that is upon you from the effect upon myself, who had a less burdensome task than you, for yours is the last word, of my effort to discharge my duty in the conduct of these proceedings.

Gentlemen, I propose at the outset to call your attention to and try and make plain to you what is the matter that is charged against the prisoner at the bar. You are not asked to pronounce any opinion of approbation or reprobation of any general conduct of the man who stands before you. The charge against him may be stated in a few words, that whatever you think of his general conduct, whatever you think of his views of policy or of public affairs, or of the propriety of introducing one view of public affairs rather than another as the uppermost in his mind in regulating his actions, in the end your verdict must come back to this—Did the prisoner at the bar adhere to the King's enemies in Germany?

Sir Roger Casement.

Mr. Sullivan

You have heard the indictment read out to you, but perhaps to your mind the indictment has conveyed little. In a few words the charge is this, that Sir Roger Casement aided the military power of Germany in the war waged against His Majesty the King. That, I think, may fairly epitomise the charge. The indictment sets out what are called overt acts, but are merely instances of evidence with regard to the main charge, for the indictment is supposed to give warning to the man who is arraigned upon it. What is the nature of the evidence and what are the facts sought to be proved from which the jury is to be asked to draw the inference that he aided the military power of Germany in this war against the Crown?

Now, gentlemen, the acts that are alleged in the indictment are six in number. I need not read to you in detail what they amount to, for again I can shortly and fairly state to you in plain language what they mean. Most of them deal with the allegation that while in Germany Sir Roger Casement recruited a number of Irishmen, alleged in the evidence to be about fifty or fifty-two, to aid Germany in the war against the Empire. That is the real substance of the charge against him, and I want you clearly to understand what is the meaning of the charge and what is the meaning of the evidence of the charge as given in the overt acts.

It would be wasting time if I were to pass on to a consideration of the case before you had clearly before you the end to which my observations are addressed, and if I appear to labour them you must pardon me. I shall necessarily occupy your time far longer than I would wish; you must excuse me for that. I shall say much perhaps that will strike a jarring note in your minds. I only ask you to believe that I am trying to do my duty. I appreciate how difficult it is that you should be put into a position—I doubt my power to do it—to understand what goes on in the mind of an Irishman. I am conscious of a strange atmosphere as I stand here. You have to try the man for his intentions; you have to judge of his motives; and there is no task so difficult as judging of the motives or intentions of a man who is not of your race and is not one of yourselves. Now, the intention of the prisoner is the whole substance of the offence of treason. It is his view of his own acts which must justify him or condemn him. Unless he intends treachery to the King, the fact that others may use with advantage that which he does, against his intention, perhaps to the public detriment of the realm, does not make him guilty of treason. The essence of treason is the evil mind that plans it.

Therefore, when you come to consider what is alleged against Sir Roger Casement here, you will always have to weigh it so far as it is humanly possible for you to do so, for the purpose of ascertaining with regard to each act, what did Sir Roger Casement do that for? What was in his mind? What was his motive? And I do not ask you to reject, because I think it is most unfair that you should ever consider as bearing on that, what might be in the mind of any other human being, or that you should digress into the interminable inquiry what might be the ultimate result of any human act, and to whom might ultimate benefit or ultimate loss occur. There will be very little dispute about what are the true facts of the case. I hardly believe there will be any, because I am happy to say that my duty compels me to comment upon one part of the evidence of one witness alone in the address which I have to present before you.

Now, gentlemen, what is proved that Sir Roger Casement has done? He went to the camp at Limburg. He did. He appealed to Irishmen to join an Irish Brigade. He did. Did any human being ever hear him ask an Irishman to fight for Germany? Not one. Subject to a comment that I shall have to make upon a new piece of evidence, introduced, I hope, as much to the surprise of the Crown as to myself, for I would in fair play have been entitled to notice of it if the Crown could have given me notice —subject to that, no human being, although you have evidence of four or five or six speeches of Sir Roger Casement in the Limburg camp, in no one of these pronouncements did he ever ask that an Irishman should fight for Germany. He asked that they should join an Irish Brigade. I will read to you in detail the evidence of each witness that has spoken about it, but I ask you to come to the conclusion that in the main the fact is this: he asked that they should join an Irish Brigade, that when the war was over or when the seas were clear—and until the war was over, the seas, you know, would never be clear—either when the war was over or the seas were clear—and he spoke in a context of the war being over soon—the men who enlisted with him would be landed in Ireland to fight for Ireland. To fight for Ireland.

I will deal with the allusion to the enemy in Ireland afterwards, and I hope, if you accept the view of the evidence that I put forward before you, corroborated by a number of witnesses, speaking of different speeches, speaking of different occasions, yet, strange to say, almost all reproducing almost in exact terms the same adjuration: "If you are "Irishmen, join the Irish Brigade; when the war is over I will land you in "Ireland, and there you may serve your country, and you may have to "fight for it": if you take that view, later in my address to you I hope to convince you that that is not treason. If the object was to have in Ireland at the close of the war men in arms and skilled in arms for the purpose of protecting what were the rights of the people of Ireland against unlawful tyranny, no matter in whose name it was sought to be exercised, that is not treason. It may be some offence in Ireland. You know nothing of that. When I come to deal with the position of affairs there I will have to point out to you that in this Court nothing is known of what the law of Ireland on such a subject may be. You cannot assume that it would be right or wrong unless the act is done within this indictment, an act done for the purpose of aiding Germany in this war to carry on her warfare against His Majesty's Empire.

Now, gentlemen, am I right in the version I have presented to you of the terms upon which Sir Roger Casement sought to enlist the service of the Irishmen in Limburg? They were in truth soldiers. That makes no difference in the offence save in making it somewhat easier for the Crown to prove that they were subjects of His Majesty, so far as that may assist them. But if he recruited anywhere people of any nationality, of any occupation, for the purpose of aiding Germany in this war against the Empire, that is the offence with which he is charged. Their individu-

Mr. Sullivan

ality matters nothing, their situation matters nothing, save in so far as it gives you an insight into his motives, save in so far as it may assist you to determine what was his intention in seeking to enlist the services of these men. Observe, the charge is to aid Germany in the war. Observe, for I state at the outset—I will have to come back to it again—not one atom of assistance in the war did Germany ever get from any human being in consequence of Sir Roger Casement's intervention. No man ever fired a shot for her. Of the fifty-two men who were recruited not one ever appeared in the German ranks or in the command of any German officer. No man has been seen in the service of Germany as a result of Sir Roger Casement's action—not one—and I shall have to comment on that when I come to deal with another part of the evidence. What aid or assistance is he alleged to have given? We have the particulars. They amount to this, that he recruited practically for the German Army or for an army to be used by Germany for German purposes directed against the Empire of His Majesty. There is no mention of them. You find them nowhere.

So far from being of service to Germany, Germany, whatever good she may have expected to get out of the episode, has at all events heretofore been solely at a loss by treating these men somewhat better than she treated prisoners of war and having them living in idleness at greater expense to Germany than other foreigners that she had within her camps. You will ask yourselves therefore when it comes to that what is the military aid that Sir Roger Casement gave them.

But, gentlemen, before I come to deal with that in detail I will pass to the evidence of what Sir Roger Casement said he wanted the Irish Brigade for. The first witness to that is, I think, Cronin. In answer to the Lord Chief Justice he says[1]—

He said that he was going to form an Irish Brigade, and he said, "Why live "any longer in hunger and misery in this camp when you can better yourselves by "joining the Irish Brigade which I am going to form; you will be sent to Berlin "as the guests of the German Government."

Examination continued—Did he say what this Irish Brigade was to do?—He said in the event of Germany winning a sea battle he would land them in Ireland, and would equip them.

What were they to do in Ireland?—Free Ireland.

Did he say who they were to fight against?—Against England.

Did he say what would happen to them if Germany did not win?—They would be sent to America; they would get £10 or £20 pocket money and a free passage. I have told the jury now what I remember of the speech he made on the first occasion when I saw him. He was asked who he was, and he said that he was Sir Roger Casement, the Organiser of the Irish National Volunteer movement.

That is Cronin's description. Then he deals with the matter again[2]—

Did he speak of raising the Irish Brigade in Limburg in connection with the Irish Volunteers in Ireland?—Yes.

Did he say that they would fight in Ireland?—Yes.

That they were to fight in Ireland?—Yes.

And for Ireland?—Yes.

And for nobody else?—For nobody else, only for Ireland.

That is Cronin's evidence of what he said. Is that confirmed by the others? Remember, when you have different speeches there will be a little variation of a phrase or a word, or a sentence here and there, but

---

[1] P. 17. [2] P. 20.

Speech for Prisoner.

Mr. Sullivan

I think you will find that that evidence runs steadily confirmed by each succeeding witness, and I ask you to accept that evidence as being the truth. The next witness dealing with the matter is the witness O'Brien[1]—

I heard him say, "Now is the time for Irishmen to fight against England; "now is their opportunity for doing so; join the Irish Brigade." He said he came to form an Irish Brigade, and he wanted all Irishmen to join the Irish Brigade and become guests of the German army. He said that if they were successful in winning the war they would land the Irish Brigade, along with the German army, in Ireland, and they would fight against England there. If Germany did not win the war, then they would be sent by the German Government to America, with a guarantee of £5 and a situation.

Then in cross-examination[2]—

You only heard a small part of his speech?—Yes.

But in what you did hear did he speak of the Irish Brigade fighting in Ireland?—Yes.

Did he say the Irish Brigade would be used in Ireland only?—In Ireland.

Did he say they were to be transferred to Ireland when Germany had won the war?—Yes.

And if Germany failed to win the war they should go to America?—To America, yes.

The next witness who deals with it is Robinson, who says in answer to the Lord Chief Justice[3]—

He said he was very glad to see so many Irishmen here, that now was our time to fight for Ireland and strike a blow, and he hoped we would all join the Irish Brigade.

Examination continued—Did he say with whom the Irish Brigade were going to fight?—Fight against England. He said that if Germany had a victory on the sea they would land the Irish Brigade in Ireland; but if Germany did not win at sea then we were all to go to America.

Then in cross-examination[4]—

Can you remember all he said?—No.

Or do you only remember bits?—A few words or so.

He wanted you to join an Irish Brigade?—Yes.

Did he say that the Irish Brigade was to fight for Ireland?—Yes.

Did he say it was to fight in Ireland?—Yes.

And did he address you? Did he say it was to go to Ireland when the Germans had won the war?—No; he said if Germany had a victory on sea.

Did he speak about Germany winning the war?—Yes.

What did he say about Germany winning the war?—He always said that Germany would win, but we contradicted him and said they would not.

The next witness dealing with it is Michael O'Connor.[5] I cannot find in the evidence of William Egan, who was examined, any particulars of the statement of Sir Roger Casement bearing on this question.

I remember seeing Sir Roger Casement at Limburg about the end of December, 1914. I heard him addressing some men. He said, "Now is the time for to fight "or strike a blow for Ireland" and that England was nearly beaten. I should think there were about 70 men listening to him.

Then in cross-examination[6]—

Did you remain on the outskirts of the crowd only a few minutes?—Yes.

You stayed there as long as there was anything going on I suppose?—No.

Did you go away after a few minutes?—Yes.

You heard him say that England was nearly beaten. Did you hear him suggest the war was nearly over then?—No, I did not.

England was nearly beaten?—He could have said it, but I did not know.

---

[1] P. 23. [2] P. 24. [3] P. 26. [4] P. 27. [5] P. 32. [6] P. 33.

Sir Roger Casement.

Mr. Sullivan

If England was nearly beaten, was not it in the context that the war was nearly over?—It might have been.

Then, whatever he was talking about, he spoke of it in the context that the war, at all events, was nearly over?—Yes.

Do you assent to that?—I assent to that.

The war being nearly over, he was recruiting an Irish Brigade?—Yes.

The next witness is Michael Moore[1]—

Sir Roger Casement asked those men to join the Irish Brigade, I being among the men, and he said any man that would join the Irish Brigade he would give him uniform, better food and better housing. He also said in case of the Germans losing the war he would send those men to America, give them a free passage and £10 or £20 pocket money, and guarantee employment in America. The Irish Brigade was to be sent from Limburg to a camp outside Berlin; he said they were to be guests of the German Government. He also said the first German victory on the water he would land the Brigade in Ireland. He said what kind of victory; naval victory. The Irish Brigade were to be landed in Ireland. I expect they were to be landed in Ireland from German vessels. I did not hear him say how the Irish Brigade were going to get to Ireland, but he said he would land them in Ireland.

Then in cross-examination[2]—

Apparently, Sir Roger Casement discussed what was to happen to the Irish Brigade if Germany lost the war, did not he?—Yes.

In that event the Irish Brigade would go to America?—Yes.

If Germany lost the war. I suggest to you that he said that he would land them in Ireland if Germany won the war?—If there was a sea battle, and if Germany came out victorious in the first sea battle he would land the Irish Brigade in Ireland.

Did he speak of the Irish Volunteer movement?—Not to my knowledge.

Or did he speak of the Home Rule movement in Ireland or getting Home Rule for Ireland?—I have never heard him.

Was there no reference to Home Rule in the event of Germany winning the war; was there no reference to Home Rule?—There was one, that Germany would give Ireland Home Rule.

If she won the war?—If she won the war.

But do you tell me that there was no reference to Home Rule to be won by the Irish Brigade?—No.

Are you sure of that?—I have never heard him say it.

The next piece of evidence on the matter that I intend to read—I am going back to another part of his evidence afterwards for the purpose of comment—is the evidence of John Neill[3]—

You heard him say he was the organiser of the Irish Volunteers, did not you?—Yes.

That he was raising an Irish Brigade?—Yes.

Was it in connection with the Irish Volunteers?—Yes.

Did you hear him say that it had been subscribed for by Irish Americans in America?—Yes.

And that they were to fight in Ireland?—Yes.

To win Home Rule?—Yes.

Did he say fight in Ireland only?—At that time only to fight in Ireland.

That was the basis upon which they were being recruited?—Yes.

Did he say that the war was nearly over?—No, he never mentioned anything about the war being nearly over.

Did he speak of what might happen when the war was over?—Yes.

When the war was over, if Germany won, did he say that the Irish Brigade could easily be landed in Ireland?—Yes.

Did he say, if Germany lost the war, on the other hand, they should go to America?—Yes.

So if Germany won, they were to go to Ireland?—Yes.

And if they lost, they were to go to America?—Yes.

Was there any mention of helping them in America, whether they could get any money to help them along in America?—Yes.

---

[1] P. 33. [2] P. 34. [3] P. 42.

How much?—From £10 to £20.

If they landed in America?—Yes.

Was that speech made more than once in your presence?—Only once in my presence.

I will have to deal with some other matters in that witness's testimony, but I postpone that for the moment in order to read another overwhelming piece of evidence, namely, the circular which has been admitted in evidence against the prisoner[1]—

Irishmen, here is a chance for you to fight for Ireland. You have fought for England, your country's hereditary enemy. You have fought for Belgium in England's interest, though it was no more to you than the Fiji Islands. Are you willing to fight for your own country with a view to securing the national freedom of Ireland? With the moral and material assistance of the German Government, an Irish Brigade is being formed. The object of the Irish Brigade shall be to fight solely the cause of Ireland, and under no circumstances shall it be directed to any German end. The Irish Brigade shall be formed, and shall fight under the Irish flag alone; the men shall wear a special distinctively Irish uniform and have Irish officers. The Irish Brigade shall be clothed, fed, and efficiently equipped with arms and ammunition by the German Government. It will be stationed near Berlin and be treated as guests of the German Government. At the end of the war the German Government undertakes to send each member of the brigade who may so desire it to the United States of America with necessary means to land. The Irishmen in America are collecting money for the brigade. Those men who do not join the Irish Brigade will be removed from Limburg and distributed among other camps. If interested, see your company commanders. Join the Irish Brigade and win Ireland's independence! Remember Bachelor's Walk! God save Ireland!

Now there, gentlemen, I pause for a moment. There is an enormous mass of testimony of different men speaking to different speeches, and many of them at different times, and a most extraordinary thing about it is, as far as I have read, Sir Roger Casement's speeches were obviously all of them on the same line, that the Irish Brigade was being formed, and would remain at Berlin under Irish officers in Irish uniform, the guests and not the servants of Germany. When the war was over, if Germany won they were to be landed in Ireland. Under no circumstances were they to be asked to fight for any country except their own. They were to be landed in Ireland, and in Ireland alone was the Irish Brigade to be used if their use became necessary. All are agreed on that, every witness that I have read. They cannot agree as to phrases, dates, and matters of that kind; but there is a most extraordinary cohesion of separate stories told by different men that the Irish Brigade was being recruited on a solemn undertaking, and that they were appealed to as Irishmen to enter into the service of their own country, they were never to be the servants of any other nation, they were not to be the servants of Germany, and they were under no circumstances to be used for any German end. You will bear that in mind, because, as I told you before, you will see how you will have to deal with that as showing what was in Sir Roger Casement's mind. Oh, says the Attorney-General, the German Government were interested in his succeeding. What cared he? He was not a German. It was nothing to him what were the calculations of any German as to what would be the result of anything he did. It is relevant to inquire what might be the result, but only relevant to inquire that in order to ascertain what was truly in his mind, because if what

---

[1] *See* Appendix, Exhibit 4.

Mr. Sullivan

he stated again and again with variations to every man who was called as a witness about his speeches, if that represented truly what was in the man's mind, I will show you, I confidently hope, that that represented no form of treason. I hope to justify it; if you accept that view, I hope to justify every word he said and every act he did.

As against that mass of testimony there is only the evidence, or a portion of the evidence, of the witness, John Neill. I will read it to you again. I say that I hope and believe that it was as much a surprise to the Crown as to anybody else; it introduces a note that absolutely contradicts everything that was said by every other witness; more than that, it introduces a matter which under his own hand is contradicted by Neill himself, and here and here alone is the smallest suggestion upon which ultimately I suggest to you the Crown case may hinge, if they wish to rely upon such testimony. Here and here alone, I will submit to you at the close of my address, is the only real evidence, if real evidence such can be called, of any proposal ever made to any human being in the camp at Limburg to go and assist the German war in any shape or form[1]—

> He wanted to see 50 names in this book [that is to join the brigade]. He also said the German Government would equip the brigade with arms and ammunition and uniforms. He also mentioned something about pay; he said the Irish Brigade would get something about from £10 to £20.

All the witnesses are agreed when the war was over, if the result was the Germans were beaten, the members of the brigade were to get £10 to £20 if they wished to go to America—

> He did not say where they would get that from. He also told the Irishmen on that Sunday that they were all to join this brigade, and that if Germany ever gained a naval victory they would land the Irish Brigade in Ireland, and to strike a blow for old Ireland once again and to gain Home Rule. He also said how the Germans were very much like the Irish and the Irish very much like the Germans. Personally I did not believe that.

So far he has confirmed, in the main, everything that has been said by other witnesses, and in a later part of his evidence I have already read, the evidence of this same man, he has confirmed in detail everything that was said by every other witness. He comes back on this occasion[2]—

> He told the Irishmen then, when he came back, that he was very disappointed to see that there were no names entered in his book for this Irish Brigade, and he also wanted to know what were the Irishmen thinking of if they said they would not go and fight for their country now at this time, and that England was completely beat, and that there was no danger of their not being landed in Ireland, and that he was the head man over the Irish Volunteers in Ireland, and that he was very proud to see how smart looking they looked, and he also hoped to see the Irish Brigade would soon be formed, and to go and fight for Ireland.

So far a little more corroborative detail, perhaps, but no divergence from the main story told by all the other witnesses and by himself. But then there comes a matter of surprise and a note that we have not heard before[3]—

> He came back in about a month after, and a clergyman, Father Nicholson, came there next. When Casement came back he just told these people that joined the Irish Brigade, when this Irish Brigade was formed they were first to go to help the Turks against the Russians.

---

[1] P. 37. [2] P. 38. [3] P. 38.

I will suggest to you later on, I do not know what the opinion of the Turks may be here, but certainly the man who went to recruit Irishmen to fight for the Turks deserved recognition for splendid courage.

After he came back, Sir Roger Casement spoke to the men, in my hearing, in the camp in No. 1 Lines, No. 1 Company, No. 2 Battalion. He used to come into the barrack rooms. He made a speech in several places—outside and inside in the barrack rooms he made these speeches. Those are the words that passed from Casement on this occasion. First of all, the Irish Brigade were to go and help the Turks against the Russians; and secondly, they were to go and help the Germans against the British; and thirdly, they were to go and shed blood for their own native country.

This is the first mention we have of this expansive programme, and, as I will show you in a minute, the witness himself had testified to totally different speeches in agreement with all the other witnesses, and he, under his own hand, gave a statement of his evidence that he was coming into the box to prove that, directly contradicts what he swears when he gets into the box.

I heard him say those things. I never saw Casement after that.

Observe the answer: "I never saw him after that." Just bear that in mind, because in order to escape from his written statement he suggested that his written statement only referred to that particular day, and that on that particular day, or that particular evening, he did not see him, but that he often saw him afterwards, and, believing that he was triumphing over the foe, when re-examined by the Attorney-General, I think not to the Attorney-General's pleasure, he said he saw him forty-six times. I will turn now to his cross-examination[1]—

Can you fix the date you arrived at Limburg?—As far as I can go, we arrived at Limburg early in December, 1914. That is as near as I can go.

How long after that did you hear this talk about the Turks?—I have heard the talk about the Turks several times.

How long was that after you had arrived at Limburg? Listen, is this true, "Casement came back about the 1st of February, 1915."

I was reading his own statement of his evidence to him—

Is that true?—Yes.

And Father Nicholson came at the same time. Is that true?—Yes, that is true. Father Nicholson came there about that time.

I suggest to you that the witness saw that he was coming into rather deeper water, and he commences to qualify his answers a little.

Then that is true. Would this be true, that you saw Casement in the camp at this time, but he did not speak to you, and you never saw him again? Is that true?—At the time I never saw him. He went away. I have seen him several times in Limburg.

He obviously was well aware of what was coming, I suggest to you, gentlemen—

On this occasion, will you fix the date of the occasion, the only occasion, so it should be rooted in your mind, that you heard him speak of the Turks?—I cannot speak to the date that I heard him speak of the Turks because I disremember.

He had himself fixed the date in his evidence prior to that, and he commences to disremember it when he sees he is in difficulties.

You disremember the dates?—Yes.

You cannot say was it early or late?—I cannot say.

---

[1] P. 39.

Mr. Sullivan

Was it the time he came with Father Nicholson?—Yes.
It was the time he came with Father Nicholson?—Yes, it was on his third visit.
Did he come with Father Nicholson more than once?—No.
Did you yourself fix the date of Father Nicholson and Sir Roger Casement coming back to the camp as the 1st February, 1915?—I did not.
Do you remember making the statement of the evidence that you were to give?—I remember, yes.
To whom did you make the statement?—To some one at the War Office.
How long ago?—On the 27th May last.
Was it taken down in writing in your presence?—Yes.
And you signed it?—Yes.
Was it true?—Well, there was a lot of it; very nearly it all was true.

Gentlemen, do you remember the pause when I asked him was it true; can you remember it? I suggest to you that he paused a long time before he answered: "Well, there was a lot of it, very nearly it all was true." That was a very carefully considered answer.

Am I to understand there was a lot of it that was not true?—You are not to understand there was a lot of it that was not true.
Was it all true?—Yes, it was all true. My statement I gave there, yes, it was all true, only I did not give them all my statement; I forgot something, but brought a lot of it back to my memory since then.
Listen to the statement that was all true at the time: "Casement came back "about the 1st February, 1915, and Father Nicholson came at the same time." Was that true?—Yes, that was true.
About the 1st February, 1915?—I cannot fix the date, you know.
Did you fix the date?—To the best of my opinion it was about that time he came there.

Then, reading again from his statement, I say—"When Casement came "back we were marched up to barrack No. 41 by sections as usual, and "Quinless told us"—then there is the statement about the Turks coming from Quinless, that Casement had told him to tell the Irish Brigade about the Turks—

Did you say that?—Yes.
Was that true?—Yes.

The statement is further read; that is not what Sir Roger Casement told him at all, but somebody else told him, and said it was Sir Roger Casement said he was to be told; that is a very different story. Then it is read to him again: "'I saw Casement in the camp at this time'—"this was about the 1st February, 1915, when he came back with Father "Nicholson—'but he did not speak to me. I never saw him again.'" Observe, he had sworn in his direct evidence, before I cross-examined him about his statement, that after this day, whatever be the date, he never saw Sir Roger Casement again. Then he says it and repeats it, or, rather, it is read out to him from his statement that he had given, taken down in writing, and had signed on the 27th May—"I saw Casement in the "camp at this time, but he did not speak to me. I never saw him "again." That was in the written statement; he is asked—"Was it "true?" and he says, "On the previous evening I did not see him." Then I say—

Let me give it to you again: "I saw Casement in the camp at this time"—this was about the 1st February, 1915, when he came back with Father Nicholson—"but he did "not speak to me. I never saw him again." Is that true?—He did not speak to me on that evening. I did not see him, he went away out of that camp on that evening, but I saw him afterwards. I did not see him again on that evening.

Speech for Prisoner.

Mr. Sullivan

Having on the 27th May dictated that evidence, that after that day he never saw Sir Roger Casement again, having in answer to the Solicitor-General sworn that never after that speech, conversation, or whatever it was, did he see Sir Roger Casement again, he now states that he did not see him that evening. He says, "He went away out of "the camp on that evening, but I saw him afterwards. I did not see "him again on that evening." I read again to him what he said—"I "never saw him again." That is what he stated was going to be his evidence. Then he answers, "On that evening." Then I say[1]—

Was it true? I will go further. "I heard that he gave an address to the "Munsters in their barracks, and that they shouted him down. I could hear the "shouting going on." Do not you see you are pointing the fact that you never saw him again, although you heard he was in a different part of the camp?—On that evening he did address the Munster Fusiliers in the barracks.

But you were not there?—I was not in the lines.

You could only hear shouting?—He was a free man in Germany and could go about where he liked.

Follow me again. I will give you every opportunity of understanding. Was it true, of the 1st February occasion, that he came to the camp with Father Nicholson, you saw him in the camp, but he did not speak to you, and you never saw him again?—On that evening I never saw him again, but he was in the camp several times afterwards, and I saw him in the camp. I never saw him again on that evening.

You heard he gave an address to the Munsters, and could hear the shouting?—Yes.

But you never saw him?—On that evening after.

Will you give me the date you next saw him?—He was in the camp every day, I might say.

By this time he has parted from the statement he never saw him after the occasion in question; the statement that he saw him several times afterwards, and we have the statement that he might say that he saw him every day afterwards. "But only once with Father Nicholson." That was about the 1st February. Then he is cross-examined about it again[2]—

If he did not speak to you that day, he could not have said anything about the Turks or Russians or anything else?—He spoke about the Turks and Russians, and also left orders with this man that joined the Irish Brigade to tell the Irishmen that joined the brigade——

Are you telling us what you heard him say, or repeating what somebody else told you; what is it?—I am telling you now about him, what he said.

By the LORD CHIEF JUSTICE—Who is "he"?—Sir Roger Casement.

By Mr. SULLIVAN—Was it what he said in your presence?—In my presence and in the presence of about 50 more of our men—that when they joined this Irish Brigade they were to go and help the Turks against the Russians on the Turkish frontier, then after that they were to go and help the Germans against the British, and then after that they were to go and shed blood for their own native country.

And after that?—He said no more then. He said that in the presence of my comrades and myself.

Then he is asked about the Volunteer movement, and so forth. But you see, gentlemen, that witness is the only witness who gives an account of a speech which, if delivered, contradicts every single word that Sir Roger Casement had ever said in the presence of any other human being, and contradicts every other speech that this witness heard him make.

---

[1] P. 40. [2] P. 41.

Mr. Sullivan

Being, I suggest to you, a little worn by his cross-examination, the learned Attorney-General re-examined him to re-establish his credit, and observe the questions that were put to him to give him an opportunity of explaining how he came to have so many variations of the same thing[1]—

How many times do you think you saw Casement altogether?

Of course, the witness might confuse either one person with another, or one visit with another, or something of that kind, if he was in a confused state, in which a thing was happening two or three or four times, and he might pick out one occasion rather than another, but the witness was evidently under the impression that he had not sworn to enough visits of Sir Roger Casement.

How many times do you think you saw Casement altogether?—I have seen him a lot of times.

About how many?—I disremember how many times; he was there so often in that camp.

How long were you there?—I was there for seven months.

Was he there at intervals?—He was there the first time I landed at Limburg.

How many times—not exactly—but roughly, do you think you heard him speak?—I have heard him speak several times, for every time he was in the camp he was all the time talking.

Three, four, or six times, or how many?—Nearer forty-six times.

This is the only witness who gave testimony to a state of affairs which I most confidently ask you not to believe. On every other occasion this man, whatever you think of his politics and his views of public affairs, had made the only appeal that I have ever heard made to any of my countrymen, to invite to take up arms on any occasion, an appeal that has recruited a quarter of a million of them to the Colours at the present moment, that they should take up arms to fight for Ireland, and I would most respectfully subscribe to the doctrine that no Irishman has a right to take up arms or risk his life for any cause that is not in the service of Ireland.

Gentlemen, the event upon which, and upon which alone, the transfer of these troops to Ireland was to take place has not yet happened, even on the most grim view of Admiralty despatches. There are these men remaining in idleness in Germany. You never catch a glimpse of them afterwards, except to hear that they still walk about Limburg in the new and perhaps somewhat gaudy uniform. No one has seen them marching or countermarching, or even indulging in sham fights under the command of any German officer. They have never appeared in arms to the detriment of any one of His Majesty's subjects, and, accordingly, I ask you to believe that what was done there never in fact afforded the smallest military aid or any other aid or comfort to the German Government; but if you will believe what is far more important, whether he is right or wrong in what he did, that the man who sought to recruit them honestly asked them to join in a cause which was to be the service of their own country, and their own country alone, and repudiate any idea that whatever benefit any other country may have thought they would gain, or wished they would gain, out of such a transaction, his motive and his intention were clean and clear, that he, at all events, would be no party to his countrymen being used at the risk of their lives in any cause that was not the cause of their own land. There is suggested, and I do submit to you it is a mean and im-

[1] P. 42.

proper suggestion, that in some way the prisoner at the bar was responsible for rations being reduced in the prison camp in Germany at the end of February, a reduction made in the amount of bread, a couple of months afterwards—I think the date was fixed in April, but at the moment I forget it—a reduction in the quality of their rations, and the substitution for potatoes of some other food. The man who testified to it testified to this, that at the time of these reductions Sir Roger Casement was not in the camp, but that the recruiting went on after the reduction of rations as before it. No man was ever threatened, no man that came before you was ever threatened with reduction of rations if he did not do what Sir Roger Casement asked him to do. Those who joined were liberated from the camp, they were better clothed, and I have no doubt they were better fed than the ordinary prisoner. No man has testified in this Court to any whisper of a threat from any human being that his rations would be reduced if he did not comply with the request of Sir Roger Casement, but it was said that after Sir Roger Casement's visits rations were in fact reduced, and if they were not, gentlemen, you would not think much of your Navy. If rations are not reduced in Germany, you might as well scuttle your ships. Of course, when you are dealing with a people in the position of the Germans, the first who will feel the pinch of hunger if supplies run short in Germany, you may be perfectly sure, will be the soldiers who had fought against the Germans. Are you to believe when rations are reduced—I do not suppose it can be all a joke to suggest that they are pretty short of some foodstuffs in Germany—when rations are reduced in a country in which, gentlemen, we have reason to believe food is not so plentiful or as cheap as you may thank God it is in your own country, is it creditable to attribute to this man in the dock the mean and malicious motives that any failure on his part to achieve his object amongst these men who, whether they agree with him or disagree with him, are his countrymen—that he was any party to starving them in order to vindicate his own conceit and his self-sufficiency? Is there any evidence of anything so mean or ignoble about what he has said or done if the version of what he has said and done be as I ask you to believe it has been established to be? Is that consistent with the mind of a man who out of petty spitefulness and wickedness would starve 2500 men because some few or many of them declined to oblige him in one of his political projects; is that the opinion you have of him? Is humanity so mean and so small that the man with the talk of high principles, the talk of patriotism that my learned friend scorns, behind the backs of those who do not listen is intriguing that they will linger on in starvation, and merely because they have not listened to him? I ask you to scout that from your minds and not to allow your judgments which have to be exercised upon what I submit to you are broad issues in this case, for, believe me, you will not find me pettifogging—do not let your judgment be warped by insinuations of this kind, which have not found expression in any clear-cut charge from the lips of any human being that I have heard speak in this Court.

I have dealt with the evidence of what happened in Limburg, at all events, with so much of the evidence as has occurred to me to be the material portions for the themes upon which I shall have to address you later. I come now to the evidence from Ireland to see how it affects the prisoner. Gentlemen, I wish you clearly to understand there is not in this case any allegation against Sir Roger Casement of the commission of any illegality in that part of His Majesty's United Kingdom called Ireland. This Court has no cognisance of such. If he has offended in that part of the realm, in that part of the realm let him be adjudged and tried before the community against whom he may be supposed to have sinned; but, so far as this case is concerned, there is no allegation in this case triable before you, that Sir Roger Casement, in fact, committed any illegal act within Ireland. He was charged, though no evidence was given of the charge here, and could not be given of the charge here, for you could not try it here—he was charged, which was the high-water mark of the guilt alleged against him there, we have it in evidence, with breach of the regulations made under the Defence of the Realm Act, and nothing more, and the breach of the regulations with which he was charged was that, contrary to those regulations, he landed in Ireland those three pistols and that box of ammunition. That represents, so far as we have heard, a charge formulating the high-water mark of his Irish illegality. But you cannot inquire into anything connected with his movements in Ireland save so far as they are relevant to the charges made of the acts he has alleged to have committed in Germany, for in the indictment upon which he stands arraigned he is not charged with doing anything illegal in any other portion of the world's surface than in the Empire of Germany, and therefore it is that I have put in the forefront of my address the consideration of the German evidence, because on the German evidence I will submit to you the case must stand or fall. He arrived in Ireland, and, as I suppose we may take cognisance of the fact that Ireland is an island, I presume he travelled over the sea. He is found in Ireland near a lonely strand, some place 10 or 12 miles west of the town of Tralee.

As I understand the Crown's case with regard to the Irish witnesses, they are really seeking to deal with the sixth paragraph of the overt acts alleged in the indictment against the prisoner. As you have heard it read to you, you will perhaps remember that he was charged with setting out from Germany, in order to carefully keep every treasonable act charged outside the realm of England, and I venture to suggest outside also that part of His Majesty's Kingdom called Ireland, and well within the frontiers of the German Empire, and the Crown do not allege that outside of the German Empire Sir Roger Casement committed any overt act connected with the treason charged here, namely, connected with his recruiting for the German Army, for that is the plain meaning of what they suggest against him. There was given in evidence a peculiar fact, the bearing of which I am at a loss now to understand because we have got the details. I nearly called him a seaman, but a signaller on board the sloop "Bluebell" was examined, and he has told you that on the 21st of April, at half-past six in the evening, the "Bluebell" sighted a steamer in the Atlantic Ocean. The Attorney-General, in opening the case, stated that it was somewhere near Tralee, but it now appears from the evidence of Signaller Waghorn that this steamer was in the Atlantic Ocean at a point which is very easily defined, because it is about 138 miles from Daunt's Rock and it is about 90 miles from the land, and I think there can be no doubt that that represents a position, roughly speaking, 90 miles south of Cape Clear, on the south coast of Ireland. Tralee is on the west of Ireland; Tralee Bay is a large indentation running almost down east and west, and you see from the map if you look down the bay you look almost straight at the setting sun. The ship is found in the Atlantic Ocean, 90 miles off Cape Clear, which is on the south coast of Ireland, and how is she heading? You gather that from the explanation that the ship attempted to give of her own motion, because whether it was true or false, and some of it was certainly false, you will probably be of opinion that her captain told no more lies than were necessary, and none that were inconsistent, when he stated that he was bound from Bergen to Genoa as being the explanation of his position in the ocean and the course that he was steering. It would hardly be of any use to represent to one of His Majesty's sloops of war that you were bound from Bergen to Genoa if the course you were steering would bring you into the Bristol Channel or any other direction than the track by which you could reach Genoa. Accordingly, you may take it as reasonably well-established, that at 6.30 that evening this ship was travelling in a direction which was leaving Ireland further and further away from her; she was 90 miles from the south coast of Ireland, and not anywhere in the neighbourhood of Tralee. It was because of that that I attempted to make some objection to the evidence of the witness, because, gentlemen, there is no connection whatever between Sir Roger Casement at M'Kenna's Fort, 12 miles west of Tralee, on the west coast of Ireland, and a ship apparently heading for the Straits of Gibraltar, 90 miles from the south coast of Ireland. I do not understand that it is suggested that perhaps Sir Roger Casement travelled by this ship; that can hardly be the suggestion. It would be a peculiar suggestion that apparently this ship, coming down the west coast of Ireland on her course from Bergen to the Straits, threw him overboard with two companions in that cockleshell of a boat of which you saw the picture, and let them shift for themselves; that is hardly the suggestion; but certain it is that all that we know of this ship in the present case is that she was found at 6.30 on the 21st April out in the middle of the Atlantic, far out of sight of land, on a course which the captain, at all events, hoped would be believed to be the course to Genoa, when he told the "Bluebell" that that was where he was making for. She had on board a number of rifles, and we have had an interesting discussion upon what rifles they are, the pattern they are, the pattern of the cartridges, the cartridge clips, and the bayonet case; the strange thing being, as far as I recollect, that these articles were of different nationalities. One was Russian, another was South American, the cartridge clips, I think, were Russian; the cartridges could not be identified as being any definite cartridge that fits the Russian gun. How that ship, whose fate we know, can in any way be brought into our story in connection with Sir Roger Casement, I have no idea, because the statement upon which the story was introduced by the Attorney-General has certainly not been verified, that off Tralee and in the neighbourhood of Sir Roger Casement this mysterious ship was seen and captured. We know, in fact, that she was nowhere in the neighbourhood of Tralee at all.

Sir Roger Casement.

Mr. Sullivan

Now, gentlemen, I pass from a consideration of the evidence to state to you what I know you will listen to with attention, what is the explanation of what these men have testified to? Gentlemen, one gets in the habits of phrase from the country and the neighbourhood in which one lives. I presume, and it is perfectly evident, that an Englishman speaks of this Empire under the name of England, an Irishman calls his own country by its own name, so does a Scotchman, and, I think the habit also prevails in Wales. I want you to understand the position that Ireland bears towards your country, because a great deal of the present case, and the explanation of the present case, depends upon your forming a perfectly true, proper, and just appreciation of the position of Ireland with regard to yourselves. I think the Attorney-General spoke of Sir Roger Casement's services to England. Sir Roger Casement was not in the service of England. Sir Roger Casement was in the service of the United Kingdom; he was in the service of His Majesty in respect of the whole Empire of His Majesty's Dominion. In Ireland you have not only a separate people, you have a separate country. An Irishman's loyalty is loyalty to Ireland, and it would be a very sorry day for the Empire when loyalty to one's own native land should be deemed to be treason in a sister country. There is no English authority in Ireland, however improperly for the sake of political factions the name of your country may be invoked. No English official exercises the smallest authority when he crosses the Channel. Those who hold high offices here have no position or no official position in Ireland. His Majesty, under the Act of Union, in fact, exercises the right preserved by the articles of the Treaty, and he appoints his Irish officers under the great seal of Ireland. No person has any constitutional right in Ireland to seek to bully or dictate to any Irishman in the name of any other section of His Majesty's United Kingdom. We are your fellow-citizens, but by no means your inferiors or your slaves. You respect our rights in Ireland as we should respect yours, but when you step inside that part of His Majesty's Kingdom, His Majesty rules there not by any title of King of your land, but in respect of his title as King and ruler of the United Kingdom.

Gentlemen, if in Ireland you cannot find within the constitution anything that has any right to call itself England, in the conduct of Irish affairs, you will then ask yourselves what was there in Ireland in 1914 and 1915 purporting to act in the name of England that required to be fought to secure Home Rule. I would be most unwilling to say anything that might in the slightest degree seem to be trespassing or infringing on the opinions of any person in this Court or outside it, but you will have to answer that question, and look back and seek to find upon the evidence what was the power that called itself England in Ireland in 1914, for, as I have already pointed out, under the constitution there is no English power in Ireland. You have got a glimpse from two or three or four witnesses of the state of affairs existing in that country, almost within gunshot of your own country, that casts a reflection and a disgrace upon our civilisation. It is a dreadful thing, gentlemen, a dreadful thing to contemplate that any one within the King's peace in any part of his United Kingdom should be subjected to the bullying and intimidation and threat of armed force to be exercised against the liberties secured to him by the constitution and by the Parliament of Great Britain and Ireland; and yet that was the state of affairs in Ireland as you see by the evidence. What was the necessity of arming men in Ireland? As one witness says, to secure Home Rule, another to free Ireland, another to secure the freedom of Ireland. To protect the liberties of Ireland against whom had you to arm? Was there in Ireland in those years an armed body which most improperly used the name of your country behind which to shelter the invasion of the liberties secured to Irishmen under the constitution? You have evidence that there was, unless indeed you believe, being constitutionally ignorant in this Court of what barbarous law may in fact prevail beyond the Channel—unless indeed you would assume from the immunity with which armed bands paraded the country north and south for the avowed purpose of attacking one another sooner or later, unless you believe from their immunity that these things may be done under the laws in Ireland, and that we who desire to live at peace and to possess what we are entitled to, our own opinions, may not form them in Ireland save at the bayonet's point of some faction or other. Does not that show you in one gleam what it was that Sir Roger Casement was doing in Limburg when he recruited the Irish Brigade? Observe the state of affairs as you have it proved in evidence. There was in the north of Ireland an armed body of men ostensibly marching about, as Robinson proves, in Belfast, deliberately originated with the avowed object of resisting the operation of an Act of Parliament which had the approval of the rest of the country. They armed, and nothing was said to them; they drilled, and nothing was said to them; they marched and countermarched; the authorities stood by and looked at them. The police were powerless. They had great forces behind them, great names and men of high position. Imagine the feeling in the country testified to, reaching as far south as what we anciently called the Kingdom of Kerry, now County Kerry. To the County of Kerry, in dread of these men, there came a rumour of the police being powerless, the civil power being paralysed, the civil Government practically abdicated—there came a rumour that all that stood between peace and the rifles of those men, His Majesty's Army, might not perhaps be relied upon.

What are you to do when, after years of labour, your representatives may have won something that you yearn for, for many a long day, won it under the constitution, had it guaranteed by the King and the Commons, and you are informed that you should not possess it because those that disliked it were arming to resist the King and Commons and to blow the statute off the book with powder? The civil police could not protect you, and the military force would perhaps prove inadequate for your support. You may lie down under it, but if you are men, to arms; when all else fails defend yourself. If the civil government will not protect you, if the constabulary cannot secure your rights, if you cannot rely upon brigades, the ultimate resort for any man in the protection of his constitutional freedom is to stand with arms in his hands, and if a civil government can be terrorised into obtaining his rights, try if his

Mr. Sullivan

attitude will not inspire them with sufficient respect to do what is right without fear, favour, or affection.

That, gentlemen, is the case that I present to you on behalf of Sir Roger Casement; that is the explanation of everything that he has done. What is to be said against him? Gentlemen, this condition of affairs had indeed been reached prior to this war that has broken out with the Empire of Germany. There was indeed an understanding and a convention between the greater leaders of these factions arming and counter-arming that for a while, while the danger to the Empire existed, this dreadful state of affairs should be put an end to; that, in the meantime, faith has been kept let us all thank Providence, for it enabled my countrymen in the service of Ireland, for they are serving the glorious traditions of their own land, to write their names in every battlefield in Europe, a thing that would have been impossible without such understanding. Do not imagine, though you may live in a great city of the Empire, that you can sneer at the loyal patriotism of these men. We recruited none of them to fight for England; no man ever made such an appeal as that to an Irish audience. Each man went forth believing that in serving in this war, serving the Empire, he was in truth rendering the best service he could to his own little country. But how about at home? If you are indeed to scrutinise the intention of Sir Roger Casement in what he did abroad, not by what he intended or what was passing in his mind, but the profit the German politicians might calculate that they might ultimately get out of it, you might go back and find that German calculations do not all come right, for you might well think that the enterprising commercial country that filled Ulster with Mausers in 1914 expected a better dividend than she got. The truce was kept in the main, but, gentlemen, not a single rifle was given up. As we have heard from the witnesses, so far from armaments ceasing, on the 16th August the sole obstacle to the importation of arms into Ireland was dropped immediately after the outbreak of the war. No arms were given up—more arms were coming in. The only security for peace, for real and permanent peace in any country, is such confidence in the administration of justice as will cause men to feel that they run no risk that requires their bearing arms in any part of His Majesty's dominions. Well, the arms were still there, the purpose still undisavowed. The truce was on the face of it but a temporary arrangement, a postponement of the threat of bloodshed and outrage which was promised to the country when the war was over; and can you blame that there were found in Ireland fortunately a minority of Irishmen who thought, and, so far as formula goes, they thought right, that their first duty of loyalty was to the land of their birth, but who thought that she was still in danger while the country remained divided in armed camps, and there was only to be postponed until the war ended the time when Ireland was to become the foundation for two hells? Many may have thought so honestly and loyally; we who differ from them have no right to criticise their judgment because we disagree with it. They have a right to think, and such men have a right if in their judgment the country was in such danger, that it was better to stay at home and provide against this ultimate happening than it was to go forth and serve in the Irish Brigades; men have a right to think that, and in view of the dreadful state of affairs which you have established in evidence before you, how can you blame a man for thinking that? And accordingly there were found men who, distrusting the truce proclaimed in Ireland, seeing that one man would observe his neighbour had not given up his rifle, another that another had got a new gun, he would arm himself, and one by one in small quantities you have the danger of the arms still coming in, and people fearing that the truce was not real, and that any moment there might break out——

The Lord Chief Justice—Where is there evidence of this?

Mr. Sullivan—The evidence of the sergeant and the evidence of Robinson.

The Lord Chief Justice—Of what you are now saying?

The Attorney-General—I was most loath to intervene, but I have heard a great many statements which are wholly uncorroborated.

The Lord Chief Justice—You have the right to intervene.

The Attorney-General—Statements as to the importation of rifles into the north of Ireland.

The Lord Chief Justice—We have allowed you very great latitude. I confess for myself I have found it rather difficult not to intervene on several occasions, and I intervene at this moment because I think you are stating matter which is not in evidence or which I have no recollection of being stated in evidence. I know the general passages to which you refer.

Mr. Sullivan—I am exceedingly sorry your lordship did not intervene sooner; I was referring to the evidence of Sergeant Hearn. I am exceedingly sorry I have gone outside what I ought, but what I was referring to was this[1]—

Do you remember in 1914, before the war, the Arms Proclamation?—Yes.

As an officer of the Constabulary were you concerned in acting under it for a while?—Yes.

Prior to that had there been considerable importation of arms?—Yes.

Was it in consequence of what happened in the north of Ireland that the people were arming so far south as Tralee?—I could not say that.

Did they, at all events, purport to be arming?—They did.

As against the armed persons in the north of Ireland?—Yes.

Were they bearing arms openly?—They were.

Without interference by the public authorities?—Yes.

And actually on the outbreak of war was the proclamation against the importation of arms withdrawn on the 16th August?—Yes, that is so.

And your directions, even so far as they went to interfere with the importation of arms, ceased on the 16th August on the withdrawal of the proclamation for the time being?—Yes.

And the arming of the population went on then unrestricted for a while?—Yes.

And the parade of arms uninterfered with by any authority?—Yes.

People drilling?—Yes.

Marching?—Yes.

Skirmishing through the country?—Yes.

Without any action taken on behalf of the police? This arming, of course, commenced before the war, did it not?—Yes it did.

It commenced some time in 1913, in the south, did it not?—Yes.

---

[1] P. 49.

Mr. Sullivan

It had commenced earlier in the north?—Yes.

Was there a great deal of excitement in the south with regard to the reports of what was going on in the north of Ireland?—There was.

I suppose at the police barracks, even in Ardfert, they read the papers?—Yes.

Then the papers are referred to.

The LORD CHIEF JUSTICE—If you look at the question I put, I think it brings home the point of my intervention now. I put to you the question after you had gone through this matter: "Are you speaking of "before or after the war?" and your answer was, "Before the war."

Mr. SULLIVAN—That is so with regard to that evidence.

The LORD CHIEF JUSTICE—No doubt you stated it quite rightly. You have stated the effect of the facts before the war, and there has been no intervention, but what you are dealing with now apparently is the period some time after the war; the period with which we have to deal is 1915; that is what we are dealing with.

Mr. SULLIVAN—It is this question.[1]

In that state of affairs, having neither police nor military competent to protect one, it was left to people in Ireland to protect themselves; is not that the truth of it?—Generally speaking it is.

Generally speaking that was the truth of it? Now, as you say, when the war broke out the Arms Proclamation was withdrawn and the arming went on as before?—Yes.

And continued right up to last month?—Yes.

Except so far as hampered by the Defence of the Realm Regulations?—Yes.

I was under the impression I was referring to that. I am sorry if I transgressed, and regret that the rein was not applied to it.

The LORD CHIEF JUSTICE—I felt so anxious not to intervene when you were making your speech, and, of course, doing the best you could for your client, but you were dealing with matters which not only were not stated in evidence—but with regard to which I will say nothing more.

Mr. SULLIVAN—I pass from that at once. If I have been carried away too far, I am exceedingly sorry. All that I was trying to lay the foundation for was in view of the condition of affairs existing at the outbreak of the war, to ask you to consider what then might be the explanation after the outbreak of the war, and the condition at the close of the war of the prisoner at the bar, because we are all agreed—I mean nearly all the witnesses are agreed—that the prisoner at the bar frequently referred in Limburg to the fact that the war was coming to a close. When the war was over the Irish Brigade was to be used in Ireland, and used in Ireland, one witness used the phrase, to secure Home Rule, others said to free Ireland, others said to secure the freedom of Ireland.

I suggest to you the inference to be drawn is that the Irish Brigade moving to Ireland after the war—it was recruited, according to a number of these witnesses, in connection with the Volunteer movement in Ireland—you should come to the conclusion that the intention expressed by Sir Roger Casement was the intention of using the Irish Brigade in Ireland in connection with the Irish Volunteer movement, which, as you have heard, had been recruiting in Ireland before the war. Now is that a reasonable suggestion? Is not it what he said? What other explanation can you give of the terms that he used? Under what circumstances were

[1] P. 51.

Irishmen to fight in Ireland, under Irish officers? For no German purpose. Whether you use it to free Ireland, to secure Home Rule, or for any other purpose mentioned, what other explanation is there, except it was in connection, as was stated in Limburg by a number of witnesses, with the Irish Volunteer movement? I intended to go no further than that, and I intended to test whether that involved any of the charges made in the present case. In that event there is no military aid to Germany; none whatever. However much Germany might like to see, after the war, or at any other time, a precipitation of a state of affairs in which there should be armed camps in any part of His Majesty's dominions, that is not the view put forward by Sir Roger Casement to the Irish Brigade. It was not to please Germany that he sought to recruit. He purported to recruit them in order to serve their own country. Is there any other way in which he could fulfil his pledge? Where else could he use them in connection with the Irish Volunteer movement or in connection with any Home Rule controversy? Where else could he use them for, whatever you call it, the freedom of Ireland or of freeing Ireland? In Ireland alone they were to fight; under Irish officers they were to fight. The documents are perfectly specific on that point, and, accordingly, I do most earnestly impress upon your consideration, that in view of the state of affairs at the commencement of the war, going no further than that, is there not a perfectly proper and reasonable explanation of what it was desirable to provide for at the conclusion of the war? The matters that I have spoken of had occurred since Sir Roger Casement left the Consular Service. They would explain the position. As I say, those matters had occurred since Sir Roger Casement left the Consular Service. [After a pause.] I regret, my lord, to say that I have completely broken down.

The LORD CHIEF JUSTICE—Then, of course, we will adjourn until to-morrow morning.

The Court adjourned.

Sir Roger Casement.

Fourth Day—Thursday, 29th June, 1916.

Mr. Artemus Jones—My lords, I regret to say that my learned leader is in a condition this morning which does not permit of his appearance in Court. I have just seen him. He is in consultation with his medical adviser, and the effect of the advice is that he must not go on. In these circumstances will your lordships grant me the indulgence of allowing me to conclude his speech and deal with the points he has not quite covered?

The Lord Chief Justice—Yes, certainly. I am sorry Mr. Sullivan is not able to be here; it was obvious that he was labouring under a strain yesterday afternoon. Will you kindly proceed with his address?

Mr. Artemus Jones—If your lordship pleases. Gentlemen of the jury, the responsibility of defending a man in a criminal Court is always a serious responsibility for the counsel who appear for him, and when the charge against him is a capital charge, and is one which involves the dread issue of life or death, that responsibility becomes still greater and heavier. Rising as I do in these circumstances to resume the speech made by my learned leader, Mr. Sullivan, yesterday, I hope that you will grant to me the same measure of sympathetic hearing, at any rate, which you have been good enough to give him.

Now, let me, if I may, resume my learned leader's argument at the point where he left off yesterday. Mr. Sullivan was pointing out to you that the evidence called by the prosecution with reference to these acts of high treason which it is said he committed in Germany was quite consistent with an entirely different view of the case; that is to say, the view of an Irishman, a loyal and patriotic Irishman, who, stirred to the depths by events, of which there is evidence in this case already, which had taken place in Ireland in 1913, had in the midst of this great war gone to Germany, not for the purpose of helping Germany to fight England, but for the purpose of forming an Irish Brigade to strive for something they had a right to strive for, the protection of their countrymen if they were coerced or tyrannised by armed forces in Ireland which were not controlled by the Executive Government. I suggest, with all respect to my lord, that it is open for you to form that view of the case on the evidence as it stands. Gentlemen, let me, if I may, answer the question which was addressed to you by the learned Attorney-General in his opening speech. He commented, as he had a right to do, upon the distinguished record which Sir Roger Casement enjoyed in the service of this great Empire. He had played a part, as the Attorney-General said, in consolidating the Empire in one sense, that in different parts of the Empire he had been trying to do his best in the responsible position he occupied. In the year 1911 he retired on a pension, which, as Sir Roger Casement said, he had honourably earned, and with a title, which it was not in his power to refuse, which his Sovereign conferred upon him. As the learned Attorney-General asked yesterday, what had happened since 1911 to convert that loyal and dutiful son of the Empire into the traitor which the Crown wishes you to believe that he is? What had happened? That was the question which the Attorney-General asked, and I promise to give the learned Attorney-General his answer in the evidence which has been already given, namely, the speeches which the sergeant of police has already said in evidence that he had read, read in the south of Ireland, and which, as he said, were being circulated all over Ireland. Let me read the state of feeling there at that time—" What he would urge upon them " was that they should go forward in the same solemnity as that with which " they devoted themselves in the cause of Protestantism when they signed " the covenant twelve months ago. Their leaders asked them to run no " risk and to do no deed which they on their part were not prepared to " run and to do."

The LORD CHIEF JUSTICE—Was this read in the evidence? There were some passages that were read, but I do not remember that part of it.

Mr. ARTEMUS JONES—I beg your lordship's pardon; your lordship remembers certain passages were marked in ink.

The LORD CHIEF JUSTICE—Some parts undoubtedly were read.

Mr. ARTEMUS JONES—It may be that I have not begun at the right point. The part I did read out was the part coming within the two black lines, which were marked at the time and shown to the witness, if your lordship will remember.

The LORD CHIEF JUSTICE—As I recollect the evidence, this was all a little irregular, but, of course, was permitted; at any rate, it was permitted by us for the defence, but the witness certainly did not say he remembered seeing those newspapers at all. What he did say was that he remembered words somewhat to the effect that were suggested by Mr. Sullivan, and we allowed those passages to be read. I think if you are going to read other parts of the speech it becomes a very different proceeding.

Mr. ARTEMUS JONES—I only intended to read those passages that appear in the shorthand notes. The mistake I made was in picking up the newspaper and reading the passages marked in black ink. I read it on the assumption that it represented all that appeared in the shorthand notes, Let me draw your lordship's attention to the passages.

The ATTORNEY-GENERAL—I do not want to take any unnecessary objection, but I should like references to be made to the answers of the witnesses upon which this argument is based. It is a strange way to prove that a speech was made by asking a witness in a criminal case whether he read a report, even if he said he read that report. My recollection of the answer is that the only answer made by the witness was he read something to that effect.

The LORD CHIEF JUSTICE—That is how I understood it, and that is what I was pointing out to Mr. Jones. Strictly, it was irregular, but it was a latitude allowed to the defence because they might have been in a difficulty in getting strict proof; and it was not objected to by the Crown, for that reason no doubt. Therefore I think it is that we must confine it to the precise questions and answers which were obtained. At most it comes to this, that speeches to that effect were issued; that is all.

The ATTORNEY-GENERAL—The question arises, if the only answer was that a speech to that effect was made, how far that justifies the reading of what purports to be a newspaper report as showing exactly what was said which was never read out to the witness at all.

The LORD CHIEF JUSTICE—All that I think is properly admissible is what Mr. Artemus Jones is proposing to read, the precise words put to the witness in the question and accepted by him as words to that effect.

Mr. ARTEMUS JONES—I am obliged to your lordship. One eminent judge once observed that a thing most notorious outside a Court of law was the thing most difficult to prove inside a Court of law. I only propose now to read to you the passages in which Mr. Sullivan questioned the police sergeant as to whether he saw statements there being made which, as the sergeant said, were influencing the minds of peasantry and people in other parts of Ireland.

I will read the whole of the cross-examination to meet the observation properly made by the Attorney-General[1]—

What is your headquarters?—Tralee.
How long are you stationed in Tralee?—Five years.
I suppose you read the papers?—Sometimes.
What paper do you read?—Anything I can get hold of—the *Irish Times*, the *Independent*.
The *Irish Times* is the one that you take for preference, I think?—Yes.
I want to know whether you read the *Irish Times* of July 14th, 1913. I can give you a copy to look at. (Newspaper handed to witness)?—I could not tell you.

The LORD CHIEF JUSTICE—I am not sure you quite appreciated what I said; you need not trouble to read all the introductory passage. I think you are entitled, and I so stated, to read the particular passages read to the Court from the newspapers as they appear here.

Mr. ARTEMUS JONES—If your lordship pleases.[2]

"We can rely not only on thousands but tens of thousands of people in England "who are prepared to assist us." There was any amount of that sort of speaking going on?—In the papers.
Some of them were perhaps more definite. Then in the very last paragraph of the meeting that is reported there, do you see a passage beginning—"In England they were prepared to stand"?—Who is speaking; whose speech is it?
I will give you the name if you wish, but I am a little diffident about it. It is the very last paragraph of the eloquent speech that closed the meeting except the vote of thanks?—There are so many meetings in different parts of Ireland, and they are mixed up together.
I will mark the passage for you if you wish it. (Counsel having marked the passage.) That is the passage I want you to look at. Did you read passages of this kind circulating in your district? "They would be right in resisting it by force, "and in their determination to resist it they would have the sympathy and support "of thousands of people in England, and amongst those thousands he had the "greatest pleasure in reckoning himself." You remember speeches to that effect at all events?—Either speeches or comment to that effect.
They were circulated broadcast through the country?—No doubt.

Then the other passage is read in another question[3]—

"He could add this as a word of partial assurance, that they had many powerful "friends in England who thought as he did. It was all very well to talk of the "great forces which were marshalled behind the Government, and which could be "used in the event of extreme necessity in Ulster. The reply to that was that the "forces of the Crown were the servants of the nation, and at least one half of the "nation believed that the employment of this force would be a monstrous crime."

Then follows this passage in the next question—

"If the resolution of Ulster were put to the test, they would find those in "England who had felt it their duty to encourage the men of Ulster in their attitude, "and who would be prepared to prove by their deeds that when they said that Ulster "was right they meant Ulster was right, and who would be prepared to share the risk.'

---

[1] P. 55. [2] P. 56. [3] P. 57.

Speech for Prisoner.

Then I propose to read from the cross-examination of Sergeant Hearn[1]—

Do you remember in 1914, before the war, the Arms Proclamation?—Yes.

As an officer of the constabulary, were you concerned in acting under it for a while?—Yes.

Prior to that, had there been considerable importation of arms?—Yes.

As a matter of common knowledge in the country, was there prior to that a very large importation of arms in the north of Ireland?—Yes.

Was it in consequence of what happened in the north of Ireland that the people were arming so far south as Tralee?—I could not say that.

Did they at all events purport to be arming?—They did.

As against the armed persons in the north of Ireland?—Yes.

Were they bearing arms openly?—They were.

Without interference by the public authorities?—Yes.

And actually on the outbreak of war was the proclamation against the importation of arms withdrawn on the 16th August?—Yes, that is so.

And your directions, even so far as they went to interfere with the importation of arms ceased on the 16th August, on the withdrawal of the Proclamation for the time being?—Yes.

And the arming of the population went on then unrestricted for a while?—Yes.

And the parade of arms uninterfered with by any authority?—Yes.

People drilling?—Yes.

Marching?—Yes.

Skirmishing through the country?—Yes.

Without any action taken on behalf of the police? This arming of course commenced before the war, did it not?—Yes, it did.

It commenced some time in 1913, in the south, did it not?—Yes.

It had commenced earlier in the north?—Yes.

In re-examination by the Solicitor-General certain questions were put. So much for these passages. Now, I should like to read one passage in the evidence of Britten, but before I do that I should like to read the statement made by the witness, that they went on arming both against the armed forces in Ulster and against conscription.

The Lord Chief Justice—Yes, partly against one and partly against the other; it was in re-examination by the Solicitor-General.[2]

Mr. Artemus Jones—Yes.

By the Solicitor-General—What effect would the landing of a cargo, I do not say three pistols, but a cargo of arms and ammunition, in that country have had upon the population?—It would have had a very grave effect.

It has been put to you that the people were arming only against the Ulstermen from the north, is that so?—Partly against Ulster and partly against conscription.

Gentlemen, I have troubled you with those passages for the purpose of emphasising the fact that the state of things which, according to the police themselves, prevailed in Ireland prior to the war must have gone on subsequently, because the reference to conscription, you know, stamps it as being the date when that question came before Parliament and before the public. I think that is a perfectly legitimate observation to make, and therefore I am entitled, I think, to make this point. Given a community such as you have in Ireland, with deep and bitter memories of what they consider to be wrongs, having by their constitutional movement secured their political rights, then being menaced on the one hand by citizens in the same island, Ireland, marching through the land prepared to resist lawful authority, what effect could that have upon the minds of

---

[1] P. 49. [2] P. 52.

these peasantry and others down in the south of Ireland? Gentlemen, it is important for you to bear that fact in mind, because it was only then that this loyal servant of the Empire, as the Attorney-General called him, up till 1911, first became connected with anything in the nature of arms; and if the learned Attorney-General wants a complete answer to the question which he put, and properly put, in his opening speech, I suggest to him that he will find the answer in these newspaper extracts that have been read out, and, above all, in the fact which is now, I think, beyond dispute, that it was in that way Sir Roger Casement started the Irish National Volunteer movement. Gentlemen, you must bear that circumstance in mind, because, you know, there are two views, as I suggested before, for you to take on the evidence as it stands. *Prima facie* those in Court listening to the impressive speech of the Attorney-General might have thought this was a case which was absolutely undefended. They may have thought because of this, probably the most momentous crisis through which this island has passed, and when the fields of Europe are reddened with the blood of some of the best men in the world, that it does seem at first sight an outrage that a man who served the Empire for so long should go to the enemy country and commit high treason as against his own Sovereign. That was one picture which the learned Attorney-General drew; but it is your duty, when you are sitting in that box as citizens of this land, to inquire into what the facts of the case are and into what the circumstances of the case are. It is open for you to form your own view as to what this man's motive and what this man's intention were when he is alleged to have committed these acts.

Now, let me bring you, if I may, to the crucial question you have got to determine when you retire to consider your verdict. He is charged with committing high treason by adhering to the King's enemies in Germany, giving aid and comfort to the King's enemies. Gentlemen, you are dealing with the language of a statute passed almost six hundred years ago, and the meaning of those words "aid and comfort" at that time, I suggest to you, was something rather different from the words "aid and comfort" as they are used to-day. Aiding and comforting the enemy means supplying them with information or with forces or with material for the purpose of levying war against the King, and you have to be satisfied in your own mind that Sir Roger Casement's intention when he was in Germany was to use the Irish Brigade for the purpose of fighting Germany's battles as against England.

The Lord Chief Justice—The words of the statute, Mr. Jones, are, of course, to be interpreted according to law, and therefore they are not for the jury, but for us. I only interpose because I want to tell you the meaning that we attribute to those words, and upon which I shall direct the jury, so that you may address your mind to it. I should not adopt the language which you used just now, but I shall tell the jury that "giving "aid and comfort to the King's enemies" means assisting the King's enemies in the war with this country, and that any act which strengthens or tends to strengthen the enemy in the conduct of the war against us would be giving aid and comfort to the King's enemies, and that any act which weakens or tends to weaken the power of this country to resist or to attack the enemy equally is giving aid and comfort to the King's enemies. That is the direction of law that I intend to give.

Speech for Prisoner.

Mr. Artemus Jones—I am much obliged to your lordship. Gentlemen, you have to be satisfied, bearing in mind, of course, the terms in which my lord will address you when it comes to his part of dealing with the case, and you will remember the terms of what he said, and also remember the essence of the offence is that it was Sir Roger Casement's intention in going to Germany. Gentlemen, just consider the position. Here he was in Cork, according to the evidence, in the years 1913 and 1914, certainly before the war broke out, addressing a meeting there, as one of the witnesses said, with regard to the Irish National Volunteer movement. You remember what I am referring to, because the police witness referred to the fact that the name of Sir Edward Carson was mentioned, and that brought the meeting to an end. That was the movement with which he became associated. And now mark this, you and I may hold our own views as to the propriety of what he did then before the outbreak of war. With whom the responsibility lies for the terrible state of things in Ireland, when the executive of the realm failed to deal with that which they ought to have dealt with, this menace of armed resistance to lawful authority, whoever may have been responsible for that I care not, but the fact remains, the witnesses have already proved that that state of things had produced in the mind of the Irish peasantry a genuine fear that they might have to take that step in case of being attacked by some armed force in Ireland. That was Sir Roger Casement's position before the war broke out. After the war broke out what happens? He goes to Germany, as we know, and addresses these Irish prisoners of war and forms the Irish Brigade. What were the first words that he used to them? Mr. Sullivan yesterday dealt exhaustively with the witness who said he urged them to fight against Russia, and so on. I do not think you will pay much attention to the evidence of that witness. All the other soldiers were agreed that he made one object clear to them, that they would go to Ireland to fight for Ireland alone, not for any purpose of Germany, but for Ireland alone, after the war was over or after a triumph at sea had been won. I suggest to you, and I do it in all earnestness, that that supplies the keynote to the motive which actuated this man in the course he took.

The Crown has to satisfy you by evidence, not by surmise, not by suggestion, not by insinuation, but by evidence and facts proved to your satisfaction, that when he did this thing in Germany he did it acting from a motive of desiring to strengthen, to adopt the language of my lord, or to tend to strengthen, the position of Germany in her war against England.

Now, let me, if I may, deal with one point upon which no doubt the Crown will lay a good deal of emphasis. I ask you to form this opinion upon the evidence as it stands, that Sir Roger Casement's object when he addressed these prisoners of war in Germany was precisely the same object that he had in mind when, long before the war broke out, he addressed that meeting in Cork to form the National Volunteer movement. I have no doubt what the Crown may suggest in answer to that—they will point to what they consider to be a very damning piece of evidence in the case, namely, the code. Gentlemen, let me deal, if I may, with that. According to the evidence called by the prosecution there was a German vessel somewhere near the coast of Ireland then. I suggest to you that that code is quite consistent with its being used with that vessel for the purpose of landing arms. Gentlemen, that was a wrong thing to do, it may have been a wicked thing to do, but that is irrelevant to the charge that you have to consider, which is high treason. That is importing into Ireland arms, which is made an offence by the Defence of the Realm Act, and the proper proceeding against Sir Roger Casement for that act would be a charge framed under the Defence of the Realm Act. The point I make on that is that that is not high treason or adhering to the enemies of the King within the Empire of Germany. Gentlemen, that is an important point I suggest to you for you to bear in mind, because it is a sort of evidence, you know, which sometimes misleads a jury into returning wrong verdicts. I suggest that that circumstance alone is a matter which might have formed the subject of a charge under the Defence of the Realm Act, a charge against him of being a rebel; but, gentlemen, that is not treason. What the Crown have to satisfy you upon is that what he did in Germany was treason in the sense that it was designed, and designed by him, to strengthen the forces of Germany as against England. I suggest to you with all respect there is no such evidence. I suggest upon the evidence called by the prosecution, when you consider the light that it throws upon the man's character and upon his motive, that it is open for you to form the view that the object with which he did this act in Germany was exactly the same object as he had when he addressed that meeting in Cork in 1914. It is open for you to form a view of the case upon the evidence which would entitle you to return a verdict of not guilty in this case. If you are satisfied that what he did in Germany was not intended by him to aid and strengthen Germany as against England, if you are satisfied that the object with which he did these things in Germany, and what he did do in fact, was exactly the same object and with regard to the same work which he was carrying on in Ireland before the war, it is open for you to return a verdict of not guilty.

Gentlemen, whom was the Irish Brigade formed to fight for? They did not leave Germany with Sir Roger Casement; they were left behind, as some of the witnesses have referred to. Thy did not come over to Ireland. When you bear that fact in mind, I suggest it is some evidence on which you can act at any rate when you are considering your verdict. That is a question I suggest to you respectfully you must answer, and I suggest also that the verdict you give must be an answer to that question. Whom was the Irish Brigade intended to fight for? It certainly was not Germany. If it be true, as the evidence shows it is, that there was in Ireland a number of people, I care not what position of life they were in, whether peasants or anybody higher, who really thought they had to arm themselves for the purpose of doing that which the lawful and constituted authority of the realm ought to have given them for the protection of themselves, if that be the case, it is open for you, as I said, to return a verdict of not guilty in this case.

I am not going to make any appeal to you on behalf of the prisoner which is founded upon anything except those considerations that the law allows. I am not going to address you upon the terrible responsibility that rests upon you in considering this case. It is, as I said before, a matter of life and death, and it would ill become me to dwell upon that aspect of the matter as far as you are concerned. I spoke just now of the responsibility which devolves upon counsel who are pleading for the life of a fellow-creature. That responsibility is small compared with your responsibility. Each one of you must be satisfied beyond a reasonable doubt that the Crown have made out their case. The law demands, as the Attorney-General said, a forfeit; but that is not all the law demands. That man has a right to demand from you the same care and scrutiny in weighing the evidence as any one of you would expect to get were you standing in that dock. It is said that life is a comedy to those who look on, and it is a tragedy to those who feel. This trial may mean a tragedy to the prisoner on account of the terrible responsibility which rests upon your shoulders. Each one of you must be satisfied, and satisfied beyond all reasonable doubt, that the Crown have made out their case. I am not going to address any appeal to you based upon sympathy or upon anything like an emotional plea in the way of mercy. The ancient and valiant race from which this man springs does not produce the type of man who shrinks from death for the sake of his country. The history of Ireland contains many melancholy and sad chapters, and not the least sad is the chapter which tells and speaks so eloquently of so many mistaken sons of that unfortunate country who have gone to the scaffold, as they think, for the sake of their native land. I am not going to base any appeal to you upon emotions. If the Crown have made out their case, it is your duty as lawful citizens to return a verdict of guilty; but I claim this, that the law requires that the Crown should prove their case, and prove it up to the hilt, and you must with sure judgment and with clean consciences consider if you be satisfied upon that point; and if you do that, if you approach the case in that spirit and apply that test to it, dark and heavy as the case may be as far as the defence is concerned, I do suggest to you that there is a way open to you to return a verdict which would be none the less just because it is humane.

Closing Speech for the Crown.

The Attorney-General—May it please your lordships, gentlemen of the jury—The case for the defence here has been presented to you, in the main by Serjeant Sullivan, with an ability and propriety and an eloquence which his distinguished career at the Irish bar entitled us to expect at his hands, and I, as all of us, most greatly regret the indisposition which at the last moment has deprived the prisoner of the advantage of his closing sentences, though not, I am glad to recall, of the main argument upon which he relied.

Gentlemen, my learned friend who has just sat down has made an observation with which I entirely concur. He told you that you must demand of the Crown in this case and at the conclusion of this case that it shall have proved beyond all reasonable doubt the charges which it has made against the prisoner. I accept and I repeat the observation. It is the duty of the Crown to prove conclusively, and so that no doubt can linger in the mind of any man amongst your number, that the prisoner has been guilty of these acts for which the Crown arraigns him to-day.

Sir Roger Casement.

Attorney-General

It will be my duty, I hope not at length, to satisfy you that at every stage of this case the Crown has proved every material statement which I made to you when, on behalf of the Crown, I opened this case some days ago.

It is proper that I should make some general references to the only defence which has been attempted in this case before I trouble, as I fear I must trouble, you with a more detailed reference to the evidence that has been given. Gentlemen, when I opened this case I was of opinion, and I am still of opinion, that I opened a simple and intelligible case, susceptible of a very clear answer, if indeed any answer could be made to the charges which it outlined. You have now heard counsel for the prisoner, and have heard the questions which they put to the witnesses who were called by the Crown, and you have heard the observations by which the defence has been made in the speeches of learned counsel. Let me summarise to you, as I conceive it, what the nature of that defence, now that we know it, is. I understand it to be this—the prisoner did not attempt to seduce Irish soldiers from their admitted allegiance to the King in order that they might assist Germany, he did not attempt to seduce those soldiers from their allegiance in order that they might fight against England; but he was so struck, his mind was so affected by the growing lawlessness in Ireland, by the constantly increasing accession of military equipment and strength to the Volunteers in the north of Ireland, that with the object of establishing an equipoise, to become effective after the war, between the strength of the Volunteers in the north of Ireland and the strength of those opposed to this view in the other parts of Ireland, he made attempts to procure men under the oath of military allegiance to the Sovereign of this country, to pledge themselves that at the end of the war they would go to Ireland, not for the purpose of assisting Germany, not for the purpose of fighting England, but for the purpose, as I have said, of holding themselves as a balance against the military power of the Volunteers of the north of Ireland, which, in the view of the prisoner, had attained excessive proportions. Now, you have listened to the speech, you have heard the rhetoric, and I make no complaint of it, by which that speech was supported, and you are in a position to judge whether in a few sentences I have not given you the whole substance of the defence. It is a very simple issue. Whether, even if every fact in it was proved, it would be a good reply to the charges made by the Crown is another matter, and a matter on which for the moment I postpone discussion, because it is more convenient, and it would be a course more economical of your time, if I first examine into this question whether the evidence of what the prisoner actually did supplies the slightest support to the theory so elaborately placed before you to-day.

Now, consider the case quite shortly. Consider the two alternatives, and then I will call your attention to the evidence, and you can choose between those alternatives. The case that is presented to you by the Crown is this short case, that the prisoner, a man who, as you know well, was long in the service of this country, and a man who well understood public affairs, that this man on the outbreak of war, the greatest struggle in which the country to which he had so long belonged had ever been engaged, went to the country of our principal enemy, that he found there captured soldiers of His Majesty the King, that he set himself then and there to seduce those men from their allegiance with the object of using them in violation of their military duty and at the risk of their lives in any enterprise which might injure the country to which they owed that allegiance. That is the charge made by the Crown, and a very specific charge. The answer is that they were not to be used to assist Germany in any way, but they were only to be used on the conclusion of the war for matters concerned with the internal politics of Ireland. Those are the two cases. Let us examine them in the light of the evidence.

First of all, let me call attention to an eloquent passage in the speech of my learned friend, Mr. Sullivan, in which you may, I think, find some indication that even he was conscious of some of the weaknesses of the case which he was recommending to your convictions. He said[1]—

> Gentlemen, what are you to do when, after years of labour, your representatives may have won something that you yearn for for many a long day, won it under the constitution, had it guaranteed by the King and the Commons, and you are informed that you should not possess it because those that disliked it were arming to resist the King and Commons and to blow the statute off the book with powder? The civil police could not protect you, and the military force would perhaps prove inadequate for your support. You may lie down under it, but if you are men, to arms when all else fails, defend yourself. If the civil government will not protect you, if the constabulary cannot secure your rights, if you cannot rely upon brigades, the ultimate resort for any man in the protection of his constitutional freedom is to stand with arms in his hands, and if a civil government can be terrorised into obtaining his rights, try if his attitude will not inspire them with sufficient respect to do what is right without fear, favour, or affection.

Gentlemen, I read that passage because I am anxious that the defence as I put it to you should be put, not in language of my own, but in the very language used by my learned friend, and immediately followed in his speech by this observation, "That, gentlemen, is the case that I "present to you on behalf of Sir Roger Casement; that is the explanation "of everything that he has done." What is contained in the paragraph that I have just read to you? I will summarise it again, I hope with complete accuracy. It means this. Ireland had obtained Home Rule, or had at least secured the result that the Home Rule Bill was upon the Statute Book. They saw arming in the north of Ireland great forces, proclaiming their intention of resisting it, and finding that the military were apparently inadequate for the support of those who desired the Home Rule Bill to become law, they judged it necessary that Irishmen should adopt the ultimate resort in the protection of their constitutional freedom and stand with arms in their hands. I quote that particular speech of my learned friend, because I desire at once to make this observation upon it. Had the acts for which the prisoner stands arraigned been committed before the war took place, had they been committed at the time when the acts which he alleges on the part of the Ulster Volunteers were taking place, these words might have been a good defence or a bad defence, but they would at least have had great relevance.

I do not desire, and I hold it be wholly irrelevant, to go into old and unhappy controversies that have ceased to maintain any contact with the march of events, but I remind you of this, that there had intervened one circumstance which had altered the whole phase of Irish politics,

---

[1] P. 151.

and my learned friend in the very next paragraph, to which I will presently draw your attention, shows that he realised it had altered the whole phase of Irish politics. What was that fact? It was that the greatest military power which the world has ever known was trying to destroy this country and trying to make an end of this Empire. Since these controversies arose, what honest citizen was thinking or talking of whether or not there might at some future day be resistance to the Home Rule Bill? From the moment that Germany made her tiger spring at the throat of Europe, I say from that moment the past was the past in the eyes of every man who wished well to England, and my learned friend knew it; he was oppressed by the difficulty, and he goes on in his speech, and he says this[1]—

Gentlemen, this condition of affairs had indeed been reached prior to this war that has broken out with the Empire of Germany.

Now, listen to this, showing what the real facts were, and showing how clearly my learned friend realised them—

There was indeed an understanding and a convention between the greater leaders of these factions arming and counter-arming, that for a while, while the danger to the Empire existed, this dreadful state of affairs should be put an end to; that, in the meantime, faith has been kept, let us all thank Providence, for it enabled my countrymen in the service of Ireland, for they are serving the glorious traditions of their own land, to write their names in every battlefield in Europe, a thing that would have been impossible without such understanding. Do not imagine, though you may live in a great city of the Empire, that you can sneer at the loyal patriotism of these men.

Observe the remarkable admission made in those words, and, indeed, a necessary admission for any candid and reasonable advocate. My learned friend himself reminds you there that on the outbreak of the war there was an understanding and a convention between the greater leaders of these factions that while the danger to the Empire existed this dreadful state of things should be put an end to. Then my learned friend points out, and quite truly, that in the meantime

Faith has been kept, let us all thank Providence, for it enabled my countrymen in the service of Ireland to write their names in every battlefield in Europe.

So that we have it admitted, and this is the case of my learned friend himself, that while there were unhappy controversies and profound antagonism of opinion, acts done on both sides, as to which I do not ask now whether the one was right or the other was right, for the inquiry would be long, bitter, and irrelevant, we have it admitted that with the outbreak of this war, with the danger to the Empire which the outbreak of this war involved, there was an arrangement and a convention between the leaders of these factions which would enable Irish soldiers to do what Irish soldiers have done in every great war in which this country has been engaged—write their names with their swords on the battlefields of Europe.

Yes, gentlemen, but how do these reflections help the prisoner? How do these reflections support what and what alone is the case made here before you on the prisoner's behalf? Old controversies and dangers which might have arisen from those controversies had this war not broken out. The outbreak of war, the swift menace to everything this

---

[1] P. 152.

country possesses, to everything that our ancestors have bequeathed to us in our long history, the swift menace to all those things, I say, the realisation by the responsible men of all parties in Ireland of the menace, required that these controversies should be composed as long as the danger lasted. Is that the view the prisoner took? What was the quality of the prisoner's acts? At the very moment that these Irish soldiers who in my learned friend's eloquent address have written their names on the battlefields of France, in that glorious retreat which marked the early days of the war, at the very moment when they had been taken into captivity, his idea of observing the truce, the existence of which has been plainly stated to you by my learned friend, of avoiding the danger to the Empire of raising these matters as long as the war lasts, was to go over to Germany under circumstances on which I shall say more in a moment, and attempt to seduce those men from their allegiance, and to arrange then and there that at some period, which I will show presently was not the end of the war, they were to land in Ireland in order to evoke there once again the hideous spectre of disunion, disloyalty, and armed insurrection. My learned friend has put before you, as I have told you, a suggestion as to the proposal that the prisoner made to these Irish prisoners of war from which I dissent from first to last. He has told you that what the prisoner said to these Irish soldiers at Limburg was that at the conclusion of the war they should go to Ireland in order to fight for Ireland.

Now, I have an observation to make to you at the very outset before I challenge and test that claim, and the observation I wish to make to you is this—I shall put it in the form of a question. I have already asked that question in this case and received no answer to it; the question can be put thus shortly—Why did the prisoner ever go to Germany at all? That is the first question, and I follow it by a second—How did he get to Germany? What was the nature of the arrangement and of the assurance that was given to him before he went to Germany? How was it that when his country was at war with Germany, when these Irish soldiers on the field of battle had just been made prisoners by the German Army, that we find him for months a free man in Germany, moving without restriction in whatsoever part of Germany those Irish soldiers were confined, able, without control or interference, to go amongst them and attempt to seduce them? Why in this view of the case did he go to Germany at all? What suggested motive is there? Gentlemen, it is not through inadvertence, I apprehend, that no answer has been given to that question by my learned friends, because when I opened this case to you I tell you plainly it struck me this question was the crux of the whole matter of the prisoner's activities. Let me remind you of what I said, and how pointedly I said it when I opened this case to you. I said this very deliberately, "If it be possible "to give an explanation of the original journey of the prisoner to "Germany which is consistent with the duty which he owed, and which "he has so recently professed to his Sovereign and to his country, I hope "that this explanation will be put forward by the very experienced counsel "by whom he has the advantage of being defended."

The question that I asked, as I then said, deliberately and pointedly, has never been answered. Why has it never been answered? I can tell you. It has never been answered because no answer to that question could

Attorney-General

be given which is consistent with the integrity of the prisoner. Why did he go to Germany? His case made before you and through the lips of his counsel is that he went there to make sure there would be some men who would be strong enough to balance the Volunteers in the north of Ireland after the war. Where do you think would be the place in which his efforts might be most fruitful if that really was his object? Do not you think that if that really was his object he might possibly have stayed in Ireland where he would still have been in the King's dominions? Why go to Germany? Why go and corrupt other men, to make them in breach of their duty incur grave penalties? Why go there? How arrange with that Government which gives very little for nothing? How arrange with that Government that as the Irish prisoners were taken they should be addressed by him? How was all this arranged, on what terms, and in what documents were those terms conveyed? Gentlemen, if we knew the full story of the circumstances under which this man went to Germany, if we knew what negotiations had taken place and what safeguards were given, what plans were made, perhaps this defence would be even more difficult than it is to-day.

Now, let me, as I promised you I would, show you in a moment how wholly inconsistent the evidence given by the Irish witnesses is with the case put forward to-day. I will follow them much in the same order as my learned friend, Mr. Sullivan, followed them yesterday. I take first of all the witness Cronin. He had said there were seventy or eighty men in a crowd.[1]

By the LORD CHIEF JUSTICE—He said that he was going to form an Irish Brigade, and he said why live any longer in hunger and misery in this camp when you can better yourselves by joining the Irish Brigade which I am going to form; you will be sent to Berlin as the guests of the German Government.

I pause there to ask whether, in your reading of the habits of the German Government, you think that the German Government were taking the same view of the activities of the prisoner that apparently the prisoner, according to the evidence put forward on his behalf to-day, was taking. I am unaware of anything in the history of the German nation during this war which would lead me to accept with enthusiasm the suggestion that they would be prepared to offer unlimited hospitality to a number of Irish soldiers in order that when the war was over they would be able to write a new page in the purely domestic history of their country; I am unaware of anything in the suggestion that leads me to accept with alacrity the theory, by whomsoever it is brought forward.

Examination continued—Did he say what this Irish Brigade was to do?—He said in the event of Germany winning a sea battle he would land them in Ireland.

Then I have in the print, "And Ireland would equip them"; I do not know how that may be, I do not recollect that answer. The words I want to lay stress on are these, "He said in the event of Germany winning "a sea battle he would land them in Ireland."

What were they to do in Ireland?—Free Ireland.

Did he say who they were to fight against?—Against England.

Did he say what would happen to them if Germany did not win?—They would be sent to America. They would get £10 or £20 pocket money and a free passage.

---

[1] P. 17.

Closing Speech for the Crown.

Attorney-General

If the nature of the activities which were contemplated for these men were of the character which it is now suggested to you on behalf of the prisoner they were, here again I pause to express my surprise that the German Government, in return for such prospective services after the war, were found advancing or promising them £10 or £20 pocket money at the end of the war and a passage to America. It may be so, but it would surprise me if it were so. What is involved in that uncontradicted evidence—never forget that—and therefore evidence, as my lord will tell you, to be received by you? What is involved in that? If Germany won a sea battle they were to be landed in Ireland. Does he say at the end of the war they were to be landed in Ireland? He says nothing of the kind. My learned friend, Mr Sullivan, says, if Germany wins a sea battle that would be the end of the war. He is quite wrong. It does not necessarily follow: it might be or it might not; there is not the slightest indication in the speech he was making to them that the prisoner is convinced of it; it might be not a decisive German success, but it might be such a success as to give Germany such a temporary control of the sea as would enable her to send these men over to Ireland. There is not a single word in the evidence of this man (I will deal with the story of the other witnesses later) which lends support to the view that the prisoner said a word to them showing that their intervention in Ireland was to be at the end of the war. Their intervention was to be if Germany wins a sea battle. Why do you suppose he took that as the period? For obvious reasons. Until Germany won a sea battle it was clear that it would be extremely difficult, if not impossible, to take any considerable body of men to Ireland, and therefore there would be no serious or practical proposal at all if he had not made this proviso. And so the proposal was at the earliest moment which made it possible, when success, temporary or complete, made it possible to make an invasion of Ireland, and when you make that invasion to fight against England—not against Volunteers in Ulster, not at the end of the war to see fair play between the various factions and to see that Ireland is not robbed of her birthright. If he said that, wholly different considerations would have arisen; but he did not say that; he said to these men, as I told you before, attempting to corrupt them, in effect: "At the first moment you can safely get to Ireland will you go there; "will you join this brigade and fight against England?" Gentlemen, you can sweep away all these belated after-thoughts and sophistries about old Irish politics and the Volunteers in the north of Ireland. They were never in his mind when he made these speeches, they never inspired the appeals he made, they had no relation to it, and, as I have said, they are after-thoughts when it is necessary to attempt to exhume some defence, however remote from the facts, in the position in which the prisoner finds himself.

So much for Cronin's evidence. Now, let me take the evidence of the next witness, O'Brien[1]—

> He said that if they were successful in winning the war they would land the Irish Brigade along with the German army in Ireland.

Mark that, "Along with the German Army." Does that look very

[1] P. 23.

much as if the invasion was only to be at the end of the war? That is uncontradicted evidence, and I think uncross-examined too. My learned friend reminds me of a passage before that[1]—

I heard him say, "Now is the time for Irishmen to fight against England, now is "their opportunity for doing so; join the Irish Brigade." He said he came to form an Irish Brigade, and he wanted all Irishmen to join the Irish Brigade and become guests of the German army.

Gentlemen, I pause to make the comment there that I am not one of those who, in dealing with the memory of private soldiers, of words said to them many months ago, under circumstances of great stress and anxiety on their part, would ask you or any other jury to accept with verbal precision their recollection of what was said, but I would confidently ask you to accept their recollection as to the broad and salient features of the speech so often made to them. That is the recollection of this man O'Brien.

My lord reminds me of a question, and it is convenient I should read it, in the cross-examination by my learned friend[2]—

Did he say they were to be transferred to Ireland when Germany had won the war?—Yes.

And if Germany failed to win the war they should go to America?—To America, yes.

Arrangements would be made to have them go to America. Did you speak to Sir Roger Casement at all yourself?—No.

The Lord Chief Justice—Then there is the re-examination.

The Attorney-General—There is the re-examination by my learned friend, the Solicitor-General[3]—

To take you back for a moment to the speech you heard Sir Roger Casement make, he said the Irish Brigade were to fight in Ireland?—Yes.

Did he say who were to take them to Ireland to fight?—The German Army.

Did he say against whom they were to fight?—To fight against England.

It is quite obvious that the phrase, "When the war is over," in such a connection has no meaning at all. If they were to be taken over to Ireland to fight against this country by any German agency, military or civil, whether they were also accompanied by German soldiers or not, it is quite obvious that if one war was over that was the commencement of a new war; it was an act of hostility, it was just as much an act of treason to this country to arrange at a moment when a particular phase of a war was concluded as it was if it were terminated immediately, by the agency of your late enemy, to transport armed men accompanied by German soldiers to Ireland; it was just as much an act of hostility as if there never had been a temporary conclusion of the existing hostilities. The truth is, as one must recognise when you look closely and collate the evidence of the various witnesses, that the real application and appeal that was made to them was that they should go to Ireland when the naval victory was won.

Now, gentlemen, I come to the evidence of Robinson[4]—

I remember him saying, "Now is your chance to fight for Ireland and free it. I "am very glad to see you here. This is the only chance you will have to fight for "Ireland. Why do not you join the Irish Brigade?" Then he spoke about the treatment of Ireland in England. That is all I remember.

---

[1] P. 23. [2] P. 24. [3] P. 25. [4] P. 26.

Closing Speech for the Crown.

Attorney-General

What was the Irish Brigade to do?—They were supposed to land in Ireland and free Ireland.

By the LORD CHIEF JUSTICE—Tell us what you heard him say, not what they were supposed to do?—That is about all I can remember at the present time. He said he was very glad to see so many Irishmen here, that now was our time to fight for Ireland and strike a blow, and he hoped we would all join the Irish Brigade.

Examination continued—Did he say with whom the Irish Brigade were going to fight?—Fight against England. He said that if Germany had a victory on the sea, they would land the Irish Brigade in Ireland.

This statement repeated by that witness is what I ask you to conclude was actually said by the prisoner. Those are the terms of the proposal, which the submission of the Crown puts before you, dealing with the facts; that was the proposal, that if Germany had a victory on the sea then and there they would land the Irish Brigade in Ireland. My learned friend reminds me that in cross-examination he adhered to that story[1]—

And did he address you? Did he say it was to go to Ireland when the Germans had won the war?—No, he said if Germany had a victory on sea.

Did he speak about Germany winning the war?—Yes.

What did he say about Germany winning the war?—He always said that Germany would win, but we contradicted him and said they would not.

I suggest to you that he represented when Germany had won the war that the Irish Brigade was to go to Ireland unless there was a victory at sea meantime. Was that what he said?—I cannot remember that. I remember him saying if Germany had a victory on sea he would land us in Ireland.

So that he adheres to his story under the stress of cross-examination. I am reminded of another question in my learned friend's re-examination[2]—

You told the jury that you heard Sir Roger Casement say that if Germany won a victory at sea the Irish Brigade would be landed in Ireland?—Yes.

Did he say who would send the Irish Brigade to Ireland?—Germany would send us to Ireland.

Did he say whether they would have any fighting to do?—He did not go into that; he said it was to free Ireland when they got there.

Did he say from whom they were to free Ireland?—From England.

So much for his evidence. Then Michael O'Connor was the next witness. He heard the prisoner addressing some men[3]—

He said, "Now is the time to fight or strike a blow for Ireland," and that England was nearly beaten.

You notice the exaltation in that statement.

I should think there were about seventy men listening to him. I was on the outskirts of the crowd. I have told all that I heard him say. I saw him on that later occasion, but I did not hear what he said. The people were hissing and booing him down the lines that day. He said that those that hissed him were followers of Johnnie Redmond, the recruiting sergeant of the British Army. A sergeant-major of the 4th Dragoon Guards called Casement a traitor. That sergeant-major was sent to Giessen or some other camp for punishment, along with Corporal Robinson.

Then the next witness is Moore[4]—

Sir Roger Casement asked those men to join the Irish Brigade, I being among the men, and he said any man that would join the Irish Brigade he would give him uniform, better food, and better housing.

---

[1] P. 27. [2] P. 29. [3] P. 32. [4] P. 33.

Attorney-General

The theory, I may pause to say, put forward by the defence has not explained to us why a German uniform should have been immediately provided for the men then if the fighting was to be in Ireland after the war; that is a link that is somewhat missing in the explanations that have been given. I resume reading now[1]—

He also said, in case of the Germans losing the war, he would send those men to America, give them a free passage and £10 or £20 pocket money, and guarantee employment in America. The Irish Brigade was to be sent from Limburg to a camp outside Berlin. He said they were to be the guests of the German Government. He also said the first German victory on the water he would land the brigade in Ireland.

Then he was asked what was to be done with the Irish Brigade, and he said they were to be landed in Ireland. Then he was asked: who was going to land them in Ireland, but that he does not know—

I did not hear him say how the Irish Brigade were going to get to Ireland, but he said he would land them in Ireland.

There again you find the statement very clearly recollected and spoken to by this witness, that it was to be sent to Ireland when the German naval victory was gained.

I come now to the evidence of Neill. I do not propose to read that, because I have to make an observation upon it. Neill, you will remember, is the witness who spoke about the Russians and the Turks. Without throwing the slightest reflection upon his good faith and desire to tell the truth, comparing the statement which he made with the statements that had been made by the other military witnesses who have been called before you, I do not ask you to place any reliance at all upon the isolated and unsupported evidence of Neill as to these observations about the Russians and the Turks. I say that to clear the ground, because I want you to deal with the case upon matters which are established, and not upon matters which are disputable or may be questioned. In justice to Neill, I only make it clear that while I do not ask you to accept his recollection, unsupported as it is, upon this point, I make and I should concur in no reflections at all upon the man's credibility or his desire to tell the truth as he remembered the facts.

I have given you now the clear recollection of the witnesses, collecting it together so that you may have it all before your minds, at the same time, as to what was actually said to them by the prisoner. What becomes of the defence, and what becomes of the only defence which has been attempted to be made? Is there one witness to whom it was suggested that all they were to do was to come and be ready in order to watch the Volunteers in the north of Ireland? Can any man who has listened to that evidence as to what the prisoner actually said doubt that it is an invented story that is put forward that he was concerned to obtain the services of these men remotely in the future, in order that they might deal with the situation as it emerged in Ireland after the war? There is not a single witness who has made any statement consistent with that view, and all the witnesses have made statements that are wholly inconsistent with that

[1] P. 34.

view. He was not asking them anything of the kind. What he was asking them was this, if Germany gained a naval success, in other words, if Germany acquired the facilities for landing troops in Ireland, are you prepared to go and fight in Ireland against England? That is what he said, and that was all that he said, that was what he always said, that is what all these witnesses speak to. What is the nature of that attempt? I respectfully accept, as I should be bound to accept, the indication which my lord, the Lord Chief Justice, gave to my learned friend as to the direction which he proposed to give you on the question of law, which is for my lord. I do not pretend to recall with precision the admirable language in which my lord stated the direction which he proposed to give to you, but I remember that my lord said this, that he should direct you that anything was an aiding and comforting of the King's enemies which strengthened the enemy for the purpose of his struggle with this country, or which weakened this country for the purpose of its struggle with the enemy. I ask you to apply that test to what we know now and while it is fresh in your mind on the uncontradicted evidence of what was said by the prisoner Casement to these men. There is no other evidence, and I have read to you all the evidence which there is. Apply that test. Supposing that Germany did win a naval success, giving her temporary control of the seas, giving it her for long enough to land Irish and German soldiers in Ireland, supposing that had taken place, would that or would it not have strengthened the enemy Germany in her struggles with this country; I ask you, would it or would it not? Would it or would it not have weakened this country in her struggle with Germany, supposing that happened which I ask you to imagine? If you answer those questions as I ask them, only one answer is possible. Of course, Germany must have been necessarily strengthened if they could have landed troops in considerable numbers, and arms and ammunition in Ireland; just as Germany would have been necessarily strengthened, so this country would have been necessarily weakened.

When we are considering these contingencies, when we are attempting to understand motives and appraise expectations, we must not confine our views to what we know now, that in fact these men retained their loyalty, starving as we know they were, starving as the evidence shows us they were, starving as the prisoner's address to them shows that he knew at the moment, when he made his appeal to them, they were. It is true that, in spite of those circumstances, only 50 men were seduced and corrupted from the soldierly duty which they owed to their Sovereign; that is true. But, gentlemen, supposing they had all been seduced, supposing they had stampeded in a body, supposing the attempt which he desired to succeed had wholly succeeded, and there had been thousands of these Irish soldiers who in Germany had consented to eat the bread of Germany, and wear the uniform of Germany, and to hold themselves in readiness to come and invade Ireland on the first opportunity, what do you think would have been the moral effect on the strength of this country? Do you think it would have weakened her in this war that it should have been known that thousands of Irish soldiers, forming the flower of that small Expeditionary Force, of which all Englishmen were so proud, had stampeded into the arms and the camps of Germany, and were now to be seen walking at will in

Germany wearing Germany's uniforms and anxiously awaiting the moment when a German success at sea might enable them to be transported to Ireland, in order that they might take up arms against England; would that strengthen Germany and weaken England? Have you any doubt in your minds that considerations of that kind passed through the minds of Germany, a country of which I have said you will probably draw the view that they are not guilty, as a rule, of disinterested acts of generosity or charity. If that was the view the prisoner shared with the German Government, that would explain their readiness to provide them with superior rations and uniforms, and their readiness to promise £10 or £20 to each man if the war went unfavourably for Germany and he had to be sent back to America.

I have said, I hope, enough upon this part of the case, and now I come to another point on which I certainly hoped and believed that my learned friends in their speeches would have at least suggested some theory. We now know that the prisoner on his view, such is his case, had only asked these Irishmen to hold themselves in readiness to go to Ireland, at the conclusion of the war, for the purpose which has been stated to you so frequently. I should like to have heard some explanation as to why he went to Ireland, having been in Germany, before the end of the war. I cannot tell you how he went to Ireland. I agree with my learned friend Serjeant Sullivan's observation on this point that the Court and the jury may reasonably take cognisance of the fact that Ireland is an island, and therefore the probability is that he went there by sea. To that view I assent. I have not been in a position to inform you, or to call evidence before you, showing how he got to Ireland. My friend disputes altogether, I will not say my theory, but my supposed theory, because if he had examined my opening speech a little more clearly he would have observed that I did not commit myself to any theory upon this point; I studiously and carefully avoided doing so; but my learned friend disputes the supposed theory of the Crown that the "Aud" had any direct connection with the landing of the prisoner in Ireland. He says, and I think the observation he makes here upon my opening is well founded, that I put it too high when I said the "Aud" was taken near Tralee. I think that criticism made by him is well founded upon that statement in my opening speech, and to the extent to which I will indicate to you I withdraw it. It is quite true, as the evidence stands before you, that the "Aud," consisting of a crew of German bluejackets and German officers, was not captured near Tralee; it was captured about 90 miles, I think it was put, from Queenstown.

The Lord Chief Justice—138 miles from Queenstown, 90 miles from the coast.

The Attorney-General—90 miles from the coast of Ireland. I did not happen to be in Court when that evidence was given. That, gentlemen, makes it very necessary to ask what was the "Aud" doing on the view of the defence. I will state to you in a moment the view of the Crown as to what the "Aud" was doing quite clearly, and I do not care whether she was within 3 miles of Tralee or within 90 miles of Tralee. The theory of the Crown is this, that it was all part of a concerted enterprise, concerted in Germany. I stated that in opening, and I state it now. I made a geographical error, such as it was, but I re-state the theory of the Crown that it was part of a common enterprise. Whether or not the "Aud" was to be landed in a different part of Ireland I do not argue, and I am not concerned to argue. It does not matter to me where it was going to land if you accept the view that it was going to land, to carry arms to Ireland. I do not know that my learned friend, Serjeant Sullivan, did accept that view. On the contrary, I think some of the observations he made support an entirely different view. My learned friend, Mr. Jones, on the other hand, when dealing with the question of the code, said it may have been intended for the purpose of communication with the "Aud." It may be; I do not know. I note a suggestion which may prove helpful in this tangled mass, when so much is left to conjecture and so little can be alleged with certainty. It may be that my learned friend is right. The fact that this code, as to which I shall make some further observations to you in a moment, was available, as my friend suggests, for communication with the "Aud," would not prevent it being available for communication with other people in Germany; but the mere fact that such a suggestion should be possible shows really that there is no doubt in the mind of anybody that there was a connection between the "Aud" and the landing of the prisoner in Ireland. If the prisoner did not come in the "Aud," and I have never suggested that he did, then it is obvious, I think, that, coming from Germany, as we know he did (at least, we must draw an irresistible inference; we have the railway ticket from Berlin to Wilhelmshaven, dated 12th April, a few days before the date of landing), he came in some other German vessel, or some neutral vessel arranged for by the Germans. I cannot tell you what the vessel was. But you will remember that the witness Hussey saw a red light out at sea at half-past nine on Thursday evening, which may have been connected with the actual landing of Casement. One of my learned friends reminds me that in the diary, where there are evidently false names used to indicate places, on the 12th April, the very date of the ticket from Berlin to Wilhelmshaven, this entry appears, "Left Wicklow in Willie's yacht." False names are used for places which will satisfy you, I think, as to what the meaning of that entry is. That entry is on the 12th April, the day when the ticket was actually issued in Germany. I do not waste any further time upon these points, as to which I cannot give you assistance, because I have not the knowledge. I do waste time, because, from my point of view——

The Lord Chief Justice—Mr. Attorney, you mentioned a passage in the diary. Is there any evidence as to whose diary it is?

The Attorney-General—It was a diary. I will give your lordship the evidence of it. It was a diary found.

The Lord Chief Justice—I know, but as far as my recollection goes there was no further evidence given beyond the fact that it was found. Whose writing it is, or whose diary it is, there is no evidence.

The Attorney-General—My lord, I did not say that it was a diary of any particular person. I said "the diary." By "the diary" I mean the diary which was found, and is in evidence as having been found.

The Lord Chief Justice—I thought it right to indicate that, because

Attorney-General

it might have conveyed to the jury that it was Casement's diary. There is no evidence of it.

The Attorney-General—You have heard, gentlemen, what my lord has said. If there was any misunderstanding I am glad it should be removed. It was a diary found with three men as to whom I make the suggestion that they had all come from Germany. There is no evidence before you as to which of the three the diary belonged, but whoever kept the diary made the note that on the 12th April, the day when the ticket was issued from Berlin to Wilhelmshaven, they left Wicklow in Willie's yacht, Wicklow being an assumed name, on the suggestion of the Crown, and whether "Willie's yacht" was a flippant way of describing a vessel commissioned in the name of the Kaiser is a matter as to which you can form your opinion.

Now, gentlemen, I have called attention to one or two points in the matters in respect of which the defence have wholly failed to give any explanation at all consistent with the innocence of the prisoner. I come now to the most striking case of all. I come to the matter which, if there was nothing else in the case, would show in the most conclusive manner possible that the whole defence, and the only defence relied upon here, is wholly without basis or foundation, and that is the code which, as my learned friend, Mr. Jones, anticipated, would be a matter upon which the Crown would lay stress. In order that you may fully understand the damning effect of the code upon the prisoner's defence you must once again consider the circumstances as they are known to us under which he came to Ireland. He came to Ireland, if the defence is true, as a man who never had contemplated, and did not, in fact, contemplate, that anything should be done in Ireland until the conclusion of the war. That is his case. So he must have come merely in the capacity of one who was about to concern himself with domestic problems in Ireland. If his defence be well founded, it must be said that he came to Ireland in order to carry on his work for the purpose of strengthening the National Volunteers. That case conceivably might have been put forward. But what is certain is this, that if the defence made here to-day is well founded, he could not have had any arrangement with the Germans by which the Germans would support him then and there. That is plain. If he went to Ireland under arrangements by which the Germans were to send him ammunition, were to send him arms, were to send him more ammunition and more arms, it is quite plain he was going there for the purpose charged by the Crown, and that he could not have been going there for the purpose indicated or suggested by the defence. I hope that is clear. To me it is so plain that it requires no further emphasis. What has he got with him? What does he try to get rid of when arrested? He tries to get rid of the code, an arranged code between himself and the Germans. What did he want with a code between himself and the Germans when he left Germany? His counsel has told us in eloquent language that he was not going at any time to associate Ireland with the Germans; that he did not want to help Germany. His counsel has told us that his only concern was with the Volunteers of the north. Why in the name of sanity did he on this view

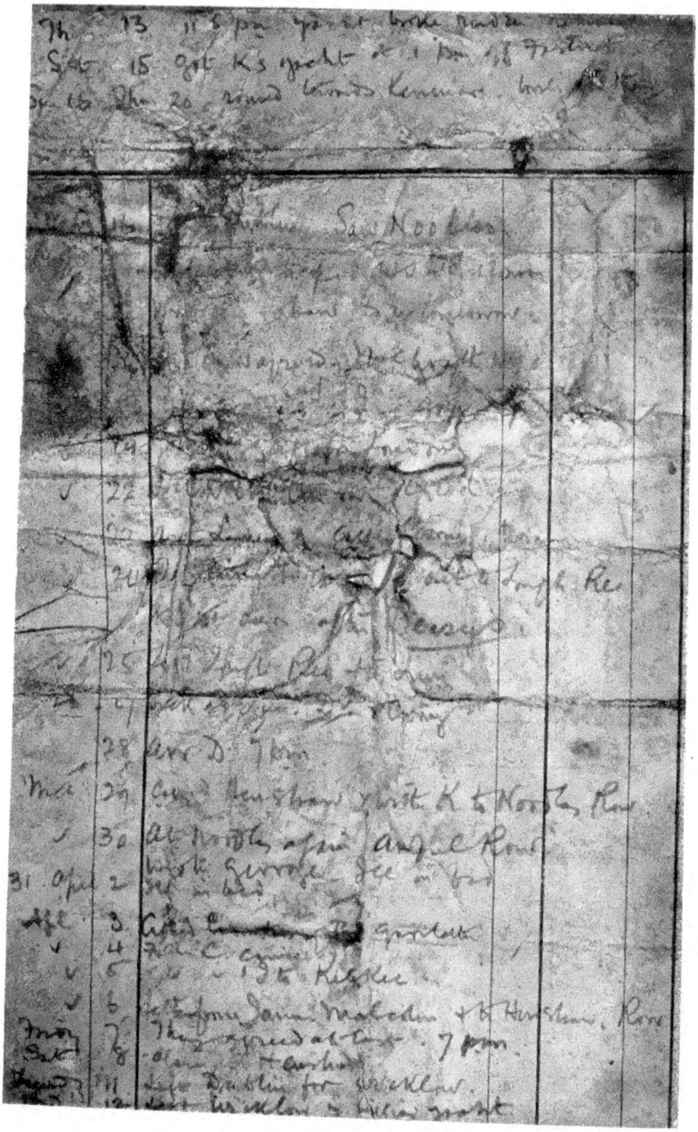

Part of the Diary, with disguised names and places.

(Page 2.)

want to arrange a code with the Germans? There is no theory consistent with the defence which will explain to you why any code was necessary at all. But look at this code. Consider the nature of the communications which, when he left the country of our enemy for Ireland, he knew to be required by his purpose and their purpose to pass between him and them.

Look at this code—"Railway communications have been stopped. "Our men are at ." It would be very interesting to the German Government, on the theory of the defence, to know that railway communications had been stopped. What had they got to do with it? "Further ammunition is needed." Does that throw any light upon the cargo of the "Aud"? Why does Germany send some ammunition in addition to which it is contemplated that further ammunition may be required? The mere message that further ammunition may be required or is needed, the mere language in which that message is couched, presupposes and renders necessary the conclusion that some ammunition has already been given. Why is the prisoner arranging that Germany shall send ammunition to Ireland, not at the end of the war, but during the war, and at the very moment of the bitterest struggles in the war? Why is that being done? Is it being done in order that at the end of the war some steps may be taken to meet the Ulster Volunteers? Gentlemen, it does not end there. "Further rifles are needed. How many "rifles will you send us? How much ammunition will you send us?" Then listen to this—"Will send plan about landing on ." It might be filled in as the exigencies of the moment might require. What does it mean without being filled in? It means a plan will be necessary to prepare for another landing, a landing of troops, a brigade, whatever it might be, ammunition, explosives; and the prisoner, who is only concerned with the Volunteers in the north after the war, leaves Germany in the middle of this war with a code in which he and the Germans acting in concert have carefully prepared themselves with messages, secret messages by which he from Ireland can send to them a plan for hostile landings in the middle of this war, and then we are told fairy tales about what is going to be done after the war with the Volunteers of the north of Ireland. What had the Germans to do with a landing made *pendente bello* if there was any basis or substance in the only case that has been put before you? Then listen to another—"Send ship to " ." You will understand now why I thought I might deal with some economy of time with the character and mission of the "Aud." "Send another ship to . Send rifles and ammunition to . "Cannons and plenty of ammunition are needed. Send them to . "Send more explosives to . Send a vessel if possible." What does all that mean? It is no good my repeating it and elaborating and over-elaborating it. What it means is obvious. Then, as I am reminded, "This code holds good from 22nd April to 20th May," a period I need hardly point out to you all of which was actually engaged in hostilities.

One further word and I will say no more about this code, because its meaning is clear, and no useful purpose can be served by repetition. This code, on the submission of the Crown, shows that there is no substance at all in the case put forward by the defence. This code, on the submission of the Crown, shows that the prisoner Casement, who went under circumstances unexplained to us, and which I cannot explain, to the enemy country while hostilities were in progress, who was allowed his freedom in that country while hostilities were in progress, who left that country for Ireland while hostilities were in progress, had agreed with the Germans to send them messages arranging for a landing, asking for another ship, and asking for explosives, for cannons, and for ammunition. Gentlemen, if you can reconcile those facts with the duty which the prisoner owed to this country, if you can reconcile those facts with the submissions which have been made to you on behalf of the defence, do so. If those facts taken together, his journey to Germany, his speeches when in Germany, the inducements he held out to these soldiers, the freedom which he there enjoyed, the course which he pursued in Ireland, the messages which he contemplated as likely to take place between himself and the Germans, satisfy you of his guilt you must give expression to that view in your verdict.

My learned friend, Mr. Sullivan, said in the early period of his observations that he hoped this case would be heard by you with a fair and impartial mind. The Crown hopes nothing else. You have a duty to discharge as serious and in many ways as testing as the duties which are discharged by any other men serving the State in these bloody and critical days. If you should come to the conclusion that the Crown has proved its case, however painful the duty, it is one from which you cannot, and you dare not, shrink. I have discharged my responsibility in this case; do you discharge yours.

The Lord Chief Justice's Summing Up.

The Lord Chief Justice—Gentlemen of the jury, this is a trial of supreme importance. The charge against the prisoner is the gravest known to the law. You have had the advantage, shared by us with you, of hearing the case presented to you by the Attorney-General, assisted by the Solicitor-General and other counsel, on behalf of the Crown. You have had the advantage also of hearing the defence in this case conducted by Mr. Sullivan until this morning, with the assistance of his juniors. There are some persons who, perhaps a little thoughtlessly, are inclined to rebel against the notion that a member of the English bar, or members of it, should be found to defend a prisoner on a charge of treason against the British State. I need not tell you I am sure, gentlemen, that if any one has those thoughts in his mind he has but a poor conception of the high obligation and responsibility of the bar of England. It is the proud privilege of the bar of England that it is ready to come into Court and to defend a person accused, however grave the charge may be. In this case, speaking for my learned brothers and myself, we are indebted to counsel for the defence for the assistance they have given us in the trial of this case; and I have no doubt you must feel equally indebted. It is a great benefit in the trial of a case, more particularly of this importance, that you should feel as we feel, that everything possible that could be urged on behalf of the defence has been said in this case after much thought, much study, much deliberation, and particularly by one who has conducted the defence in accordance with the highest traditions of the English bar. Mr. Sullivan made a speech of most striking power and eloquence. You heard it. You must have felt its effect, and, not only in the force of his argument in the speech, but also in the legal presentment of the case, it would be impossible to find anything that could be urged on behalf of the defence that has not been said with the greatest skill, and, let me add, with commendable courage.

Now, gentlemen, you will remember in considering this case that in a trial of treason what must be in your mind is that it is a very grave offence. At all times, to betray the King, that is the State, that means the country, and that means those of us who are subjects of the King who live in a common society, is and must ever be a most odious charge. But treason in time of war by adhering to the King's enemies, by aiding and comforting the King's enemies, when all persons are making sacrifices in this country to resist the enemy, and are all combining, whatever their views may be, to defeat the common enemy—treason in these times is almost too grave for expression. Gentlemen, it is because one must feel that that I desire to caution you in this case. This case, like all criminal cases, must be considered and judged calmly and dispassionately. We must be careful to deal with it according to the evidence in the case. You must banish from your mind everything you may have read or heard outside of this Court. You have sworn by the oaths that you took when you went into the jury-box to deal with the case according to the evidence; and let me remind you of it, because it is not very easy in a case of this description, where the defence have thought it right and necessary for the purposes of their case to introduce political considerations, to concentrate your attention closely and exclusively upon the evidence that has been given before you. Let me also tell you what has been said by the learned Attorney-General, endorsing the view presented to you by Mr. Artemus Jones this morning, that it is for the Crown to satisfy you beyond all reasonable doubt that the prisoner is guilty of the charge made against him. It is not for the defence to disprove the charge. Before you find a verdict of guilty against the prisoner, you must be satisfied that the prosecution has proved it.

Before I consider the evidence there is one other observation I want to make, and that is this. We have heard much in this case about politics in Ireland. It is impossible to refrain from making some observation upon the evidence that has been given. For myself, I always feel anxiety in a Court of justice when there is any possibility of the introduction of political passion. Justice is ever in jeopardy when passion is aroused. To deal with this case you must consider it, as I am sure you will, quite calmly and dispassionately, according to the evidence. Pay no more attention to what has been said with regard to the condition of Ireland before the war or after the war than is necessary in order to understand the circumstances of this case, and more particularly to do justice to the defence which is set up. Mr. Sullivan said to you yesterday in the observations he made upon the defence, that he was afraid he might be saying some things that would

Lord Chief Justice

startle you in this Court. He indeed said that he felt almost in a strange atmosphere. Well, gentlemen, with regard to those observations, let me urge you, without knowledge for one moment of the views of any one of you in regard to a subject upon which opinion is divided in this country, and even more so in Ireland, not to allow yourselves to be influenced in any way by any political opinion which may have been discussed or which may even have been put forward and urged by Mr. Sullivan in his address to you. I cannot but think that he paid the highest compliment to an English jury when he had the courage to address you as he did yesterday upon Ireland. It is all to the good that it was done. He did it in the interests of his client, to present to you his client's point of view, so that you might be able to gauge his client's mind, and, in order to do it, it was necessary that he should fearlessly put certain contentions before you. Gentlemen, one may dismiss the greater part of them very quickly, because we are not even on debatable ground. That there was conflict, Parliamentary conflict, with regard to Irish affairs for a few years before the war is only to say what has happened for a very long period. That it became acute between the north of Ireland and other portions of Ireland equally is beyond question. That during the passage of the Home Rule Bill, particularly, as we are told on the evidence, after the second reading, there were heated speeches made, parts of which have been quoted to you, is again quite outside the region of controversy. That even the situation was acute immediately before the war, you make take as established by the evidence, and one may say, from common knowledge. But, gentlemen, when you get to the war, from the 4th August, 1914, although we have evidence in this case that some persons did continue arming, that there was marching, counter-marching, and skirmishing, as it has been termed, for the purpose of exercise, yet at least it can be said, and must be said, that all parties united, not only in Great Britain, not only in the British Dominions, but also in Ireland, where, much to the consternation of the common enemy, it was found that, however deep the gulf might be between the north of Ireland and other portions of Ireland in times of peace, when war came against the British Empire there was a union of forces which would resist any attack made upon the Empire. With that, I think, for the moment at any rate, it is unnecessary that we should go further into the history of Irish politics. Except, perhaps, I may remind you of this. We have been told in the course of the evidence that steps have been taken to preserve the position, at any rate during the war, up to the present moment, and for some further period, and that every attempt is made to allay any bitterness and to prevent any disunion during the continuance of the war.

With those facts in mind, let me just tell you what the charge is in this case. It is that of adhering to the King's enemies in the Empire of Germany contrary to the Treason Act of 1351. The particulars of the offence are that Sir Roger Casement, a British subject, did on various dates and whilst this country was at war with the German Emperor contrive and intend to aid and assist the enemies of the King against the King, and did traitorously adhere to, aid and comfort the King's enemies in the Empire of Germany. That is using language which is not only well known

Lord Chief Justice

in Courts of law, but is simple enough, although part of it is old-fashioned phraseology. You heard a very lengthy discussion as to the meaning of words in the statute yesterday. We have ruled in this Court, following, as we think, the law as laid down certainly for centuries, that to do an act which amounts to adhering to the King's enemies, is an offence of treason, although the act is committed without the realm, that is, in the Empire of Germany. You need not trouble yourselves about the law. It is for us as judges to direct you as to the law. It is for you to decide the facts. Those are for you and for you only, and the direction that I shall give you of the law will enable you to understand the case and to devote attention to the special points necessary, in order to determine whether or not the prisoner is guilty or not guilty of this offence. When I deal with the facts I beg of you to remember that I am not the judge of the facts, nor are my learned brothers; that the judges of the facts are you gentlemen who sit in the jury-box. I shall make observations to you upon the evidence for the purpose of assisting you to arrive at a just conclusion, but you will remember that in so far as they may reflect any view which I may have formed of the facts, it is for you to come to the conclusion, and if you do not agree with any observation I may make upon the facts, then, it is for you not to pay further attention to it than to consider it. If you agree, then, you must, of course, act accordingly.

Now, gentlemen, the offence of adhering to the King's enemies is described in the words of the statute as "giving aid and comfort to the "King's enemies." I direct you as a matter of law, that if a man, a British subject, does an act which strengthens or tends to strengthen the enemies of the King in the conduct of the war against the King, that is, in law, the giving of aid and comfort to the King's enemies. Again, if a British subject commits an act which weakens or tends to weaken the power of the King and of the country to resist or to attack the enemies of the King and the country, that is, in law, the giving of aid and comfort to the King's enemies. If I may put it to you, the real point to which you must direct your attention in this matter when you are considering whether or not the acts done amounted to adhering to the King's enemies in the sense of giving aid and comfort to the King's enemies is: "Were the acts done such as would strengthen the German "Emperor or such as would weaken His Majesty the King?" You must consider, in coming to a conclusion as to the evidence, whether, as has been pointed out to you by the Attorney-General for the Crown, the stirring up of a strife in Ireland between the north and the Nationalists, or the fomenting of an armed insurrection, or, indeed, the procuring or causing any result in Ireland which would cause disturbance and trouble of a serious character there, would have been of assistance to Germany in the conduct of this war. It does not need a very vivid imagination to see that if Germany could introduce arms and ammunition into Ireland for the purpose of helping to create a rebellion there, or strife of a serious character, so as to occupy the attention of the British Executive, and also to necessitate the maintaining of a considerable number of His Majesty's soldiers in Ireland, that that would be assisting Germany. It would certainly be weakening the power of the Crown to the extent, at any rate,

Lord Chief Justice

that it made it necessary to keep soldiers in Ireland instead of sending them out to the Front.

The defence in this case does not really dispute the main facts of the case. The one part of the evidence which was seriously contested by Mr. Sullivan yesterday is not insisted upon by the Crown to-day. You will remember that Mr. Sullivan did attack vehemently that part of Neill's evidence which was to the effect that the prisoner had told those who were to join the Irish Brigade that they were first to assist the Turks against the Russians, and then they were to assist the Germans against the English, and then they were to fight for their own country. You may dismiss that part of the evidence from your mind altogether. The Crown does not insist upon it, and, without making any reflection whatever upon the witness Neill, says it does not ask you to act upon that, and, therefore, you may leave that part of the case out of consideration. It brings us to the real point in this case. It does not arise so much upon the evidence, that is, on the particular words used, as on the inferences that you draw from the evidence as given. If I may put it as simply as possible, the defence says that Sir Roger Casement only asked persons, these soldiers, to become members of the Irish Brigade for the purpose of assisting to resist the Ulster Volunteers after the war had concluded. The whole importance of this for the moment is whether it is right to say that that is the true effect of the evidence. The Crown says to you that that is not the true effect; that every fact that you examine points to the contrary; and that what was intended was that at the first sea victory Irish soldiers should be landed, and that the Irish Brigade should then be introduced into Ireland; and the comment is naturally made that until there had been a sea victory of Germany it would be impossible for Germany to land, at any rate, any considerable number of Irish soldiers, even if they could have enrolled them in the brigade—if not impossible, at least extremely difficult; and the suggestion made to you by the Crown is that the inducements held out and the statements made were that as soon as Germany had won a sea victory those who became members of the Irish Brigade were to be introduced into Ireland; and the Crown says that if that is the true view there is only one conclusion possible. Those are the two contentions. I shall have something to say to you before I close this case upon the view presented to you by the defence, even if you accept the version contended for by the defence, but I will leave that for the moment.

Gentlemen, the evidence establishes the history of the prisoner, which is now familiar to you, and which I shall not repeat, but which substantially is to the effect that he was in the employ of the British Crown, that he served in the Foreign Office, that he acted as His Majesty's Consul, that he came to the period when he retired, that he was knighted as an honour to him in recognition of the services that he rendered to the King and the State, and that he was subsequently employed in a Commission which went abroad to South America to inquire into the atrocities of Putumayo, and that that was the condition of things till just a little before the war. Until this moment, a little before the war, there is nothing to indicate that there was any want of allegiance in him. That was the position then. Later, after the war, on a date which we do not really know, he went to Germany. How, why, in what circumstances we have no information; but he went there, and the contention with which you are now familiar is that whilst there he committed the treason with which he is charged.

High treason is an offence committed against the duties of allegiance to the Sovereign. It is founded on the relation of the person to the Crown, and on the privileges he derives from that relation. There is a passage, and the only passage with which I shall trouble you, in Sir Michael Foster's Discourse on the Law of High Treason, a very high authority, written by a very distinguished author, in which he says, "Natural "allegiance is founded in the relation every man standeth in to the "Crown, considered as the head of that society whereof he is born a "member; and on the peculiar privileges he deriveth from that relation, "which are, with great propriety, called his birthright. This birthright "nothing but his own demerit can deprive him of. It is indefeasible and "perpetual; and, consequently, the duty of allegiance, which ariseth out "of it, and is inseparably connected with it, is, in consideration of law, "likewise unalienable and perpetual." Now, there are various kinds of treason. There may be the act known as compassing the King's death; it may be levying war against the King; or it may be that form of treason with which you are concerned in this case, the only one, therefore, with which you need trouble yourselves. The history of the law of treason in this country is of extreme interest. It shows that throughout centuries there has always been the attempt made, and successful attempt in many cases, to protect the liberty of the subject against encroachments of their liberty, and particularly in much more remote periods fortunately against encroachments of the Crown. Statutes have been passed of which you have heard some read. I only mean to refer to that portion of the law which is applicable to the case now before you in order to tell you that the law requires in this case that the overt acts (and I will explain to you what they mean in a moment) which are charged against the prisoner should be proved by two witnesses to an overt act, or one witness to one overt act, and another witness to another overt act, both of the same form of treason. In this case you need not trouble yourselves about that direction, except to bear in mind when you are considering the evidence and determining whether you can rely upon it that there must be two witnesses to an overt act in order to justify you in finding the prisoner guilty—either two witnesses to one overt act or one witness to one and another witness to another overt act, both of the same treason.

You may say, and probably have asked yourselves during the course of the case, what are overt acts? Overt acts are such acts as manifest a criminal intention and tend towards the accomplishment of the criminal object. They are acts by which the purpose is manifested and the means by which it is intended to be fulfilled. According to our law it is necessary in charging a prisoner with this offence to state in the indictment the overt acts upon which reliance is placed; and, again, the greatest care is taken that a man shall not be taken by surprise in a charge of this character; and the law says that no evidence shall be given of any overt act which is not charged in the indictment; the full effect, therefore, being

Lord Chief Justice

that when the prisoner comes into Court to answer the indictment of treason he has the particulars given to him in writing, and at some time before he comes into Court, in order that he may be ready to defend himself. Gentlemen, I am not going to read to you the overt acts, for the reason that they can be summarised, I think, very briefly. You may divide them into two parts, the first part dealing with what I may call the Irish Brigade incidents, the second part dealing with the 21st April, 1916, and the incidents connected with that date. It is quite possible for you to come to the conclusion—it is entirely for you—that both of the sets of overt acts are really part and parcel of the same scheme and of the same set of operations. The first five overt acts alleged deal with the period between December, 1914, and February, 1915. The substance of the charge is that the prisoner solicited and incited and endeavoured to persuade soldiers of the King to forsake their allegiance and to join the armed forces of the enemy, and to fight against the King; further, the charge is of circulating and distributing a leaflet, to which I will direct your attention later, with the object of soliciting, inciting, and persuading the Irish soldiers to forsake their duty to the King and to aid and assist the enemy in the prosecution of the war against the King; and then another form of the same charge is that of, in fact, persuading and procuring certain persons—some of them are named, Bailey, Quinless, O'Callaghan, Keogh, Cavanagh, Greer, Scanlan, and others whose names are unknown, to the number of about fifty, to forsake their allegiance to the King and to join the forces of the enemy with a view to fight against the King and his subjects in the war. That substantially deals with what I call, for convenience and brevity, the Irish Brigade incidents. The second part of the charge is that in April, 1916, the prisoner set forth from Germany as a member of a warlike and hostile expedition undertaken and equipped by the enemies of the King, having for its object the introduction into and landing on the coast of Ireland of arms and ammunition intended for use in the prosecution of the war by the enemies against the King.

Now, gentlemen, when considering your verdict you will also bear in mind that if one overt act out of the six alleged is, in your judgment, proved against the prisoner, that means a verdict of guilty. It is not necessary that you should find that all six overt acts are proved. You may, in your opinion, come to the conclusion that all six are proved, or that only some or one of them can be proved. If you do, that is sufficient to constitute treason. One overt act properly proved is all that is necessary to constitute the offence.

The last observation I will make to you upon the law is that you must be satisfied before you convict the prisoner of the intention and purpose of the act. We were told by Mr. Sullivan yesterday that you had to arrive at the mind of the prisoner, and he suggested that it was difficult, almost impossible, for an Englishman to divine what was passing in the mind of an Irishman, or to understand it. You never really can get at the actual thought passing through a man's mind, except by considering his actions, including, of course, his statements. A man's intentions are to be gathered from his acts. A man must be held to have intended the natural and reasonable consequences of his act. That is one of the fundamental principles of our law, and, after all, it is only plain common sense. When a man, particularly an intelligent man, does an act which would appear reasonably to involve certain consequences you are entitled to assume that he intended those consequences. You therefore have to ask yourselves, did he do an act or acts of the nature which I have described to you, of adhering to the King's enemies, giving aid and comfort to the King's enemies? And you must ask yourselves, did he intend the reasonable consequences of this act? I will put it to you again so that you may understand it quite clearly. You have to determine whether the prisoner was contriving and intending to aid and assist the enemy. If what he did was calculated to aid and assist the enemy, and he knew it was so calculated, then, although he had another or ulterior purpose in view, he was contriving and intending to assist the enemy. It is necessary you should pay particular attention to this direction, which is a direction of law to you. The questions of fact upon it, of course, you will determine for yourselves, but it is necessary that you should understand that if what he did was calculated to aid the enemy, and if he knew or must have known that it was so calculated, then, he would be contriving and intending to assist the enemy, notwithstanding that he had another or ulterior purpose in view. Let me put it to you in another way. If he knew or believed that the German authorities were taking the steps they did in collecting the Irish prisoners into one camp, distributing literature amongst them, forming an Irish Brigade, and providing them with uniforms, &c., for their own purpose, and to serve their own ends in the war, and he in concert with them was promoting the enterprise, then he was contriving and intending to assist the enemy, though he had another purpose to serve. If he knew or believed that the Irish Brigade was to be sent to Ireland during the war with a view to securing the national freedom of Ireland, that is, to engage in a civil war which would necessarily weaken and embarrass this country, then he was contriving and intending to assist the enemy. Gentlemen, I trust I have made clear to you what is the meaning of contriving and intending to assist the enemy, and how you must judge it.

I propose now to consider very briefly the evidence which has been given. Again, I must point out to you that the statement which was made by the prisoner yesterday was a statement which was not made on oath, and it is right that I should also tell you that it was open to the prisoner, if he chose to avail himself of the opportunity, to go into the witness-box and give evidence. Let me deal with the facts. I am not going to read the evidence to you, because in substance, except for one point to which I have called your attention, there is no real dispute about it. I will only read such passages as deal very closely with the controversial element. I am now going to direct your attention to the evidence in the case more particularly to help you to determine whether the inducements held out by the prisoner to the Irish Brigade were to go to Ireland after the war had come to a close in order to resist the domination of the north of Ireland party, the Volunteers, or whether, as the Crown contends, the inducement held out was to go to Ireland after the first sea victory of the Germans to fight England, to free Ireland from England, and with the assistance of Germany. It is only in regard for the moment to that question that I am going to read to you certain passages of the evidence.

The story as to what happened is now quite beyond dispute. At some time before the end of December, 1914, the prisoner is found in Germany whilst Germany is engaged in this gigantic and terrible war with this country among others. How the prisoner, a British subject, came there, why he was there, or for what purpose he was allowed during this time to remain in Germany, if he was there any time, we do not know. We do know that in December, 1914, there had been a number of soldiers taken prisoner during the war; that the Irish soldiers—men supposed to be Irish, as one witness explained it, probably meaning that everybody was not known to be Irish, but generally they were—were gathered together in one camp. You have heard how they were taken from particular camps and brought to this camp at Limburg Lahn, and whilst at that camp the prisoner came to them. They were then suffering all the torment no doubt of a prisoner of war. This man addressed them. I will not comment upon the language that he used. I will read it to you according to the testimony of the witnesses. It is for you to judge whether that language was not calculated and intended to seduce these men from allegiance to their Sovereign. You may ask, and not unreasonably, how comes it that when these prisoners are segregated into the one camp that the prisoner, Sir Roger Casement, is introduced into that camp or allowed to enter into it by the Germans? He could not get there without their permission. He was there, according to the evidence, coming and going freely according to his own will, and addressing these prisoners of war. You are asked to believe that that was because the Germans thought that the effect of his addressing them might be that a number of these British soldiers would become members of the brigade which would be known as the Irish Brigade, formed for the purpose, at any rate, I will assume for the moment, of being taken to Ireland and of fighting for Ireland only. But you may ask, what would the effect of the formation of that brigade be upon Germany and upon the British Empire? The Attorney-General said to you, apart altogether from military effect, that the mere result of British soldiers having formed into a brigade in Germany, not to fight for England, because nobody suggests that, but to be equipped with arms and ammunition by Germany, and then to go to Ireland, if announced, if known, must create injury to this country; that it is calculated to strengthen Germany, because it would show the success that had happened in Germany over British prisoners of war, and would tend to weaken this country, because it would be shown that our soldiers were not to be relied upon, and that when they were taken prisoners of war they then yielded to the seduction in the German camp. You must consider for yourselves whether the Attorney-General's observations are well warranted in that when he says, "Conceive the effect either upon "belligerents or upon neutrals in any war," meaning, conceive the effect as reflected upon Germany or reflected upon England.

Gentlemen, the passages of the evidence have been read to you, I am afraid, more than once. The very short passages to which I am going to call your attention I read because they are so important on this part of the case. Because if you come to the conclusion that the true view of the facts is that the prisoner was soliciting and attempting to persuade these prisoners of war to join the Irish Brigade to be landed in Ireland after the first sea victory of Germany, and if you come to the conclusion that that does not mean after the war had come to an end, then, you will probably think that the Attorney-General has made good his contention; and it is for the purpose of enabling you to come to a conclusion on that that I read these very short passages. Cronin was called, the soldier. This is his statement[1]—"Sir Roger Casement said "he was going to form an Irish Brigade, and he said, 'Why live in "'hunger and misery in this camp when you can better yourselves by "'joining the Irish Brigade which I am going to form; you will be sent "'to Berlin as the guests of the German Government.' . . . He said "in the event of Germany winning a sea battle he would land them in "Ireland," and then, according to the shorthand note, "and Ireland would "equip them." I do not think that is a true transcript of the note. I will treat it as struck out, and read it, "He said in the event of "Germany winning a sea battle he would land them in Ireland." It does not matter for the purposes of the case whether it is right or wrong.

What were they to do in Ireland?—Free Ireland.

Did he say who they were to fight against?—Against England.

Did he say what would happen to them if Germany did not win?—They would be sent to America. They would get £10 or £20 pocket money and a free passage

That is Cronin's statement. You remember Cronin. He was the first of the soldiers called. You remember his giving evidence, and you will judge whether there is anything that has happened in this case which should lead you to disbelieve Cronin. You must judge whether his evidence is reliable or not. Then he was cross-examined. The use of cross-examination is for the purpose of enabling you to test the evidence of the witness. The cross-examination on this part of the case is to this effect[2]—

Did he speak of raising the Irish Brigade in Limburg in connection with the Irish Volunteers in Ireland?—Yes.

Did he say that they would fight in Ireland?—Yes.

That they were to fight in Ireland?—Yes.

And for Ireland?—Yes.

And for nobody else?—For nobody else, only for Ireland.

Did he say they were to be landed in Ireland after the war was over?—No; in the event of Germany winning a sea battle.

In the event of Germany winning a sea battle they might be landed before the war was over?—The war could not be over till the sea battle was won.

Did not he speak of Germany having won the war before the brigade was to move to Ireland?—No.

But the seas were to be clear before the brigade was to go to Ireland?—Yes.

That is the whole of the evidence of Cronin upon this point. Gentlemen, when you are considering the testimony of a witness you may think, and it is entirely for you, that you place more reliance upon the actual words used by the witness himself than words which are put into his mouth. That is entirely for you. A witness comes, and he tells his own story in his own language, according to his own recollection, and then questions are put to him perfectly legitimately and properly in cross-examination

---

[1] P. 17. [2] P. 20.

which may be a variation of the form in which the witness has given his answer. You have to consider the whole of the evidence together and form an opinion as to whether his statement on this point was reliable or not.

The next witness was O'Brien. His evidence upon the point is to this effect. He, that is the prisoner, came in February, 1915.[1]

I heard him say, "Now is the time for Irishmen to fight against England; now is their opportunity for doing so, join the Irish Brigade." He said he came to form an Irish Brigade, and he wanted all Irishmen to join the Irish Brigade and become guests of the German Army. He said that if they were successful in winning the war they would land the Irish Brigade along with the German Army in Ireland, and they would fight against England there. If Germany did not win the war, then they would be sent by the German Government to America with a guarantee of £5 and a situation.

You must consider there the meaning of this statement if you accept it, "They would land the Irish Brigade with the German Army in Ireland." Then in cross-examination he is asked[2]—

In what you did hear, did he speak of the Irish Brigade fighting in Ireland?—Yes.

Did he say the Irish Brigade would be used in Ireland only?—In Ireland.

Did he say they were to be transferred to Ireland when Germany had won the war?—Yes.

And if Germany failed to win the war they should go to America?—To America, yes.

Then, again, in re-examination[3]—

He said the Irish Brigade were to fight in Ireland?—Yes.

Did he say who were to take them to Ireland to fight?—The German Army.

Did he say against whom they were to fight?—To fight against England.

That is the evidence of O'Brien. The next witness is John Robinson. He says[4]—

He said he was very glad to see so many Irishmen here, that now was our time to fight for Ireland and strike a blow, and he hoped we would all join the Irish Brigade.

Examination continued—Did he say with whom the Irish Brigade were going to fight?—Fight against England. He said that if Germany had a victory on the sea they would land the Irish Brigade in Ireland.

Then in cross-examination[5]—

How long was Sir Roger Casement speaking on the occasions you have detailed to us—the first time you heard him speak, for instance?—About a quarter of an hour to twenty minutes.

He wanted you to join an Irish Brigade?—Yes.

Did he say that the Irish Brigade was to fight for Ireland?—Yes.

Did he say it was to fight in Ireland?—Yes.

And did he address you? Did he say it was to go to Ireland when the Germans had won the war?—No, he said if Germany had a victory on sea.

Did he speak about Germany winning the war?—Yes.

What did he say about Germany winning the war?—He always said that Germany would win, but we contradicted him and said they would not.

I suggest to you that he represented when Germany had won the war that the Irish Brigade was to go to Ireland unless there was a victory at sea meantime. Was that what he said?—I cannot remember that. I remember him saying if Germany had a victory on sea he would land us in Ireland.

But there is no doubt it was in Ireland you were to serve?—Oh, yes, at that time.

---

[1] P. 23. [2] P. 24. [3] P. 25. [4] P. 26. [5] P. 27.

Lord Chief Justice's Summing Up.

Then there is one further passage in re-examination[1]—

Did he say who would send the Irish Brigade to Ireland?—Germany would send us to Ireland.

Did he say what they were to do when they got there?—Free Ireland.

Did he say whether they would have any fighting to do?—He did not go into that; he said it was to free Ireland when they got there.

Did he say from whom they were to free Ireland?—From England.

Then there was one more witness, Michael O'Connor[2]—

Can you tell us anything you heard him say?—He said, "Now is the time to fight "or strike a blow for Ireland," and that England was nearly beaten.

Then there was some evidence about hissing and booing him along the lines.

Did he make any remark to those that hissed him and booed him?—He said those who hissed him were followers of Johnnie Redmond, the recruiting sergeant of the British Army.

That is a statement by the witness which did not seem to have so much force when it was made in the witness-box. It is not so unimportant. It is for you to consider whether that was said, because if it was said, that is to say, "Those who hissed him were followers of Johnnie Redmond, "the recruiting sergeant of the British Army," it does not seem quite to tally with the suggestion that is made that the prisoner was seeking to obtain recruits for the Irish Volunteers to resist attacks or domination by the Ulster Volunteers in Ireland after the war. That is a matter for your consideration. I merely make the observation to you, this reference to Johnnie Redmond, "the recruiting sergeant of the British Army." Then he is cross-examined[3]—

If England was nearly beaten, was not it in the context that the war was nearly over?—Yes.

Do you assent to that?—I assent to that.

The war being nearly over, he was recruiting an Irish Brigade?—Yes.

Then the next witness is Michael Moore[4]—

He also said the first German victory on the water he would land the Brigade in Ireland.

Did he say what kind of victory?—Naval victory. The Irish Brigade were to be landed in Ireland.

And then he said he expected, and I stopped him and said he must not tell us what he expected, and he said, "He said he would land them in "Ireland." Then in cross-examination he says[5]—

Apparently, Sir Roger Casement discussed what was to happen to the Irish Brigade if Germany lost the war, did not he?—Yes.

In that event the Irish Brigade would go to America?—Yes.

If Germany lost the war? I suggest to you that he said that he would land them in Ireland if Germany won the war?—If there was a sea battle, and if Germany came out victorious in the first sea battle he would land the Irish Brigade in Ireland.

Was there no reference to Home Rule in the event of Germany winning the war; was there no reference to Home Rule?—There was one, that Germany would give Ireland Home Rule.

If she won the war?—If she won the war.

But do you tell me that there was no reference to Home Rule to be won by the Irish Brigade?—No.

Are you sure of that?—I have never heard him say it.

---

[1] P. 29. [2] P. 32. [3] P. 33. [4] P. 34. [5] P. 34.

That is all that there is in this connection. I will not read Neill's evidence.

Now, gentlemen, you have got really the whole of the evidence which you need consider upon this point. It is not suggested to you that you should disbelieve these witnesses entirely. Indeed, Mr. Sullivan has told you that he accepts in the main the evidence that was given, and the only point upon which he does ask you to disregard their evidence is as to that part of it in which they say that they were to be landed in Ireland if Germany or as soon as Germany won a sea victory. Mr. Sullivan argued that that really meant the same thing as saying "If the war was over." But it is clear at any rate that that was not the view of the soldiers, or some of them, because of the answers which I have read, and of which you will judge, because when the question is put to them about the close of the war, at least one or two said, "Oh, no, not at the close of the war, if "Germany won the first sea victory."

In this connection there is one document to which I must call your attention. It is a document as to which there was some controversy during the course of the trial, the document known as exhibit No. 4. It is a leaflet which was distributed. There is no evidence in this case directly connecting Sir Roger Casement with this document. There is evidence that after Sir Roger Casement had come upon the scene and had made a speech or speeches of the character stated in the evidence that this leaflet was distributed amongst the Irish prisoners of war in Limburg Camp. There is evidence that some of these leaflets were posted up in the barrack room. There is evidence that the men gathered round and read them. There is evidence that German soldiers brought this leaflet in and introduced it in the camp. You will remember that evidence. I am not proposing therefore to read it to you. But this is the leaflet, and in considering whether or not the prisoner was acting with Germany for the purpose of seducing these men from their allegiance you must take into account this document given in evidence, that is to say, it is a matter which you must consider. Discard it if you like. If you think right to say, "Well, we are not satisfied upon "this, that Sir Roger Casement had anything to do with it, or knew of it," you are quite entitled, then, if you come to that conclusion, to disregard it. But equally, if you think, looking at the matter fairly, and drawing a fair and reasonable inference from the circumstances stated in the evidence, that, although it was distributed by Germans after Sir Roger Casement came upon the scene, it was part of the plan of operations between the Germans and the prisoner Casement, then, you must take it into your serious consideration.

This is the language of it—"Irishmen, here is a chance for you to fight "for Ireland! You have fought for England, your country's hereditary "enemy. You have fought for Belgium in England's interest, though it was "no more to you than the Fiji Islands! Are you willing to fight for your "own country with a view to securing the national freedom of Ireland? "With the moral and material assistance of the German Government an "Irish Brigade is being formed"—you must consider that passage—"with a view to securing the national freedom of Ireland." You must consider whether that meant to free Ireland from England during the war, or whether it meant only to free one political party, what I may call the Home Rule Party in Ireland, and all those persons in Ireland who held the same view, from the domination of the Ulster movement in Ireland, which is what is suggested: whether that simply means—it is the object of every man to secure his own freedom so that he may defend himself against Volunteers who may be marching up and down, as you have heard described, in the country and possibly over the lands of these persons. "With a view to securing the national "freedom of Ireland, with the moral and material assistance of the German "Government an Irish Brigade is being formed." That seems to show beyond all doubt on the face of the document that there was material assistance of the German Government. Then comes this passage—"The "object of the Irish Brigade shall be to fight solely the cause of Ireland, "and under no circumstances shall it be directed to any German end." What is suggested and what you have to consider is, that may be a very good way of getting Irishmen to join the Irish Brigade, particularly men who had been soldiers, with the notion that they would only be fighting for Ireland. You must consider whether if a man was fighting for Ireland during the war it was possible to do that against England without giving aid and comfort to the King's enemies. You will come to a conclusion as to what you think that means. Then it proceeds—"The Irish Brigade "shall be formed, and shall fight under the Irish flag alone; the men shall "wear a special distinctively Irish uniform and have Irish officers. The "Irish Brigade shall be clothed, fed, and efficiently equipped with arms "and ammunition by the German Government. It will be stationed near "Berlin, and be treated as guests of the German Government." You must ask yourselves, again, why Germany should be ready to feed and equip and clothe these men, provide them with uniforms, and with arms and with ammunition, if the sole object of the Brigade was to resist the march and counter-march and domination of an opposed political party, of the Ulster Volunteers. It is not very easy to understand what the suggestion is with regard to that. You must consider it for yourselves. Why should Germany be ready to do this? If it was to happen during the war, it is comprehensible, enough. It would be to the interest of Germany, because it would be sowing seeds of dissension of the strongest kind in Ireland. But why, if it was only to happen after the war, when war between this country and Germany had come to an end, Germany should be interested in doing these acts to enable, what I may call for brevity, Home Rulers to get the benefit of the Home Rule Act, is not quite easy to understand. There it is. It is for you to consider. Then, "At the "end of the war the German Government undertakes to send each member "of the Brigade who may so desire it to the United States of America "with necessary means to land. The Irishmen in America are collecting "money for the Brigade. Those men who do not join the Irish Brigade "will be removed from Limburg and distributed among other camps. If "interested, see your company commanders. Join the Irish Brigade and "win Ireland's independence! Remember Bachelor's Walk! God save "Ireland!"

Gentlemen, that really is the whole of the evidence to which it is necessary that I should call your attention on these first five overt acts which are connected with what I have termed compendiously the Irish Brigade incident. I now proceed to deal with the evidence as regards the April, 1916, incidents. Before I do so, let me tell you that the mere fact that the prisoner had, by the acts proved in the evidence, committed an offence or offences against the law is not relevant to this charge. The facts relating to the 21st April, and for the few days thereafter, are only material to this charge if you think that these acts were committed in concert with Germany in pursuance of a plan of operations formed in Germany. If you come to that conclusion, then these acts are directly material on the charge of treason.

Now, the first incident is on the night between the 20th and 21st April. There is the finding of the boat and the seeing of the light. A light is seen about half-past nine on the Thursday night, whatever it is. We know no more than that. On the morning of Good Friday, the 21st April, M'Carthy, the farmer, the man who had been to the well to say his prayers, noticed the boat; he also found the tin box which had been covered with earth, according to his statement, but from which the earth had been displaced; he also saw the footprints of three men; he traced them going in the direction of his house from the sea. Later he found his little girl, about eight years of age, playing with revolvers. There are the bags which are discovered shortly after. In those bags there was the green flag which was produced to you, and a piece of a map, and in other bags other portions of a map of Ireland. Mary Gorman, at about half-past four in the morning, saw three strange men passing, going from the sea and going towards Ardfert. She identified one of the men as the prisoner, and said they were carrying overcoats. Where the boat came from we do not know. There is no evidence to show how that boat had got to the point where it was found. You have seen the photograph of it. You realise the kind of boat it is. It was there with the ammunition and the pistols and the other things, again there is nothing to show except the evidence of their being found as described to you by the witnesses. The tin box contained some 900 rounds of pistol ammunition. There was a flash lamp, field glasses, 40 rounds of ammunition in a bag, and three pistols.

I do not propose to follow through the incidents of taking the various things that were found to the police station. It really does not help. That is all for the purpose merely of identification. Later on the prisoner is found at about twenty minutes past one in the afternoon of 21st April, Good Friday, at M'Kenna's Fort. But before that the two officers, Riley and Sergeant Hearn, had loaded their carbines and gone out to search the country. After searching the country for some little time they came to M'Kenna's Fort, which you have heard described to you. It seems to be a circular Irish ruin. It was described as with trenches round it, or a trench 9 to 14 feet deep, and covered with brushwood. Riley has told you that he saw the prisoner, that he covered him with his rifle, and that thereupon he was asked who he was, and he gave the name of Richard Morton, Denham, Bucks. He said he had arrived at Dublin, came on to County Kerry, then to Mount Brandon, and from there to the fort, and had arrived there, that is, at the fort, in the morning, and said he intended to go to Tralee. The whole of this incident requires your careful examination and consideration. You must ask yourselves why was it

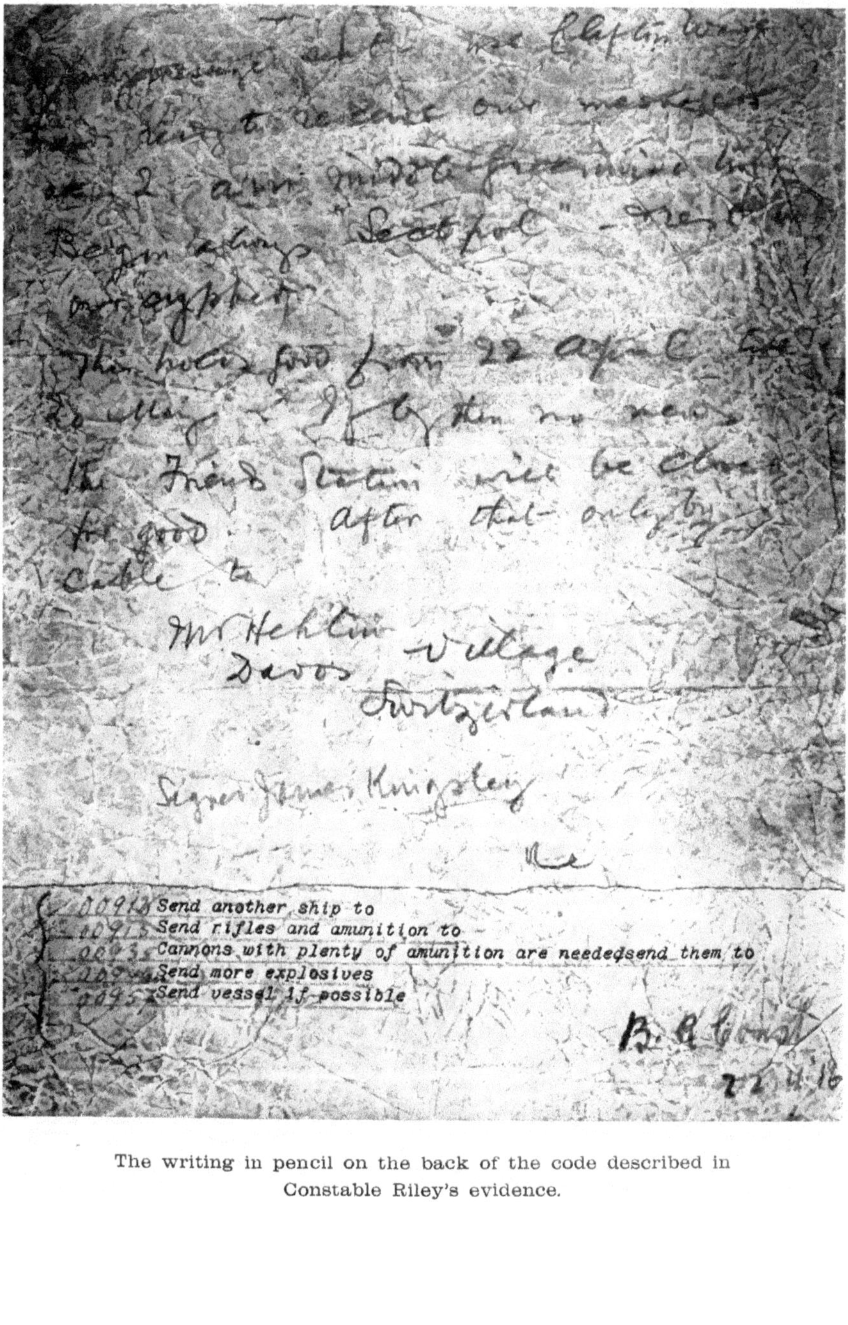

[illegible]
[illegible] our messages
[illegible] middle [illegible]
Begin always "[illegible]" [illegible]
our cypher
This holds good from 22 April to
[illegible] May. If by then no news
the Friend Station will be closed
for good after that only by
Cable to

Mr Hehler Village
Davos
Switzerland

Signed James Kingsley

0091 Send another ship to
0091 Send rifles and amunition to
0093 Cannons with plenty of amunition are neededsend them to
009 Send more explosives
0095 Send vessel if possible

B. A. Const
22.4.16

The writing in pencil on the back of the code described in Constable Riley's evidence.

Lord Chief Justice's Summing Up.

Lord Chief Justice

that the prisoner arrived in this way in Ireland? Why was it he arrived in this boat with this ammunition, and was found afterwards at this fort where, according to his own statement, he had been for some hours, and why did he give a false name? The boy Collins who was called before you told you about the piece of paper that he saw drop from the prisoner's hand at his back, and it was subsequently picked up by the boy. He went on with his pony and trap, as he was told to do, or asked to do, I think, to Mary Gorman's for the purpose of Mary Gorman identifying the prisoner as one of the three men she had seen. Then he goes back at some later stage with another boy, or has another boy with him, Tom Doone, and he tells Doone to pick up that piece of paper which was, he says, where it had been dropped; it was given to him, and then he took it back and handed it to the police. That piece of paper is exhibit 18, of which you have a photograph. That is the code. You remember the evidence about that code. There are the figures first, and then the words in English showing what the figures meant. You have heard the criticism which has been passed upon that code by the Attorney-General. Reference has been made to the various orders that there are, or requests, and you are asked to say that that cannot have been done with any innocent intention, but, moreover, and what is more material and important, can only have been done in concert with Germany, and that the object of this code, and of the carrying of this code by the prisoner, was to enable him to send messages somewhere to some one which could not be given openly, which had to be given in a code which nobody could understand, and therefore these figures were adopted in the code so that the person receiving them should know what was meant and nobody else. Your attention was directed to just a few of the sentences or part sentences—"Further ammunition is needed. Further rifles are needed. How many "rifles will you send us? How much ammunition will you send us? "Will send plan about landing. Await details about sending. Send "another ship to . Send rifles and ammunition. Cannons "and plenty of ammunition are needed. Send them. Send more "explosives. Send vessel if possible."

Those are some of the salient features of this code. Then there is the statement, which is rather difficult to decipher, at the back of the document, which says—"This holds good from 22nd April till 20th May. "If by then no news, friends' station will be closed for good, after that "only by cable to," then an address, Davos Village, Switzerland. You must ask yourselves what is the meaning of that? Why was the prisoner carrying it? And, more important, why did he drop it in that way when the police arrested him? There was also evidence of the finding of a piece of paper at the place where he had been, which has no relevancy to the matter into which you are inquiring, except that it is written in German characters and in the German language. Then there is further the finding of the sleeping car ticket from Berlin to Wilhelmshaven. That is a ticket for the night of the 11th to the 12th April, and is quite clearly a ticket issued by the German railway, and apparently to Wilhelmshaven. That was found, you will remember, in the pocket of one of three overcoats. There is nothing to show that that was the prisoner

Casement's overcoat. It is only evidence that it is one of the three. You will also bear in mind in this connection that there was some evidence—you must judge of the value of it—that in the figures on the code which were to be used as the cypher, the "7" is a German "7," or at least a "7" such as is usually written in German. It is rather striking if you look through it, as I have no doubt you have done, that all these "7's" are made in that particular way, and certainly not as a "7" is usually written in this country.

From all that evidence you are asked to draw the inference, and if you think right you are entitled to draw the inference, that the prisoner had come from Germany; that he was acting in concert with the Germans. In this connection you naturally would ask yourselves, how is it that Germany allowed this man, and at least one other, who has been identified, and who was in the Irish Brigade, to leave Germany and to land, if you are satisfied they did land, from that boat on this wild seashore in Ireland? The suggestion made to you is that, of course, it was permitted because it was part of the plan of operation.

Later in the day of the 21st April, somewhere about six o'clock in the evening, in the Atlantic Ocean, about 90 miles from the southern coast of Ireland, the vessel "Aud" is discovered. She was sighted by H.M.S. "Bluebell" off the south-west coast. She was painted with Norwegian colours, two forward and two aft. She was signalled by the "Bluebell," and she replied that she was bound for Genoa from Bergen. The "Bluebell" thereupon told her to follow. You remember the incident, the firing of the shot across her bows, and then she followed. The "Bluebell" was taking her to Queenstown. Queenstown was about 138 miles, as was described, to the east of the spot where the "Aud" was found. Due east clearly not, as Mr. Sullivan was quite right in contending. It is apparent to any one with very little knowledge of Ireland that this vessel would have to go further to the southward and then turn to the east to get to Queenstown. Then when she is within 3½ miles of Queenstown she seemed to stop her engines, and then a cloud of white smoke appeared; two boats were lowered; flags of truce were carried in these boats; in these boats were twenty German bluejackets and three officers, two of them being identified as German naval officers; and they are taken on board the "Bluebell" as prisoners of war. Within a very few minutes, some ten minutes, of the cloud of white smoke being seen the "Aud" blows up and sinks. We have the evidence of Dempsey, the diver, of what he found when he went there, I think, on 10th May or about that time. He produced to us here in Court a rifle which, he said, was typical of a number of rifles which he saw there, not pledging himself to this one rifle being exactly like the others, but he said all similar in pattern; and that has been identified by the colonel in the Russian Army as a rifle of the Imperial Service of Russia made in the year 1905. A cartridge and clip were also produced to us. The clip is made in Russia, and identified as being the clip that was used by the Imperial Service. The cartridge is not identified because, as the colonel told us, it has not the marks on it which he would expect to find if it had been made in the Russian Service; but it is a cartridge which he says would fit the Russian rifle. Rifle butts were found, and one of them was produced to you here in Court. A bayonet sheath was also produced, of which, as far as one knows, there is very little evidence. It seems to have come from South America, but, at any rate, we do not know. That is the safest way to put it. I ought to have told you—it comes in at this moment—that just before the vessel sank and before the white smoke was seen to issue—about that time—two flags were broken at the masthead, and they were then seen to be German naval ensigns.

Upon that evidence you are asked to conclude that this vessel was not a vessel bound from Bergen to Genoa, but that she was, in fact, a German vessel, or a vessel used for German purposes, and that she was painted with Norwegian colours in order to deceive the ever-vigilant British Navy; that she was engaged in an operation of landing arms and ammunition in Ireland, because besides the cartridge that was produced, Dempsey told us there were thousands of cartridges which he saw lying by the ship when he went to the bottom of the sea. He was only able to conduct his operations for one day, or at one time, because the weather got very bad, and then he had to abandon it. But that is what he told you he saw. He described it as "thousands of cartridges "lying about in the neighbourhood of the ship," and the question for you upon this is, whether you think right to draw the inference that this vessel was engaged in this operation for the Germans of landing arms and ammunition in Ireland. It is said she was not going to Genoa. What would she be doing at Genoa with these old rifles and ammunition? Why was she painted in this way? When you get the two naval ensigns at the masthead, at least, it makes it quite plain that she was engaged in German and naval matters. If there remained any doubt about it, the fact that twenty German bluejackets and two officers were on board and taken prisoners of war, puts the matter beyond all doubt.

You may very naturally say to yourselves, well, how perfectly absurd to suggest that a vessel of this kind was going from Bergen to Genoa carrying these German sailors, naval men, and German officers with all this ammunition. Of course, if this vessel were found hundreds or thousands of miles from Ireland that would not justify you in coming to the conclusion that they were intended for Ireland, but when she is found, as she was, 90 miles from the south-west coast of Ireland on the evening of this very 21st April, Good Friday, you probably will ask yourselves, was it a pure coincidence that that vessel happened to be there so soon after the prisoner Casement and another man had been seen in Ireland with all the attendant circumstances which I have already described to you, and which you have heard stated in evidence? The Crown says to you it is not a coincidence. The Crown says this is part of the concerted operation which was then taking place; it was all in pursuance of the scheme, of a similar scheme which had been formed from December, 1914, to February, 1915, and onwards, when these speeches were made by the prisoner, to get Irish soldiers to join the Irish Brigade. They suggest to you that this is not a mere chance, that Germany should just at that moment and on that day have been engaged in landing arms or in attempting to land arms and ammunition at some point on the coast of Ireland. It is not suggested, and certainly the evidence does not establish, that this vessel was going to

Lord Chief Justice

Tralee. But that really does not matter at all. It is quite immaterial to what points in Ireland she was going if you come to the conclusion that she was making for Ireland and intending to land there when she found a favourable opportunity in order to put her arms and ammunition on the shore. That matter is entirely one for you. It is purely a matter of fact. I can give you no direction on law about it except the one I have already given to you, and that is, that if on this evidence you think fit to draw the inference the Crown asks you to draw, you are entitled to do it. If you think that it is not sufficient, you are entitled to reject it. It is entirely for you.

Now, gentlemen, the only other incident in connection with this matter that is worth referring to is the maps. We have not examined them, but they are here in Court. There are a number of portions of a map of Ireland which were put together by Colonel Gordon, and, as he has told you, they contain evidence, according to the view that he presented to you, that they were not made in this country, because he said the meridian was numbered from Ferro, and not from Greenwich, and also because the scale was slightly different from that adopted in this country. The meridian of Ferro, he told us, is used in the maps of Central Europe, and that is as far as we can get with it, and there we must leave it. It all forms part and parcel of the one story which is suggested to you in connection with this matter, and if on consideration, having regard to the evidence that has been given, drawing such inferences as you think are fair and reasonable inferences to be drawn in the circumstances, you come to the conclusion that the position of the "Aud" at this time, really synchronising as it did with the advent of the prisoner a little earlier in the morning on the coast of Curraghane, all pointed to an attempt to land arms and ammunition for the purpose of assisting Germany by helping those who wished either to create discontent, or, it might be, to rebel in Ireland, and that if there were such persons, and Germany could manage to land her arms and ammunition at that time, it would all be very useful, and would assist in that way, and consequently would be a weakening of the forces of the King, then you would draw the inference the Crown asks you to draw. That is the substance of this matter, and it is not necessary that I should read to you in any detail or at any length the evidence upon it.

Gentlemen, that really concludes the whole of the evidence in this case. I have already said to you all that I think it necessary to say upon the law. I shall not repeat it. I will conclude only by impressing upon you that if you have a reasonable doubt in the matter after considering the evidence it is your duty to acquit the prisoner. But if, after viewing all the facts and circumstances, the conviction is borne in upon you that this prisoner has committed the offence with which he is charged, then, gentlemen, it is your duty to return a verdict to that effect, and to take no regard of the consequences which must follow. Will you consider your verdict?

Mr. Justice Avory—Gentlemen, if you want any of the exhibits that have been referred to you can have them by asking.

The jury retired at 2.53 p.m.

Lord Chief Justice's Summing Up.

The Lord Chief Justice—There is some request about a map. There is no map of Ireland that has been proved in the case except the one to which Colonel Gordon deposed.

Mr. Bodkin—Except the one which is in pieces.

The Lord Chief Justice—The jury would like to see the original code found and an authentic specimen of the initials and signature of the prisoner. None such has been proved. The original code, of course, they can have. That we will send in to them. They also ask for an original copy of the circular posted at Limburg Camp, but I understand that was not proved.

Mr. Artemus Jones—No.

The Attorney-General—I think there is a specimen of the signature and handwriting of the prisoner, the letter written when he received his knighthood, exhibit 32.

The Lord Chief Justice—That is quite true. I think it is better not to put it in. I think really what they want is the initials. One sees why they may have been asking for it. I think it better to treat it that there is no evidence of it and leave it there. The original code, exhibit 18, shall be sent in, and also the map.

At a later stage,

The Lord Chief Justice—The jury have asked for a copy of the indictment, which we will send them, and they also ask for a copy of the evidence, but we do not propose to send that.

The Attorney-General—If your lordship pleases.

The jury returned into Court at 3.48.

The King's Coroner—Gentlemen of the jury, will you answer to your names?

The names of the jury were called over.

The King's Coroner—Are you agreed upon your verdict?

The Foreman of the Jury—We are.

The King's Coroner—How say you; do you find the prisoner, Sir Roger David Casement, guilty or not guilty of the high treason whereof he stands indicted?

The Foreman of the Jury—Guilty.

The King's Coroner—You find Sir Roger David Casement guilty of high treason, and is that the verdict of you all?

The Foreman of the Jury—Yes.

The King's Coroner—Sir Roger David Casement, you stand convicted of high treason. What have you to say for yourself why the Court should not pass sentence and judgment upon you to die according to law?

The Prisoner—My Lord Chief Justice, as I wish to reach a much wider audience than I see before me here, I intended to read all that I propose to say. What I shall read now is something I wrote more than twenty days ago. I may say, my lord, at once, that I protest against the jurisdiction

Sir Roger Casement

of this Court in my case on this charge, and the argument that I am now going to read is addressed not to this Court, but to my own countrymen.

There is an objection, possibly not good in law, but surely good on moral grounds, against the application to me here of this old English statute, 565 years old, that seeks to deprive an Irishman to-day of life and honour, not for "adhering to the King's enemies," but for adhering to his own people.

When this statute was passed, in 1351, what was the state of men's minds on the question of a far higher allegiance—that of a man to God and His kingdom? The law of that day did not permit a man to forsake his church or deny his God save with his life. The "heretic" then had the same doom as the "traitor."

To-day a man may forswear God and His heavenly kingdom without fear or penalty, all earlier statutes having gone the way of Nero's Edicts against the Christians, but that Constitutional phantom, "The King," can still dig up from the dungeons and torture chambers of the Dark Ages a law that takes a man's life and limb for an exercise of conscience.

If true religion rests on love, it is equally true that loyalty rests on love. The law I am charged under has no parentage in love and claims the allegiance of to-day on the ignorance and blindness of the past.

I am being tried, in truth, not by my peers of the live present, but by the peers of the dead past; not by the civilisation of the twentieth century, but by the brutality of the fourteenth; not even by a statute framed in the language of an enemy land—so antiquated is the law that must be sought to-day to slay an Irishman, whose offence is that he puts Ireland first.

Loyalty is a sentiment, not a law. It rests on love, not on restraint. The Government of Ireland by England rests on restraint and not on law; and since it demands no love it can evoke no loyalty.

But this statute is more absurd even than it is antiquated; and if it is potent to hang one Irishman, it is still more potent to gibbet all Englishmen.

Edward III. was King not only of the realm of England, but also of the realm of France, and he was not King of Ireland. Yet his dead hand to-day may pull the noose around the Irishman's neck whose Sovereign he was not, but it can strain no strand around the Frenchman's throat whose Sovereign he was. For centuries the successors of Edward III. claimed to be Kings of France, and quartered the arms of France on their royal shield down to the Union with Ireland on 1st January, 1801. Throughout these hundreds of years these "Kings of France" were constantly at war with their realm of France and their French subjects, who should have gone from birth to death with an obvious fear of treason before their eyes. But did they? Did the "Kings of France" resident here at Windsor or in the Tower of London, hang, draw, and quarter as a traitor every Frenchman for 400 years who fell into their hands with arms in his hand? On the contrary, they received embassies of these traitors, presents from these traitors, even knighthood itself at the hands of these traitors, feasted with them, tilted with them, fought with them—but did not assassinate them by law. Judicial assassination to-day is reserved only for one race of the King's subjects, for Irishmen; for those who cannot forget their allegiance to the realm of Ireland.

The Prisoner's Speech.

Sir Roger Casement

The Kings of England as such had no rights in Ireland up to the time of Henry VIII., save such as rested on compact and mutual obligation entered between them and certain princes, chiefs, and lords of Ireland. This form of legal right, such as it was, gave no King of England lawful power to impeach an Irishman for high treason under this statute of King Edward III. of England until an Irish Act, known as Poyning's Law, the 10th of Henry VII., was passed in 1494 at Drogheda, by the Parliament of the Pale in Ireland, and enacted as law in that part of Ireland. But if by Poyning's Law an Irishman of the Pale could be indicted for high treason under this Act, he could be indicted only in one way and before one tribunal—by the laws of the realm of Ireland and in Ireland. The very law of Poyning's, which, I believe, applies this statute of Edward III. to Ireland, enacted also for the Irishman's defence, "All those laws by which "England claims her liberty." And what is the fundamental charter of an Englishman's liberty? That he shall be tried by his peers. With all respect I assert this Court is to me, an Irishman, not a jury of my peers to try me in this vital issue, for it is patent to every man of conscience that I have a right, an indefeasible right, if tried at all, under this statute of high treason, to be tried in Ireland, before an Irish Court and by an Irish jury. This Court, this jury, the public opinion of this country, England, cannot but be prejudiced in varying degree against me, most of all in time of war. I did not land in England; I landed in Ireland. It was to Ireland I came; to Ireland I wanted to come; and the last place I desired to land in was England. But for the Attorney-General of England there is only "England"—there is no Ireland, there is only the law of England—no right of Ireland; the liberty of Ireland and of Irishmen is to be judged by the power of England. Yet for me, the Irish outlaw, there is a land of Ireland, a right of Ireland, and a charter for all Irishmen to appeal to, in the last resort, a charter that even the very statutes of England itself cannot deprive us of—nay, more, a charter that Englishmen themselves assert as the fundamental bond of law that connects the two kingdoms. This charge of high treason involves a moral responsibility, as the very terms of the indictment against myself recite, inasmuch as I committed the acts I am charged with, to the "evil example of others in "the like case." What was this "evil example" I set to others in "the "like case," and who were these others? The "evil example" charged is that I asserted the rights of my own country, and the "others" I appealed to to aid my endeavour were my own countrymen. The example was given not to Englishmen, but to Irishmen, and the "like case" can never arise in England, but only in Ireland. To Englishmen I set no evil example, for I made no appeal to them. I asked no Englishman to help me. I asked Irishmen to fight for their rights. The "evil example" was only to other Irishmen who might come after me, and in "like case" seek to do as I did. How, then, since neither my example nor my appeal was addressed to Englishmen, can I be rightfully tried by them?

If I did wrong in making that appeal to Irishmen to join with me in an effort to fight for Ireland, it is by Irishmen, and by them alone, I can be rightfully judged. From this Court and its jurisdiction I appeal to those I am alleged to have wronged, and to those I am alleged to have injured by my "evil example," and claim that they alone are competent to decide my guilt or my innocence. If they find me guilty, the statute may affix the penalty, but the statute does not override or annul my right to seek judgment at their hands.

This is so fundamental a right, so natural a right, so obvious a right, that it is clear the Crown were aware of it when they brought me by force and by stealth from Ireland to this country. It was not I who landed in England, but the Crown who dragged me here, away from my own country to which I had turned with a price upon my head, away from my own countrymen whose loyalty is not in doubt, and safe from the judgment of my peers whose judgment I do not shrink from. I admit no other judgment but theirs. I accept no verdict save at their hands. I assert from this dock that I am being tried here, not because it is just, but because it is unjust. Place me before a jury of my own countrymen, be it Protestant or Catholic, Unionist or Nationalist, Sinn Feineach or Orangemen, and I shall accept the verdict and bow to the statute and all its penalties. But I shall accept no meaner finding against me than that of those whose loyalty I endanger by my example and to whom alone I made appeal. If they adjudge me guilty, then guilty I am. It is not I who am afraid of their verdict; it is the Crown. If this be not so, why fear the test? I fear it not. I demand it as my right.

That, my lord, is the condemnation of English rule, of English-made law, of English Government in Ireland, that it dare not rest on the will of the Irish people, but it exists in defiance of their will—that it is a rule derived not from right, but from conquest. Conquest, my lord, gives no title, and if it exists over the body, it fails over the mind. It can exert no empire over men's reason and judgment and affections; and it is from this law of conquest without title to the reason, judgment, and affection of my own countrymen that I appeal.

My lord, I beg to say a few more words. As I say, that was my opinion arrived at many days ago while I was a prisoner. I have no hesitation in re-affirming it here, and I hope that the gentlemen of the press who did not hear me yesterday may have heard me distinctly to-day. I wish my words to go much beyond this Court.

I would add that the generous expressions of sympathy extended me from many quarters, particularly from America, have touched me very much. In that country, as in my own, I am sure my motives are understood and not misjudged—for the achievement of their liberties has been an abiding inspiration to Irishmen and to all men elsewhere rightly struggling to be free in like cause.

My Lord Chief Justice, if I may continue, I am not called upon, I conceive, to say anything in answer to the inquiry your lordship has addressed to me why sentence should not be passed upon me. Since I do not admit any verdict in this Court, I cannot, my lord, admit the fitness of the sentence that of necessity must follow it from this Court. I hope I shall be acquitted of presumption if I say that the Court I see before me now is not this High Court of Justice of England, but a far greater, a far higher, a far older assemblage of justices—that of the people of Ireland. Since in the acts which have led to this trial it was the people of Ireland I sought to serve—and them alone—I leave my judgment and my sentence in their hands.

The Prisoner's Speech.

Sir Roger Casement

Let me pass from myself and my own fate to a far more pressing, as it is a far more urgent theme—not the fate of the individual Irishman who may have tried and failed, but the claims and the fate of the country that has not failed. Ireland has outlived the failure of all her hopes—and yet she still hopes. Ireland has seen her sons—aye, and her daughters too—suffer from generation to generation always for the same cause, meeting always the same fate, and always at the hands of the same power; and always a fresh generation has passed on to withstand the same oppression. For if English authority be omnipotent—a power, as Mr. Gladstone phrased it, that reaches to the very ends of the earth—Irish hope exceeds the dimensions of that power, excels its authority, and renews with each generation the claims of the last. The cause that begets this indomitable persistency, the faculty of preserving through centuries of misery the remembrance of lost liberty, this surely is the noblest cause men ever strove for, ever lived for, ever died for. If this be the case I stand here to-day indicted for, and convicted of sustaining, then I stand in a goodly company and a right noble succession.

My counsel has referred to the Ulster Volunteer movement, and I will not touch at length upon that ground save only to say this, that neither I nor any of the leaders of the Irish Volunteers who were founded in Dublin in November, 1913, had quarrel with the Ulster Volunteers as such, who were born a year earlier. Our movement was not directed against them, but against the men who misused and misdirected the courage, the sincerity, and the local patriotism of the men of the north of Ireland. On the contrary, we welcomed the coming of the Ulster Volunteers, even while we deprecated the aims and intentions of those Englishmen who sought to pervert to an English party use—to the mean purposes of their own bid for place and power in England—the armed activities of simple Irishmen. We aimed at winning the Ulster Volunteers to the cause of a united Ireland. We aimed at uniting all Irishmen in a natural and national bond of cohesion based on mutual self-respect. Our hope was a natural one, and if left to ourselves, not hard to accomplish. If external influences of disintegration would but leave us alone, we were sure that Nature itself must bring us together. It was not we, the Irish Volunteers, who broke the law, but a British party. The Government had permitted the Ulster Volunteers to be armed by Englishmen, to threaten not merely an English party in its hold on office, but to threaten that party through the lives and blood of Irishmen. The battle was to be fought in Ireland in order that the political "outs" of to-day should be the "ins" of to-morrow in Great Britain. A law designed for the benefit of Ireland was to be met, not on the floor of Parliament, where the fight had indeed been won, but on the field of battle much nearer home, where the armies would be composed of Irishmen slaying each other for some English party again; and the British Navy would be the chartered "transports" that were to bring to our shores a numerous assemblage of military and ex-military experts in the congenial and profitable business of holding down subject populations abroad. Our choice lay in submitting to foreign lawlessness or resisting it, and we did not hesitate to choose. But while the law breakers had armed their would-be agents openly, and had been permitted to arm them openly, we were met within a few days

Sir Roger Casement.

of the founding of our movement, that aimed at united Ireland from within, by Government action from without direct against our obtaining any arms at all. The manifesto of the Irish Volunteers, promulgated at a public meeting in Dublin on 25th November, 1913, stated with sincerity the aims of the organisation as I have outlined them. If the aims contained in that manifesto were a threat to the unity of the British Empire, then so much the worse for the Empire. An Empire that can only be held together by one section of its governing population perpetually holding down and sowing dissension among a smaller but none the less governing section, must have some canker at its heart, some ruin at its root. The Government that permitted the arming of those whose leaders declared that Irish national unity was a thing that should be opposed by force of arms, within nine days of the issue of our manifesto of goodwill to Irishmen of every creed and class, took steps to nullify our efforts by prohibiting the import of all arms into Ireland as if it had been a hostile and blockaded coast. And this proclamation of the 4th December, 1913, known as the Arms Proclamation, was itself based on an illegal interpretation of the law, as the Chief Secretary has now publicly confessed. The proclamation was met by the loyalists of Great Britain with an act of still more lawless defiance—an act of widespread gun-running into Ulster that was denounced by the Lord Chancellor of England as "grossly illegal and utterly unconstitutional." How did the Irish Volunteers meet the incitements of civil war that were uttered by the party of law and order in England when they saw the prospect of deriving political profit to themselves from bloodshed among Irishmen?

I can answer for my own acts and speeches. While one English party was responsible for preaching a doctrine of hatred designed to bring about civil war in Ireland, the other, and that the party in power, took no active steps to restrain a propaganda that found its advocates in the Army, Navy, and Privy Council—in the Houses of Parliament and in the State Church—a propaganda the methods of whose expression were so "grossly illegal and utterly unconstitutional" that even the Lord Chancellor of England could find only words and no repressive action to apply to them. Since lawlessness sat in high places in England and laughed at the law as at the custodians of the law, what wonder was it that Irishmen should refuse to accept the verbal protestations of an English Lord Chancellor as a sufficient safeguard for their lives and their liberties? I know not how all my colleagues on the Volunteer Committee in Dublin reviewed the growing menace, but those with whom I was in closest co-operation redoubled, in face of these threats from without, our efforts to unite all Irishmen from within. Our appeals were made to Protestant and Unionist as much almost as to Catholic and Nationalist Irishmen. We hoped that by the exhibition of affection and goodwill on our part towards our political opponents in Ireland we should yet succeed in winning them from the side of an English party whose sole interest in our country lay in its oppression in the past, and in the present in its degradation to the mean and narrow needs of their political animosities. It is true that they based their actions, so they averred, on "fears for the Empire," and on a very diffuse loyalty that took in all the peoples of the Empire, save only the Irish. That blessed word "Empire" that bears so paradoxical a resemblance to charity! For if charity begins at home, "Empire" begins in other men's homes, and both may cover a multitude of sins. I for one was determined that Ireland was much more to me than "Empire," and that if charity begins at home so must loyalty. Since arms were so necessary to make our organisation a reality, and to give to the minds of Irishmen menaced with the most outrageous threats a sense of security, it was our bounden duty to get arms before all else. I decided with this end in view to go to America, with surely a better right to appeal to Irishmen there for help in an hour of great national trial than those envoys of "Empire" could assert for their week-end descents upon Ireland, or their appeals to Germany. If, as the right honourable gentleman, the present Attorney-General, asserted in a speech at Manchester, Nationalists would neither fight for Home Rule nor pay for it, it was our duty to show him that we knew how to do both. Within a few weeks of my arrival in the States the fund that had been opened to secure arms for the Volunteers of Ireland amounted to many thousands of pounds. In every case the money subscribed, whether it came from the purse of the wealthy man or the still readier pocket of the poor man, was Irish gold.

Then came the war. As Mr. Birrell said in his evidence recently laid before the Commission of Inquiry into the causes of the late rebellion in Ireland, "the war upset all our calculations." It upset mine no less than Mr. Birrell's, and put an end to my mission of peaceful effort in America. War between Great Britain and Germany meant, as I believed, ruin for all the hopes we had founded on the enrolment of the Irish Volunteers. A constitutional movement in Ireland is never very far from a breach of the constitution, as the Loyalists of Ulster had been so eager to show us. The cause is not far to seek. A constitution to be maintained intact must be the achievement and the pride of the people themselves; must rest on their own free will and on their own determination to sustain it, instead of being something resident in another land whose chief representative is an armed force—armed not to protect the population, but to hold it down. We had seen the working of the Irish constitution in the refusal of the army of occupation at the Curragh to obey the orders of the Crown. And now that we were told the first duty of an Irishman was to enter that army, in return for a promissory note, payable after death—a scrap of paper that might or might not be redeemed, I felt over there in America that my first duty was to keep Irishmen at home in the only army that could safeguard our national existence. If small nationalities were to be the pawns in this game of embattled giants, I saw no reason why Ireland should shed her blood in any cause but her own, and if that be treason beyond the seas I am not ashamed to avow it or to answer for it here with my life. And when we had the doctrine of Unionist loyalty at last—"Mausers and Kaisers and any King you "like," and I have heard that at Hamburg, not far from Limburg on the Lahn—I felt I needed no other warrant than that these words conveyed—to go forth and do likewise. The difference between us was that the Unionist champions chose a path they felt would lead to the woolsack;

while I went a road I knew must lead to the dock. And the event proves we were both right. The difference between us was that my " treason " was based on a ruthless sincerity that forced me to attempt in time and season to carry out in action what I said in word—whereas their treason lay in verbal incitements that they knew need never be made good in their bodies. And so, I am prouder to stand here to-day in the traitor's dock to answer this impeachment than to fill the place of my right honourable accusers.

We have been told, we have been asked to hope, that after this war Ireland will get Home Rule, as a reward for the life blood shed in a cause which whoever else its success may benefit can surely not benefit Ireland. And what will Home Rule be in return for what its vague promise has taken and still hopes to take away from Ireland? It is not necessary to climb the painful stairs of Irish history—that treadmill of a nation whose labours are as vain for her own uplifting as the convict's exertions are for his redemption—to review the long list of British promises made only to be broken—of Irish hopes raised only to be dashed to the ground. Home Rule when it comes, if come it does, will find an Ireland drained of all that is vital to its very existence—unless it be that unquenchable hope we build on the graves of the dead. We are told that if Irishmen go by the thousand to die, not for Ireland, but for Flanders, for Belgium, for a patch of sand on the deserts of Mesopotamia, or a rocky trench on the heights of Gallipoli, they are winning self-government for Ireland. But if they dare to lay down their lives on their native soil, if they dare to dream even that freedom can be won only at home by men resolved to fight for it there, then they are traitors to their country, and their dream and their deaths alike are phases of a dishonourable phantasy. But history is not so recorded in other lands. In Ireland alone in this twentieth century is loyalty held to be a crime. If loyalty be something less than love and more than law, then we have had enough of such loyalty for Ireland or Irishmen. If we are to be indicted as criminals, to be shot as murderers, to be imprisoned as convicts because our offence is that we love Ireland more than we value our lives, then I know not what virtue resides in any offer of self-government held out to brave men on such terms. Self-government is our right, a thing born in us at birth; a thing no more to be doled out to us or withheld from us by another people than the right to life itself—than the right to feel the sun or smell the flowers, or to love our kind. It is only from the convict these things are withheld for crime committed and proven—and Ireland that has wronged no man, that has injured no land, that has sought no dominion over others—Ireland is treated to-day among the nations of the world as if she was a convicted criminal. If it be treason to fight against such an unnatural fate as this, then I am proud to be a rebel, and shall cling to my " rebellion " with the last drop of my blood. If there be no right of rebellion against a state of things that no savage tribe would endure without resistance, then I am sure that it is better for men to fight and die without right than to live in such a state of right as this. Where all your rights become only an accumulated wrong; where men must beg with bated breath for leave to subsist in their own land, to think their own thoughts, to sing their own songs, to garner the fruits of their own labours—and even while they beg, to see things inexorably withdrawn from them—then surely it is braver, a saner and a truer thing, to be a rebel in act and deed against such circumstances as these than tamely to accept it as the natural lot of men.

My lord, I have done. Gentlemen of the jury, I wish to thank you for your verdict. I hope you will not take amiss what I said, or think that I made any imputation upon your truthfulness or your integrity when I spoke and said that this was not a trial by my peers. I maintain that I have a natural right to be tried in that natural jurisdiction, Ireland, my own country, and I would put it to you, how would you feel in the converse case, or rather how would all men here feel in the converse case, if an Englishman had landed here in England and the Crown or the Government, for its own purposes, had conveyed him secretly from England to Ireland under a false name, committed him to prison under a false name, and brought him before a tribunal in Ireland under a statute which they knew involved a trial before an Irish jury? How would you feel yourselves as Englishmen if that man was to be submitted to trial by jury in a land inflamed against him and believing him to be a criminal, when his only crime was that he had cared for England more than for Ireland?

The Usher—Oyez. My lords, the King's Justices do strictly charge and command all manner of persons to keep silence whilst sentence of death is passing upon the prisoner at the bar, upon pain of imprisonment.

The Lord Chief Justice—Sir Roger David Casement, you have been found guilty of treason, the gravest crime known to the law, and upon evidence which in our opinion is conclusive of guilt. Your crime was that of assisting the King's enemies, that is the Empire of Germany, during the terrible war in which we are engaged. The duty now devolves upon me of passing sentence upon you, and it is that you be taken hence to a lawful prison, and thence to a place of execution, and that you be there hanged by the neck until you be dead. And the Sheriffs of the Counties of London and Middlesex are, and each of them is, hereby charged with the execution of this judgment, and may the Lord have mercy on your soul.

Mr. Justice Avory—Amen!

II.—THE APPEAL.

IN THE COURT OF CRIMINAL APPEAL, LONDON,
MONDAY, 17TH JULY, 1916,

BEFORE

MR. JUSTICE DARLING,
MR. JUSTICE BRAY,
MR. JUSTICE A. T. LAWRENCE,
MR. JUSTICE SCRUTTON, and
MR. JUSTICE ATKIN.

Counsel for the Crown—

THE ATTORNEY-GENERAL (The Right Hon. Sir Frederick Smith, K.C., M.P.),

THE SOLICITOR-GENERAL (The Right Hon. Sir George Cave, K.C., M.P.),

MR. A. H. BODKIN,

MR. TRAVERS HUMPHREYS,

MR. G. A. H. BRANSON,

Instructed by SIR CHARLES W. MATHEWS, K.C.B., Director of Public Prosecutions.

Counsel for the Appellant—

MR. A. M. SULLIVAN (K.C. and Second Serjeant of the Irish Bar),

MR. T. ARTEMUS JONES,

MR. J. H. MORGAN,

Instructed by MR. G. GAVAN DUFFY, assisted by MR. MICHAEL FRANCIS DOYLE, of the American Bar.

Sir Roger Casement.

First Day—Monday, 17th July, 1916.

Mr. SULLIVAN—My lords, in this case the prisoner was indicted under the statute of Edward III., the offence being stated in the following terms:—"Sir Roger David Casement is charged with the following "offence:—High treason by adhering to the King's enemies elsewhere "than in the King's realm—to wit, in the Empire of Germany—contrary "to the Treason Act, 1351 (25 Edward III., statute 5, chapter 2)." The matter of the appeal, my lords, will involve two questions—first, whether the matter described in the charge is in truth an offence within the statute cited, and a second point will arise as to whether the definition of the offence of adhering given by my lord the Chief Justice at the trial at the bar was an accurate definition or was defective as an instruction to the jury.

My lords, I propose to consider first of all the state of affairs at common law at the time of the passing of the Act of Edward III. If I may briefly outline my argument, which I am afraid will occupy a little while, as the case is of much importance, I propose to argue that the statute of Edward III. was passed for the purpose of limitation of legal decisions that were cropping up and extending the doctrine of treason at the time of the statute; that it dealt only with treasons that were triable at the time at common law. There is authority that the statute was to be declaratory of the common law. I propose to show that at the time, even under the most extending construction of the common law then prevalent, which the statute was passed to prune and not to enlarge, under no circumstances could there have been such a crime as that described in the indictment here, namely, adhering to the King's enemies elsewhere than in the King's realm. I intend, on the construction of the statute, to submit that if we had to construe this statute as though it had passed yesterday, the first reading of it would convey a perfectly clear view of the provisions of the statute to the mind of everybody, and that that clear view would be inconsistent with the matter charged in the indictment being an offence under the statute. I then propose to show how there crept into text-books, because only into text-books the matter originally crept, an error with reference to the purview of the statute; I think I will be able to show the source of that error and the explanation of it. I intend to show from the statutory development of the law of treason, running through a very great number of statutes since the time of Edward III., an extraordinary history of expansion and contraction going back again and again to the statute of Edward III., as being the law of the land, but I intend to submit that on the consideration of those statutes it was perfectly clear that the statute of Edward III. itself did not in any degree purport to legislate for any territory that was outside the King's realm; that it was extended beyond the realm by special statutes, and that these special statutes have in their due course disappeared; and that going outside the statute itself, which is all that is charged in the present instance, and

The Hon. Mr. Justice Darling.

I think all that remains owing to the repeal of all others, that statute itself never did of its own motion extend to anything done outside of the realm, and that its extension beyond the realm was statutory extension, and that that extension has disappeared with the disappearance of the statutes which created it.

The first matter to be considered is the terms of the statute, because the terms of the statute show that it was passed with reference to matters theretofore triable by common law. "Whereas divers opinions have been "before this time in what case treason shall be said, and in what not, the "King at the request of the Lords and of the Commons, hath made a "declaration in the manner as hereafter followeth; that is to say"—then we can pass on—"or if a man do levy war against our Lord the King "in his realm, or be adherent to the King's enemies in his realm, giving "to them aid and comfort, in the realm or elsewhere, and thereof be "probably attainted." I have passed three matters which do not arise in the present instance. The first important matter is the recital that "divers "opinions have been before this time in what case treason shall be said and "in what not." I would have your lordships bear in mind that at the time of the statute there were at least four different codes of law regulating the affairs of subjects within the realm of England, and some of these codes of law extended far beyond England. The common law I hope to show was purely local, dependent in its essence on venue, and the common law could have cognisance of nothing that did not arise within the body of some county; there are statutes subsequently passed to enable the common law to deal with matters that have not arisen within the bodies of counties, but as far as I know there has not yet been cited any authority for such a proposition that the common law at the time of Edward III. was capable of informing itself of something amounting to a transgression which had completely taken place in a territory that was not in a body of a county, which was the foundation of the jurisdiction of common law.

My lords, the opinions of what was treason and what was not, some of them we can trace. The opinion that compassing the King's death was treason was the most ancient of them. Compassing the death of the King went back probably to the reign of Alfred; it was certainly an ancient offence at the time of the statute. In the year 1285 we get an instance of adhering, and a typical instance of adhering. There are seven or eight others in the reports, and they are all of the same type, because they are all cases in which a person within the King's peace and within the realm has been seeking to assist enemies of the King, in some cases within the realm, but in most cases outside the realm, by the subject utilising his position in the realm to give information and to send intelligence, or, as we see from statutes later on, perhaps even send material aid to the King's enemies outside the realm, but the offender is always within the realm.

The first case I mention of adhering—I am now dealing with within the realm—was before the statute was passed. I have a typical case as to adhering, which is taken from the documents of the city of Oxford; they are not available here so far as I know. I am quoting from the extract of them that is set out in the History of English Law, by Professor Holdsworth, where he cites the case at some length of Nicholaus de Wautham, and his offence, roughly, was as follows:—In that case the offence was—

Mr. Sullivan

the prefatory averments are almost identical with what remained for hundreds of years afterwards—that Nicholaus de Wautham conspired with Guy de Monteforti and his brother, and Llewellyn of Wales, an enemy of our Lord the King, and that he did come to the King's Council or Court to privately find out the secrets of the King and all those secrets which he could, and when he had ascertained them he conveyed them to the King's enemies; and it says that he was one of the adherents, the terms in which it is alleged in the subsequent indictments for adhering, continuing for a couple of hundred years. Strange to say, in the second volume of Pollock and Maitland, at page 505, your lordships will find the opinion expressed that of the offences mentioned in the statute, probably the most recent in the development of the law of treason, was levying war against the King in his realm. That provision, my lords, and the limitation of it is important when one comes to consider the position of offences with regard to which the statute was passed.

My lords, at the time of the statute there were in England among the great landowners and nobles a number of persons who were under two allegiances, one in England, and, in respect of lands which they extensively owned in France, another allegiance in France. The limitation of levying war, and I submit also the clear limitation of adhering, arose from the fact that, being feudal subjects of the King of France in respect of French lands and of the King of England in respect of English lands, the barons themselves would be anxious to limit the decision of treason in such a way as that their English lands should not be forfeited in respect of service and homage rendered in respect of their possessions outside the realm rendered to the King's enemies. At page 460 of the first volume of Pollock and Maitland there is this passage, "The territory within which, "according to later law, subjects would be born to the King of England "was large; under Henry II. it became vast. It comprehended Ireland; "at times (to say the least) it comprehended Scotland; it stretched to "the Pyrenees. Then, again, the law even of Bracton's day acknowledged "that a man might be a subject of the French King and hold land in "France, and yet be a subject of the English King and hold land in "England. It was prepared to meet the case of a war between the "two Kings; the amphibious baron might fight in person for his liege "lord, but he must also send his due consignment of knights to the "opposite army. In generation after generation a Robert Bruce holds "lands on both sides of the Scotch border; no one cares to remember on "which side he was born." The reference to Bracton is folio 427B. It was the Parliament that was seeking to have a definition of treason, which, of course, at that time was very largely a matter affecting title to property, and developed, indeed, in the early days as part of the law of real property.

The distinction between treason and felony was, as we all know, who should get the lands of the barons confiscated, whether the King, who, of course, was anxious to extend everything to being treason, whether it should be others who would be anxious to limit the cases of treason within the narrower compass. This furnishes an instance of why there should be special mention both in the case of adhering to the King's enemies and of levying war, and a limitation that it should be within the realm, otherwise bound as the owner of land in France would be bound under pain of forfeiture of his lands in France, he being in most cases a legislator in England, bound as he would be to furnish actual military service to the King of France, under whom he held his French lands as a condition to retain them, he would forfeit his English lands if that amounted to treason with reference to his allegiance to the English King. I submit that it is a very plain reason why the Parliament would be most anxious to see that the persons who very largely constituted the Parliament should be put in a position of having to elect, with two feudal claims upon them, which of their territories they should forfeit in case their two feudal lords disagreed and went to war. At all events there is no doubt whatever, I submit, that the limitation of levying war was confined to within the realm. The provisions of the statute have been re-enacted on subsequent dates, and I will point out to your lordships on one occasion, and on one occasion only, was the levying of war extended to without the realm, and that was a statute of Charles II., and for a brief period. One of the matters that will have to be considered here if levying war was to be treason only when committed within the realm, is why should mere adherence to another person without the levying of war elsewhere have been constituted treason, when the actual taking up of arms beside him would not have been treason within the appropriate limit of the statute?

The quotation from the Oxford City documents will be found in Pollock and Maitland, volume ii., page 507, at the bottom. That is the case of adhering I was reciting. Now, at common law, both before and after the statute, trial had to proceed according to a process which was so rigidly settled that process was everything, and the essence of common law, the foundation of common law was venue. It is most important in the construction of the statute to note that procedure is not dealt with, because I will point out to you when it comes subsequently to be extended, as the statute was periodically extended to operate outside the confines of the realm, procedure was always looked upon in the statute, and hundreds of years afterwards when venue was loosening in civil actions, and was indeed becoming a matter that might be alleged falsely and not controverted, nevertheless you find that in criminal matters the question of venue is attended to whenever there is statutory enlargement of offences and bringing them outside the confines of the realm or outside the body of counties. There being no provision in the statute, the question at once arises, if a statute is to operate outside the kingdom how is the statute to be put into operation? Venues, we know, went back certainly to the Constitutions of Clarendon, which are in 1164, where we get the essence of venue, and the essence of the first step in process against a person against whom a crime is subsequently to be alleged. We find all through that twelve men from the neighbourhood of the occurrence became the standard of opinion as to whether a man is even to be put to trial or not, and as late as 35 Henry VIII., chapter 6, apparently six men should come actually from the very county in which the offence had taken place. Your lordships will find in Viner, volume xxi., page 3, under "Trial," at the first line of the page, "If an act be to be done all beyond sea, it "cannot be tried in England; but where part is to be done in England and "part beyond sea it may be tried in England." In the same volume, at page 130, under "Trial," you find a suggestion of trying crimes committed in two counties in either county. That, as a matter of fact, contrasts with the opinion of Stephen, that, until there was a statute of Edward, crimes that were not committed in either county could be tried in neither.

Mr. Justice Darling—The opinion of Sir Fitzjames Stephen?

Mr. Sullivan—Stephen's Commentaries.

Mr. Justice Darling—What did he say?

Mr. Sullivan—That until the statute was passed, at common law a man being shot in one county and traversing the boundary and dying in another, the murder not being completed in either, it was possible at common law the murderer should escape trial.

Mr. Justice Darling—It was impossible. Does he indicate what did become of him?

Mr. Sullivan—I should say he did it again.

Mr. Justice Darling—Did he always commit murder on the edge of the county?

Mr. Sullivan—As a matter of fact, Viner says he may be tried in either county. That is what I referred to Viner for at page 130.

Mr. Justice Darling—Stephen said he thinks he could be tried in neither.

Mr. Sullivan—Till the statute of Edward I. was passed, a very early statute. At all events, as we know, there have been statutes passed, a long series going back to Edward I., dealing with crimes committed on the borders of counties or in more than one county. Your lordship knows with regard to venue there are a large number of venue statutes with regard to crimes that are partially committed in one place and partially in another. They are very ancient statutes, and they are consistent with the fact that venue was originally such a rigid doctrine. Viner, of course, is writing after the statute had cured that, and he may be expressing the opinion of the statute. At all events, they were triable in either county eventually, but there certainly was a statute passed to deal with it at a very early period, and, at all events, undoubtedly until the passing of the statute there was difficulty in laying a venue, and venue was the very essence of trial.

Mr. Justice Darling—How do you know that that statute did not declare the common law, the statute which made the crime triable in either county?

Mr. Sullivan—It may have done so; I cannot say that I know it did not; I do not seek to make any such proposition, but at the same time it is exceedingly difficult when one studies the relation of venue to jurisdiction under the old common law to see how he could be indicted in either county, because, my lord, the jurors in one county had no means of informing themselves of the circumstances under which the blow was given, and the jurors in the other county had no means of informing themselves of what had been the ultimate consequence of the blow.

Mr. Justice Darling—Are you speaking of the time before there were witnesses, when the jurors were the witnesses?

Mr. Sullivan—Yes.

Mr. Justice Darling—Or of a time when jurors were jurors, and witnesses could be summoned before them?

Mr. SULLIVAN—I will take the time when the jurors were the persons who first presented and subsequently tried on their own presentment; they were the witnesses and the proof.

Mr. JUSTICE DARLING—Once you arrive at the time when the juror was a juror and witnesses were summoned, do you mean there was no means even in early days of getting witnesses from Worcestershire, say, to come before a jury of Herefordshire?

Mr. SULLIVAN—No, I think that would be the cure. Once you get to the development of the witness of something that had happened in the county, once the law developed into the practice of outside witnesses apart from the neighbours, once you have jurisdiction to inquire into something having happened that was against the peace, that was within the county, then there came the inquisition, and they might inform themselves of what had been the ultimate result. The essential thing for inquiry in either county must still be that something had happened in the county which gave the juror a right to inquire. You are still within venue; whether, having your venue, your inquiry may go into facts outside the venue is a different matter. I am only dwelling on this so as to show that when you get outside the body of the county, at the time of Edward I., I submit it was impossible that any county could inform itself of a matter which had happened completely outside the body of any part of His Majesty's realm.

Mr. JUSTICE DARLING—Perhaps you have not arrived at it, but, at all events, you have not mentioned that people were tried by Commissioners.

Mr. SULLIVAN—I am coming to them. The Commissioners were merely a development. That will be a part of my argument upon which I shall rely most strongly, that the statutes proceeded to provide for offences outside the realm, and with the same provisions making offences outside the realm, the statutes, conscious of the incompetence of common law to deal with them, provided statutory tribunals to deal with them; the same statute which extended treason outside the realm also provided for its trial within.

Mr. JUSTICE DARLING—Do you mean the statute of Henry VIII.?

Mr. SULLIVAN—The 26 Henry VIII., not 35 Henry VIII. 35 Henry VIII. was passed to explain doubts that had arisen on the previous statute of 26 Henry VIII. At page 178, volume xxi., of Viner, under "Trial"—"If a man be stricken upon the high sea, and dies of the same stroke "upon the land, this cannot be inquired of by the common law, because "no venue can come from the place where the stroke was given (though "it were within the sea pertaining to the realm of England, and within "the ligeance of the King), because it is not within any of the counties "of the realm; neither can the admiral hear and determine this murder, "because though the stroke was within his jurisdiction, yet the death was "*infra corpus comitatus*, whereof he cannot inquire; neither is it within "the statute of 26 Henry VIII., because the murder was not committed "on the sea. But by the Act of 13 Richard II. the constable and "marshal may hear and determine the same." That emphasises what I was saying with regard to the statute referring to offences at common law only, because as we know both the constable and marshal and the admiral had jurisdiction outside the realm of England altogether in other cases.

Mr. Justice Darling—Serjeant Sullivan, in the case you put, suppose neither the assizes nor the admiral could investigate this case, what about the coroner; ought not he to inquire where the man died and how he came by his death?

Mr. Sullivan—The coroner could inquire, no doubt, into how the man died, but, the coroner being also shackled by his jurisdiction, I submit it is perfectly clear that he could not hold investigation as to circumstances that arose outside the body of the county, any more than the common law could.

Mr. Justice A. T. Lawrence—What is the authority for that?

Mr. Sullivan—Viner—" If a man be stricken upon the high sea, and " dies of the same stroke upon the land, this cannot be inquired of by " the common law, because no venue can come from the place where the " stroke was given (though it were within the sea pertaining to the realm " of England and within the ligeance of the King)." That was cured by the statute.

Mr. Justice Darling—Yes, but a dying declaration made by a man was always evidence. Suppose a man was wounded in Herefordshire and fled into Worcestershire and fell dead, but before dying stated that So-and-So and So-and-So in Herefordshire struck him the blow of which he died, could not good evidence be given before the coroner in Worcestershire?

Mr. Sullivan—I submit not. The coroner of Worcestershire did not inquire into what had been done in the adjoining county.

Mr. Justice Darling—He must inquire of the death on view of the body; if it was found that the man before he died made a deposition which said So-and-So and So-and-So half a mile away at the other end of the village in the other county struck him the blow, do you say that that evidence could not have been given?

Mr. Sullivan—There certainly was a period in which it could not be. The evidence must be given just as anything might take place, but the Coroner's Court could express no opinion upon whether the evidence with regard to an act done outside his jurisdiction was true or false. But there is the case, if the coroner could not inquire, the common law could not inquire. Of course, the difficulty is in transporting one's mind to a state of legal development in which that might be so, because hundreds of years ago these anomalies were redressed all by statute; when it came to crimes they were redressed by statutes; they were redressed in the law between man and man in contracts to commence with, at a very much earlier period, or rather in a very different way by the allegation of false venue, but the very allegation of false venue of contracts which were partly to be performed within the realm is an illustration of how rigid was the rule of venue and the limitation of venue upon a matter which had not been redressed by any such device and in which the venue had to be true, down to the end, except when it was altered by statute. You have to get a true venue, for venue was of the very essence of criminal jurisdiction.

Then at page 180—" If two of the King's subjects go over into a " foreign realm, and fight there, and the one kills the other, this murder "being done out of the realm cannot be for want of trial heard and determined by the common law, but it may be heard and determined before "the constable and marshal." Then volume xiv., at page 376, "Every "indictment at common law must expressly show some place wherein the "offence was committed, which must appear to have been within the "jurisdiction of the Court in which the indictment was taken, and must "be alleged without any repugnancy; for if one and the same offence be "alleged at two different places, or at B aforesaid, where B was not "before mentioned; or if the stroke be alleged at A and the death at B, "and the indictment conclude that the defendant *sic felonice murdravit* "the deceased at A, the indictment is void; so is it also if it lay not both "at a place of the stroke and death, or if any place so alleged be not such "from whence a venue may come."

With regard to venue there is a very interesting case, I believe not heretofore printed, which my colleague, Professor Morgan, has found in the Coram Rege Roll, Easter, 2 Henry IV., Membrane 18; that will be in the year 1401. The Roll is in the Record Office, and your lordships can inspect it. It is a very peculiar case. It is the case of one John Kynaston, who was charged with being an accessory to the treason of compassing in Wales and with certain felonies in Shropshire committed.

The record begins by reciting that Owen Glyndwr and other Welshmen had imagined, conspired, and intended the death and deposition of the King and of the Prince of Wales, and John Kynaston was indicted for consenting to the aforesaid treasons—this is not a literal translation, it is the pith of the document—he was charged with having traitorously sent his son in arms to assist Owen Glyndwr at Oswestry, and with having received and comforted two Welshmen, traitors, and with having feloniously stolen cattle. He was indicted in Shropshire; the indictment was returned into the Court of King's Bench at Westminster. It was there given in evidence that Oswestry and other places laid in the indictment of treason were in Wales and outside Shropshire, and the laws of the realm—that is, the place of the treason, the assemblage under Owen Glyndwr. The Attorney-General appeared, and upon this contended that the King's justices in Shropshire could not inquire into treasons in Wales, nor were they triable by the law of England. The position of the Attorney-General was, as we all know, not the same as the position which the Attorney-General occupies in more recent years; I rather fancy the chief Crown representative was the King's Serjeant at the time. As I have said, the Attorney-General appeared, and upon this contended that the King's justices in Shropshire could not inquire into treasons in Wales, nor were they triable by the laws of England. This was admitted, and the jury were required to try the issue of only those felonies that were committed in Shropshire; the jurors were summoned from Shropshire to the Court of King's Bench. The plea to the jurisdiction appears to have been admitted, because the jurors were asked to try and inquire into the felonies committed in Shropshire only. Accordingly, my lords, he is tried for that; he is not tried for the treason, and, my lords, as a matter of fact, the jury acquitted him of the charge against him. I have here a complete copy of the roll if your lordships would like to see it.

Mr. Justice Darling—It does not say that he could not be tried for treason outside England. It may say he could not be tried for it except he was tried in Wales, but it does not say he could not be tried for treason.

Mr. SULLIVAN—Wales is there alleged in the plea to have been outside. They could not inquire into treason in Wales, nor were they triable by the law of England.

Mr. JUSTICE DARLING—It does not say it was not treason within the realm; it was within the realm, of course.

Mr. SULLIVAN—I think not. I think when your lordship looks at the record the argument is that Wales is not within the realm of England; a very strange state of affairs prevails.

Mr. JUSTICE DARLING—Who was King over Wales at that time?

Mr. SULLIVAN—Owen Glyndwr claimed to be.

Mr. JUSTICE DARLING—But Henry IV. did not recognise it, else why did he fight him?

Mr. SULLIVAN—I admit their minds were not *ad idem* on the subject, but the position of Wales, my lord, was a very peculiar one; the position of Wales was very similar to that of the position of the French provinces.

Mr. JUSTICE DARLING—Would you hand up the record you have there?

Mr. SULLIVAN—Yes, my lord, it is in Latin. Wales was part of the realm, but it was in this most anomalous position, it was not in the body of any county. It is all the stronger for me if it was part of the realm. It was not in the body of any county, and the King's writ did not run in Wales until a very much later period of history, so much later that there is a case in Burrows' Reports which I cannot give the reference to at the present time, another case of the venue statutes that applied both to England and Ireland, in which a venue was removed from Carlow to a Midland county in England, as being the nearest county in which the King's writ did run. There is actually a statute to which I will refer your lordships, if I may be permitted to deal with the statutes in a different branch of the argument. You find, with regard to this matter, that Owen Glyndwr's case is one where the statute provided for the trial of the offence in Wales and other places where the King's writ did not run. Now, that defect is cured by statute after the case; but there is the case that until provision was made by the statute—take Wales as being within the realm, which is all the stronger in my view—I submit, for want of the body of a county within the realm an offence is untriable, and it takes a statute to cure it; the date is subsequent to the Treason Act that we have to construe in the present instance. Now, I propose to go shortly through the statutory development.

Mr. JUSTICE DARLING—Do you mean to say that is an authority for this proposition, that at the time of Henry IV. a man might commit treason within the realm and could not be tried anywhere within the realm for it?

Mr. SULLIVAN—I think that it shows that Wales was considered to be without the realm. I am taking your lordship's view that Wales was within the realm, and I am saying it is an authority that an offence committed in Wales was not triable in an English county.

Mr. JUSTICE A. T. LAWRENCE—Were not there Courts in Wales that could try at that time?

Mr. SULLIVAN—I think not. I may be a little confused in my dates, but just at the instant it occurs to me that that was at a time when the King's writ was not running in Wales. Will your lordships permit me to look it up afterwards? I cannot give the exact date now. There was a statutory provision with regard to the King's writ not running.

The ATTORNEY-GENERAL—This matter of Kynaston, it was said, was not reported, but I find there is a report of it given, a short report, on page 155 of the first volume of Hale's Pleas of the Crown, the 1800 edition.

Mr. SULLIVAN—What Hale says is, "As touching treason committed "in Wales before the statute of 26 Henry VIII., chapter 6, no treason, "murder, or felony committed in Wales was inquirable or triable before "Commissioners of oyer and terminer, or in the King's Bench in England, "but before justices or Commissioners assigned by the King in those "counties of Wales where the fact was committed." That is Henry IV. Then he quotes the Kynaston case. Then he says that by the statute 26 Henry VIII., chapter 6, that was cured. The proposition in Hale suggests that it requires statutory provision, and, indeed, there is a statute dealing with trials of matters in Wales and other places where the King's writ runneth not. Subsequently to the statute of Edward III. there was a great number of statutes passed regulating the law of treason, and a great number of those statutes extend the law of treason outside the realm. Where they did so you find them providing for its trial. The first statute is 2 Henry V., chapter 6; that would be in 1414. The matters dealt with in the statute were matters chiefly arising on sea, and the matters made treason were principally violation of safe conducts granted by the Crown, breaches of truce in time of truce. The important matter is that they were merely offences committed outside the bodies of counties, there committed, and so committed abroad.

Mr. JUSTICE DARLING—Serjeant Sullivan, have you noticed this in Hale's Pleas of the Crown, at page 158, after discussing this very case of Kynaston, "But certainly Wales is within the kingdom of England, "and therefore not within the statute of 35 Henry VIII., chapter 2, for "trial of foreign treasons"?

Mr. SULLIVAN—That was certainly true at the time that Hale wrote it. Henry VIII. incorporated Wales just as he incorporated Ireland. It was incorporated in the reign of Henry VIII.

Mr. JUSTICE DARLING—On page 155 or 156, if you look at the inset in the margin, he says this in dealing with this case that you have been citing, "As touching treason committed in Wales before the statute of "26 Henry VIII., chapter 6, no treason, murder, or felony committed in "Wales was inquirable or triable before Commissioners of oyer and "terminer, or in the King's Bench of England, but before justices or "Commissioners assigned by the King in those counties of Wales where "the fact was committed."

Mr. SULLIVAN—That is after 2 Henry IV.

Mr. JUSTICE DARLING—Then he cites the Act of Henry IV. That is in the *John Kynaston* case. There you have a distinct statement that it was treason against the King of England to levy war against him in Wales; that he could be tried; he could not be tried at the assizes of Shropshire, he could not be tried at the King's Bench in London, but he could be tried by a special Commission issued by the King of England to go and try him in Wales.

Mr. SULLIVAN—By statute; that is the very argument that I am going to address to your lordship.

Mr. JUSTICE DARLING—Hale does not say it is by statute that the Commissioners act, except that they try him under the statute of Edward III.

Mr. SULLIVAN—No, my lord, when you come to the Commissioners I think you find the Commissioners are purely statutory.

Mr. JUSTICE DARLING—" Before justices or Commissioners assigned by " the King in those counties of Wales where the fact was committed."

Mr. SULLIVAN—Your lordship will find that the provision of assigning both Commissioners and venues is statutory, and I am going to open a series of statutes to your lordship.

Mr. JUSTICE BRAY—Let it be so; supposing it is so, that merely regulates the mode and the place of trial. It does not say it is not treason; the Act that you have referred to does not make it treason. If any Act makes it treason it is the Act of Edward III.

Mr. SULLIVAN—What I submit is this, that nothing is treason unless it can be so adjudicated treason. When you are dealing with the Courts of law it is not a matter of morals, but of law. Unless there is some Court that can say whether a treasonable act has been committed or not, in the inquiry into the matter, it cannot be treason to do an act which you can do without being punishable for it or triable for it in a Court of law. There cannot be what in law amounts to a crime of which no Court can inform itself. You must not be presumed to have committed a crime until you have been lawfully condemned, and if there exists no machinery, not only for condemnation, but for inquiry, I submit that is overwhelming proof that the act cannot be a crime when its legal quality cannot be inquired into.

Mr. JUSTICE DARLING—How can you say there was no machinery if, although it could not be tried at the ordinary Commission of Assize nor in the King's Bench, it was within the King's legal power to issue a Commission to people to try the person for the particular treason?

Mr. SULLIVAN—I think, my lord, that I will show your lordship where the Commission came from that went into Wales, but, at all events, we have not yet come to a case; until after 26 Henry VIII. I think we shall not come to a case. I submit that the common law Commission would be a Commission of oyer and terminer. When you find that they are not triable at the common law Commission, not triable by the Court of Queen's Bench, and are triable by a different body, I think you will find that that body is a statutory body appointed *ad hoc*, and I think I will find the statute. I think that Hale must have been speaking of the statute passed in 32 Henry VIII., chapter 4, where there are special provisions made for the trial of treasons in Wales, where the King's writ runneth not.

Mr. JUSTICE BRAY—Hale was speaking of something which happened before Henry VIII. Where is the statutory authority for trying people, as you say, by Commission; where do you find that?

Mr. SULLIVAN—Hale admits that the Court of common law was incapable of trying it.

Mr. JUSTICE BRAY—But at the same time he says the King may appoint Commissioners or judges to try it.

Mr. SULLIVAN—Unless the King had some peculiar power in Wales he could only appoint special Commissioners to try criminal cases under special statute.

Mr. JUSTICE A. T. LAWRENCE—Why do you say that?

Mr. JUSTICE BRAY—Therefore it was that I asked to see what the statute was and when.

Mr. SULLIVAN—Until 32 Henry VIII. I find no statute.

Mr. JUSTICE A. T. LAWRENCE—He could always do it at common law. It has always been so understood.

Mr. SULLIVAN—The common law Courts were the Courts sent out from the King's Bench into the country or the King's Bench itself.

Mr. JUSTICE A. T. LAWRENCE—Those were the ordinary Courts, but just the same power that enabled those Commissions to be issued could issue a special Commission to try in a particular place a particular case.

The ATTORNEY-GENERAL—Hale has a reference to that at page 154. In dealing with offences committed on the high seas before that statute, that is 28 Henry VIII., chapter 15, they might be tried by special Commission under the common law, and according to the course of the common law.

Mr. SULLIVAN—I am going to point out that Hale is wrong. The passages in Hale treat this matter as if the law was against me, but I am going to deal with Hale. Hale follows Coke, and I am going to put it that the authorities cited by both Coke and Hale for the propositions they advance do not support the propositions for which they are cited.

My lords, I was pointing out that owing to the absence of venue (and I have cited the authorities) the common law could not try cases that arose outside the realm, or even outside the bodies of counties. I find that I omitted one passage from volume xxi. of Viner, page 180, with regard to treasons. "Treasons committed out of the realm cannot be "tried by the Courts at common law." At the time these text-writers were writing they had a little catalogue of statutes passed to remedy the defect of the common law. I was calling attention to the statute 2 Henry V., chapter 6, which I will only refer to shortly. That created offences of treason by acts done outside of the realm, and as it did so it provided a tribunal to try them, and it provided that they should be tried by a conservator and two men learned in the law, and they were to be tried according to the practice prevailing in trials before the admirals of the Kings of England. That was not common law, as your lordships know. So there, which is the first case I find after the statute of Edward III., where the statute clearly was creating offences in respect of acts committed entirely outside of the King's dominions, a statutory Court with statutory jurisdiction not dependent upon venue at all is appointed to try them according to a code of law which did not require venue for its jurisdiction. 26 Henry VIII., chapter 13, is, I submit, the foundation of all that has been said in Hale and Coke with regard both to procedure and to treason out of the realm.

That statute your lordships will find if you have before you the Collection of Treason Statutes, ordered by Parliament to be printed in

1709, at page 7—"It shall be high treason to wish or desire by words "or writing, or to imagine, invent, or attempt any bodily harm to be "done to the King, the Queen, or their heirs apparent." The 1 Henry IV. restored the statute of Edward III., the reign of Richard II. having gone completely outside the statute both in interpretation or without interpretation, and by statutory offences, but they were all within the realm, and that is why I am not citing them on this branch of my argument. Here you have a repetition of treasonable offences. There is compassing and publishing of the King that he is a heretic, "detaining from the King "his castles or holds or his ships or munition of war. And to the intent "that all treasons should be the more dread, hated, and detested to be "done by any person or persons . . . be it therefore enacted that "no offenders in any kinds of high treasons whatsoever they may be, their "aiders, consentors, councillors, nor abettors, shall be admitted to have "the benefit or privilege of any manner of sanctuary . . . and that "if any of the King's subjects, denizens, or other do commit or practice "out of the limits of this realm in any outward parts any such offences, "which by this Act are made or heretofore have been made treason, that "then such treasons whatsoever they may be or wheresoever they shall "happen to be done or committed shall be inquired of and presented by the "oaths of twelve good and lawful men upon good and probable evidence "and witness, in such shire and county of this realm and before such "persons as it shall please the King's Highness to appoint by Commission "under his great seal, in like manner and form as treasons committed "within this realm have been used to be inquired of and presented; and "that upon every indictment and presentment found and made of any "such treasons and certified into the King's Bench, like process and other "circumstance shall be there had and made against the offender, as if the "same treasons so presented had been lawfully found to be done and "committed within the limits of this realm. And that all process of out-"lawry hereafter to be made," and so on. I submit that that is the foundation of the law of foreign treasons that are afterwards to be found in the books, that statute and another statute which I will come to later. There are two important matters to be noticed there—"That if any of "the King's subjects, denizens, or other do commit or practice out of the "limits of this realm in any outward parts"——

Mr. Justice Darling—Where are you reading from now?

Mr. Sullivan—I am reading from the Parliamentary Collection of Statutes.

The Attorney-General—I have it in my note as chapter 13, section 3.

Mr. Sullivan—"That if any of the King's subjects, denizens, or "other do commit or practice out of the limits of this realm in any outward "parts, any such offences which by this Act are made or heretofore have "been made treason, that then such treasons whatsoever they may be or "wheresoever they shall happen so to be done or committed shall be "inquired of and presented by the oaths of twelve good and lawful men "upon good and probable evidence and witness, in such shire and county "of this realm and before such persons as it shall please the King's "Highness to appoint by Commission under his great seal, in like manner "and form as treasons committed within this realm," and then there is process of procedure and the outlawry section which I need not pursue. There you have, as you had in 1414, legislation clearly applying beyond the limits of the realm, and as soon as you find that state of affairs you find a statutory tribunal with jurisdiction to inquire into it.

Mr. Justice Darling—Do you say that there was no tribunal to inquire into it before this?

Mr. Sullivan—Not with regard to offences committed within the territory of any foreign prince. There were two tribunals that could inquire into it. I shall have to develop that later on. The admiral could try anything that was committed on the high seas or below the bridges of the great rivers. He had a civil law jurisdiction, and he could always try treason, although being civil law treason the result was not the same as at common law. Then also the constable and marshal could try treasons committed outside the realm, and he could try them within the realm as long as the appeal of treason remained and wager of battle. As long as that remained there was jurisdiction in the constable and marshal to try appeals of treasons of persons within the realm in respect of treasons committed outside the realm. But, when I come to read the next statute, even now the common law does not know it, notwithstanding the statute of 26 Henry VIII., and it requires another statute to give jurisdiction to the common law Court to inquire into treasons committed outside the realm.

The next statute in order of date deals with the matter I was speaking of with regard to the admiral, but, as in *The King* v. *Lynch*, there appears to have been considerable confusion as to the scope of this statute, I will draw your lordships' attention to it, the Act 28 Henry VIII., chapter 15. The statute recites that, "Where traitors, pirates, thieves, robbers, and "so forth, many times escaped unpunished because the trial of their "offences hath heretofore been ordered, judged, and determined before "the admiral or his lieutenant or commissary after the course of the "civil laws"—I told your lordships that it is established by clear authority that the admiral had jurisdiction to inquire into anything that happened on a ship below the bridges and on the high seas all over the world—"the "nature whereof is that whatever any judgment of death can be given "against the offenders, either they must plainly confess their offences "(which they will never do without torture or pains), or else their offences "be so plainly and directly proved by witness indifferent, such as saw "their offences committed (which cannot be gotten but by chance at few "times), because such offenders commit their offences upon the sea, and "at many times murder and kill such persons being in the ship or boat "where they commit their offence, which should witness against them in "that behalf," and then, "For reformation whereof be it enacted by the "authority of this present Parliament that all treasons, felonies, robbers, "murders, and confederacies hereafter to be committed in or upon the sea "or in any other haven, river, creek, or place where the admiral or "admirals have or pretend to have power, authority, or jurisdiction, shall "be inquired, tried, heard, determined, and judged in such shires and "places in the realm as shall be limited by the King's Commission or "Commissions to be directed for the same in like form and condition as "if any such offence or offences had been committed or done in or upon "the land; and such Commission shall be had under the King's great "seal directed to the admiral or admirals or to his or their lieutenant "deputy and deputies, and to three or four such other substantial persons "as shall be named or appointed by the Lord Chancellor of England for "the time being from time to time and as oft as need shall require "to hear and determine such offences after the common course of the laws "of this land used for treasons, felonies, robbers, murders, and con-"federacies of the same done and committed upon the land within the "realm." That statute is most important to bear in mind for two reasons. Your lordships again see a Commission was issuable under it to try, among other things, treasons and treasons committed within the realm of England, one of them a reported case cited by the late Lord Chief Justice as being a conclusive authority in *The King* v. *Lynch*, *The King* v. *Vaughan*, which I shall have to deal with afterwards.

The statutory Commission supersedes the admiral in his theretofore unlimited jurisdiction in trying everything that happened on ships on the high seas or in estuaries below the great bridges. The Commission still goes to the admiral, but he has associated with him three or four substantial persons, who, as your lordships know, are the judges who are, in fact, common law judges, and they are to proceed according to the course of the laws of the land used for these offences when the same were done and committed upon the land, and they may be tried in any shire or county appointed by the Commission. If the King had power to appoint by Commission overriding the law of venue that the offence should be tried in any county, I submit you would not have had that provision there, still less would you have had the provisions, both in the year 1414, 26 Henry VIII., and what I am coming to next, 35 Henry VIII.

Mr. Justice Darling—Does that do more than change the procedure before the admiral for cases which the admiral by virtue of his jurisdiction had hitherto tried and would continue to try?

Mr. Sullivan—The admiral no longer proceeds to try them as admiral. He now tries them as president of a Commission, consisting of himself and three or four substantial persons nominated by the Lord Chancellor—a new Court.

Mr. Justice Darling—Yes, but it was to try the cases which the admiral used to try.

Mr. Sullivan—It was.

Mr. Justice Darling—Then it was found that the admiral tried them——

Mr. Sullivan—He tried them by civil law.

Mr. Justice Darling—Yes, and then it was decided to associate with him people who knew the common law, and they altogether tried these cases by a different procedure.

Mr. Sullivan—There being a new Court.

Mr. Justice Darling—There was a jury provided.

Mr. Sullivan—Yes, I am coming to that.

Mr. Justice Darling—The admiral had not been accustomed to sum up, so they put a couple of judges with him to help him, but it only goes to procedure.

Mr. SULLIVAN—I am labouring the point that it goes to procedure; it supplies a statutory venue which without it did not exist.

Mr. JUSTICE DARLING—You mean, if you are going to say there must be a jury to try the case, you leave the admiral, but you put with him a jury and a couple of common lawyers, and because you are going to have a jury you must say where the trial is to take place, because you have to summon them.

Mr. SULLIVAN—Certainly. That is part of my argument. Once you get a trial according to common law, even where you have a tribunal, which is not a common law tribunal, but a statutory tribunal, it must proceed on the lines of the common law, and you must have a venue, and the statute provides that venue. That is why I submit this is a very strong authority, that without venue, even at that date, the common law in crimes had no jurisdiction, and accordingly, where you are to proceed according to common law, you must have a statutory venue when the true venue was one from which you could not summon the jury. I am labouring the point of process and procedure even at such a late date as this as showing that without such provision the common law could not go on, and could not try anything that was alleged to be an offence. That is why I am, perhaps, at some length insisting on the process and procedure sections of that statute as throwing light upon the inability of the common law to get on without a venue. I have called your lordships' attention to the provisions of 26 Henry VIII. That made acts committed outside the realm treason which would have been treason if they had been committed within the realm. It also provided for the trial of them, and I have read the section dealing with the trial of them. Apparently they were again in difficulty as to procedure under the statute of 26 Henry VIII., and after nine years they had to pass a statute giving the true common law jurisdiction.

Mr. JUSTICE ATKIN—Pardon my interrupting you for a moment. Is what you have stated as the effect of 26 Henry VIII., chapter 13, this, that an act which if done within the realm is treason, was declared to be treason if done outside the realm?

Mr. SULLIVAN—It was.

Mr. JUSTICE ATKIN—That is to say, it was not merely a law dealing with procedure, but it also altered the description of treason.

Mr. SULLIVAN—Yes. It extended the law of treason, as I submit, for the first time that you can trace, outside the limits of the realm. Having done that, they were faced with the question of how they were to proceed in cases that came within that part of the statute.

Mr. JUSTICE ATKIN—You will have to consider later on, if that is the meaning of 26 Henry VIII., chapter 13, how it bears upon the statute of Edward III.

Mr. SULLIVAN—Yes, my lord.

Mr. JUSTICE ATKIN—Because if it made that treason outside the realm which was treason within the realm, then if the Act of Edward III. only made adhering within the realm treason, this made treason adhering outside the realm.

Mr. SULLIVAN—That is not absent from my mind. I have not overlooked it, and I will deal with it. What I am pointing out at the moment is that the statute of 26 Henry VIII., which I submit for the first time, extended this law to acts done completely outside the realm in the territory of another prince, was conscious of the fact that it could not stop there, and had to provide for this new departure by the constitution of a new tribunal with a statutory venue, to be appointed by the King's Commission; and I use that as an argument that the common law, even at that date, could not have proceeded, and they had to provide a statutory tribunal to deal with what had become clearly an offence, but an offence which required a statutory tribunal to try it, the common law being powerless for want of a venue.

Mr. Justice Bray—Is this right, that the statute provided, first of all, that certain acts which were not treasons should be treasons?

Mr. Sullivan—That, I submit, is the construction of the statute.

Mr. Justice Bray—It did not deal with the treason of adhering to the King's enemies in that part of the statute at all, and then by a later section it dealt with the mode of trial to those treasons and all other treasons. Is not that right?

Mr. Sullivan—No. Will your lordship turn to the section?

Mr. Justice Bray—"Be it enacted that if any of the King's subjects, "denizens, or other do commit or practice out of the limits of this realm "in any outward parts, any such offences which by this Act are made "or heretofore have been made treason"——

Mr. Sullivan—That is omnibus.

Mr. Justice Bray—"That then such treasons, whatsoever they be or "wheresoever they shall happen so to be done or committed, shall be "inquired" into by a jury.

Mr. Sullivan—Yes, it created foreign treasons, and then inasmuch as you could not proceed, the procedure shall be according to the custom of the law in the realm, and the law of the realm could not inform itself without a venue, and then it provides a statutory tribunal with a statutory venue for the purposes of summoning the jurors and proceeding according to common law. By 35 Henry VIII. doubts seems to have arisen as to whether that procedure section was sufficient.

Mr. Justice Bray—This statute did assume that before the Act 26 Henry VIII. there were treasons committed out of the limits of the realm which might be tried.

Mr. Sullivan—I submit not.

Mr. Justice Bray—"Do commit or practice out of the limits of this "realm in any outward parts any such offences which by this Act are "made or heretofore have been made treason." Therefore it clearly implied that there were treasons committed out of the realm which were offences before the Act, and then it made them triable in a certain way.

Mr. Sullivan—I submit the construction of the statute is somewhat different. I submit what it enacts is this. It uses the word "offences" when it clearly shows that the offences, as they call them, namely, the acts, which your lordship sees are of a peculiar character, for instance, publishing of the King that he is heretic, and matters of that kind—that these acts, or, as they call them, offences, if done out of the realm, are to have some quality of crime, as if they were done within the realm; and, again, the word "offences" being applied simply means acts which have been declared within the realm to be offences, if now done outside the realm, shall be crimes, although done outside the realm.

The importance of that construction, if it is the right construction, is that you would then need to have some tribunal to take some cognisance of this extension of crime, namely, an extension to the inquiry into the criminal nature of the acts wholly committed outside of the realm, which, I submit, you find no trace of prior to 26 Henry VIII.; and in order that some one may inquire into them—the twelve men from the vicinity cannot inquire into them, because *ex hypothesi* the matter arises where there are no twelve men corresponding to the statute to inquire—and accordingly the statute itself constitutes a new tribunal, constitutes a venue that could not have existed at common law, and then provides procedure whereby in the new tribunal a trial may be had of the new offences. If they were not new offences and the argument is unsound, there would have been no necessity for setting up this peculiar and awkward tribunal. I submit there is no such thing known to the law as a crime which the law is incapable of pronouncing a crime after procedure. No man is a criminal who has not been condemned according to the course of law.

In 35 Henry VIII., the Act of 26 Henry VIII. had obviously created difficulty in procedure even at that date. "Forasmuch as some doubts "and questions have been moved that certain kinds of treasons, mis-"prisions, and concealments of treasons done, perpetrated, or committed "out of the King's Majesty's realm of England and other His Grace's "dominions cannot nor may by the common laws of this realm be "inquired of, heard, and determined within this his said realm of "England." Your lordships see that the statutory tribunal under 26 Henry VIII. was not the common law; it was a statutory tribunal. "For "a plain remedy, order, and declaration therein to be had and made, be "it enacted by authority of this present Parliament that all manner of "offences being already made or declared, or hereafter to be made or "declared, by any of the laws and statutes of this realm to be treasons, "misprisions of treasons, or concealments of treason, and done, perpetrated, "or committed, or hereafter to be done, perpetrated, and committed by "any person or persons out of this realm of England shall be from hence-"forth inquired of, heard, and determined before the King's justices of "his bench for pleas to be holden before himself by good and lawful men "of the same shire where the said bench shall sit and be kept, or else be "before such Commissioners and in such shire of the realm as shall be "assigned by the King's Majesty's Commission, and by good and lawful "men of the same shire in like manner and form to all intents and pur-"poses as if such treasons, misprisions of treasons, or concealments of "treasons had been done, perpetrated, and committed within the same "shire whereof they shall be so inquired of, heard, and determined as is "aforesaid." There the common law comes in, and comes in, I submit, for the first time.

Mr. Justice Darling—It might be so, except that you leave out, as it seems to me, the power of the Crown to issue Commissions for the trial of these offences, not the judges of assize, oyer and terminer, but Commissions for the trial of treasons done outside the realm.

Mr. SULLIVAN—By this time there has been, on both sides, such a search made that if in truth you could find anterior to the date of the statutes I have mentioned such Commissions issuing they would have been produced. Records much anterior to that are produced here, and at the trial below were debated and touched upon. When you cannot find these Commissions, and if you do find that where such Commissions are issued, they are issued under statute in every case, as far as I know—I speak, of course, subject to correction—that, I submit, is a very strong argument that it required statutory authority.

Mr. JUSTICE DARLING—When do you find a Commission which was issued by statutory authority? Which is the first of them?

Mr. SULLIVAN—I cannot tell you.

Mr. JUSTICE DARLING—When you find what Hale, Coke, and Hawkins thought about this matter it really will not do to say, "Find the par-"ticular Commission; find the document." It will not do. The War of the Roses took place in England, and this statute of Henry VIII. was passed when England was only just settling down from a long period of devastating civil war.

Mr. SULLIVAN—I will have to deal with the authority of Coke and Hale, and I hope to show your lordship that Coke is an authority which from the earliest times has been open to comment, especially Lord Coke's views on the laws of treason.

Mr. JUSTICE DARLING—You rely on the passage in Stephens' Commentaries, do you, where he deprecates Lord Coke?

Mr. SULLIVAN—It goes away behind Stephens—Pulton and Keeling in the early part of the eighteenth century are not less severe than Stephens. You find Stephens, and you find all the historians rather deprecating Coke, and suggesting that he exercises no judgment of his own with respect to these matters.

Mr. JUSTICE DARLING—Did Lord Coke only go wrong about the law of treason, or are his other conclusions wrong?

Mr. SULLIVAN—Some of them. It is as impossible for a man to be always wrong as it is for him to be always right.

Mr. JUSTICE DARLING—Many judges have ascertained that for themselves.

Mr. SULLIVAN—Coke is referred to as the foundation of this, and when I come to deal with him I will point it out. We have investigated the authorities cited by Coke for the proposition he advances, and it certainly is peculiar that they have nothing to say to the case, and certainly justify the observation made both in Stephens, Keeling, and Pulton, and others that Lord Coke was rather fond of citing a case as being a precedent and authority that had nothing whatever to say for the proposition for which he cites it. That is certainly true of his passages on treason, and I will deal with his authorities, and show that he cites a number of authorities as justifying his text that have no relation whatever even to the subject-matter of the text.

Mr. JUSTICE ATKIN—Is this the argument so far, that the Act of 26 Henry VIII. had made a foreign treason for the first time, and had not provided a satisfactory means of dealing with it except by a special Commission?

Mr. SULLIVAN—Yes.

Mr. JUSTICE ATKIN—And that 35 Henry VIII. provided that these foreign treasons should be tried at common law?

Mr. SULLIVAN—Yes.

Mr. JUSTICE ATKIN—And from that you infer that it could not have been tried at common law before 35 Henry VIII.?

Mr. SULLIVAN—Yes, my lord, that is my argument. 35 Henry VIII. was passed obviously because doubts had arisen. I have already read to your lordships 26 Henry VIII. Obviously doubts had arisen about procedure, which even at that comparatively late period was still a crucial matter in criminal proceedings.

Mr. JUSTICE ATKIN—It would follow, would it not, that after 35 Henry VIII. was passed those treasons which by 26 Henry VIII. had been made treasons for the first time—foreign treasons—could be tried at common law?

Mr. SULLIVAN—Yes. It certainly is strange if the common law had seizin of such matters that a statute should be passed with regard to foreign treasons in 35 Henry VIII., notwithstanding the statute of 26 Henry VIII., giving jurisdiction to the Court of King's Bench, the Court of King's Bench not having been the Court to which on three previous occasions Parliament had assigned the trial of foreign treasons where Parliament had dealt with foreign treasons. "Where the bench shall "sit and be kept, or else before such Commissioners as shall be assigned "by the King's Commission"—there is kept alive the power to assign by Commission—"and by good and lawful men of the same shire in like "manner and form to all intents and purposes as if such treasons, mis-"prisions of treasons, or concealments of treasons had been done, per-"petrated, and committed within the same shire where they shall be so "inquired of, heard, and determined as is aforesaid." My lords, the matter is confirmed by a statute of 5 & 6 Edward VI., chapter 11, which is, "That if any of the King's subjects, denizens, or other do commit or "practice out of the limits of this realm"—it is practically a repetition with a slight variation, which is an important variation, of 26 Henry VIII.

Mr. JUSTICE ATKIN—It first of all makes certain acts treasons within the realm, declaring by words that the King is a heretic.

Mr. SULLIVAN—Yes, and it constitutes some new treasons.

Mr. JUSTICE ATKIN—Declaring it by writing is made a treason, and detaining from the King his castles within the realm is made a treason.

Mr. SULLIVAN—There are a number of new treasons.

Mr. JUSTICE ATKIN—And then it proceeds to section 6.

Mr. SULLIVAN—That is the section I was coming to. The earlier sections are not printed.

Mr. JUSTICE ATKIN—You may take it that they are substantially the same as the treasons in 26 Henry VIII.

Mr. SULLIVAN—Yes, it was practically a repetition, teaching that the King is a heretic, writing that the King is a heretic, depriving the King of the castles within the realm, and so on. Then it proceeds, "And, "moreover, be it enacted that if any of the King's subjects, denizens, or "other do commit or practice"—the next words are important—"out of "the limits of this realm in any outward parts"—that is still 26 Henry VIII.—"any of the offences which by this Act are made or heretofore now

Mr. Sullivan

"standing in force have been made treasons, that then such treasons, "whatsoever they may or wheresoever they shall happen so to be done or "committed, shall be inquired and presented by the oaths of twelve good "and lawful men upon good and probable evidence and witness in such "shire and county of this realm, and before such persons as it shall please "the King, his said heirs or successors, to appoint by Commission under "his great seal in like manner and form as treasons committed within "this realm have been used to be inquired of and presented; and that "upon every indictment and presentment founden and made of any such "treasons and certified into the King's Bench like process and other cir- "cumstance shall be there made." Again you get back to the Commission going out rather than to the Court of King's Bench. But it is in terms practically the same as 26 Henry VIII., and it extends to new treasons, and/or theretofore declared treasons out of the realm.

Mr. Justice Atkin—I suggest that the procedure in 26 Henry VIII. and in this section is procedure for getting the presentment rather than for getting a trial. It provides that they shall be presented, and then it shall be certified to the King's Bench.

Mr. Sullivan—Yes, and then by 5 & 6 Edward VI. you would proceed under 35 Henry VIII. It was the absence of procedure in 26 Henry VIII. probably that necessitated the passing of 35 Henry VIII. That would appear to be the stumbling-block as to procedure between the two sections. Then, my lords, the Act of Mary I. swept away all statutory treasons, and restored Edward III., and 1 & 2 Philip and Mary, chapter 10, dealt, among other things, with the case of minors, which I need not trouble about, and it provided that all trials of treasons shall be according to the course of the common law. In the statutes again and again you come across the two matters of compassing death and levying war within the realm. The exception I previously cited to your lordships is 13 Charles II., chapter 1, where, apparently, having dealt with compassing, it provides as high treason the levying of war within or without the realm. Except for that statute, although the levying of war is dealt with in three other statutes, it is always within the realm, and 13 Charles II., chapter 1, is notable as having extended the office of levying war to without the realm. When you come to the Williamite statutes they also necessarily deal with war outside the realm, but they deal with it in a somewhat different manner. 9 William III., chapter 1, dealt with offences which are probably offences to be committed abroad, because it is an offence to go into France without a licence or to return from France without a licence, and to serve the Pretender in France, and the statutory provision is that the offence may be triable in any county—again the procedure which is always the concomitant of the statute which purports to create a crime outside the body of the county, "And be it further enacted that where any "of the offences against this Act shall be committed out of this realm "the same may be alleged and laid, inquired of, and tried in any county "of this realm." That enables you to allege a fictitious venue with regard to the crimes. As I have pointed out, up to the present the venue is never a fictitious venue, it is always a statutory venue to be fixed by the King's Commission; but here the words are, "The same may be "alleged and laid, inquired of, and tried in any county of this realm."

That enables the prosecution to lay a venue which is something akin to the fictitious venues in civil proceedings. Then, my lords, 13 William III., chapter 3, is also a statute which deals with correspondence with the Pretender, giving assistance to him, and sending money to him. It winds up, "That where any of the offences against this Act shall be "committed out of this realm, the same may be alleged and laid, inquired "of, and tried in any county in this kingdom of England." Soldiers are on a somewhat different basis. In 1 Anne, Statute II., chapter 20, you find it made high treason with regard to persons in military service, an officer or soldier out of England, to correspond with the enemy or to give advice or intelligence.

Mr. Justice Darling—Did the statute of 9 William III. create new treasons?

Mr. Sullivan—I submit it did.

Mr. Justice Darling—New treasons, and said they should be tried in any county?

Mr. Sullivan—Yes, my lord.

Mr. Justice Darling—What was the necessity for it? If you look at 35 Henry VIII. that statute says, "For as much as some doubts and "questions have been moved," and so on, "for a plain remedy, order, "and declaration therein to be had and made, be it enacted that all "manner of offences being already made or declared, or hereafter to be "made or declared, by any of the laws and statutes of this realm to be "treasons, misprisions of treasons, or concealments of treasons, and done, "perpetrated, or committed, or hereafter to be done, perpetrated, or "committed by any person or persons out of this realm of England, shall "be from henceforth inquired of, heard, and determined before the King's "justices of his bench for pleas to be holden before himself by good and "lawful men of the same shire, where the said bench shall sit and be kept, "or else before such Commissioners and in such shire of the realm as shall "be appointed by the King's Majesty's Commission." What was the necessity of that statute?

Mr. Sullivan—The change of venue. Under the statute 35 Henry VIII. it was either where the King's Bench were sitting, or else in a venue to be fixed by the Commission, if there was a special Commission.

Mr. Justice Darling—Not where the King's Bench were sitting.

Mr. Sullivan—"Where the said bench shall sit and be kept."

Mr. Justice Darling—"The King's justices of his bench."

Mr. Sullivan—"To be holden before himself by good and lawful men "of the same shire, where the said bench shall sit and be kept." Or, alternatively, such county as the Commissioners are appointed to sit.

Mr. Justice Darling—My brother Lawrence suggests this probably means Middlesex—"Where the justices of his bench"—that means the King's Bench—"shall sit and be kept." The King's Bench long ago followed the Sovereign.

Mr. Sullivan—Yes, my lord. Alternatively, it is by special Commission in the shire appointed by the special Commission. There is a change made in William III. You may allege the venue.

Mr. Justice A. T. Lawrence—Could you put it in any county?

Mr. Sullivan—You could put it in any county, and try it at common law, alleging what might be called a fictitious venue.

Mr. Justice Darling—That is practically all it does, is it not? It says you might have tried them, because this statute 35 Henry VIII. applies to treasons to be created, and therefore it would apply to treasons created in the reign of William III.

Mr. Sullivan—Yes, my lord.

Mr. Justice Darling—If it had not been for that statute they would have been tried in the King's Bench sitting in Middlesex, or wherever the King might happen to be with his judges.

Mr. Sullivan—Yes, my lord.

Mr. Justice Darling—That statute says they may be tried in any county.

Mr. Sullivan—Yes, I agree, 35 Henry VIII. would have enabled them to have been tried either where the King's Bench was, or any special venue fixed by the special Commission. But at common law they would only have been tried in Middlesex. What I am pointing out is that by 1 Mary all trials of treasons were to be at common law, and then when you come to the subsequent legislation for the purpose of complying with the common law, if you are going outside Middlesex, where the King's Bench sat, you need a statutory provision that you may allege the venue as being in the place where you are trying him under the common law, otherwise you cannot try him under the common law.

On the other hand, I was mentioning that soldiers were under a different code. Apparently the first statute with regard to soldiers is the statute of Anne, with the two different chapters, making it high treason for a soldier on land out of England or upon the sea to correspond with the enemy, or enter into relations with him, as it was extended by 3 and 4 Anne. There also the trial was to be as if committed in a county to be assigned by the Commission that tries it. Those were to be Commission trials. That is in the case of soldiers. In 3 & 4 Anne there is a similar provision that it is triable in any county. 7 Anne, chapter 4, is important, because one of the cases cited is a case of soldiers. It is section 48, I think, but again I am citing from the collection of Queen Anne statutes, and they do not print the numbers of the sections. "And "forasmuch as there is not any effectual provision made for the govern-"ment of Her Majesty's land forces out of the realms of Great Britain "and Ireland, be it further enacted and declared that if any officer or soldier "in Her Majesty's army shall either upon land out of Great Britain or "upon the sea hold correspondence with any rebel or enemy of Her "Majesty, or give them advice or intelligence either by letters, messages, "signs, or token, or any manner of way whatsoever, or shall treat with "such rebels or enemies, or enter into any condition with them without "Her Majesty's licence or licence of the general, lieutenant-general, or "chief commander, then every such person so offending shall be deemed "and adjudged to be guilty of high treason, and suffer such pains and "penalties as in the case of high treason." There we get into a special code of laws, which we know grew into the Army Act which commenced with the Mutiny Act, and made provision for high treason triable at common law, presumably under 1 Mary by a combination of the two statutes with regard to soldiers. Then 7 Anne, chapter 21, provides specially for the trial of Scotsmen for treason, and they are to be tried "by good and lawful men of the same shire in like manner to all intents "and purposes as if such treason had been done or committed in the "same shire, where they shall be inquired of, heard, and determined." That is practically the same power to lay the venue as in the statutes of Anne.

Mr. Justice Bray—Do these later statutes throw any light on the question?

Mr. Sullivan—No, except to this extent, that even when you get to these later statutes, probably from too great caution, but still the caution is there, to provide venues—even when you get to the eighteenth century—wherever you have a provision dealing with an outside crime (it is that feature that I am seeking to impress)—when you get into the eighteenth century you have the question of venue still being laboured to safeguard the administration of the statutes, notwithstanding all that had gone before. That question of the venue surviving so late does, I submit, throw a light on what the question of venue must have been when you go back some hundreds of years, and consider what was the state of affairs at the time of Edward III., when, even in the time of Queen Anne, Parliament is careful to see that there is a venue to try a foreign offence.

Now, my lord, I propose to deal with the authorities in the nature of text-books, and also with such cases as we have been able to find bearing on this subject. It is right that I should tell your lordships that between the years 1860 and 1870, at all events, subsequent to the passing of the Treason Felony Act, all the special statutes I have been quoting from, 28 Henry VIII. and those extension statutes, have been repealed.

Mr. Justice A. T. Lawrence—Repealed by the Statute Law Revision Act?

Mr. Sullivan—26 Henry VIII. and 5 & 6 Edward VI. were repealed by the Statute Law Revision Act of 1863.

Mr. Justice A. T. Lawrence—That is the method of repeal to which you are alluding?

Mr. Sullivan—Yes, and as I mentioned in the course of my review of the statutes (I have not cited the statutes), again and again they have gone back to the statute of 25 Edward III. by clearing out all what I might call fancy treasons from time to time; I think four times in the course of the period I have covered.

Now, my lord, the original idea, that adhering to the King's enemies was an offence that might be committed out of the realm, is, I think, to be traced to Coke, page 3 of the Third Institute. Having quoted the statute, he sums up the different heads of offence which, he says, are created by the statute. I want to call attention not only to the case of adhering to, but to the case immediately preceding it, which, I presume, is the same authority, each part of the sentence having the same authority. He says the first concerneth death; the second concerneth—and he sets out his catalogue; the third is levying war against the King. That is his sole statement of it. I submit that, except under the statute of Charles II., which I gave your lordships as a notable exception, levying war against the King was limited by the statute of Edward III.

Mr. Sullivan

to levying war against the King within his realm. But Lord Coke states it at page 3, "The third is levying war against the King," without any limitation of any sort, kind, or description. The words are always the same. "Or if a man do levy war against our Lord the King in his "realm, or be adherent to the King's enemies in his realm, giving to them "aid and comfort in the realm or elsewhere, and thereof be probably "attained of open deed." Coke, at page 3, sums up the third as levying war against the King without any limitation of any kind, sort, or description. The fourth is adhering to the King's enemies within the realm or without, and declaring the same by some overt act. Your lordships see that it is not a quotation of the words of the statute, but he purports in the following pages to cite the statute verbatim, and to comment upon each sentence and phrase of it, but the strange thing is that at the bottom of page 10, paragraph 15, where he deals with this matter which we have to discuss before your lordships he misquotes the statute, "*Ou soit* "adherent as enemies *nostre seigniour le Roy*, a *eux donant aide et* "*comfort en son roialme et aylors.*"

Mr. Justice Darling—Is that the way he cites it?

Mr. Sullivan—Yes.

Mr. Justice Darling—He leaves out the words "*en son roialme.*"

Mr. Sullivan—He does.

Mr. Justice Darling—Does he put it in inverted commas?

Mr. Sullivan—Has your lordship the Third Institute before you?

Mr. Justice Darling—No. I have a print of the statute. My brother Atkin and I have been to the Record Office, and we have read the original of this statute in Norman French, and, more than that, we have compared it——

Mr. Sullivan—Compared it with the reproduction?

Mr. Justice Darling—No, compared it with the Parliamentary Roll of the same date, which probably was written rather before it; and we carefully observed the writing and the punctuation, if that is worth anything. There is a little difference. It is not only Lord Coke who misquotes things, because, if you take the Statute Roll and the Parliamentary Roll, which the Record Office people treat as quite contemporary—nobody knows for certain which is the earlier, but, from inquiries made, they think that the Parliamentary Roll was the original, and that the Statute Roll was copied from it—the Parliamentary Roll says, "*Donant a eux ou comfort* "*en son roialme ou par aylors,*" and the Statute Roll says, "*Donant a* "*eux aide et comfort en son roialme ou par aylors.*"

Mr. Sullivan—I conceive there might be a question arising on that limb of the sentence, but what I wish to point out is that in the Third Institute, printed in italics, and purporting to be the statute when he comes to deal with it, sentence by sentence, he prints the statute bit by bit in inverted commas, in brackets, and in italics.

Mr. Justice Atkin—I do not think it was in inverted commas in the original. I am looking at the fourth edition, and I fancy it was almost the same printed in bold print in a kind of bracket.

Mr. Sullivan—It is italicised in the edition I am reading from.

Mr. Justice Atkin—What is the date of your edition?

Mr. Sullivan—1809.

Mr. JUSTICE ATKIN—The fourth edition is 1669.

Mr. SULLIVAN—In paragraph 15 the words "In his realm" are left out, and if, indeed, the statute is quoted truly at the top of the dissertation part the dissertation is justified in all its entirety. If you leave out those words "in his realm" of the statute, leaving them out in the first part, and including them in the second only as being descriptive of the whole sentence, then I could have no case on this branch of my argument at all. But it is because the statute includes those words that I submit the meaning of the statute is perfectly plain, and you can only arrive at a conclusion in favour of Lord Coke's statement of the law by arriving at the conclusion that in truth the words "in his realm" ought to be left out of the statute in order to make the sense that Lord Coke says the statute bears; because I do submit first and last that what your lordships have to do is to read the statute and form your opinion, in the first instance, whether, on your first reading of the statute, it does not convey a perfectly clear meaning to your mind. If it does that, that is the meaning of the statute.

Mr. JUSTICE DARLING—What becomes of the maxim, "Second thoughts "are best"?

Mr. SULLIVAN—It does not apply to the reading of statutes, because I think what Lord Esher said in the construction of a will is perfectly true also with regard to statutes. "This case," he said, "would be a per"fectly plain case to any man who did not commence by confusing his "mind with reading a large number of other cases."

Mr. JUSTICE DARLING—That is a dangerous doctrine when you have been addressing the Court for two hours.

Adjourned for a short time.

Mr. SULLIVAN—When the Court adjourned I was pointing out that when it comes to the detailed commentary on page 10, Coke first of all fails to quote in what obviously purports to be a quotation from the statute the limitation "within the realm," and leaves it "or be adherent to the "King's enemies, giving to them aid and comfort in the realm or else"where." That, of course, completely alters the meaning of the statute. It is right to say that the dissertation upon the statute then follows as a matter of course upon lines which have been apparently approved by citing the statute with a clause omitted. If the clause were included the comment on the whole of the statute as it would then stand would, I submit, be more valuable, but for any writer to comment on a clause which he first misquotes is a dangerous proceeding, which is apt to lead him astray.

Mr. JUSTICE ATKIN—He has already at page 1 set out the statute correctly, and he has translated it correctly, and this is only a part of his commentary where he purports to set out some of the words.

Mr. SULLIVAN—That I had stated. He quotes the whole statute on page 1, and at page 3 he summarises, and on page 10 he purports to deal with this clause. It is the commentary under this clause which has become the foundation of what I submit is the plain error of the writer. "This "is here explained, viz., in giving aide and comfort to the King's enemies "within the realm or without; delivery or surrender of the King's castles "or forts by the King's captaine thereof to the King's enemie within the "realme or without for reward, &c., is an adhering to the King's enemy, and "consequently treason declared by this Act." These cases that he cites of the delivering of castles are cases, I submit, not at common law at all, but within the jurisdiction of the constable and marshal without doubt or question, and therefore no difficulty applies to those cases, for the jurisdiction of the constable and marshal was not limited by any question of venue or by the rules of the common law. It is for that reason that I cited the passages from Viner.

Mr. JUSTICE ATKIN—You could appeal a man for a crime committed abroad before the constable and marshal. You could not have an appeal for a crime unless it was a crime.

Mr. JUSTICE A. T. LAWRENCE—Your argument is that it is not a crime.

Mr. SULLIVAN—My argument is that it is not a crime in the sense in which we are dealing with it, namely, it is not a matter to which the statute refers, because, I submit, the statute refers to the administration of the King's Courts of the common law within the realm.

Mr. JUSTICE ATKIN—If you could have an appeal before the marshal for treason committed abroad, what was it that gave you power to appeal him for treason, except on the footing that it was a crime or a wrong?

Mr. SULLIVAN—The jurisdiction of the marshal was really a jurisdiction for persons, originally, at all events, who were serving His Majesty in a military expedition.

Mr. JUSTICE DARLING—Take the very case you are arguing now, the case of Casement. Is your point this, that he could not be tried in the King's Bench, as he was tried, but he could have been lawfully tried by virtue of a special Commission issued by the Crown?

Mr. SULLIVAN—No, that is not my argument.

Mr. JUSTICE DARLING—Why not?

Mr. SULLIVAN—My argument is that he is indicted as having committed an offence against the statute of Edward III., and that the matter alleged is not an offence within the statute of Edward III.

Mr. JUSTICE DARLING—The statute of Edward III. says that it may be an offence to commit certain treasons outside the realm—"within the "realm or elsewhere," that is outside. The statute says there may be such crimes, there may be such treasons, how could they have been tried?

Mr. SULLIVAN—I submit the statute does not say that.

Mr. JUSTICE A. T. LAWRENCE—You read the word "elsewhere" out of the statute altogether.

Mr. SULLIVAN—No. I had better deal at once with the construction as I submit of the statute. The statute deals first of all with levying war, and it is limited within the realm.

Mr. JUSTICE A. T. LAWRENCE—It begins by compassing or imagining the King's death.

Mr. SULLIVAN—Yes.

Mr. JUSTICE A. T. LAWRENCE—It does not limit that to within the realm.

Mr. SULLIVAN—It is unlimited in terms, but would have to be administered by the common law Courts, and in respect of the limitation of the declaration of treason theretofore made by the common law Courts, so that men within the King's peace may know what acts are treason and what are not. That would be limited in the way I argued this morning. It would be limited to the Courts that could take cognisance of such acts as would constitute evidence of compassing, but in terms it is not limited as to place, and is outside the realm, probably because the King's dominions extended far outside the realm, and with regard to compassing might apply to compassing both in Scotland, Ireland, Wales, and France and other of the King's dominions.

Mr. Justice Darling—You say the King's dominions extended far outside the realm. Were the counties which ultimately became the United States of America within the realm or without?

Mr. Sullivan—They were without.

Mr. Justice Darling—New Hampshire was one of them. That was without the realm.

Mr. Sullivan—Outside the realm.

Mr. Justice Darling—There was no doubt about that.

Mr. Sullivan—I do not like to affirm that any proposition is without doubt. Lord Coke has not dealt with it. But I submit they were not part of the King's realm. They were part of the King's dominions, and when you read the statutes, as far as the statute of Edward III. goes, I think you will see that there is a clear line of demarcation both of administration and of principle as to what acts are committed within the realm and what acts are committed outside the realm.

Mr. Justice Darling—You are asking us to adopt the view of this statute which many people have considered before any of us here present. Have you got Archbold among your other books?

Mr. Sullivan—Yes, my lord.

Mr. Justice Darling—If you turn to page 1033 you will see this, and that is why I asked you where New Hampshire was—"In 1775 the law "officers (Thurlow, A.G., and Wedderburn, S.G.) had been informed that "in 13 Anne an Act against high treason had been passed in the province "of New Hampshire; that the said Act was disallowed by Order in "Council in 1718; that it was conceived there was no law of that province "at present existing for the trial and punishment of that offence. They "were asked in what manner it was proper to proceed against persons for "high treason committed in New Hampshire. They replied, 'We are "'humbly of opinion that it requires no Act of a provincial Legislature "'to constitute the offence of high treason in any of His Majesty's planta- "'tions. The crimes may be prosecuted in the Superior Court of New "'Hampshire (which by 2 William III. hath the full criminal jurisdiction "'within that government which His Majesty's Court of King's Bench "'exercises here), or in this country in the statutes of 35 Henry VIII., "'as the occasion may require.'"

Mr. Sullivan—Yes. Surely, does not that confirm the view I presented to the Court, that New Hampshire was outside the realm?

Mr. Justice Darling—Yes, but what becomes of your argument? New Hampshire is outside the realm, and Lord Thurlow and Lord Loughborough, as I think he was afterwards, say that for treason committed there you may indict him and prosecute him here, because he has committed the treason outside the realm, he has committed it elsewhere.

Mr. SULLIVAN—Yes, under 35 Henry VIII.

Mr. JUSTICE SCRUTTON—What made it treason in New Hampshire?

Mr. SULLIVAN—26 Henry VIII.

Mr. JUSTICE ATKIN—No, according to you, the effect of that was done away with by 1 Mary.

Mr. SULLIVAN—No, 1 Mary I did not open in terms to your lordships. 1 Mary provided that no acts should be treason except the acts mentioned in the statute of Edward III.

Mr. JUSTICE ATKIN—But it still leaves it treason if committed abroad.

Mr. SULLIVAN—Yes, I submit that is the meaning of the statute. No act is to be deemed an act of treason except such acts as are specified—"From henceforth no act, deed, or offence being by Act of Parliament or "statute made treason, petit treason, or misprision of treason by words, "writing," and so forth, "but only such as be declared and expressed "to be treason, petit treason, or misprision of treason in or by the Act "of Parliament or statute made in the twenty-third year of King Edward "III." What I have been quoting from is a "collection of the several "statutes and parts of statutes now in force relating to high treason and "misprision of high treason," ordered to be printed by Parliament on the 20th April, 1709, and to be published when subscribed by the judges. So that I have just read to your lordships the statutes which include that statute of 26 Henry VIII., and that is subscribed, as you will see, at the end by all the judges as being in their opinion, at all events, the statutes then current and in force. That is the view, I submit, of 26 Henry VIII. Such acts as were treasonable acts under the statute of Edward III., under the statute of Henry VIII. were treasonable acts wherever they were committed.

Mr. JUSTICE ATKIN—I still do not follow what your answer is to my brother Scrutton. If this opinion is correct, this assumes that there is such a thing as committing treason out of the realm.

Mr. SULLIVAN—That is perfectly true.

Mr. JUSTICE ATKIN—And that it could be tried in England.

Mr. SULLIVAN—Yes, in 1775.

Mr. JUSTICE ATKIN—You say it does not follow that the form of treason is adhering to the King's enemies out of the realm.

Mr. SULLIVAN—That is one of my arguments, that compassing being unlimited is a thing that might take place anywhere, but that treason of adhering is limited by the statute to taking place within the realm, and it is triable so long as being adherent is the offence, which is the state of mind existing in the individual; and the extent of the jurisdiction given by the statute was that you might try and inquire into his state of mind in the light of events which might have taken place either within the realm or without the realm. That is to say, the aid or comfort he might have given which would be evidence of his adherence need not be aid and comfort in the place where he is, in fact, adhering within the realm, but might be rendered to the enemy outside the realm.

Mr. JUSTICE A. T. LAWRENCE—Do you say there are two substantive treasons in that branch of the section?

Mr. SULLIVAN—No, one. Being adherent is the only one.

Mr. Justice A. T. Lawrence—If that is so, the "elsewhere" applies to it.

Mr. Sullivan—The "elsewhere" applies to the aid and comfort, which is the overt act by which you prove the adhering.

Mr. Justice A. T. Lawrence—You cannot have a trial for treason without an overt act, can you?

Mr. Sullivan—No.

Mr. Justice A. T. Lawrence—You say the first branch of the thing is a treason which you cannot try?

Mr. Sullivan—Oh, no.

Mr. Justice A. T. Lawrence—Either it is one and the same treason, or it is two treasons, one of which you cannot try.

Mr. Sullivan—I submit that there is only one treason.

Mr. Justice A. T. Lawrence—That is adhering.

Mr. Sullivan—Yes. You may prove that he is adhering within the realm, but acts which have taken place outside the realm—inside or outside. The offence is, "Or be adherent to the King's enemies in his realm, "giving to them aid and comfort in the realm," or outside of it. His adherence may manifest itself by his giving aid and comfort either within the realm or outside of it.

Mr. Justice A. T. Lawrence—But you have to say that it cannot be an adherence within the realm as a triable offence.

Mr. Sullivan—If he is in the realm and is adhering to the King's enemies he is, being within the realm and within the King's peace, giving aid and comfort to the King's enemies anywhere. The idea of treachery which underlies it is there apparent. The treachery consists of the man being within the protection of the King's peace, in his realm, and nevertheless assisting the enemies of the realm by giving them aid and comfort. He assists them by his presence in the realm, just as in the first case, and, indeed, the six other cases reported. His being within the realm enables him to get the information or to get the material which becomes useful to them, although they may not be within the realm at all, and his adherency and his work within the realm may not be manifested within the realm, although the offence is committed within the realm, and, in order to prove the offence, it may be necessary to show the events taking place in places not within the realm. But the offence which you are proving by evidence of acts outside the realm is nevertheless an offence taking place within the realm by the man who within the realm is collecting information of a private character, matters of that description, or perhaps it may be stores, and letting that information or letting that aid or comfort go to the enemies of the realm who may be outside. But the man must be inside. It is his action, his state of mind, his treachery, that is being committed within the realm where he is, although it is manifested by something which takes place, owing to his agency, outside.

Mr. Justice A. T. Lawrence—I do not follow you. You can only show it by some overt act or other.

Mr. Sullivan—Take the overt acts in the cases that have arisen. The reported cases that have arisen have all been cases of persons within the realm collecting information as to the disposition of the King's forces or ships within the realm, or matters of that kind, which would be useful for an enemy to know, and transmitting that to the enemy outside; just as in the first case I quoted of the person who came into the King's Council and ascertained the King's secrets and then transmitted them.

Mr. Justice Atkin—In those cases of sending information, is not the overt act laid as being within this country, as a rule?

Mr. Sullivan—In the reported cases, yes.

Mr. Justice A. T. Lawrence—Every act done within this country must be an overt act within this country.

Mr. Sullivan—But, my lord, the statute would provide that even if you could prove no overt act within this country, and if your offence was something which took place elsewhere, in Flanders or in France, you could prove that the man was adhering within the realm by reason of something set on foot by his agent within the realm that manifested itself outside the realm. You might show, for instance, that he within the realm had contrived that stores and munitions or something of that sort had reached the enemy outside the realm where the enemy was. You could show that he within the realm had collected information, and although you could prove no overt act within the realm, you could show that he was doing that and adhering by showing that information which only could have been collected by him, and for a treasonable purpose, had, in fact, reached an enemy that was never within the realm at all. There the overt act was outside, but the crime was committed by the treachery of the man who never left the realm.

Mr. Justice Scrutton—In your view may the crime of adhering within the realm be proved by overt acts entirely elsewhere?

Mr. Sullivan—Yes.

Mr. Justice Scrutton—What meaning do you give to "within the "realm" supposing all that was proved was that a man elsewhere had assisted the enemy? Is it necessary to prove presence in the realm, or what?

Mr. Sullivan—It is necessary to prove that he was within the realm. He must be present within the realm in committing the offence, although the overt act by which you show what he was concerned in within the realm might be an overt act completely outside the realm. He must be within the realm. The adherency is a matter personal to the man. It is the man who is doing the adhering, and he must be within the realm.

Mr. Justice A. T. Lawrence—It is the man who is doing the treason.

Mr. Justice Bray—If the indictment in this case had been for adhering within the realm, that could have been proved by the acts he did in Germany.

Mr. Sullivan—Not that he did, but if you found that he was within the realm you might prove by acts in Germany that he who had never been in Germany at all—that X.Y.Z., who had never been in Germany at all, was guilty of adhering to the King's enemies who were in Germany, and assisting them, although he himself never went there and never went outside the realm; and you could prove that by events which took place in Germany from which an inference could be drawn that he remaining at home was, in fact, assisting them and adhering to them.

Mr. Justice A. T. Lawrence—How could you do that? It is an

impossibility. It would not admissible evidence. Unless he was connected with the act he could not be charged with it.

Mr. Sullivan—Take any concrete case of sending information.

Mr. Justice A. T. Lawrence—That is an act done in this country.

Mr. Sullivan—The overt manifestation of that act done within this country might not be manifest within the country at all.

Mr. Justice A. T. Lawrence—It is either an act of his or it is not. If he is within the country doing the act, then the act is done within the country.

Mr. Sullivan—The overt act by which you show that he within the country was adhering may involve the investigation of things that happened not within the country, but in Germany. Take the case of conveying information as in the nine reported cases in which there has been adherence. They are all cases of supplying information by a person within the realm to the use of persons not within the realm. The overt act may be proved by the receipt outside the realm of information. You may prove acts done in Germany from which a jury would be entitled to infer that the man within the realm was responsible for these overt acts that happened outside the realm.

Mr. Justice A. T. Lawrence—How could he be responsible except for acts done by him?

Mr. Justice Atkin—Are you suggesting the case of a man sending out an agent with a general authority to give money to the enemy?

Mr. Sullivan—I was going to answer, my lord—*The Queen* v. *Mulcahy*.

Mr. Justice Atkin—Every time he gives money to the enemy through his agent who is abroad there is an overt act by the principal within the realm.

Mr. Sullivan—In *The Queen* v. *Mulcahy* the man who was convicted of treasonable practices in Dublin had never been within 3000 miles of Dublin at the time the acts were committed. His agent had done them. The accused was, in fact, in America during the rising of 1867, and he was tried and convicted for it.

Mr. Justice Scrutton—Is there any case in which there is an overt act of adherence without the realm where the prisoner has not done some act within the realm?

Mr. Sullivan—Some overt acts, yes.

Mr. Justice A. T. Lawrence—How? I cannot think of it.

Mr. Sullivan—Take it that the prisoner being in America appoints an agent to do certain acts in Germany with the assistance of the Germans, and then the prisoner comes and remains within the realm. He is within the realm, and his agent is doing acts outside the realm. He does nothing within the realm. But if *The Queen* v. *Mulcahy* is rightly decided the acts of his agent may be proved to show that he, although doing nothing overtly himself, was adhering to the King's enemies all the time he was within the King's peace.

Mr. Justice Atkin—*Mulcahy* was a case of compassing.

Mr. Sullivan—Yes.

Mr. Justice Atkin—He was not indicted for adhering, and the overt act was a conspiracy.

Mr. Sullivan—It was a peculiar case.

Mr. Justice Atkin—I am looking at the report of the case of three English and Irish appeals. I have no doubt the indictment is set out correctly. The first count was feloniously compassing to deprive and depose the Queen, and then it sets out the overt act, that he did conspire to raise money and levy insurrection, and that he conspired to move and stir up certain persons in the United States of America to invade Great Britain. The second count was feloniously compassing and intending to levy war against the Queen in order to compel her to change her measures and counsels. The third count was feloniously compassing to move and stir certain foreigners to invade the United Kingdom.

Mr. Sullivan—I think your lordship will find that the levying war was, in fact, done in Dublin, where the prisoner was not. You will find that is so in the Court of Error. It only went to the Lords on a technical ground.

Mr. Justice Atkin—These were all felonies under the Act of 2 Victoria.

Mr. Sullivan—Yes, under the Act of 1848. I pointed out at the commencement of my argument there was no procedure in this statute of Edward III., and accordingly procedure would have to be at common law under this statute. "Be adherent to the King's enemies in his realm" is a clear definition of the offence. It is a state of being. It is solely a question of being adherent, relating to the attitude of the man.

Mr. Justice A. T. Lawrence—You must read on beyond that to make it intelligible.

Mr. Sullivan—I am going to.

Mr. Justice A. T. Lawrence—It has to be "probably attainted of "open deed by the people of their condition." How could you get a treasonable deed unless you get the state of his mind?

Mr. Sullivan—Giving them aid and comfort in the realm or elsewhere is, I submit, a description of the nature of his adherency.

Mr. Justice Darling—Is it not quite reasonable to suppose that these words, "giving to them aid and comfort," are words in apposition, words which explain what adherent is?

Mr. Sullivan—Reading then in that way they are descriptive of the adherence.

Mr. Justice Darling—Do you agree that is the way to read them?

Mr. Sullivan—That is the way I think I am reading them.

Mr. Justice Darling—Then let us see how you can read them. You can read them that it means this, if a man be adherent to the King's enemies in his realm by giving to them aid and comfort in his realm, or if he be adherent to the King's enemies elsewhere by giving them aid and comfort elsewhere.

Mr. Sullivan—I submit that is a method of reading which would do violence to the context. I submit the way to read them truly as descriptive of what is adhering is to read them as being adjectival; and reading it without the adjective it is, if a man be adherent to the King's enemies in his realm.

Mr. Justice Darling—That may be, but the thing to be explained is, what is meant by adherent? I thought you agreed just now that the words "giving to them aid and comfort" were to explain the adhering. Supposing somebody had said, "What do you mean by adhering? Do "you mean my simply saying I approve of the King's enemies?"—no, that is not treason. The treason is defined as adhering, and adhering is giving to them aid and comfort. If they are enemies within his realm you are adhering to them if you give to them aid and comfort within the realm, and if they are enemies outside the realm you are adhering to them if you give to them aid and comfort outside the realm. My brother Atkin and I took the trouble to look at the Parliamentary Roll and the Statute Roll. They are both the same in this respect, that you get the words "adherent as enemies *nostre seigniour le Roy,*" and then there is a break. I mention this because there was a great deal of argument at the trial about commas and brackets. If you look at the original Norman French you will find there is a break. You do not see brackets or commas, but they put a transverse line right through. There is a break after "*le Roy en le roialme,*" and then comes "*donant a eux eid ou confort en son roialme ou par aillours.*" But if you look at the Parliamentary Roll there is just the same break after "*en* "*le roialme,*" and then comes "*donant a eux eid et confort en son* "*roialme,*" and then another break, the equivalent of the bracket contended for at the trial by the Attorney-General. That break is drawn right through the line, and you get the words "*ou par aillours.*" If you look at the Statute Roll in that place where there is an undoubted break in the Parliamentary Roll there is a mark which we looked at very carefully with a magnifying glass. It is not certain that it is a break just as it appears in the Parliamentary Roll, but we were inclined to think it was a break, not made with a pen, but a break which had come by the folding in the course of all these six centuries. If you put that break after "*donant a eux eid ou confort en son roialme*" it is very much the worse for your argument.

Mr. Sullivan—If anything can be inferred from that, but I understood brackets did not exist in the sense of brackets.

Mr. Justice Darling—They are not brackets in the sense that they have not got a transverse line that runs at right angles, but there is a very distinct line drawn right through the line of writing, and that occurs every here and there where we should now perhaps put what I think are called breaks in the print. Where we should put brackets these old scribes put a transverse line. It was very natural. They were doing it with a pen.

Mr. Justice Atkin—I think they really are to represent commas; they are reproduced in the reprint of the statute as commas. The Statute Roll is printed in the revised statutes exactly correctly. I suppose you would infer, if there was any importance to be attached to the difference, that they corrected the Parliamentary Roll from that which is the authority, namely, the Statute Roll.

Mr. Sullivan—It ought to be so, but I submit you cannot draw any inference from punctuation. The whole matter will have to be determined without any theory as to punctuation arising from a fortuitous circumstance which is not the same in the two rolls, and, at all events, when your lordships are dealing with a penal statute, I humbly submit that crimes should not depend on the significance of breaks or of commas. If a crime depended on a comma, the matter should be determined in favour of the accused, and not of the Crown.

Mr. Justice A. T. Lawrence—If you can give an intelligible reading to the words disregarding them, then that might be so.

Mr. Sullivan—I submit the meaning to be given is perfectly intelligible. Although the statute has been in force so many years, there is only one case in which even an indictment can be found, and until the year 1903 there is no case in which there had been an argument or judgment upon the meaning of this part of the statute. Although there had been on this limb of the statute nine cases, they were all cases of adherency within the realm, and the proof of communications and information collected within the realm, or attempted proof to the enemies outside. The meaning, I submit, is perfectly clear, and you must get rid of the words "in "his realm" altogether, and leave them out, as Lord Coke does, in order to arrive at his translation of them.

Mr. Justice Darling—Lord Coke sets out first of all the statute quite correctly, and then he wants to tell you how it is to be understood, and when he comes to tell you how it is to be understood, seeing that at that point the words "*en son roialme*" are not necessary to the understanding, he leaves them out, as one often does in reading the section of a statute in order to make clear what the meaning is, and then you read it in two branches. If the man is indicted for aiding and comforting the King's enemies within the realm, then it is necessary to say that the aid and comfort must be given within the realm; if he is indicted for aiding and comforting the King's enemies outside the kingdom, then you do not need the words within the kingdom.

Mr. Sullivan—I submit if it is necessary in order to give it that meaning, or rather to prevent another meaning being apparent, to leave out these words, the Court in construing the statute cannot leave them out, but must take the meaning with those words in. If the words being in do not alter Coke's meaning of the phrase, there is no harm in inserting them, and there would be no object in leaving them out if they were consistent with his phrasing of it. I submit that is the case, and "giving "both aid and comfort in the realm or elsewhere" is descriptive of adhering.

Mr. Justice Darling—I agree with you personally if you stop at "comfort." If you stop at "giving aid and comfort," yes, that describes the crime of adherence; but you do not want "elsewhere" for that. You want the "elsewhere" when you are describing the crime to be committed elsewhere.

Mr. Sullivan—Stopping at "comfort" and leaving out the adjectival phrase, "giving to them aid and comfort," how does the statute run? It runs "or by adhering to the King's enemies within his realm, in the "realm or elsewhere." Why is there any repetition of "in the realm"? I submit it is impossible to stop at the word "comfort," because then you would have a repetition of the words "in the realm," which would clearly be superfluous and unmeaning. Accordingly, to avoid repetition of the phrase, the repetition being unneeded, it is absolutely necessary, I submit, to read the whole phrase as being adjectival, as being descriptive of the fact of being adherent, which act of being adherent is then clearly defined as being within the realm. But let us consider this. What about levying war—"Or if a man do levy war against our Lord the King in his realm"?

There the limitation, I submit, is perfectly clear. Is the adherency to be something wider than levying war? If he takes up arms, and you indict him under that limb of the statute, it would be levying war against our Lord the King in his realm. If he does not take up arms he does something short of it; but there is a much wider construction of the statute, according to Coke, and the man who takes up arms outside the realm is not guilty of levying war within the realm, but the man who gives him the information is guilty of the offence of high treason under the same statute. That is an anomaly.

Mr. Justice Darling—Do you say that if a man levied war against the King in one of his Colonies he would not be guilty of treason, if he raised an armed force and levied war against the King, say, in Australia?

Mr. Sullivan—In every one of the Colonies he would now be guilty of treason. There is no doubt about it.

Mr. Justice Darling—Guilty of treason under this statute. Never mind any other legislation.

Mr. Sullivan—The levying of war was confined by this statute to the realm for the reasons I have pointed out. The phrase "levying war" is repeated in Philip and Mary when we come to deal with compassing and levying war. Adherence does not seem to have been dealt with by statute at later periods, but compassing and imagining and levying war have been dealt with by legislation again and again. Levying war in the time even of Philip and Mary was within the realm. Within the realm means something both with regard to levying war and adherence, and it is a strange thing that the matter never until 1903 came up for argument, and was the subject of argument or judicial consideration prior to 1903, when *The King* v. *Lynch* was decided, and in *The King* v. *Lynch* there was a ruling on this point on a basis which I do not think can be contended as sound.

Mr. Justice Scrutton—In most of these cases the gentlemen who adhered to the enemies outside the realm took very good care not to come in again afterwards.

Mr. Sullivan—That would be the reason why no proceedings would be taken except for outlawry.

Mr. Justice Scrutton—In one case an attempt was made to try him.

Mr. Sullivan—That was a military governor, and, what is more, it was the castle at Calais, at that time an English borough returning two members of Parliament.

Mr. Justice Scrutton—I was thinking of *The King* v. *Hulton*.

Mr. Sullivan—In that case it was a process of outlawry, but it was the same thing. Of course he could have come back and traversed his indictment, and if he had stood his trial on the indictment his outlawry would have been quashed. He is not tried and condemned on the indictment, but he is outlawed by process. The crime for which he was outlawed is that he did not answer to the King's writ. He did not come and stand his trial, and therefore he was outlawed. On the return to the writ he was outlawed for not coming forward to stand his trial.

Mr. Justice Darling—If he had come to stand his trial he had, according to you, a perfectly good legal objection to the indictment.

Mr. Sullivan—He had according to me.

Mr. Justice Darling—Why did not he come and take it?

Mr. Sullivan—In those days confidence in the administration of justice was not so well rooted as at present. This question of adherency was considered in *The King* v. *Hulton*, and in the trial in Ireland it was expressed that the adherency was in the person, although the enemies to whom he had adhered might be outside the realm.

Mr. Justice Scrutton—I have not been quite clear as to what you are doing. I thought you were starting with the text writers, and were then going to deal with the authorities. Would it be possible to do it in some sort of order?

Mr. Sullivan—I stand reproved.

Mr. Justice Scrutton—It is our fault, I think, because we have been asking questions about all sorts of things.

Mr. Sullivan—I did intend to deal with Lord Coke and his authorities. With regard to his authorities, he cites for his interpretation 43 of the Book of Assizes, items 28, 29, and 42. None of those cases has any reference at all to the statute or to the words of the statute.

Mr. Justice Scrutton—He begins with *John Britton's* case. Is that one of the castle cases?

Mr. Sullivan—The first reference I have is 43 of Assizes, item 15 (*a*).

Mr. Justice Scrutton—You seem to be beginning in the middle, if I may respectfully say so.

Mr. Sullivan—Apparently that is so. I took the reference as being there. Then the next is 43 of Assizes. Then there are references to the Rolls of Parliament, 7 Richard II., items 15, 17, and 24, and 7 Henry IV., item 47. That has nothing to do with treason at all. 7 Richard II., item 15, was not a case of treason, but impeachment of the Bishop of Norwich for a number of offences, including peculation and breach of contract and general corruption, in respect of an agreement with the Crown to supply an army and to provide it. 7 Richard II., item 17, is a case of the custodian of a castle in Flanders who was put in arrest for surrendering the castle. There is no treason mentioned. One of them was released, and the other was committed to prison during the pleasure of the King. It certainly is not a proceeding on the statute. The earlier ones could not have been. Then item 24 is a case of surrendering a castle. There is an allegation that one of them was encroaching the Royal power by issuing letters of safe conduct. There is certainly no conviction of treason, and they are committed to prison until they pay a fine or ransom. With regard to those cases, my friend on the other side did not cite below any of the other cases there.

Mr. Justice Scrutton—I am interested in the *John de Brittaine* and *Robert de Werkes* cases. Those are cases that Lord Coke cites for his propositions. It cannot be fair for you to begin in the middle of the note.

Mr. Sullivan—I agree it is not fair to the commentator.

Mr. Justice Scrutton—Lord Coke probably put his best cases first.

Mr. Sullivan—He might have done, but they have not been cited in argument. The Roll of Parliament, 20 Edward I., would not help us.

Mr. Justice Scrutton—Have you not looked, or has not your junior looked at it?

Mr. SULLIVAN—It is entirely my own oversight if I have not had my attention directed to it; I regret I have not been a little more industrious recently as I might have been. One case referred to is 20 Edward I., and the other is 32 Edward I. Then there is one in 8 Richard III., and one in 38 Edward III. Those might be referable.

Mr. JUSTICE SCRUTTON—33 Edward I. looks as if it were common law; it is before the statute.

Mr. SULLIVAN—That would be before the statute, and so would be 20 Edward I. Your lordship sees they are all Rolls of Parliament.

Mr. JUSTICE SCRUTTON—They are none the worse for that.

Mr. SULLIVAN—They are not common law. The Courts of Parliament, my lord, were not common law.

Mr. JUSTICE A. T. LAWRENCE—They are not proceedings of the common law Courts, but it does not follow that they did not administer the common law.

Mr. SULLIVAN—They may have administered the common law, but they were not bound or limited by the common law. I endeavoured to point out on the statute of Edward III. that it had to be administered by the common law. One of the consequences, I submit, if you are compelled to hold the statute dealt with offences committed by persons within the realm, is that otherwise until 26 Henry VIII. he was not triable. The question of how it could be tried is dealt with on page 11, "That is to "say, out of the realm of England. But then it may be demanded, how "should at this time this foreign treason be tried? And some of our "books do answer, that the offender shall be indicted and tried in this "realm where his land lieth, and so it was adjudged in 2 Henry IV. But "now by the statute of 35 Henry VIII., chapter 2 (which yet remains in "force), all offences made or declared, or hereafter made or declared "treasons, misprisions of treason, and concealments of treason, com- "mitted out of the realm of England, shall be inquired of, heard, and "determined, either in the King's Bench or before Commissioners in such "shire as shall be assigned by the King." Now, the Crown cited below for the proposition that the trial might be had where his land was, Fitzherbert's Abridgement, 5 Richard II., Trial 54—"*Quare impedit* by "the King against one P., clerk, of a church in the bishopric of Durham, "and setting forth how the bishop, who is dead, presented B.N., his "clerk, and the clerk died, and the chapel was collated upon a cardinal, "naming his name, and on account of heresy and schism the church was "void, the temporalities being in the King's hands, and therefore the "presentation belongs to the King."

There is a long argument, in which there is in the course of the argument an observation by counsel, which is the whole matter of the authority as far as can be ascertained from the perusal of it, that the trial might be held anywhere, especially where his land lies—"I say with certainty "that the Court has cognisance of this plea, and prove it because the whole "Court Christian is one Court, and if a man is accused in the arches "here in this country of a certain crime for which he is liable to "deprivation, and then he appeals to the Court of Rome, and is deprived "over there, this deprivation is triable in the King's Court in the same "way as if he had been deprived in the arches, inasmuch as it is all one

"Court; and if a man be an adherent to the King's enemies in France his "land is forfeitable, his adherence will be tried where his land is, as has "often been done with the adherents of the King's enemies in Scotland; "and, sir, on my faith, if a man be a traitor his land is forfeitable, and "the lord has it by way of escheat; and it is reasonable, for if, when a "man is out of the faith of his Sovereign Lord the King, his land is "forfeitable, *a multo fortiori* when he is out of the faith of God." That is the authority cited against us below, and the authority for the proposition in Coke, that he could be tried where his land was. When you come to deal with Hale, and especially with Hawkins, there was so much opinion as to how he should be tried that it is quite clear nobody knew how he could be tried.

Mr. Justice Darling—Is that the authority referred to by Sir Edward Coke?

Mr. Sullivan—Yes; 5 Richard III., Trial 54.

Mr. Justice Atkin—Before you go to Hale, there is a passage in Coke's Institutes, page 11, "It was resolved by all the judges of England "that for a treason done in Ireland the offender may be tried by the "statute of 35 Henry VIII. in England, because the words of the statute "be, all treasons committed out of the realm of England, and Ireland "is out of the realm of England."

Mr. Sullivan—That is after 35 Henry VIII. The question that Coke is putting is prior to 26 Henry VIII. How could you try any of these treasons; what were you to do? If the thing was a crime it ought to be triable, and apparently they are casting about to try and imagine how it could be tried; but with all the opinions how it could be tried, so far as can be ascertained, I am not aware in that period that it ever in truth was tried, and when you get to Hawkins, Hawkins finds himself faced with a number of different methods in which, it is alleged, it might be tried; and I submit the observation of Hawkins, so far from being an observation against me, is, in truth, a confession that nobody knew how you could try it until 25 Henry VIII.

Mr. Justice Atkin—I thought it was the decision in Dyer that it could not be tried.

Mr. Sullivan—There was the opinion that it could not be tried. The opinion in Viner's Abridgement is that it could not be tried, and there it ended. It is 2 Dyer, 131*b*. In Coke, on piracy, he says this on page 113, "Note, treason done out of the realm is declared to be treason by "the statute of 25 Edward III., and yet at the making of this Act of "26 Henry VIII. it wanted trial (as by the preamble of this statute it "is rehearsed) at the common law." So apparently he expressed two different opinions in two different parts of the same volume.

Mr. Justice Darling—Does he say it wanted trial?

Mr. Sullivan—Yes, it wanted trial.

Mr. Justice Darling—What do you take that to mean?

Mr. Sullivan—That there was no way of trying it.

Mr. Justice Darling—Why should not it require to be tried?

Mr. Sullivan—The context is, I think, perfectly clear; as I say, it is on page 113, under the heading "On Piracy," "Note, treason done out "of the realm is declared to be treason by the statute of 25 Edward III., "and yet at the making of this Act of 26 Henry VIII. it wanted trial "(as by the preamble of this statute it is rehearsed) at the common law." That is to say, it lacked trial.

Mr. Justice Darling—Do you understand that to mean that it could not be tried at all?

Mr. Sullivan—That it could not be tried at common law.

Mr. Justice Darling—What does that mean? It could not be tried at assizes?

Mr. Sullivan—It could not be tried by common law Courts; it could not be tried within the realm by any of the common law Courts when committed outside the realm.

Mr. Justice Darling—Why could it not be tried by the Commission issued by the King?

Mr. Sullivan—They could go to such places in Wales and Ireland in the King's dominions, not shires and counties—places that had not the bodies of counties.

Mr. Justice Darling—Why could not they go anywhere?

Mr. Sullivan—Because, your lordship sees, an act within the body of a county is got into the county; that could only proceed on venue.

Mr. Justice A. T. Lawrence—Once you have got a Commission to try it in a county you would have a venue. There would be no difficulty about venue then.

Mr. Sullivan—Before the matter came to trial there had to be the procedure anterior to trial by which the accused would be brought before the Court, and, as we know, the accused was brought before the Court by procedure, which necessitated his neighbours bringing him before the Court. Of course, there were Courts which sat by Commission within their own jurisdiction. A constable, I take it, could act with regard to a matter which was not within the body of the county; that is the case mentioned in Viner. If the matter was not within the cognisance of the body of the county, you might have tried him at civil law in certain instances, but at common law a thing had to be done in the body of a county.

Mr. Justice Scrutton—Perhaps I have misunderstood your argument, but Lord Coke says, at page 11, in the passage I think you read, "And "some of our books do answer that the offender shall be indicted and "tried in this realm where his land lieth, and so it was adjudged in 2 "Henry IV." Was it so adjudged according to the law in 2 Henry IV.?

Mr. Sullivan—As far as can be ascertained, I am instructed that that turns out to be the Welsh case; we have tried to trace it.

Mr. Justice Scrutton—Lord Coke evidently thought he had authority for that proposition.

Mr. Sullivan—The reference, as far as we can discover, is in Henry IV., Coram Rege Roll. That is what I cited and handed to your lordship. I am told that that is so. If it is the Welsh case, it is rather hard to see why it is cited in such company.

Mr. Justice Scrutton—They were going to try him when he stole sheep, but when they proceeded to try him nobody appeared to offer evidence, and so he was acquitted.

Mr. Sullivan—He was charged.

Mr. JUSTICE SCRUTTON—He was charged with a number of things.

Mr. SULLIVAN—He was charged with a sufficient number of things to have given the Court some work to do.

Mr. JUSTICE SCRUTTON—They could try him for stealing the sheep, but the prosecution did not call any evidence.

Mr. SULLIVAN—The object of the proceedings against him was different, and the sheep formed a very small portion. The peculiar thing is the admission that he was not triable.

Mr. JUSTICE ATKIN—Do you mean this admission in his Comment on Piracy? You refer to the inconsistency in Sir Edward Coke's comments on what he says in the part dealing with treason, and what he says when dealing with piracy. At page 113 he says, "And yet at the making of "this Act of 26 Henry VIII. it wanted trial (as by the preamble of this "statute it is rehearsed) at the common law." If you look at the preamble of the statute, all that the statute said was that the traitors at sea could not be tried; it goes no further than that.

Mr. SULLIVAN—He is obviously wrong.

Mr. JUSTICE ATKIN—They could be tried before the admiral, who had exclusive jurisdiction, as I understand, over the high seas, and therefore they could not be tried at common law; it is only by reason of the exclusive jurisdiction of the Lord High Admiral as it existed over the high seas.

Mr. SULLIVAN—Yes, the statute itself expressly provides it is only referring to offences that were triable by the admiral according to the course of the civil law.

Mr. JUSTICE ATKIN—That is traitors at sea, on the high seas.

Mr. SULLIVAN—Yes, it is to remedy the course of procedure according to civil law.

Mr. JUSTICE ATKIN—I do not suppose Lord Coke's Commentary proposed to go beyond the preamble.

Mr. SULLIVAN—He refers to them as being traitors out of the realm. Will your lordships look at the strange references he gives? He refers to it as being treason done out of the realm.

Mr. JUSTICE ATKIN—Yes, he does.

Mr. SULLIVAN—If you transpose the statute and refer to it as 26 Henry VIII. it would be more accurate, but even in that event it would not be accurate either. Certainly the statute he refers to only refers to it by the preamble set out. He is inaccurate whichever way you read it; it is by no means an accurate statement of the law, as it stood, if I may say so.

Then the next matter in the text-books is in Hale, with reference to the same.

Mr. JUSTICE ATKIN—Before you leave the Institutes, do you know the date of the Third Institutes?

Mr. SULLIVAN—That I do not know, but I came across a passage in Kelyng, which suggested that part of the Third Institutes was posthumous, and the treason portion is mentioned in Kelyng.

Mr. JUSTICE ATKIN—If you do not know, do not trouble to find it now.

Mr. SULLIVAN—It is mentioned in Kelyng, and especially with reference to treason it says his posthumous statements are not accurate, above all, with reference to his article on treason.

Now, Hale deals with the matter at page 167 of the first volume—"If an Englishman during the war between the King of England and "France be taken by the French, and there swear fealty to the King of "France, if it be done voluntarily, it is an adhering to the King's enemies; "but if it be done for fear of his life, and that he returns, as soon as he "might, to the allegiance of the Crown of England, this is not an "adherence to the King's enemies within this Act. Clause 7, Edward "III., Part I., membrane 15." The references he deals with are 6 John, membrane 19, and 7 Edward III., Part I., membrane 15 and membrane 9. The dates of all those are prior to the statute. The first matter he refers to is 6 John, membrane 19, in reference to the confiscation of the lands of the barons in the time of John; they are all prior to the statute. So far as I can see there is nothing in that which involves the construction of what we are debating here, or the question of adherence without the realm by acts done completely without the realm; it is the forfeiture of the baron's land, who elected to serve the French King instead of John. Then 7 Edward III., membrane 9 and membrane 15. Those are two cases in which there is a direction to deal with land which has been forfeited on the ground, apparently, that the two parties had been charged with having joined the Scots, whatever that may be at that date, and they were to get back their lands on the ground that they had not joined the Scots. There is nothing to assist us in the smallest degree in that. Possibly the charge against them was levying war in the realm, or it may have been.

Mr. Justice A. T. Lawrence—Against the Scots.

Mr. Sullivan—The other items are taken from the Rolls of Parliament; they are impeachments, and he deals with them; they are inquiries into the loss of castles. Your lordships see the sentences are not sentences pronounced in respect of treason. Then at page 168, just above the shoulder note to page 169, "And note, though the charge were treason, "and possibly the proofs might probably amount to it, and Walsingham "tells us it was done by treason, yet the reason expressed in the judgment "against Weston only"—then the judgment is set out—"and the like "reason is expressed in the judgment against Gomeneys." Then, "The "truth is"—and this, my lords, is most instructive—"if it were de-"livered up by bribery or treachery, it might be treason, but if delivered "up upon cowardice or imprudence without any treachery, though it were "an offence against the laws of war, and the party subject to a sentence of "death by martial law, as it once happened in a case of the like nature "in the late times of trouble, yet it is not treason by the common law, "unless it was done by treachery; but though this sentence was given *in* "*terrorem*, yet it was not executed; it seemed to be a kind of military "sentence though given in Parliament, like unto that of the Baron "Graystock, governor of Berwick." There is also another case which he cites, and then at the top of page 169, "This also seems rather a "sentence of council of war than a judgment of high treason; and thus "far touching the treason of adhering to the King's enemies within the "land and without. Touching the trial of foreign treason, viz., adhering

Mr. Sullivan

"to the King's enemies, as also for compassing the King's death without "the kingdom at this day, the statutes of 35 Henry VIII., chapter 2, hath "sufficiently provided for it." Then he cites *Storey's* case, "But at "common law he might have been indicted in any county of England, and "especially where the offender's lands lie, if he had any." That is 5 Richard II., Trial 58, in Fitzherbert's Abridgement, the case I have cited to your lordships.

Mr. Justice Darling—What do you say to this; this is Chief Justice Hale?

Mr. Justice Scrutton—You say that Hale followed Coke, and that Coke was wrong in his law, and you say that without looking at the authorities he cites.

Mr. Justice Darling—Is not it rather a cavalier way of disposing of Coke and Sir Matthew Hale?

Mr. Justice A. T. Lawrence—It is not the way one has been accuscomed to hear them dealt with.

Mr. Justice Darling—What do you say to Lord Coke and Sir Matthew Hale, and what do you say to Chief Justice Dallas? We have read the arguments below, and one sees how Lord Coke and Sir Matthew Hale were treated; I was wondering if we ought to treat them in that way. There is a case of *Burt* v. *Conant* in the first volume of Broderip and Bingham's Reports, at page 570, where Chief Justice Dallas says this, "We are told "that we must look to the authorities, and find what we can in the books "upon the subject. Now, if the authority of Lord Hale and that of Mr. "Serjeant Hawkins are to be treated lightly, we may be without any "authorities whatever. With respect to Lord Hale, it is needless to "remind those whom I am now addressing of the general character for "learning and legal knowledge of that person, of whom it was said that "what was not known by him was not known by any other person who "preceded or followed him, and that what he knew he knew better than "any other person who preceded or followed him. With respect to Mr. "Serjeant Hawkins, we know his authority. These are books which are "in the hand and head of every lawyer, and constantly referred to on "every occasion of this sort. I must, therefore, look to these books; "and I shall proceed to examine the exposition given by text writers of "the words of those statutes and the commission of the peace." Chief Justice Dallas took a rather different view of Sir Matthew Hale and Serjeant Hawkins from that which you ask this Court to take.

Mr. Sullivan—My lord, it is not the first time that a Court has been asked to differ from an opinion expressed by Coke.

Mr. Justice A. T. Lawrence—There have been shoals of law reformers since that day, who have all had these authorities before them, and they have not reformed the law in the way one imagines they would have done if they had not treated these statements as good law.

Mr. Sullivan—Probably. My lord, what I intend to point out to the Court is this, that when you are dealing with a statute, that is the authority; the statute is there itself, and it is its own prime expositor. Lord Coke was not a contemporary with the statute, and his speculative opinion, if it turns out to be a speculative opinion, cannot possibly control the construction of a statute, which as far as research can go, until the year 1903, was never construed, after argument, by judgment. I agree that if you could find that the law has been acted on in a certain way for a great number of years, that would influence you in acting in consonance with the views of great text writers, that would influence a Court to a very great degree; but if the law as pronounced by them has not been acted on, if it has not come in question to be acted on, if the matter has not arisen, the observations even of great lawyers like Coke and Hale on the construction of a statute which has not come before a bench to be canvassed and debated, I submit, is of far less authority than their opinions upon matters of other kinds. Sir Matthew Hale purports to give authority for his propositions. One is, of course, conscious of the absurdity of the situation of declaring that there was a crime of which no Court could inform itself; the thing is contradictory. A crime that cannot be judicially pronounced to be a crime is not a legal offence of any kind, and accordingly both Coke and Hale are found facing what is clearly a difficulty in their own minds. If this were so, and there was a crime committed entirely outside of the King's dominions and outside of the realm, how did it come to be a crime, how was it pronounced to be a crime, for without pronouncement it could not be a crime? They answer it by saying the only answer we can find to it is that he might have been indicted in any county of England, especially where the offender owned land, if he had any, and there is the reference to 5 Richard II., Trial 54, which when we refer to it is the observation of counsel arguing in a case where the matter does not arise. If that is the best foundation that can be found for getting over what is obviously to the mind of every person a tremendous difficulty in extending the statute outside of the realm, and if you go to that authority on which they express that opinion, and you find that the authority carries you very little distance, if any, in that direction, and it is simply the observation of counsel arguing another case in which the matter does not arise, and is not applicable, that becomes the sole authority, because they cite it as being the authority themselves for a proposition, which I submit is contrary to the long string of statutes which I have cited to your lordship.

Mr. Justice Atkin—Does Sir Matthew Hale deal with the case in Dyer, at page 31*b*, at all? I think Lord Coke does cite that as contrary to his view.

Mr. Sullivan—He cites it.

Mr. Justice Atkin—Perhaps you will deal with that later on.

Mr. Sullivan—I am going to cite that later on. The citation from Dyer is not the same one; that is *Storey's* case.

Mr. Justice Atkin—That was foreign treason, compassing the King's death.

Mr. Sullivan—Yes, and, secondly, as your lordship sees from the date, it was clearly within the statutes then current.

Mr. Justice Atkin—Either on the footing that the Act of Edward III. made it treason, because it did not limit it to being within the realm, or on the footing of 26 Henry VIII.

Mr. Sullivan—Yes; in any event, it was clearly not demurrable in 13 Elizabeth. So far from being an authority against me, I submit the passage in 2 Hawkins, at page 306, is a strong authority in my favour—

Mr. Sullivan

"It seems to have been a great doubt before the making of the statute 35 Henry, chapter 2, in what manner and in what place high treason done "out of the realm is to be tried. For some seem to have holden that "it was triable only upon an appeal before the constable and marshal." There is the first alternative, and it negatives common law because the constable and marshal were not common law—"Others, that it might be "tried upon an indictment, laying the offence in any county where the "King pleased; and others, that it was triable by way of indictment in "that county only wherein the offender had lands." There are his authorities, and if one is right the other two are wrong; they are all brigaded to the same extent. "But, surely," says the commentator, "it "cannot reasonably be doubted but that it was triable some way or other; "for it cannot be imagined that an offence of such dangerous consequence, "and expressly within the purview of 25 Edward III., should be wholly "dispunishable, as it must have been if it were no way triable." That is looking at the matter through the wrong end of the telescope, with all respect.

Mr. Justice Scrutton—What is the authority which Serjeant Hawkins gives for the country? There is the Third Institute, which I know. What is the other authority before that?

Mr. Sullivan—We have consulted the highest authority in historical law, and we are not able to answer. Professor Holdsworth was unable to translate it, we were told.

Mr. Justice Scrutton—Have you tried the librarian of the Bar Library?

Mr. Sullivan—I do not know if my friend, the Attorney-General, knows it.

The Attorney-General—No.

Mr. Sullivan—At least, I am sinning in goodly company. With all respect to Hawkins, he looks at the matter from the wrong end. He says, this being a crime, surely it must be punishable. A consideration of the development of the laws of crime will show that it was by reason of being punishable a thing was a crime, and it was by reason of the legal consequence operating through the Courts of justice that put acts into categories of crime and felonies and treasons.

Mr. Justice A. T. Lawrence—Is that correct? Do you say it was a crime because it was punishable?

Mr. Sullivan—That, I submit, is the only test known to the law.

Mr. Justice A. T. Lawrence—I should have thought it was exactly the converse—that it was only punishable because it was a crime.

Mr. Sullivan—He assumes it was a crime, and then says it would be a dreadful thing if it were not punishable.

Mr. Justice Darling—He does not say it would be a dreadful thing. He says various lawyers have disputed, as they will, technically: here is a man guilty of a crime, how are you going to try him? Then Hawkins says these people have disputed, but surely he must be triable one way or another, and why decide amongst these people? It may be you could try in more than one of the ways. The King could certainly issue a special Commission to try him.

Mr. Justice Bray—The words are "expressly within the purview of "25 Edward III." That is clearly the strongest expression of opinion that the offence is provided for by 25 Edward III. Supposing by some mischance it was not triable after the passing of that Act until the statute of Henry VIII. it would become triable then.

Mr. SULLIVAN—I submit that you could only arrive at that conclusion in this way. He says, "Surely it cannot be imagined that an offence "of such dangerous consequence and expressly within the purview of 25 "Edward III. should be wholly dispunishable?" I submit the answer is, if it was expressly within 25 Edward III., there would not be any doubt about how it was tried.

Mr. JUSTICE A. T. LAWRENCE—The statute does not give any particular form of trial.

Mr. SULLIVAN—Because I submit it did not create the offence. I have pointed out when the offence is clearly created by statute outside the realm the statute always did provide a method of trial for it.

Mr. JUSTICE A. T. LAWRENCE—The statute is the statute treating of all these treasons; it does not give any form of trial for either. Your argument, if it destroys the one on that ground, would destroy them all, and there would be no treason left.

Mr. SULLIVAN—Except what was committed within the realm.

Mr. JUSTICE A. T. LAWRENCE—It would not leave that.

Mr. SULLIVAN—Yes, my lord.

Mr. JUSTICE A. T. LAWRENCE—Why?

Mr. SULLIVAN—Anything committed within the body of a county, within the realm, would be tried according to the law of the realm by the common law Courts. My argument does not seek for a moment to doubt that.

Mr. JUSTICE A. T. LAWRENCE—The statute does not say that.

Mr. SULLIVAN—There was no necessity for saying anything at all about trial as long as it did not purport to legislate outside the King's realm or bodies of his counties. It need not say anything; the statute operates automatically, and the judicial system was in itself competent to deal with it as long as you kept the statute within the body of the judicial system. The statute only becomes unworkable by a construction which causes it to create an offence without the limit of the judicial machinery to try it. That is why I submit your lordship would not so construe it. Then your lordships would find this enormous period covered by many statutes relating to treasons meanwhile, but you find this enormous period of legal history in which there was an offence in the air, something like a crime that no Court could take cognisance of. How could there be a crime? How could any man be said to be guilty in accordance with the constitutional doctrine of the presumption of innocence until conviction, according to the process of law? If you could not convict a man of being a criminal he was not a criminal; the crime did not exist. They are all pressed with this, and Hawkins shows there is, in truth, no solution to this obstacle that I pointed out at the outset, of venue in connection with treason. Some say that you could only try it by the marshal, others that it could be tried on an indictment laying an offence without the King's peace. There is no precedent till you get the statute.

Mr. JUSTICE A. T. LAWRENCE—I understand you to admit it would be triable by the marshal, do you? How did it become so triable?

Mr. SULLIVAN—By civil law. The statute of 13 Richard II. was limiting the marshal, and not extending him. Your lordships will find by 13 Richard II., chapter 2, and 1 Henry IV., chapter 14, the marshal was not trying anything that could be triable by the common law. According to Viner, because a matter was not triable by the common law, there being an appeal, the marshal had cognisance of it. Viner was obviously referring to the statute which forbade the marshal to take cognisance of anything that could be tried by the common law.

Mr. JUSTICE ATKIN—What statute is that?

Mr. SULLIVAN—It is 13 Richard II., chapter 2. That is the one limiting the authority. Your lordship remembers in the reign of Richard II. there was a conflict both with the admiral and with the marshal with regard to the exercise of jurisdiction in places within the bodies of counties. Up to then there was a disputed jurisdiction, and then 13 Richard II., chapter 2, as your lordships remember, confined the marshal, and another statute confined the admiral, to the trial of such offences as the common law had not cognisance of. There were complaints of encroachment of cases within the cognisance of the common law, and then the statute is passed to declare in this Parliament by the advice and assent, and so forth, the power and jurisdiction of the constable is as follows:—" To the " constable it pertaineth to have cognisance of contracts touching deeds " of arms and of war out of the realm, and also of things that touch war " within the realm, which cannot be determined or discussed by the " common law, with other usages and customs to the same matters per- " taining which other constables heretofore have duly and reasonably used " in their time; joining to the same, that every plaintiff shall declare " plainly his matter in his petition, before that any man be sent for to " answer thereunto. And if any will complain, that any plea be com- " menced before the constable and marshal, that might be tried by the " common law "—then there is the remedy of it.

Then 1 Henry IV., chapter 14, repeats the declaration that matters which are triable at common law shall not be called in question, and it says, " That all the appeals to be made of things done within the realm " shall be tried and determined by the good laws of the realm, made and " used in the time of the King's noble progenitors; and that all the appeals " to be made of things done out of the realm shall be tried and determined " before the constable and marshal of England for the time being." Apparently that statute of Henry IV., as long as it stood, and the statute of Richard II. gave jurisdiction to the constable and marshal, provided that the matter that they inquired into was outside the cognisance of the common law, and in light of that, is not the observation of Hawkins of great weight, that the first alternative as to how you are to deal with the last form of treason is to be by the constable and marshal?

Mr. JUSTICE DARLING—Have you looked at the work by Mr. Ferdinand Pulton, a barrister of Lincoln's Inn, who wrote a treatise very carefully collected, as he says, " out of the reports of the common laws of this " realm, and of the statutes in force, and out of the painful works of the " Reverend Judges Sir Anthonie Fitzherbert, Sir Robert Brooke, Sir " William Stanford, Sir James Dyer, Sir Edward Coke, knights, and other "learned writers of our laws," and so on? The copy I am reading from is dated 1609.

The ATTORNEY-GENERAL—That was the first edition.

Mr. JUSTICE DARLING—Have you seen it?

The ATTORNEY-GENERAL—Yes.

Mr. JUSTICE DARLING—Have you seen it, Mr. Sullivan?

Mr. SULLIVAN—No.

Mr. JUSTICE DARLING—I am reading from the folio between pages 110 and 111, section 4—"And because by the said statute of 25 Edward III. "it is declared to be high treason to levy war against the King in his "realm, or to be adherent to his enemies, aiding them in his realm, or "elsewhere; therefore if a subject born of the realm being beyond the "seas doth practice with a prince or governor of another country to invade "this realm with great power, and do declare where, how, and by what "means the invasion may best be made, it is high treason; for an "invasion with great power cannot be, but of likelihood it will tend to "the destruction or great peril of the King and hurt to the realm; and, "moreover, the said offender hath manifested himself to be adherent to "the King's enemy and to aid him with his counsel, though not in the "realm, yet elsewhere, and this offence shall be tried in the King's Bench, "or elsewhere, before such Commissioners, and in such county, as the "King by Commission shall appoint according to the statute of 35 Henry "VIII."

Mr. SULLIVAN—There is no doubt about that being the law at that date.

Mr. JUSTICE DARLING—Is not that exactly this case? A person being subject to the King, adheres outside the realm to a foreign prince. Pulton says that can be tried in the King's Bench, or elsewhere, as the King may direct.

Mr. SULLIVAN—According to statute.

Mr. JUSTICE DARLING—We are after the statute; we are subsequent to the statute.

Mr. SULLIVAN—The question is, what statute?

The ATTORNEY-GENERAL—He says Edward III.

Mr. JUSTICE DARLING—I will read it again. He is dealing with the statute. He begins at section 3—"The aforesaid statute of 25 Edward III. "doth confirm it to be high treason for any person to compass or imagine "the death of our Sovereign Lord the King," and so on. "And because "by the said statute of 25 Edward III. it is declared to be high treason "to levy war against the King in his realm, or to be adherent to his "enemies, aiding them in his realm, or elsewhere; therefore, if a subject "born of the realm being beyond the seas doth practice with a prince or "governor of another country to invade this realm with great power." Then it proceeds as I have read. Then he puts what is, upon the facts, exactly the case we are arguing to-day.

Mr. SULLIVAN—I take it he cannot cite any case.

Mr. JUSTICE ATKIN—That seems to be based upon *Storey's* case of compassing.

Mr. SULLIVAN—Yes.

Mr. JUSTICE ATKIN—I thought it probably was, because I noticed the word about "practising," which is the word used in *Storey's* case. He does go on to say it is adhering.

Mr. SULLIVAN—He goes on to say so. I do not know whether he quotes any case, or gives any text, more than we have been able to find up to the present.

Mr. JUSTICE A. T. LAWRENCE—As I understand you, the offence of compassing does not exist out of the realm; no punishment, no crime.

Mr. SULLIVAN—It might have been so up to 26 Henry VIII.

Mr. JUSTICE A. T. LAWRENCE—That does not create treason; it only says that treason may be tried in a particular way.

Mr. SULLIVAN—That is 35 Henry VIII. 26 Henry VIII., I point out, does create treason, and makes acts outside the realm treason that are treason within the realm, which is extending Edward III. to the world. 26 Henry VIII. is the most important of all. 35 Henry VIII. was passed in order to clear up doubts arising upon the draughtsmanship and the provision of the special tribunal that was provided by 26 Henry VIII. to try these new treasons outside of the realm. I do submit that when you come to treason outside of the realm you find treason outside of the realm begins in the Reports later than 26 Henry VIII., "That if any of the "King's subjects, denizens, or other do commit or practice out of the "limits of this realm, in any outward parties, any such offences, which "by this Act are made, or heretofore have been made, treason, that then "such treasons, whatsoever they be, or wheresoever they shall happen to "be done or committed, shall be inquired," and then it provides trial; but the Act of 26 Henry VIII. did create treasons outside the realm, and accordingly, in 1609 and after that, you find in the Reports cases cropping up of allegations of treason outside the realm, and as late as 1709, one hundred years later than the opinions stated, you find Parliament treating by the revision of the judges the statutes and parts of statutes relating to treason—and there is 26 Henry VIII. as being then in force.

Mr. JUSTICE A. T. LAWRENCE—That, you say, has been repealed?

Mr. SULLIVAN—Yes, but it refers to the period of the cases cited, and it was current as governing the realm and governing everybody within or without the realm during all the period of the cases cited since that date. They repeal it after the Treason Felony Act had been passed. I do submit that 26 Henry VIII. is the most important statute upon this, because I think you find it is after 26 Henry VIII. that you see *Storey's* case and the other cases of foreign treason.

Mr. JUSTICE ATKIN—After 26 Henry VIII., according to you, was adhering to the King's enemies beyond the realm treason or not?

Mr. SULLIVAN—It was arguable, at all events, that it was, although I submit that owing to the limitation of the statute of Edward III. itself it would be contradicting the statute to extend it beyond it, but compassing was certainly beyond. I submit that the statute was extending compassing. Then you had meanwhile, as your lordships know, in the history of the reign of Henry VIII. a whole lot of fancy treasons; in fact, one had to keep one's eyes on the Statute Book, because one's opinions, lawful to-day, might forfeit one's life to-morrow. I think 26 Henry VIII. is the most important of all the statutes. It certainly extended the law of treason outside the realm to quite a lot of new treasons within and without the realm for the first time, and it provided the trial.

Mr. Justice Atkin—I do not know why you say it was the important Act, because the Act of 5 & 6 Edward VI., chapter 2, section 6, repeats exactly the same language; it has not been repealed, and is now in force.

Mr. Sullivan—That is true.

Mr. Justice Atkin—It is set out in Archbold, at page 1033.

Mr. Sullivan—The significant thing is, I think, the compassing cases after 26 Henry VIII. I have gone through all those reported in the State Trials, and two other reports, and collected them, and I am not aware of anything before 26 Henry VIII., in which you find cropping up the allegation outside the realm. It is significant, I think, that in the State Trials, at all events, I may be corrected about it, but I think the foreign treasons as reported in the Reports commence subsequent to 26 Henry VIII., at all events, I say so until 1903. There is a reported case of adhering, and no matter, my lord, was brought forward in argument for judicial decision involving the question, and therefore I submit——

Mr. Justice A. T. Lawrence—That is only because it did not arise. There is no ground for supposing a case arose and was passed over.

Mr. Sullivan—There is only one case, *The King* v. *Cundell* in the Newgate Calendar.

Mr. Justice A. T. Lawrence—That was cited in the Court below.

Mr. Sullivan—Yes. That is the only case in which apparently the question might have arisen. It does not appear that any question did arise. Cundell had been in His Majesty's service, and he had, in fact, been guilty of treason under the second Act of Anne—not the second Mutiny Act, but the second Military Act passed in the reign of Anne. There does not appear to have been any doubt raised until *The King* v. *Lynch.* No precedent can be found of judicial opinion being called in to consider the matter, as affecting the lives or liberties of any of His Majesty's subjects. However the matter may have been canvassed in the abstract, as far as I know, until the case of *The King* v. *Lynch* judicial authority had never been exercised in manner of argument upon this clause of the statute with which I am afraid I am wearying your lordships a good deal longer than I desire to do.

Now, my lord, with reference to the observation in Hawkins, to which I have called your lordships' attention, will your lordships look at 2 Dyer, page 131*b*. It is not a judicial decision.

Mr. Justice Atkin—I thought it was under the procedure under which, before the creation of the Court for the consideration of Crown cases reserved, criminal cases were discussed by the serjeants of Serjeants' Inn. It is a very old practice.

Mr. Sullivan—It is a very old practice, and it had the authority of judgment.

Mr. Justice Atkin—It was the only way of dealing with it. Sir James Dyer states that it was argued by counsel before them; sometimes they were.

Mr. Sullivan—The history is in Mr. Holdsworth's work, and it is very interesting. It does not appear from the report in Dyer to have arisen at a net point, but all such points that arose in the Court it was undoubtedly the habit to have debated at Serjeants' Inn in the manner set out in this particular case, and in all probability, as your lordship says, it may be a judicial decision of a case discussed in that way.

Mr. Justice Atkin—Sir James Dyer was King's serjeant at that time, was he not?

Mr. Sullivan—He was Chief Justice of the Common Pleas afterwards; I do not know if he was King's serjeant; that would add authority to it.

Mr. Justice Darling—If he was a serjeant at all, that would be a good deal.

Mr. Sullivan—Of that I know nothing, but I have great respect for the King's serjeants. The King's serjeant, as we know, until the nineteenth century, led the Attorney-General until the unfortunate contretemps arose in which he accepted a minor position to the Attorney-General, and allowed himself to be led in Court. The report is in Trinity Term, 2 & 3 Philip and Mary, and it is certainly a practical contradiction of the suggestion of Coke, Hawkins, and Hale, because there was no doubt a question about what the opinion of the judges then moved was. "It was "moved for a doubt among the judges and King's serjeants, whether if "treason be committed in France, or anywhere out of the realm, it be "inquirable and triable by law at this day, by the statute of 35 Henry "VIII., chapter 2, because in the statute of 1 & 2 Philip and Mary, "chapter 10, it is enacted, that all trials hereafter to be had, awarded, "or made for any treason, shall be had and used only according to the "due order and course of the common laws of this realm, and not other- "wise." That emphasises what I pointed out this morning, and that under 26 Henry VIII. and 35 Henry VIII., although you had proceedings, you had not, till the Court of the King's Bench came in, common law— "And it seems that notwithstanding this, the statute 35 Henry VIII., "chapter 2, is in force, because no offence of treasons committed out of "the realm was triable here by the course of the common law, therefore "this statute enlarges the power and authority of the trials of the realm "in this point."

Mr. Justice Scrutton—Is the word "county" or "country"?

Mr. Sullivan—"County" is printed.

Mr. Justice Scrutton—What is a foreign county?

Mr. Sullivan—I think it is right, my lord; this was said just about the time of the statute, though I did not quote the statute with regard to foreign pleas.

Mr. Justice Atkin—I think it was called a foreign county if laid in the wrong county.

Mr. Sullivan—The foregn plea when it arose was in a county foreign to that in which it was presented; the word "county" is probably right; "but for treason committed in a foreign county and triable in the King's "Bench or in any county of the pleasure of the King, by statute 33 Henry "VIII., chapter 23, it seems otherwise." That is 33 Henry VIII., chapter 23. Strange to say, that statute is not printed in the 1709 collection, but I have a note of it.

Mr. Justice Scrutton—On the face of it it had nothing to do with treason.

Mr. Sullivan—It had something to do with treason, and if your lordships will give me a moment I will tell you exactly what it was. It was urged that great inconvenience had arisen from having to remand the accused for trial in the county where the treason was committed as the law then stood, and persons examined before the council or vehemently suspected of treason would be tried at the Commission of oyer and terminer within the shire, and it was said that the Commissioners should have power and authority to inquire, hear, and determine such treasons, and so on, within the shire and premises limited by their Commission or without wherever such offence was committed. I have a note of it, if your lordship will allow me to refer to it. I have it in my list of statutes creating offences, but somehow I must have slipped over it. It did deal with treasons.

Mr. JUSTICE SCRUTTON—Do you say " or without " refer to 26 Henry?

Mr. SULLIVAN—Yes.

Mr. JUSTICE SCRUTTON—And nothing else?

Mr. SULLIVAN—As a matter of fact, the enactment is repugnant to the recital, because the offence they purport to deal with is by persons who were sometimes examined before the council, and sometimes information was taken, and then they had to be remanded for trial to the county in which it was alleged the offence took place. The result was they might have waited trial under a Commission of oyer and terminer for an interminable length of time, and the statute purports to remedy that by enabling them to be tried in a venue directed by the King's Commissioner instead of going to a true venue. Primarily for treason committed within the realm the consequence was they had to be remitted for trial to the place where the treason was committed.

Mr. JUSTICE BRAY—After this case in Dyer all the learned judges assumed that felony could be created without and tried within this country, otherwise they were considering a point that never could arise at all.

Mr. SULLIVAN—After the opinion given, yes, certainly.

Mr. JUSTICE BRAY—At the time the opinion was given they must have assumed that for a treason committed in France the person could be prosecuted in this country; otherwise it was arguing a case that never could arise at all.

Mr. SULLIVAN—That is, of course, accurate; they were doubting it.

Mr. JUSTICE BRAY—Supposing what you are saying is right, that they had not in contemplation these treasons referred to in 35 Edward III.; is that your argument?

Mr. SULLIVAN—I cite the case as the considered opinion, that prior to the Act of 35 Henry VIII., the act would, if done within the realm, have been treason in that sense.

Mr. JUSTICE BRAY—Suppose we were in your favour upon that, I think it is an authority quite against you, upon the point whether what is a treason is what can be charged. It is clearly against you on that point. Here are all these learned judges giving their opinion and considering a point that never could arise at all.

Mr. SULLIVAN—I am afraid I have misconveyed myself.

Mr. JUSTICE DARLING—We will resume this case to-morrow morning.

Adjourned till to-morrow morning at 10.15 a.m.

Second Day—Tuesday, 18th July, 1916.

Mr. SULLIVAN—My lords, on two occasions yesterday, I find, on referring to my report, I was to some extent at cross purposes with the Court. I find, my lords, at a time when I was discussing acts committed within the realm that the members of the Court were putting to me questions which were directed to the administration of law within the King's dominions generally, and I do not think that I made myself as clear as I would wish as to the attitude of my argument towards the administration of the law without the realm but still within the King's dominions. There was, of course, a great distinction between the realm and the dominions. Within the realm you had the common law established within the ancient realm of England, and the realm was added to by statute from time to time; it had absorbed portions of Scotland before eventually it came in altogether; Ireland was added by statute, Wales was added by statute, and France nominally remained the King's dominions. For some time after all jurisdiction in France disappeared, but France was the King's realm. Now, my argument does not deny that within the King's dominions the King's law ran, and it does not deny in the smallest degree that Parliament might legislate for the King's dominions, and that the legislation of Parliament would be administered in the King's dominions, although they might be outside the King's realm of England, which was a very much more circumscribed geographical locality. In the dominions, such as in Gascony, in Ireland, in Wales, in Scotland, there was no common law; the King's law was administered in the dominions by Commissioners administering the law *ad hoc* as their Commission required, but my argument with regard to the statute of Edward III., with the limitation of "within the realm," and two of its matters, did not draw as clear a distinction as I would like between what was within the realm and what would be without the realm and still be an offence under the statute, being committed within the King's dominions and triable by the King's law as administered in his dominions outside the realm. There is no doubt that with regard to a number of the matters mentioned in the statute of Edward III., compassing, for instance—the other matters I need not mention in the next two paragraphs—they were all matters which could be committed as crimes in any part of the King's dominions, and were themselves vicious and treasonable *per se;* but with regard to two of the matters that are mentioned in the statute of Edward III., I submit they only acquired their treasonable character if they were committed within a particular part of the King's dominions, namely, within the King's realm, and their viciousness and criminality depended upon the personality who committed them dwelling within the King's realm, within the King's peace, and under his protection. For that reason those two matters, which were so circumscribed on the construction of the statute for which we contend, and being done only in a particular place, where incapable of extension by the construction of the statute of 26 Henry VIII. or of 5 & 6 Edward; but the other matters were clearly crimes wherever they were committed within the King's dominions, and were capable of being tried by the law as administered in the King's dominions, the law applicable thereto. Reference was also made to Commissions issuing within the realm of England to try crimes. As we all know, the issue of those Commissions was the subject of controversy and protest from Parliament for very many years; they did not issue under the common law. That is the ground of the Parliamentary protest, that the Commissions issued proceeded according to civil law, and not according to common law, and that was the very ground of the protest of Parliament against the issue of Commissions. Finally, the principal Commissions being issued were Commissions to the marshals, which were eventually abolished by the Petition of Right, and the question was as to the right to issue these Commissions in times of peace, trying people according to martial law.

There is another matter I made a mistake in in replying to one of your lordships. I did not notice with regard to 5 & 6 Edward VI., chapter 11, that one of your lordships asked me the result of the passing of the Act of 1 Mary. I find in the little volume of the statutes I have been quoting from all the time, the volume subscribed by the judges, that the memorandum on that statute of 5 & 6 Edward VI. is as follows:—"Memorandum.—All the particular "treasons made treason by this Act and which were not treason by the "statute of 25 Edward III. are expired or repealed by the statute of "1 Mary, chapter 1." I may also state comment was made on the verification of the authorities referred to in Coke by my colleagues, who have done all that I asked of them, and done it most loyally and well; every single reference has been verified, and we have here a memorandum showing all these reference to which attention was called yesterday. *De Brittaine's* case was a case particularly mentioned. That was a case of what Maitland calls the amphibious baron, for it was a question with regard to the title to land in England that was alleged to have been forfeited (your lordship sees by the date it was anterior to the statute) by the fact that the owner, like a great number of the barons, had also French land, and in respect of his French land he seems to have been doing suit and service to the King of France: exactly the position contemplated by Bracton, where, in respect of his French lands, he had to furnish suit and service to the King of France at times when he was at war with the King of England, and when he had to furnish suit and service to the King of England in respect of his English land. The question arose whether the deceased man had been assisting the King of France or rendering service in respect of lands at Rouen. As far as I can gather from the record, it is anterior to the statute, and it illustrates exactly the state of affairs that I suggest is the reason of the special limitation in adherence within the realm of England, because the legislators were, to a very large extent, men who owned French land, and in respect of their French land had to do suit and service in France, and they did not want to be put to their election which of their estates they would give up, because they had a tendency to hold on to both of the lands if they could.

Mr. Justice Scrutton—I still have some curiosity; what happened to it?

Mr. Sullivan—The man was dead at the time of the investigation. The question was whether there was dower still claimable out of the

Mr. Sullivan

lands; it is a petition in Parliament. I am wrong; the dower case was the next one in the note. The facts are as I have stated.

Mr. JUSTICE DARLING—This is the first case that Coke cites as his authority.

Mr. JUSTICE ATKIN—It is a case of land forfeited for adhering to the Scots.

Mr. SULLIVAN—The French, my lord. I make it out to be in respect of land in Rouen. The question arose in the case of *John de Brittaine*, that the manors mentioned ought to be declared his inheritance, and it is answered that the manors did rightly belong at some time to some person whose name I do not give, who held the manor, and that then he, the said viscount, whoever he was, adhered to the part of the King of France contrary to his allegiance to Henry. He was the Viscount of Rouen, apparently, as far as I can make out from the translation.

Mr. JUSTICE DARLING—But the viscount then was not a mere honorary title as it is to-day; it meant that he had a military duty to discharge in Rouen.

Mr. SULLIVAN—He had, my lord, of course, at that date. He was the Viscount of Rouen, and adhered to the part of the King of France contrary to his allegiance to Henry III., on which account his property was forfeited to the King; that is to say, there was a claim that all his land on both sides of the Channel had been forfeited to the King, as far as I can make out from the record. Then the allegation that the claimant's father had taken possession of the land was not to oust the King's claim. As a matter of fact the King was not a party to the proceedings, and the question was rather challenging his title on the part of some person who claimed from a prior assignment, before the forfeiture alleged.

Mr. JUSTICE SCRUTTON—I follow that he was dead; but what happened to the estate?

The ATTORNEY-GENERAL—The lands were forfeited.

Mr. JUSTICE SCRUTTON—Because of his adhering to the King of France out of the realm?

The ATTORNEY-GENERAL—Yes.

Mr. JUSTICE ATKIN—The land had been forfeited, and this was a petition by a descendant to say they inherited.

Mr. SULLIVAN—This was a petition of a descendant of a man who had entered, and who apparently had been ousted; he claimed owing to the entry.

Mr. JUSTICE ATKIN—He did not claim it under the forfeiture.

Mr. SULLIVAN—No.

Mr. JUSTICE ATKIN—He claimed against the forfeiture.

Mr. SULLIVAN—He claimed against the forfeiture in respect of an entry of a predecessor who had been ousted.

Mr. JUSTICE A. T. LAWRENCE—How was it held?

Mr. SULLIVAN—It was held that the lands had been forfeited.

Mr. JUSTICE A. T. LAWRENCE—It was held against his claim?

Mr. SULLIVAN—Yes, my lord. The date is most important.

The ATTORNEY-GENERAL—It is 1292.

Mr. SULLIVAN—The fate of the viscount illustrates exactly the state of affairs which would be most terrifying to a very large number of His

Majesty's legislators, namely, that in respect of an act done at Rouen his lands at Rouen, and in England too, had all been forfeited to the King of England.

Mr. JUSTICE DARLING—At that time who was the King of England?

Mr. SULLIVAN—Henry III. at the time of the forfeiture.

The ATTORNEY-GENERAL—Edward I. at the time of the hearing.

Mr. SULLIVAN—It is later when the allegation was made; at the time of Henry III. the forfeiture had taken place. The matter arises, I think, a generation afterwards, because it is a petition to Parliament to be reinstated in that from which his predecessor had been ousted. Then, my lords, the next authority I propose to deal with is *The King* v. *Platt*.

Mr. JUSTICE ATKIN—The next case is 33 Edward I.; that is, adhering to the Scots.

Mr. SULLIVAN—We have all these cases.

The ATTORNEY-GENERAL—That is *Robert de Ross*.

Mr. SULLIVAN—In that case it was a case of bail, and it does not appear to me that the statute 33 Edward I. is in point.

Mr. JUSTICE ATKIN—Surely the *Ross* case is a case of a claim to land, and the lands had been forfeited, because it says he died in the allegiance of the Scots, and had a right to have adhered to them. I had a look at the Roll last night.

Mr. SULLIVAN—I think we are dealing with a later case, 33 Edward I.

Mr. JUSTICE ATKIN—The case of *Robert de Ross*.

Mr. SULLIVAN—"Memorandum.—That the King caused to be liberated "the body of Ralph——"

Mr. JUSTICE ATKIN—That is not the right reference. There are several things that might come under 6; there are several references under 33 Edward I. It is almost the last entry under the date.

Mr. SULLIVAN—Then, my lord, again I am at fault.

Mr. JUSTICE ATKIN—Last night I had an opportunity of seeing the Parliament Roll, and I looked it up. It is exactly the same case as that where the lands had been forfeited; the predecessor of the claimant had his land forfeited because he had adhered to the part of the Scots, I think it is said.

The ATTORNEY-GENERAL—It was found by the King in Council that Robert de Ross, for a long time before the last war in Scotland, against his duty had removed himself from the King and adhered to the part of the Scots who were at that time enemies and rebels against the King, and never again in his lifetime did he return into the peace of his King, but remained with his enemy. The Council refused the prayer of the petitioner, which asked to be restored to the lands of Robert under a proclamation which had been made saving the rights of such persons in Scotland who came into the King's peace after the war.

Mr. JUSTICE ATKIN—That looks like a case of adhering in Scotland.

Mr. SULLIVAN—Adhering to the rebel Scots; it was in Scotland in the King's dominions.

Mr. JUSTICE ATKIN—But it was out of the realm.

Mr. SULLIVAN—It was out of the realm, certainly, of England. I was pointing out that France, Ireland, Wales, and Scotland appeared at that period to have been all in the same dominion; they were in the King's dominion, but not within the King's realm of England. As I say, you could legislate for them, and the King's law was law within them, but they were not part of the realm.

Mr. Justice Scrutton—Perhaps there is a little more to be said for Lord Coke than you thought; you will not be quite so severe on him when you next come to address us about him, will you?

Mr. Sullivan—I do not think that this case in any way bears out the proposition that the statute of Edward III. could be applied outside the realm by any case that was triable at common law. What I am pointing out to your lordships is that, whereas the law would run in the King's dominions, it would not be administrable by common law, it would be administered as the law was administered in the King's dominions; that was by Commission which would sit under civil law. This was all prior to the statute, which I submit was passed in order to relieve both the southern Scotsman, whose estates came into England, and the southern barons, whose estates were in England and France. With regard to these petitions in Parliament, they were not cases at common law in any respect, and the case in 8 Edward III., the Year Book, case 20, is a case of adhering to the Scots; but unless again he adhered to the Scots by marching into Northumberland, with his other acts, he was not only within the King's dominions at all times, but also was actually within the King's realm. There is a matter about the custom of Normandy, case 73, of the treason to the Duke; I have not looked through that, but I do not think it adds anything to the foundation of my argument. The cases prior to the statute again, you see, are all within the King's dominion; they are all triable by the King in some manner of form, but within the realm; they could not have been tried at common law.

Mr. Justice A. T. Lawrence—What law were they tried by?

Mr. Sullivan—By Commission, which proceeded according to civil law.

Mr. Justice A. T. Lawrence—What is the authority for saying that?

Mr. Sullivan—The petition to Parliament and the protests of Parliawith regard to the special Commission. They could not have a common law; they could not have the common law of the realm. They had their law. When we are speaking of the common law we are speaking of the common law of the realm at this period of the development.

Now, my lords, I will go to the case of *The King* v. *Platt*, in 1 Leach's Crown Cases at Page 157. There was an application for *habeas corpus*, as your lordships are aware, because Platt was committed for high treason committed at Savannah, Georgia. The warrant was simply high treason. There was an application for the discharge of the prisoner under the Habeas Corpus Act made to the Court at the Old Bailey, and an objection was taken by the Attorney-General that the Court had no power to try the prisoner, as he could only be tried by the King's Bench under 35 Henry VIII., because he said the treason was committed out of the realm. It was, of course, committed within the King's dominions; it was committed at Georgia. It was committed out of the realm, and the point taken is that the Court cannot entertain the application for *habeas corpus*, because the Court has no seisin of the case, the treason being committed in Georgia, and this point is upheld; but the judgment with reference to the matter we are dealing with, or rather the dictum, is as follows:—"North America is part of one of the four divisions "of the world, and that it is without the four seas of Great Britain." The four seas become important. Then, "It was the ancient opinion "that the species of treason which consists, by 25 Edward III., chapter 2, "in adhering to the King's enemies, might be tried, before the statute "35 Henry VIII., chapter 2, within the kingdom, by the rules of the "common law"——

Mr. Justice Atkin—There is a passage you have left out, and I want to see what is the bearing of it—"This warrant, therefore, contains sufficient certainty to show that the high treason which it charges the prisoner "with having committed was, in fact, committed out of the realm of "England." Then it goes on as you were reading it.

Mr. Sullivan—Yes, my lord—"It was the ancient opinion that the "species of treason which consists, by 25 Edward III., chapter 2, in "adhering to the King's enemies, might be tried, before the statute 35 "Henry VIII., chapter 2, within the kingdom, by the rules of the common "law, though the aid and comfort was afforded without the realm; but "that every other species of treason committed out of the realm must "be tried in the place where it was committed, or under the provisions of "that Act of Parliament. Perhaps, therefore, in every other species of "treason except that first mentioned it would be necessary, both in the "special Commission and in the indictment, to pursue the language of the "Act, and to aver that it was committed without the realm; but, without "giving an opinion upon this point, it is not necessary to use such an "averment in the warrant of commitment." The dictum that I have to deal with is what I have read. I think when that is considered, that, so far from being a dictum in the smallest degree conflicting with my proposition, is really an affirmance of it. It was an ancient opinion that this one particular act might be tried within, though the aid and comfort was afforded without. That is the proposition that I am labouring on the construction of the statute.

Mr. Justice Darling—Do not you see it does not say it was the ancient opinion that the species of high treason which consists by 25 Edward III. in adhering to the King's enemies within the realm; it says "adhering to the King's enemies." It does not say within the realm.

Mr. Sullivan—No, it does not.

Mr. Justice Darling—It says, "Might be tried before the statute "35 Henry VIII., chapter 2, within the kingdom, by the rules of the "common law, though the aid and comfort was afforded without the "realm." How would you adhere to the King's enemies within the realm by doing nothing but giving aid and comfort without the realm?

Mr. Sullivan—You would be adhering within the realm by reason of the aid and comfort you were affording them outside.

Mr. Justice Darling—Although you say you were outside the realm?

Mr. Sullivan—No, although you were within the realm.

Mr. Justice Darling—But this argument does not put that, which is the essence of your case.

Mr. Sullivan—Dealing with the case, if your lordships will bear with me for a moment I think I will be able to point out that my contention is the true meaning of the case. The emphasis lies in the fact that the aid and comfort might be given outside.

Mr. Justice Darling—That is common to every case where you say that the treason was committed outside the realm; the aid and comfort is assumed to be given outside. If it were given within you could prosecute him for many kinds of treason; you could prosecute him for levying war, and there are a number of cases which say that that would be sufficient.

Mr. Sullivan—In all the reported cases the adherence, in fact, the aid and comfort, has been given or said to be given to an enemy outside the realm by a person who never was outside the realm, but who was within.

Mr. Justice Darling—Does it not occur to you that it would be very rare that the person who had comforted the King's enemies outside the realm would be so foolish as to come back unless he came with the intention of levying war, and then if he did they very likely caught him and prosecuted him for levying war?

Mr. Sullivan—Within the realm.

Mr. Justice Darling—Not in every case.

Mr. Sullivan—But it is within the realm. What I am pointing out is, in fact, you have cases of aid and comfort supplied outside the realm, and the person who is prosecuted and convicted is a person who at all times was within the realm.

The Attorney-General—Not always.

Mr. Sullivan—Except compassing.

The Attorney-General—There is *Wharton's* case.

Mr. Sullivan—That we will come to.

Mr. Justice Darling—And *Lynch's* case.

Mr. Sullivan—I have prefaced all my observations by saying up to the year 1903. I am not ignoring *Lynch's* case. I intend to deal with that. Up to 1903, with the exception of *Cundell's* case, in which we have the indictment—I am speaking of the reported cases—and *Wharton's* case, which is explicable on the other grounds, you have a number of cases in which the person did not do any act of adherence in the shape of giving the enemy aid and comfort within the realm; his aid and comfort to the enemy was to be aid and comfort to the enemy who was to be outside the realm. The importance of the tracing of that is this. It treats compassing as being untriable; it treats adhering as being the only form that was triable in respect of matters, aid and comfort being given outside the realm. That is significant, and what could be the reason of that ancient opinion? What would be the significance of an ancient opinion that adhering might, but compassing and other acts might not, be triable within the realm?

Mr. Justice Atkin—In that case it is a little complicated to find out the issue, but is not the fact this, that there was a man committed for treason committed abroad out of the realm; he was brought here, and had been committed here. It was then sought to get him released under the Habeas Corpus Act, because he could not be tried before the first Court of Gaol Delivery in London. The answer to that was, "No, the Habeas "Corpus Act does not apply, because he could not be tried by the Court "of Gaol Delivery, but only in the Court of King's Bench by a special

"Commission under the Act of Henry VIII." That is what the Court held. I do not think they intended to decide it.

Mr. SULLIVAN—It is only a dictum.

Mr. JUSTICE ATKIN—But they refer to the ancient opinion that, in the case of adhering to the King's enemies part of the adhering to the King's enemies was committed within the local jurisdiction, so that you could have a local venue. All other treason out of the realm would be tried in the King's Bench or under the provisions of the Act.

Mr. SULLIVAN—That is my contention of the meaning of that passage, and that again proves how it is justified by my previous argument on venue.

Mr. JUSTICE ATKIN—Again it is only on the question where it could be tried. I think it supports you on your point, as far as I am concerned, that you could not try a treason out of the realm at common law because of the difficulty as to local venue.

Mr. SULLIVAN—That is what I use it for.

Mr. JUSTICE ATKIN—It leaves open the question that there was an offence, if only you could find a way of trying it.

Mr. SULLIVAN—Yes. I venture to say there was no other offence known to the law that could be investigated.

Mr. JUSTICE DARLING—This is a judgment of the Court, and it says the ancient opinion was that the case of adhering by giving aid and comfort outside the realm was an exception to the other rule.

Mr. SULLIVAN—Yes, and I was about to point out, but my lord anticipated me, the reason of that exception. It got over the ancient rigidity of the primary law of venue. The law developed that where only part of the transaction had taken place in a venue, that gave you sufficient seisin—I quoted Viner on that—to investigate the whole transaction. My construction of the statute of Edward III. is entirely consistent with this, provided the adherent was within the realm, although his adherence was both within and without the realm, he within being adherent, his acts without being acts of aid and comfort. In that case they had got over the difficulty of venue by having what you might call a partial venue within the realm, and that gave jurisdiction.

Mr. JUSTICE DARLING—But the Court here in stating what was the ancient opinion do not make use of your first premises; they do say that it was only the man who, being within the realm, had been adhering to the King's enemies without the realm.

Mr. SULLIVAN—They do not say that in plain terms, but I think the emphasis of the aid and comfort being rendered without rather implies that; that, at all events, is my submission, and that, of course, would be intelligible as showing that the one particular species of treason, if you read it in the way I ask you to, would be an exception to the general rule that none of these acts was triable at common law if committed outside the realm; because if the man was within the realm you had the partial venue which the Court seized upon as giving a jurisdiction to investigate the whole transaction, though portion was outside the realm. It was in that way that commercial law developed, and the allegation that something was to be done within the jurisdiction enabled Courts to try transactions partly to be done within the jurisdiction of the Court and partly on the other side of the world.

Mr. JUSTICE A. T. LAWRENCE—How can you explain their omitting that essential part of the proposition?

Mr. SULLIVAN—I do not think they have.

Mr. JUSTICE A. T. LAWRENCE—There is not a word about his being within the realm.

Mr. SULLIVAN—I submit that that is implied by the emphasis of the fact that he could be tried by the rules of the common law, though the aid and comfort was offered without the realm. The statute, I submit, creates the offence with which we are charged if it had been committed within the realm, namely, the offence of being adherent to the King's enemies. That is what I am charged with.

Mr. JUSTICE A. T. LAWRENCE—Apart from an overt act, that is no offence at all.

Mr. SULLIVAN—The overt act is only evidence.

Mr. JUSTICE A. T. LAWRENCE—You cannot charge a man with treason merely for what he thinks.

Mr. SULLIVAN—You had to have an overt act to prove your charge against him, and the peculiarity of adhering is that the Court is enabled to investigate the circumstances of an overt act that did not take place within the jurisdiction.

Mr. JUSTICE A. T. LAWRENCE—Your argument goes upon the footing that it is treason without any overt act. You say he is guilty of treason within the realm, although he performed no overt act at all anywhere?

Mr. SULLIVAN—No, I have not stated that; he is guilty of treason of adhering to the King's enemies within the realm.

Mr. JUSTICE A. T. LAWRENCE—That is not a treason in itself?

Mr. SULLIVAN—If you prove it, it is.

Mr. JUSTICE A. T. LAWRENCE—Is it? There is no authority for that that I know of.

Mr. SULLIVAN—The mere mental attitude of a man can never be treason. The adherence must be adherence manifesting itself by an overt act somewhere, but if it manifests itself by an overt act anywhere, that species of adherence, he being within the realm, is triable where you have the venue of the partially accomplished offence, although the complete accomplishment of the offence took place outside the realm. That, at all events, is my submission as to the meaning of that dictum, for it is only a dictum, in *The King* v. *Platt*, and I can only admit it for the consideration of the Court in the manner that I have presented it.

Now, my lords, the next case I have to deal with is *Lynch's* case.

Mr. JUSTICE BRAY—Before you leave *Platt's* case, how do you deal with this passage on page 168, "This warrant therefore contains suffi-"cient certainty to show that the high treason which it charges the "prisoner with having committed was, in fact, committed out of the realm "of England"? Is it not your argument that high treason cannot be committed out of the realm of England?

Mr. SULLIVAN—Oh, no, my lord, never. If I have conveyed that to the Court, I have entirely failed to convey my proper meaning.

Mr. JUSTICE BRAY—That is what this indictment charges in the present case; it charges him with adhering to the King's enemies outside the realm, "elsewhere than in the King's realm." I have understood your argument to be that that is an offence which does not exist.

Mr. Sullivan—In the present case, yes; what is charged is, adhering and doing an act completely outside the realm and the King's dominions.

Mr. Justice Darling—You say, if I understand you, it is essential that the man to be charged should be within the realm when the act of treason is committed outside it. That is the act of adherence. You say the adherence is the reason, but the person who adheres must be within the realm, and must adhere by aiding and comforting an enemy outside it?

Mr. Sullivan—Not necessarily outside, but the enemy may be outside.

Mr. Justice Darling—Either within or without?

Mr. Sullivan—Yes, either within or without.

Mr. Justice Darling—Then you say the treason is committed in England by an act of aid and comfort given outside England.

Mr. Sullivan—Yes.

Mr. Justice Darling—And that the traitor, therefore, is always within the kingdom, and because of that the local venue applies to what he did and you can try him.

Mr. Sullivan—Yes, that was my argument.

Mr. Justice Darling—And that is the whole of it.

Mr. Sullivan—That is the gist of my argument which I submit to the Court. That is the argument I present.

Mr. Justice Bray—In what they say was the ancient opinion, your argument must be that the ancient opinion was wrong.

Mr. Sullivan—I had meant to convey that that ancient opinion was right on my construction of the statute.

Mr. Justice Bray—But your argument involves this, that what they recite as the ancient opinion was, in fact, wrong.

Mr. Sullivan—Oh, no, my lord, I have again misconveyed myself, and I am exceedingly sorry. It is a lack of proper expression. The ancient opinion was right, if I am right in my construction of the statute that the ancient opinion showed adherence was peculiar in this, that the man adherent, being within the jurisdiction, he could be tried at common law, although you never could prove completion of his crime under the old law of venue where the completion of his crime was, in fact, giving aid and comfort outside the realm.

Mr. Justice Bray—How do you explain that that is not stated in the ancient opinion? They do not even say adhering to the King's enemy within the realm, which implies that adhering to the King's enemy need not be in the realm.

Mr. Sullivan—I would, I fear, only be repeating myself if I tried to put it again.

This matter, as we know, arose in *The King* v. *Lyuch*, and was there debated, argued, and pronounced upon by a Court after argument, so far as I know, for the first time. It is the first judicial decision on the construction of the statute, and is, of course, an authority. In the report in 1903, 1 King's Bench, you will find no assistance on this point that we are now discussing. An argument in *The King* v. *Lynch* is reported in 1903, 1 King's Bench, at page 444, but that is an argument entirely upon the question of naturalisation and naturalisation

Mr. Sullivan

during war. In the shorthand notes of *The King* v. *Lynch* will be found the argument upon the branch of the case with which I have been occupying your lordships' attention at such length, but there is no judgment upon it; that is to say, there is no considered judgment upon it and no pronounced judgment upon it. The question is allowed to proceed to the jury notwithstanding the objection made that the offence charged was adherence without the realm. The Lord Chief Justice, Lord Alverstone, expressly refers in two different places to *The King* v. *Vaughan* as being a complete authority against the contention that I am advancing here; in fact, *The King* v. *Vaughan* appears to have been treated by the Lord Chief Justice as being a matter, at all events in a trial at bar, which would close discussion. I propose to examine *The King* v *Vaughan*, and refer your lordships to it. I convinced the Court at the trial at bar, and they assented to the proposition, that *The King* v. *Vaughan* certainly was not an authority on this point.

Mr. Justice Darling—Serjeant Sullivan, you say you convinced the Court at the trial that *The King* v. *Vaughan* was not an authority on this point?

Mr. Sullivan—That *The King* v. *Vaughan* was not an authority against me.

Mr. Justice Darling—And notwithstanding that, they ruled against you upon this point, although they put *The King* v. *Vaughan* aside.

Mr. Sullivan—That is so.

Mr .Justice Darling—What you are appealing from is their judgment, and that did not go upon the authority of *The King* v. *Vaughan*. Why need you trouble about *The King* v. *Vaughan*?

Mr. Sullivan—Because *The King* v. *Lynch*, which is a matter to be considered, is based on *The King* v. *Vaughan*.

Mr. Justice Darling—The Court before whom the appellant was tried thought that *The King* v. *Lynch* was rightly decided, although they did not hold up the authority of *The King* v. *Vaughan*; why need you trouble with *The King* v. *Vaughan*?

Mr. Sullivan—Well, my lord, if I am right in my contention that *The King* v. *Lynch* was really based on *The King* v. *Vaughan*, and on another matter, namely, the statute of George II., which I respectfully submit is no authority against me, then I submit that would get rid of *The King* v. *Lynch* as an authority against me, if I show it is based on considerations that are not good in law. *The King* v. *Lynch* is there as an authority against me.

Mr. Justice Darling—It may be, but not upon the ground that *The King* v. *Vaughan* is an authority. At all events, the Court before whom the appellant was tried said, as I understand—we will take it to be so—"We do not follow *The King* v. *Vaughan*, but we think, for all that, "that *The King* v. *Lynch* was rightly decided."

Mr. Sullivan—What I propose to show is that since *The King* v. *Lynch* is there as an authority against me it is based on a wrong decision. If *The King* v. *Lynch* is treated as neutral, I, of course, would not be justified in taking up the time of the Court.

Mr. Justice Darling—Not neutral, an authority against you, and declared by the Lord Chief Justice and two other judges, Mr. Justice

Avory and Mr. Justice Horridge, to be an authority against you, but not on the ground that *The King* v. *Vaughan* was an authority against you. Why should you trouble with *The King* v. *Vaughan?*

Mr. Justice Atkin—What you want to do is to get rid of the authority of *The King* v. *Lynch* by saying that it was founded upon a misapprehension of a particular case.

Mr. Sullivan—Yes.

Mr. Justice Atkin—If *The King* v. *Lynch* stands as an authority we are bound by it, and everybody is bound by it.

Mr. Sullivan—That is why I was anxious to show that the decision of *The King* v. *Lynch* should not operate against me because it was on a false basis.

Mr. Justice Darling—In order that we may not argue what is not necessary to argue, on what ground did the Court before whom the appellant was tried say that *The King* v. *Lynch* was good law?

The Attorney-General—The judgment of Mr. Justice Avory is on page 130; after hearing the arguments about *The King* v. *Vaughan*, the learned judge gives his conclusion.

Mr. Justice Darling—"First of all, it is not right to say that the "point was not, in fact, decided in *The King* v. *Lynch*"; is that the passage?

The Attorney-General—Yes, that is where it begins.

Mr. Sullivan—At page 128 the Lord Chief Justice says, "Then "at last we come to the decision of *The King* v. *Lynch*, decided in "1903. There the same argument was advanced by the defence that has "been put forward before us, and it was persisted in and elaborately "argued. The Court there came to the conclusion that the defendant's "contention was wrong, and, although it gave no judgment, the then "Lord Chief Justice proceeded to sum up, and directed the jury as if it "was an offence. Lynch was convicted by the jury, and if the argument "of the defence is right in this case, Lynch never should have been con- "victed, and the Court ought to have ruled that no offence had been "disclosed either by the evidence or in the indictment. The Court did "not so rule, but on the contrary directed the jury upon the assumption "that the offence was disclosed if the jury took a particular view of the "facts. Now that is a current authority which is strong."

The Attorney-General—Mr. Justice Avory's judgment is at page 130.

Mr. Sullivan—"First of all, it is not right to say that the point was "not, in fact, decided in *The King* v. *Lynch*. While it is true that no "formal judgment was pronounced on the objection, it will be found by "reference to the report of the case in 19 Times Law Reports that the "Lord Chief Justice stopped the Attorney-General in his reply to the "argument, and said that they were satisfied on the point, and unless he "wanted to cite any further authorities they did not wish to hear him "further. That was, in fact, a decision that the point taken was a bad "one. But, further and beyond the fact to which allusion has been "made, that the prisoner in that case could not have been convicted unless "the point was decided against him, it will also be found in the same "report of the summing of the learned Lord Chief Justice that he, "towards the close of his summing up, used these words. He reminded "the jury 'that the charge against the prisoner was that of aiding the "'King's enemies; and he had already told them that the facts which "'had been laid before them amounted to aiding the King's enemies, and "'that wherever it was done this was an offence in respect of which, if "'proved, the prisoner ought to be found guilty upon the indictment.' "So that there was an express direction in terms in that case to the jury "that wherever the acts were done of adherence to the King's enemies that "was an offence within the meaning of the statute." It is solely for the purpose of disposing of the authority against me that I propose to show to your lordships that the Lord Chief Justice, whose decision in that case is alluded to by two of the judges at the trial at bar in the present case, treated it as having actually decided the point very many years ago, a case which on investigation proves to be irrelevant to the matter that the Lord Chief Justice was called upon to decide, and if it is open to me to show that the decision of *The King* v. *Lynch*, relied upon in the present case by the Court below, was, in fact, based upon foundations which were insecure, it is the only way I know, my lord, of removing a case which appears to be decided precisely in point against me; the only way I know in advocacy is to take the principles upon which a case has been decided, if one has to fly in the face of it and state that it was wrong.

Mr. Justice Darling—Where does the Lord Chief Justice in this trial deal with the case of *The King* v. *Vaughan?*

The Attorney-General—At page 83 of the second day.

Mr. Sullivan—He also dealt with it on the third day when my colleague was addressing the Court. He said that they had already expressed an opinion. On page 122 of the third day there is the particular passage I have in mind, but the learned Attorney-General refers to page 83.

Mr. Justice Darling—I have page 83, where the Lord Chief Justice says, "You need not labour that point, at any rate, as we are at present "advised that *The King* v. *Vaughan* does not bind us. Mr. Sullivan—"Very well, my lord. Now, if *The King* v. *Vaughan* does not deal with "the matter, the next argument of the Attorney-General in *The King* v. "*Lynch* was the statute of 18 George II. That is set out *in extenso* "in the shorthand notes, if I may quote from them, at page 112. *The* "*King* v. *Vaughan*, the Attorney-General said, was the chief authority "upon which he relied, and I think he puts it forward as being a matter of "considerable importance."

Mr. Sullivan—Then there is the passage at page 122 on the third day.

Mr. Justice A. T. Lawrence—What was the ground upon which the Lord Chief Justice thought that *The King* v. *Vaughan* was wrong; what was the ground upon which he laid it aside?

Mr. Sullivan—That was what I was about to open to your lordship.

Mr. Justice Bray—What he intended to say was that you need not trouble about *The King* v. *Vaughan* being an authority against you.

Mr. Justice Darling—He says that at page 122 in terms.

Mr. Sullivan—"We have already expressed our view upon that. "You are quite justified in referring to it, and there has been no argu- "ment to the contrary. *The King* v. *Vaughan* is no authority against "you." If *The King* v. *Vaughan* is no authority against me I intended to submit that *The King* v. *Lynch*, which treats *The King* v. *Vaughan* as being so exactly in point, is no more authority against me than *The King* v. *Vaughan*.

Mr. Justice Bray—Where did Lord Alverstone, in that case, say he treated *The King* v. *Vaughan* as conclusive?

Mr. Sullivan—At page 109 of the shorthand report of *The King* v. *Lynch* he says it in two different places. Interrupting the argument of Mr. Justice Avory, as he now is, the Lord Chief Justice says, "I have "no doubt you have considered it, but it seems to me that *The King* v. "*Vaughan* is a direct authority. The charge against the prisoner is "left to the jury upon the count only of adhering to the King's enemies, "that being done upon the high seas, and that point is then attempted to "be taken that he was not a British subject at all. The Attorney- "General—There is no count for compassing. My learned friend Mr. "Avory said there was. The Lord Chief Justice—It seems to me *The* "*King* v. *Vaughan* is a direct authority against you; it is in 13 State "Trials, and the passage is at page 525 and page 526. I have no doubt "you have looked at this most carefully. There are passages in "Hale and others that are against this contention. They may be relics "of a barbaric age, but you have to deal with them."

Mr. Justice Bray—Is that the only passage upon which you found the argument that *The King* v. *Lynch* was decided solely upon *The King* v. *Vaughan?*

Mr. Sullivan—I should not have said "solely," if I did say so. In *The King* v. *Lynch* the Lord Chief Justice treats *The King* v. *Vaughan* as being directly in point. He refers to it twice. There is no judgment that we can read in *The King* v. *Lynch*, because there is no judgment delivered on this part of the argument; it is therefore on the interlocutory observations of the Lord Chief Justice that one is compelled to found it.

Mr. Justice Bray—The Lord Chief Justice's suggestion that *The King* v. *Vaughan* was a direct authority was not accepted by Mr. Justice Avory. It does not follow that *The King* v. *Lynch* proceeded solely on *The King* v. *Vaughan*.

Mr. Sullivan—Not solely. There was a second argument addressed by the Attorney-General, to which also I desire to direct attention, on the statute of George II.

Mr. Justice Darling—It comes to this, does it not, that if *The King* v. *Vaughan* was an indictment framed upon the statute of 25 Edward III., then it is an authoritly, and Mr. Avory, as he then was, argued that the indictment was not framed upon the statute of Edward III., and that, therefore, was no authority? He puts it on page 110 of his argument "The indictment alleges that there was a ship sent out by the French "King to wage war upon the high seas within the jurisdiction of the "Admiralty, and that being within the jurisdiction of the Admiralty, "about 14 leagues off Deal, did then aid, help, and assist the enemies of "our Lord the King in the ship of war called the 'Loyal Glencarty.'

"There is no allegation; that would have been a bad indictment, my "lord, under the clause of the statute, because there is no allegation "that he was adhering to the King's enemies, which is the gist of this." Then the Lord Chief Justice says, "Aid, help, and assist the enemy of our "said King." Then Mr. Avory says, "That may have been a form of "treason recognised at common law apart from the statute. That is "why I said that this case was not, or did not appear, to have been a "case under this statute. The indictment does not appear to be framed "under the statute as a charge of adhering to the King's enemies, but "rather as a common law charge of treason committed upon the high "seas. That is what I thought of *Vaughan*, and I desire only to repeat "it. That does not appear to be an indictment framed under this clause "of the statute. It may be, and then I am not disputing it as an "authority that that might at common law have constituted a treason. "That is not the question here, of course." That is the whole objection.

Mr. SULLIVAN—The next observation of the Lord Chief Justice is, "Mr. Attorney, are there any authorities you wish to call our attention to?"

Mr. JUSTICE DARLING—On what ground do you say Lord Reading proceeded in saying that *The King* v. *Vaughan* was not an authority?

Mr. SULLIVAN—Because I showed him on the examination of *The King* v. *Vaughan* that *The King* v. *Vaughan* was as plainly as could be an act of adhering to the King's enemies within the realm. I proved it.

Mr. JUSTICE DARLING—The indictment did not use the word "adhering."

Mr. SULLIVAN—Pardon me, my lord, it did. There was a discussion upon the first count of the indictment. I will open it to your lordships. The second count of the indictment was in the clearest way; it begins that it was within the realm, and I showed that the place alleged was within the realm of England.

Mr. JUSTICE A. T. LAWRENCE—Did the indictment allege it?

Mr. SULLIVAN—Yes, the second count; and even against the peace.

Mr. JUSTICE DARLING—How many counts were there?

Mr. SULLIVAN—Two.

Mr. JUSTICE DARLING—The second count says, "And the said jurors "of our said Lord the King upon their said oaths farther represent," and so on.

Mr. SULLIVAN—To begin with, before we get to the counts of the indictment, will your lordship look at the Court? If you look at the Court you get an admiral and the three or four substantial persons, not under 35 Henry VIII., but under 28 Henry VIII.; that is the jurisdiction of the Admiralty.

Mr. JUSTICE ATKIN—The second count is levying war.

Mr. SULLIVAN—"As a false traitor," and so forth. The first thing is "further resigning, practising, and with his whole strength intending "the common peace and tranquillity of this kingdom of England to "disturb; and a war and rebellion against the said King upon the high "seas, within the jurisdiction of the Admiralty of England, to move, stir "up, and procure, and the said Lord the King, from the title, honour, "royal name, and imperial crown of his kingdom of England, and "dominions upon the high seas, to depose and deprive; and miserable "slaughter of the subjects of the said Lord the King, of this kingdom "of England, upon the high seas, and within the jurisdiction aforesaid, to "cause and procure; on the said 8th day of July, in the said 7th "year of the King, upon the high seas, about 14 leagues from Deal, and "within the dominion of the crown of England." There is no doubt that it was within the dominions of the realm of England.

Mr. Justice Darling—Yes.

Mr. Sullivan—Several persons would have been hanged a hundred years previously for doubting this was within the realm—"And within the "jurisdiction of the Admiralty of England aforesaid, falsely, maliciously, "devilishly, and treacherously, by force and arms with divers other false "rebels and traitors (to the jurors unknown), war against our said now "Lord the King, prepared, prompted, levied, and waged. And that the "said Thomas Vaughan in performance of his said war and rebellion, "then and there, by force and arms, maliciously, wickedly, and openly "assembled——"

Mr. Justice Darling—That is quite distinct; it was within the jurisdiction of the Admiralty, that was on the high seas; that is within the jurisdiction of the Admiralty. We all know who ruled the waves in those days, and that is the reason why it was within the dominions.

Mr. Sullivan—There are two points to be noted. First, it was within the realm of England; that was absolutely certain in those days. I could keep on quoting authorities that the narrow seas were part of the realm of England, and the ships thereon were the castles of the King within his realm. There is no doubt it was within the realm of England; and, secondly, it is not tried as a foreign treason, and although Lord Alverstone appears to have thought it was under 35 Henry VIII., as committed out of the realm, it is tried under 28 Henry VIII. You observe, although it is within the realm, it is tried under 28 Henry VIII. Why? It is not in the body of a county, and for want of being within the body of a county, although it is within the realm, it is accordingly tried, not under 35 Henry VIII. in the Court of King's Bench, but under 28 Henry VIII. by the special Commission consisting, as your lordships see, of the admiral and of the three or four substantial persons, the judges.

Mr. Justice Darling—Is the ground that Lord Alverstone misunderstood the case and that Lord Reading did not? Lord Reading says that *The King* v. *Lynch* is good law against you.

Mr. Sullivan—And therefore I want to show that, so far as any judgment was pronounced in *The King* v. *Lynch*, it was a judgment arrived at solely, or if not solely, mainly on *The King* v. *Vaughan*. Would your lordship turn to *The King* v. *Lynch*, just a few lines below where we stopped reading, where the Lord Chief Justice says, "Mr. Attorney, are "there any authorities you wish to call our attention to?" The Attorney-General says, "There is a great mass of authority." Then the Lord Chief Justice says, "I know, but are there any you wish to call our "attention to? I have already expressed my opinion, but if there are "authorities you think we ought to know of we will hear them." That is as much of a judgment as there is pronounced in the matter. The Attorney-General then goes on with authorities, and at page 115, *Sir*

John Parrot's case is approved by the Lord Chief Justice during the argument as a distinct authority again. I do not think it would be so treated now. You do not find any further judgment, and accordingly, before he heard the Attorney-General, the Lord Chief Justice had already announced that the mind of the Court was quite satisfied on the authority, so far as you can see, of *The King* v. *Vaughan*. There is no considered judgment; the matter evaporates and goes to the jury. There are the expressions of opinion of the Lord Chief Justice. *Parrot's* case I do not think will help us; we are all familiar with the trial of Parrot; that is one of the great historical trials, but it will not help us in this respect. The Lord Chief Justice had already, before his attention was called to anything else, expressed his opinion that *The King* v. *Vaughan* was a clear authority; if the Attorney-General wished to add anything to it, well and good, but he was quite convinced, and he expressed his opinion on *The King* v. *Vaughan*. Am I not at least entitled to say, if *The King* v. *Vaughan* was in fact of no authority on the matter, that the decision of *The King* v. *Lynch* is very seriously impaired? I do not know of any other passages of the Lord Chief Justice in *The King* v. *Lynch* to amend that judgment. At page 115 it says, "And so it was resolved in *Sir* "*John Parrot's* case." The Lord Chief Justice says, "Distinct authority "again." Then there is a reference to Hale, and then the Attorney-General says that the objection is a mere matter of form, and that his learned friend is really bringing forward a matter already raised on the indictment; and it really was a matter of form. The counsel for the prisoner then said, "I understand we still have the opportunity of moving "this again in arrest of judgment." Then the Lord Chief Justice says, "You first ask us to construe the statute, and then you say if the statute "is rightly construed there is no evidence." Then the Lord Chief Justice says, "That only goes to the form, not the substance." Then Mr. Avory says, "I do not want to reply to this. I see what your lordship's "view is, and we have an opportunity at a later stage of discussing those "matters." Then the Lord Chief Justice says, "Are you calling evi- "dence?" Then counsel for the prisoner says, "Yes. I propose to "call evidence"—and so the case goes on.

So far as there is any ruling upon the point which I am arguing before your lordship, if *The King* v. *Lynch* is said to be a decision against me, I am anxious to criticise the grounds of *The King* v. *Lynch*, and the matter which most influenced the Court in *The King* v. *Lynch*, and had decided the judgment of the Court before any argument was addressed on behalf of the Crown, as the President of the Court had stated.

Mr. Justice Darling—The difficulty about it is that if you get rid of *The King* v. *Vaughan*, the Court in *The King* v. *Lynch* did not rely only on *The King* v. *Vaughan*. There are specially mentioned all these authorities with which you dealt yesterday—Coke, Hale, Hawkins, and all of them.

Mr. Sullivan—I wish to call attention to the fact that these authorities are cited after the Lord Chief Justice has informed the Attorney-General that he has already expressed his opinion on the case on the authority of *The King* v. *Vaughan*.

Mr. Justice Darling—Suppose they did rely upon twenty authorities and one of them was a bad one and the other nineteen were good, the decision is a good one for all that. You can take a little poison without it killing you if the rest of the food is wholesome.

Mr. SULLIVAN—Without trying it, I will assent to that. I should suggest the converse happened. The Court said it was quite satisfied with the poison, but if they wished to add any further argument they might go on and cite anything else they thought might be drawn to the attention of the Court. The moment the Attorney-General rises he is informed that no argument is needed on his part to convince the Court, because the Court has already expressed an opinion, but they will listen to anything further he wishes to say, they having already made up their minds he has no case to meet. Up to that point the Court informs the Crown they have no case to meet. The only authority against the prisoner in the opinion of the Court, so far as the expression of the Court goes, is *The King* v. *Vaughan*, which is no authority at all. I submit you are not bound here by the trial at bar of *The King* v. *Lynch*, and in view of that history of the development of *The King* v. *Lynch* it certainly does not stand as a high authority, if the Court were satisfied that there was no case to be met by the Crown, and were satisfied on what the Court said was a conclusive authority in favour of the Crown, which upon investigation is shown to have been no authority at all.

Mr. JUSTICE DARLING—There were two other judges present besides Lord Alverstone, Mr. Justice Wills and Mr. Justice Channell, both very learned judges, who had made a considerable study of all these other authorities. Their knowledge of the law of treason was not limited to *The King* v. *Vaughan*.

Mr. SULLIVAN—Certainly. All that I wish to say with regard to *The King* v. *Lynch* in view of its acceptance of *The King* v. *Vaughan* is that *The King* v. *Lynch*, if it purports to follow the other authorities which I dealt with yesterday, if the authorities I dealt with yesterday, which I take it would be present to the minds of the Court, are good, they are good, but if they are bad, *The King* v. *Lynch* would be bad on the ground that these were bad and should be overruled.

Mr. JUSTICE DARLING—Yes.

Mr. SULLIVAN—All I wish to get rid of with regard to *The King* v. *Lynch* is that it should be cited as something in the nature of an additional considered authority after argument, when I point out that before there is any real argument of the case at all the Court makes up its mind, perhaps from their antecedent following of Coke, Hale, and Hawkins, but expressing itself to be satisfied there is an authority which would be binding on the Court because of a previous trial at bar which was conclusively in point. I have no wish to occupy the time of the Court any further upon this point. It does come back to this, that if I was right in my argument yesterday, *The King* v. *Lynch* would be wrongly decided if it followed *Vaughan*. If your lordships are satisfied that I need not open *Vaughan*, I can leave that. Whether it followed *Vaughan*, which, I submit, is a bad authority, or whether it followed the authority of the text-books, if those books are to be noticed, I submit it would fall in every event, and I think I need not further occupy the time of the Court with regard to the matter.

My lords, the only other case is *The King* v. *Cundell*. I think I mentioned it yesterday, and it will be present to your lordships' mind.

Mr. Justice Darling—Yes.

Mr. Sullivan—I will not turn back to that.

There are, my lords, a few matters that I may have omitted. We were dealing with the case of *Owen Glyndwr*, the record of which was sent up. There is a peculiar history with regard to that, because it appears that Glyndwr was proceeded against, and that subsequently it was found necessary to confirm the proceedings against Owen Glyndwr by statute, 9 Henry VI., chapter 3—"The proceedings against Owen "Glyndwr attainted of high treason shall stand," and so forth, "but "shall not prejudice his heirs." The important matter there is that it does not prejudice his heirs, for there you see at once the distinction between the confirmance of common law treason and conviction following in a common law Court and a conviction of treason at civil law where there was no attaint of blood. So you see obviously Owen Glyndwr's treason would be within the King's dominions but without the realm, and when proceedings against him are confirmed by Act of Parliament, they are confirmed to stand good as a conviction at civil law, and not at common law, which confirms the argument that I addressed to your lordships this morning.

Mr. Justice A. T. Lawrence—Is there any distinction drawn between civil law and the statute?

Mr. Sullivan—No.

Mr. Justice A. T. Lawrence—It was not uncommon for such statutes as that to be passed to save the heirs from forfeiture. There are lots of precedents for that.

Mr. Sullivan—It might be that. On the other hand, as we know, these proceedings tried before the admiral, although he had jurisdiction to try for high treason, and did convict of high treason in his trial at civil law, involved no attaint of blood.

Mr. Justice Darling—Glyndwr's rebellion was against Henry IV., was it not, and this is a statute of 9 Henry VI.?

Mr. Sullivan—Yes.

Mr. Justice Darling—Who were Owen Glyndwr's heirs at that time?

Mr. Sullivan—At any rate, they had sufficient influence with Parliament——

Mr. Justice Darling—They were good friends of Henry VI., you may depend.

Mr. Sullivan—Yes.

Mr. Justice Darling—I should not wonder in the least if they were very good relations of Henry VII. You will get to the house of Tudor directly.

Mr. Sullivan—Yes. The House of Tudor had a knack of drawing unto itself diverging elements in earlier years.

My lords, may I now shortly sum up what I have occupied your lordships' time over? First, I submit that dealing within the realm, and dealing with the common law, which is the common law of the realm, developing out of the county administration and the administration of the bodies of counties, there could not have been and there is no existence of something that is alleged to be a crime whose existence cannot be inquired into or determined by a legal tribunal. If no legal tribunal can inform itself whether the state of affairs exists, I submit such a state of affairs cannot be said to be a crime when their existence cannot become known to a legal tribunal—that for want of venue the common law could never inform itself of a matter which had arisen outside of the body of the county—that the statute of Edward III., although it would be law in all the King's dominions as far as we are dealing with it, its administration by the common law would depend on the powers of the common law to inform itself as to the facts alleged against supposed offenders, and that therefore the statute when dealing with matters within the realm should not be construed as to intend the creation of an offence on a state of affairs which again could not be tried—and that in the construction of the statute it must be borne in mind that the statute would fall to the ground so far as it is incapable of working itself out by the process and procedure of the common law. I submit on the plain reading of the statute, if we read it to-day for the first time, if you gave it to a man who knew nothing about the complications connected with it, it would convey clearly to his mind that the two matters alleged in the statute would only have the criminal element of treachery according to the statute if they were committed within the realm; and one of them had this peculiarity, that it might be proved to be committed within the realm, although the completion of the offence might have taken place outside the realm if the offender was within all the time. That was a peculiarity which distinguished it from the other matters alleged in the statute. I submit that any passing of the statute to try and make it fit with the opinion of text-writers would be outside the jurisdiction of the Court; that the statute should be expounded by each member of the Court for himself, and that the duty is to peruse the statute and to form an opinion as to what the statute means, and not to try and see if the statute can be reconciled or read in accordance with the opinion of any text-writer, no matter how eminent. I would call the attention of the Court to the fact that as far as I know—again I speak subject to correction—you do not find any effort to put in operation with regard to outside matters, these allegations of treason until subsequently to 26 Henry VIII., that in all these years, including the time when there were pretenders in France leading against the Kings of England, you do not find precedent—apart from *Cundell's* case—of any proceeding in the nature of adhering where the adherent is, and all the acts and circumstances take place, entirely without the jurisdiction, in all these hundreds of years. An examination of the cases shows that until *The King* v. *Lynch* the matter is never debated and submitted to the judgment of His Majesty's judges. There is no contemporaneous exposition, and there is no adjudication upon the meaning of the statute through all these years after debate and judicial pronouncement upon it.

My lords, for these reasons I submit that this Court is not trammelled by the speculative opinions of any text-writers where the statute has not been construed by any other Court except the Court at bar in *The King* v. *Lynch*, and accordingly that the Court should approach this statute as if the statute had passed yesterday, and if reading it as passing yesterday a clear opinion on the terms of the statute is conveyed to the mind of the Court, that should be the reading of the statute, no matter for how many years text-writers have expressed a different opinion.

Mr. JUSTICE DARLING—There are other points raised, Serjeant Sullivan, in this appeal besides this.

Mr. SULLIVAN—There are other points raised in the notice of appeal. I have not dealt with them. On investigation, whatever criticism might be directed, I do not think I should be justified in occupying your lordships' time in asking that the judgment should be reversed on them.

Mr. JUSTICE DARLING—We will let you know if we desire to hear you, Mr. Attorney.

Their lordships retired.

On resuming,

Mr. JUSTICE DARLING—We have no occasion to trouble you, Mr. Attorney.

Judgment.

Mr. JUSTICE DARLING—In this case the appellant was indicted for high treason in adhering to the King's enemies elsewhere than in the King's realm, that is to say, within the Empire of Germany; and his act was said to be contrary to the Treason Act of 1351, the statute of 25 Edward III., chapter 2. That statute says, "Whereas divers opinions have been "before this time in what case treason shall be said, and in what not; "the King, at the request of the Lords and of the Commons, hath made a "declaration in the manner as hereafter followeth," which is the statute of Edward III., and various treasons are defined; and after the treason of levying war against the King in his kingdom there is defined, because it is only, as has often been said, declaring the common law, this particular treason. I will read it first in the words in which it is written in the Parliament Roll and in the Statute Roll, now in the Record Office, in Norman French, and then I will read it in the translation which has been published long ago under the authority of the King's printers. The words are these, "May commit treason by levying war against the King," and so on, "*Ou soit adherant as enemys nostre seignur le Roi en le "roialme donant a eux eid ou confort en son roialme ou par aillours,*" and that has been translated "or be adherent to the King's enemies in his "realm, giving to them aid and comfort in the realm or elsewhere." It is the construction of those few words which has given rise to all the argument which has been addressed to the Court before whom the appellant was tried and to this Court.

Now, we desire to say, every member of this Court desires to say, that we are greatly indebted to Serjeant Sullivan, who has appeared for the appellant in this case. We desire to say that in our judgment his argument was exceedingly well considered, well delivered, and was in every way worthy of the greatest traditions of the King's Courts, in one of which it was delivered. Having said that, it is from no want of respect to his argument that we did not call upon the Attorney-General, but the Court, having considered fully and attentively every argument used by Serjeant Sullivan, and the authorities he advanced for it, have come to the conclusion that there was no need to call for any refutation of it from the Attorney-General. The authorities have been fully cited; there is no consideration which is not before the Court, because the answer, so far as it was an answer, to Serjeant Sullivan's argument had been made by the Crown at the trial, and Serjeant Sullivan himself was thoroughly aware of what might be the answer to any proposition which he put before us. We have considered, therefore, with the advantage of having known to us all that passed at the trial, the argument which he has so well, so excellently I may say, addressed to us.

Now, the main point raised in the argument of Serjeant Sullivan was that this statute had neither created nor declared that it was an offence to be adherent to the King's enemies beyond the realm of the King; and that the words meant that the giving of aid and comfort, *ou par aillours*, that is, outside the realm, did not constitute a treason which could be tried in this country unless the person who gave the aid and comfort outside the realm, in this case within the Empire of Germany, was himself within the realm at the time he gave the aid and comfort. This argument was founded upon the difficulties which must arise owing to the doctrine of venue, that people were only triable within certain districts where the venue could be alleged; that if a man committed a crime in a county he must be indicted and tried for it in that county; that if he committed a crime against the King he must be tried within the realm; and that if the aid and comfort was given outside the realm by a person being then outside the realm he could not be tried there—that follows, because it was not within the King's realm; and that, as he could not be tried by the King's Courts in the Empire of Germany, he could not be tried in the King's Courts at all for what he had done in Germany unless when he gave the aid and comfort in Germany he was himself actually resident within the realm of the King. It was said, this must be so, or one could find a case where a man had altogether outside the realm given aid and comfort to the King's enemies, and had been indicted within the realm and tried for it. Such a case would be difficult to find in the course of years, because it cannot be a very common offence. First of all, if a man did commit it—I call it an offence—if he did those things, pure and simple, it is highly improbable that he would then put himself in peril by coming within the realm where what he had done might be investigated, and where he might be punished for it. One would expect that very few people would put themselves in a position where they could possibly be charged; but if any of them did, it is so highly probable that, besides the giving of aid and comfort outside the realm, they would have done something inside the realm, if they came back it is so highly probable that they would have come back with some evil intention, such as levying war, compassing the King's death, or doing something of that sort, that they would very probably be arrested on their arrival in this country, and not charged with being adherent to the King's enemies outside the realm, but charged with some such offence as anybody being within the King's realm could commit there; it would be much more easily proved; and, therefore, if the two offences had been committed, as would be extremely probable, in the one case, any one having the direction of a criminal prosecution would be certain to charge him for the case which could be more easily proved. Therefore we are not very much impressed by the fact that there is very little precedent for such a prosecution as this.

But there is a large amount of authority for the proposition that what the jury have found was done by this appellant, and what it is not contested was done, because there is here no appeal upon the facts, is an offence triable, as this offence was triable, in the King's Bench. Taking the words of the statute themselves, it appears to us that the construction for which Serjeant Sullivan contends is not the true one. He would have it that "be adherent to the King's enemies in his realm, giving to them "aid and comfort in the realm or elsewhere," means that the adherence, because it is the adherence which is the offence, really must be by a person who, being in this country, gives the aid and comfort, it may be in this country, it may be outside of it. We agree that if a person being within this country gives aid and comfort to the King's enemies in this country he is adherent to the King's enemies; we agree (and Serjeant Sullivan admits this) that if he is in this country and he gives aid and comfort to the King's enemies outside this country he is adherent to the King's enemies. But we think there is another offence, and that these words must mean something more than that. We think that the meaning of these words is this, "giving aid and comfort to the King's enemies" are words of apposition; they are words to explain what is meant by being adherent to, and we think that if a man be adherent to the King's enemies in his realm by giving to them aid and comfort in his realm, or if he be adherent to the King's enemies elsewhere, that is by giving to them aid and comfort elsewhere he is equally adherent to the King's enemies, and if he is adherent to the King's enemies, then he commits the treason which the statute of Edward III. defines. Reasons may be given for that, but we think a very good reason is to be found in this, that the subjects of the King owe him allegiance, and the allegiance follows the person of the subject. He is the King's liege wherever he may be, and he may violate his allegiance in a foreign country just as well as he may violate it in this country. If authority were wanted for that it is to be found in *The King* v. *Cundell*, 4 Newgate Calendar, page 62. I put out of the question Serjeant Sullivan's argument as to where the person could be tried, whether he could be tried by Commission or tried by Commission of oyer and terminer, or tried in the King's Bench; but a really shocking example of what allegiance may mean is to be found in *Cundell's* case where prisoners of war, being then in the Isle of France, which I think we now call the Isle of Mauritius, were seduced from their allegiance; they had adhered to the King's enemies; being recaptured they were actually tried here in England, and one of them, Cundell, was executed for high treason, the others were pardoned. That was because he had violated his allegiance which followed him, which remained with him wherever he might be outside the King's dominions, and by which he was even bound when he was a prisoner of war. Of course, I do not cite that case to commend it for its humanity or anything of that kind, but merely to say that as a matter of strict law it is perfectly good law, and the only reason why it is not decisive of this case is that it does not dispose of the question where the person who has committed the particular treason can be tried or how he can be tried.

Now, I have said that it is the opinion of the Court that there is a great deal of authority for this proposition, that adherence to the King's enemies outside the King's dominions by a person who is himself outside constitutes the commission of this treason by the person who is elsewhere than within the King's realm. It is worth while to notice that this question must have been discussed; people may have doubted how a person could be tried, but it must have been discussed among lawyers as to how he could be tried. There is a long and ancient opinion, as I will show when I read the cases presently, for the proposition that it is treason to do what the appellant has been convicted of doing in this case.

Now, a statute was passed which has been often cited here, a statute of 35 Henry VIII., and what it says is this, "An Act for the trial of "treasons committed out of the King's dominions." There is a distinct statement that you can commit treason out of the King's dominions; it is only a question of how the person is to be tried; and it says, "Forasmuch "as some doubts and questions have been moved that certain kinds of "treasons, misprisions, and concealments of treasons done, perpetrated, or "committed out of the King's Majesties realm of England and other His "Grace's dominions cannot by the common laws of this realm be enquired "of, heard, and determined within this his said realm of England. For "a plain remedy, order, and declaration therein to be had and made. Be "it enacted by authority of this present Parliament that all manner of "offences being already made or declared or hereafter to be made or "declared by any of the laws and statutes of this realm to be treasons, "misprisions of treasons, or concealments of treason, and done, perpe- "trated, and committed by any person or persons out of this realm of "England shall be from henceforth enquired of, heard, and determined "before the King's justices of his bench for pleas to be holden before "himself," and so on; that is to say, tried in the King's Bench. Therefore this trial was rightly had in the King's Bench, provided what was done by the appellant amounted to treason by virtue of the statute of Edward III. If it was such a treason it was rightly tried. Whether it was or not depends upon the construction which we ourselves, reading this statute, put upon it. Serjeant Sullivan has asked us simply to take the statute and read it as though we had seen it for the first time, and he says that is the best way to construe any statute. Well, it is a little difficult for anybody who is a judge of the King's Bench to say that he reads for the first time the statute of Edward III. concerning treasons. We must all have read it before. But I do not know that the rule which Serjeant Sullivan lays down is altogether an acceptable one.

In Maxwell on the Interpretation of Statutes, chapter 11, there is this passage, "It is said that the best exposition of a statute or any other "document is that which it has received from contemporary authority. "*Optima est legum interpres consuetudo*," and then another maxim is given. "Where this has been given by enactment or judicial decision "it is, of course, to be accepted as conclusive. But, further, the mean- "ing publicly given by contemporary, or long professional usage, is pre- "sumed to be the true one, even when the language has etymologically

Mr. Justice Darling

"or popularly a different meaning. It is obvious that the language of "a statute must be understood in the sense in which it was understood "when it was passed; and those who lived at or near the time when it "was passed may reasonably be supposed to be better acquainted than "their descendants with the circumstances to which it had relation, as "well as with the sense then attached to it by the Legislature; and the "interpretation put upon its enactment by notorious practice may, perhaps, "be regarded as some sanction and approval of it."

Now, this statute had been understood long before to-day, has been understood by lawyers of great learning, has been understood by lawyers of very exceptional erudition who have been members of the King's Bench, and understood in the sense in which we have to-day said we understood it. Their authority has been attacked by Serjeant Sullivan. Serjeant Sullivan has attacked Lord Coke, quite properly attacked him. He has attacked his authority; he has questioned the reasons, if there be any, for the statements which Lord Coke has made concerning the law; and if we were to accede to the argument of Serjeant Sullivan we should have absolutely to disregard the opinion of Lord Coke, the opinion of Mr. Serjeant Hawkins, and the opinion of Sir Matthew Hale—all great names in the law, and persons whose opinions have long been followed in many questions of extreme difficulty which have puzzled lawyers for many generations. Let us see what Hale says. Sir Matthew Hale in his Pleas of the Crown, chapter 15, says this, "Touching the trial of foreign treason, viz., adhering "to the King's enemies, as also for compassing the King's death without "the kingdom at this day, the statute of 35 Henry VIII., chapter 2, has "sufficiently provided for it," and then he cites Dyer 31*b* and *Story's* case, "but at common law he might have been indicted in any "county of England, and especially where the offender's lands lie, if he "have any." That is a very definite statement, and if we were to allow this appeal we should be bound to say that that did not state the law. Are we entitled to throw over the opinion of Sir Matthew Hale as cavalierly as we are invited to do? Looking at this book, The History of the Pleas of the Crown, how comes it to be in our hand? I read at the very beginning of it, "Extract from the Journal of the House of Commons, the "29th day of November, 1680.—Ordered, that the executors of Sir Matthew "Hale, late Lord Chief Justice of the Court of King's Bench, be desired "to print the MSS. relating to the Crown law, and that a committee be "appointed to take care in printing thereof," and it is referred to Sir William Jones, Serjeant Maynard—a name to be reverenced in legal history—Sir Francis Winnington, Mr. Sacheverel, Mr. George Pelham, and Mr. Paul Foley; and it is because of their care and by order of Parliament that we have this book in our hand at all.

Then there is Mr. Serjeant Hawkins. At page 306 of the second volume, section 48, he says this, "It seems to have been a great doubt "before the making of the statute of 35 Henry VIII., chapter 2, in what "manner and in what place high treason done out of the realm was to be "tried. For some seem to have holden that it was triable only upon "an appeal before the constable and marshal; others that it might be "tried upon an indictment, laying the offence in any county where the "King pleased; and others, that it was triable by way of indictment in "that county only wherein the offencer had lands; but surely it cannot be "reasonably doubted, but that it was triable some way or other; for it "cannot be imagined that an offence of such dangerous consequence, and "expressly within the purview of 25 Edward III., should be wholly dis- "punishable, as it must have been, if it were no way triable." Serjeant Sullivan's argument is that it was dispunishable because you could not try it, if the kind of treason alleged were what is alleged in this case.

I mentioned yesterday, and I think it is worth reading again, because we are relying, confessedly relying, upon the authority of Sir Matthew Hale and of Serjeant Hawkins in the judgment that we are giving, and also upon the opinion expressed by Lord Coke, to which I will come presently —there is a passage in the case of *Butt* v. *Conant*, decided in 1820, and reported in first volume of Broderip and Bingham's Reports at page 570, where Chief Justice Dallas, himself no mean authority, says this, "We are "told that we must look to the authorities, and find what we can in the "books upon the subject." It seems to have been recognised that that was the proper way; if a question of law arose, look back at the old authorities and find what you can in the books upon the subject. "Now, "if the authority of Lord Hale, and that of Mr. Serjeant Hawkins, are "to be treated lightly, we may be without any authority whatever." Here we are asked to treat them lightly, we are asked to reject them altogether. "With respect to Lord Hale, it is needless to remind those "whom I am now addressing"—this was in 1820—"of the general "character for learning and legal knowledge of that person, of whom it "was said, that what was not known by him was not known by any "other person who preceded or followed him; and that what he knew, he "knew better than any other person, who preceded or followed him. "With respect to Mr. Serjeant Hawkins, we know his authority. These "are books which are in the hand and head of every lawyer, and constantly "referred to on every occasion of this sort. I must, therefore, look to "these books; and I shall proceed to examine the exposition given by "text-writers of the words of those statutes, and the commission of the "peace."

Now, with regard to Lord Coke, his opinion is precisely the same as that which is given by Sir Matthew Hale and Mr. Serjeant Hawkins, and it has been said to us that we should not follow Lord Coke, because Stephen in his Commentaries, and other writers elsewhere, have spoken lightly of the authority and learning of Lord Coke. It may be they have done so. Of course, they have all the advantage. They are his successors. If Lord Coke were in a position to answer them it may be they would regret that they had entered into argument with him; but although Stephen and others have perhaps flouted the authority of Lord Coke, he has been recognised as a great authority in these Courts for centuries, and nowhere more than perhaps in the passage I am now about to read, which I owe to my brother Atkin, in the case of *Garland* v. *Jekyll*, reported in 2 Bingham's Reports, page 296, in the year 1824—"I know it has been said that Lord "Coke in this case must be mistaken, for in the margin is a reference "to Lord Coke's Reports, and upon referring to the page you find nothing "to warrant his opinion. I have looked into the report, and the observa- "tion is correct; but it will be found that the same observation will apply

Mr. Justice Darling

"to cases that are relied on on the other side; it appears to me that the "reference was not made by Lord Coke, but that it has been introduced by "some ignorant editor, who fancied something confirmatory of the opinion "in Coke. The fact is, Lord Coke had no authority for what he states, "but I am afraid we should get rid of a good deal of what is considered "law in Westminster Hall if what Lord Coke says, without authority, is "not law. He was one of the most eminent lawyers that ever presided "as a judge in any Court of justice, and what is said by such a person "is good evidence of what the law is, particularly when it is in conformity "with justice and common sense." Those are the words of Chief Justice Best.

If one wanted an opinion of a person who was not a lawyer, one with whom I dare say Serjeant Sullivan, at all events, is perfectly familiar, it is where this same Lord Coke is alluded to by John Milton as one who—

On the Royal Bench
Of British Themis, with no mean applause,
Pronounced, and in his volumes taught our laws,
Which others at their bar too often wrench.

There are other authorities who understood this matter in precisely the same way, not authorities as great as Lord Coke, but it is worth while, I think, to show what was the volume of opinion during ages when lawyers were considering this particular matter. There is a treatise, not perhaps very commonly known—I referred to it yesterday—by Mr. Ferdinand Pulton, a barrister of Lincoln's Inn, and the particular copy I am reading from was published in 1609. He says, "These views are collected out "of the reports of the common laws of this realm, and of the statutes in "force, and out of the painful works of the reverend judges," mentioning them, and there is this passage, "And because by the said statute of "25 Edward III. it is declared to be high treason to levy war against the "King in his realm, or to be adherent to his enemies, aiding them in his "realm or elsewhere; therefore if a subject born of the realm being beyond "the seas doth practice with a prince or governor of another country to "invade this realm with great power, and do declare where, how, and by "what means the invasion may best be made, it is high treason; for an "invasion with great power cannot be, but of likelihood it will tend to "the destruction of great peril of the King and hurt to the realm; more-"over, the said offender hath manifested himself to be adherent to the "King's enemy and to aid him with his counsel, though not in the realm, "yet elsewhere, and this offence shall be tried in the King's Bench, or "elsewhere, before such Commissioners, and in such county, as the King "by commission shall appoint, according to the statute of 35 Henry "VIII., chapter 2."

A much more modern writer was of the same opinion, Sir James Fitz-james Stephen. In his Digest of the Criminal Law he says, "Every one "commits high treason who, either in the realm or without it, actively "assists a public enemy at war with the King."

A valuable opinion to the same effect was given in the year 1775, and it is referred to, and can be found in Archbold at page 1033, where this is said, "In 1775 the law officers (Thurlow, A.G., and Wedderburn, S.G.) had "been informed that in 13 Anne an Act against high treason had been "passed in the province of New Hampshire," which was in the King's dominions in America, "that the said Act was disallowed by Order in "Council in 1718; that it was conceived there was no law of that province "at present existing for the trial and punishment of that offence. They "were asked in what manner it was proper to proceed against persons for "high treason committed in New Hampshire. They replied, 'We are "'humbly of opinion that it requires no Act of a provincial Legislature to "'constitute the offence of high treason in any of His Majesty's planta- "'tions. The crimes may be prosecuted in the Superior Court of New "'Hampshire (which by 2 William III. hath the full criminal jurisdiction "'within that government which His Majesty's Court of King's Bench "'exercises here), or in this country in the statutes of 35 Henry VIII., "'as the occasion may require.'" That was exactly this case. The treason was not committed within the King's realm; it was committed elsewhere. There is no pretence that the person who committed it by being adherent, or whatever form the treason took, was within the King's realm. That is a distinct statement which covers this case exactly, and that is the opinion of two such law officers as Lord Thurlow and Lord Loughborough, absolutely consonant to the opinion which this Court is expressing to-day.

I do not know that it is worth while to allude to the paragraph to which Serjeant Sullivan called our attention in *Platt's* case, which is in the first volume of Leach's Cases in Crown Law, at page 168, but it is to be noticed that no stress whatever is laid by the Court there upon the words, which Serjeant Sullivan insists govern the whole of this particular definition of treason, that is, the words "in his realm," because what is said is, "It was the ancient opinion, that the species of treason which consists, "by 25 Edward III., chapter 2, in adhering to the King's enemies, might "be tried, before the statute 35 Henry VIII., chapter 2, within the king- "dom, by the rules of the common law, though the aid and comfort was "afforded without the realm."

We do not think it necessary to give further reasons for the conclusion to which we have come. We purposely do not rely upon a recent case which has been questioned by Serjeant Sullivan, simply for the reason that we are of opinion that there is ample authority for the conclusion to which the Court indubitably came to in that case, ample authority to be found in the decisions and in the opinions of great lawyers to which I have referred in giving the judgment of this Court.

It only remains to say that the appeal is dismissed.

The other points taken in the notice of appeal questioning the summing up of the Lord Chief Justice are entirely withdrawn by the appellant's counsel, and it is needless to say more about them.

APPENDIX I.

PRINT OF PRODUCTIONS IN TRIAL.

INDEX TO EXHIBITS.

Number of Exhibit.	Description.
1.	Warrant dated 13th May, 1916.
2.	Copy birth certificate of Roger David Casement.
3.	Supplement to *London Gazette* of 4th August, 1914.
4.	Address headed "Irishmen!"
5.	Newspaper photograph of the non-commissioned officers of Company "A," Irish Brigade, Berlin.
6.	Photographs of sands at Curraghane.
7.	Photograph of a boat.
8.	Dagger.
9.	Tin box.
10.	Three revolvers.
11.	A leather bag.
12.	Black bag.
13.	Leather bag.
14.	Three life-belts.
15.	Paper in which sausage was found.
16.	Paper found on Sir R. Casement.
17.	Paper found in Exhibit 12.
18.	Two pieces of paper (Code).
19.	Overcoat.
20.	Overcoat.
21.	Overcoat.
22.	Four sheets of notepaper found on Bailey.
23.	Maps.
24.	List of maps found.
25.	Rifle.
26.	Broken rifle butts.
27.	Bayonet case.
28.	Cartridge in clip.
29.	Copy certificate of birth of Daniel Julian Bailey.
30.	Statement of Daniel Julian Bailey, 23rd April, 1916.
31.	Ticket, Berlin to Wilhelmshaven.
32.	Letter from Roger Casement to Sir Edward Grey, dated 19th June, 1911.
33.	Official history of Sir Roger Casement.

EXHIBIT 1.

In the Metropolitan Police District.

To each and all of the Constables of the Metropolitan Police Force—

Information on oath has been laid by the Director of Public Prosecutions that SIR ROGER CASEMENT and DANIEL JULIAN BAILEY (hereinafter called the defendants) on the 1st day of November, 1914, and on divers other days thereafter, and between that day and the 21st day of April, 1916, unlawfully, maliciously, and traitorously did commit high treason within and without the Realm of England in contempt of our Sovereign Lord the King and his laws, to the evil example of all others in the like case offending contrary to the duty of the allegiance of them the said Sir Roger Casement and Daniel Julian Bailey to our said Sovereign Lord the King and against the form of the statute in such case made and provided.

YOU ARE THEREFORE HEREBY COMMANDED to bring the Defendants before the Court of Summary Jurisdiction sitting at the Bow Street Police Court forthwith to answer to the said Information.

Dated the 13th day of May, 1916.

John Dickinson.

(Seal.)

One of the Magistrates of the Police Courts of the Metropolis.

(2s. Stamp.)

On back.
Inspector Parker is to execute this warrant.

P. Quinn,
Superintendent.

Perforation.
13.5.16.

EXHIBIT 2.

17/62.

Form A.—Act 26, Vict. Cap. 11.

BIRTHS REGISTERED IN THE DISTRICT OF KINGSTOWN IN THE UNION OF RATHDOWN IN THE COUNTY OF DUBLIN.

No.	Date and Place of Birth.	Name (if any).	Sex.	Name and Surname and Dwelling Place of Father.	Name and Surname and Maiden Surname of Mother.	Rank or Profession of Father.	Signature, Qualification, and Residence of Informant.	When Registered.	Signature of Registrar.	Baptismal Name, if added after Registration of Birth and Date.
(1)	(2)	(3)	(4)	(5)	(6)	(7)	(8)	(9)	(10)	(11)
143	1st September, 1864, Doyle's Cottage, Lawson Terrace.	Roger David.	Male.	Roger Casement, Lawson Terrace, Sandycove.	Annie Casement, formerly Jephson.	Late Captain in the Antrim Militia.	Roger Casement, Father, Lawson Terrace, Sandycove.	27th September, 1864.	John Foster, Newland, Registrar.	

Certified to be a true copy taken from the Certified Copies of Entries of Births in the General Register Office, Dublin.

Given at the General Register Office, Charlemont House, Dublin, under the Seal of the Office, this 6th day of May, 1916.

(The Seal of the General Register Office, Dublin.)

Issued for Official Purposes.

Sir Roger Casement.

EXHIBIT 3.

Supplement to the *London Gazette* of Tuesday, the 4th of August, 1914, containing notification that a state of War exists between England and Germany.

EXHIBIT 4.

Irishmen !

Here is a chance for you to fight for Ireland !

You have fought for England, your country's hereditary enemy.

You have fought for Belgium, in England's interest, though it was no more to you than the Fiji Islands !

Are you willing to fight for your own country ?

With a view to securing the National Freedom of Ireland, with the moral and material assistance of the German Government, an Irish Brigade is being formed.

The object of the Irish Brigade shall be to fight solely the cause of Ireland, and under no circumstances shall it be directed to any German end.

The Irish Brigade shall be formed and shall fight under the Irish flag alone ; the men shall wear a special, distinctively Irish uniform and have Irish officers.

The Irish Brigade shall be clothed, fed, and efficiently equipped with arms and ammunition by the German Government. It will be stationed near Berlin, and be treated as guests of the German Government.

At the end of the war the German Government undertakes to send each member of the Brigade, who may so desire it, to the United States of America, with necessary means to land. The Irishmen in America are collecting money for the Brigade. Those men who do not join the Irish Brigade will be removed from Limburg and distributed among other camps.

If interested, see your company commanders.

Join the Irish Brigade and win Ireland's independence !

Remember Bachelor's Walk !

God save Ireland !

EXHIBIT 22.

Four Sheets of Notepaper found on Bailey, on one of which is written—

Castle, near Tralee, is quite a quaint old Irish structure of stone.

Appendix I.

EXHIBIT 23.

Two Maps of Ireland, each cut in Fourteen Sections.

EXHIBIT 24.

Maps Found.

Two Maps of Ireland, each cut in 14 Sections, marked in indelible pencil back and front as follows:—

Section	1,	marked	TROY.	Section	8,	marked	GALWAY.
,,	2,	,,	FOYLE.	,,	9,	,,	DUBLIN.
,,	3,	,,	STRANGFORD.	,,	10,	,,	WEXFORD.
,,	4,	,,	NEAGH.	,,	11,	,,	LIMERICK.
,,	5,	,,	DONEGAL.	,,	12,	,,	TRALEE.
,,	6,	,,	BLACKSOD.	,,	13,	,,	KENMARE.
,,	7,	,,	CLEW.	,,	14,	,,	CORK.

On the back of one of the Sections, No. 14, appear the figures and words by way of index:—

1. Troy.
2. Foyle.
3. Strangford.
4. Neagh.
5. Donegal.
6. Blacksod.
7. Clew.
8. Galway.
9. Dublin.
10. Wexford.
11. Limerick.
12. Tralee.
13. Kenmare.
14. Cork.

19/29.

EXHIBIT 29.

Form A.—Act 26, Viet. Cap. 11.

BIRTHS REGISTERED IN THE DISTRICT OF N. CITY 2 IN THE UNION OF N. DUBLIN IN THE COUNTY OF CITY OF DUBLIN.

No. (1)	Date and Place of Birth. (2)	Name (if any). (3)	Sex. (4)	Name and Surname and Maiden Surname of Mother. (5)	Name and Surname and Dwelling Place of Father. (6)	Rank or Profession of Father. (7)	Signature, Qualification, and Residence of Informant. (8)	When Registered. (9)	Signature of Registrar. (10)	Baptismal Name, if added after Registration of Birth and Date. (11)
328	1887. Seventeenth January, 143 Up. Dorset Street.	Daniel.	Male.	Jane Bailey, formerly Bollard.	Daniel Bailey, 143 Up. Dorset Street.	Grocer.	Jane Bailey, Mother, 143 Up. Dorset Street.	Twenty-ninth January, 1887.	O. C. J. Delahoyde, Asst. Registrar.	

Certified to be a true copy taken from the Certified Copies of Entries of Births in the General Register Office, Dublin.

Given at the General Register Office, Charlemont House, Dublin, under the Seal of the Office, this 16th day of May, 1916.

(1d. stamp.
A. K.
16/5/1916.)

(Seal of the
General Register
Office, Dublin.)

Appendix I.

EXHIBIT 30.

Statement of Daniel Julian Bailey taken by D. I. Britten at Abbeydorney on 23rd April, 1916.

My name is Daniel Julian Bailey. I was born in Dublin, but have not been there since November, 1906. I joined the R.I. Rifles in 1904—the regiment left Dublin in 1906 for Aldershot. I went to India in 1907—Meerut Station, came to Watford, England, in January, 1913, as a reservist, went to Canada in April, 1913, and returned in September to Watford. We moved to Craven Park, Harlesden, London, and was working as a porter in Goods Shed at Paddington Station at the outbreak of the war. I was called up to my depot in Belfast immediately, and went out with the Expeditionary Force. I was taken prisoner about the 4th September, 1914, and was sent to Senelager. They then took me with the other Irish to Limburg, where we were well treated for a time. I saw Sir Roger Casement about April, 1915, and he spoke to us about joining an Irish Brigade solely for the purpose of fighting for Irish freedom. I joined to see if I could possibly get out of the country. I signed on as D. J. Beverley. I was made sergeant straight away. We went (about 56) to Zossen, and we remained there as prisoners from May, 1915, to the end of March, 1916, when I was sent to Berlin. (I was taken by motor to Neukollen, a suburb of Berlin.) In the car with me was Mr. Monteith and some German civilian. We went to an explosives school and got instruction there from the civilian in the use of explosives. I was only there about three hours, and then went back to Zossen with Mr. Monteith. I remained there for a week or more, and was then taken to the Saxonia Hotel in Berlin. I was given civilian clothing and was taken to the Government Offices in Wilhelmstrasse, and got further instruction in explosives. Sir Roger Casement was stopping at the Saxonia, but he did not tell me what I was going to do. I stayed there about ten days. Monteith was there too. On Tuesday, the 11th inst., a car came to door and the three of us (Casement, Monteith, and I) were driven to War Office. They gave me a railway ticket and we got into a motor car and went to Zoological Gardens Station and got into the train for Wilhelmshaven. We were put on a submarine, U20, there. She steamed out and had to return, owing to accident, to Heligoland. There we boarded U19 and came round Shetland to the West Coast of Ireland. I knew now where I was going, but still got no instructions. I gathered, when near Tralee, that it was in connection with the Volunteer movement. They steamed in as near as they could, lowered the collapsible boat, and put us off. When everything was ready, we took in the boat the revolvers and ammunition, &c., which you have found, and I was ordered to bury them. It was about 1 a.m. or later when we were put in the boat. When in the surf the boat overturned and we had to wade ashore, and I went back two or three times to fetch in the stuff. We buried the arms, &c., not far from where we landed. I followed them, and we stopped in a avenue of whins off the road. We left our coats there, and I was taken by Mr. Monteith to Tralee, by the road, people were going to Mass when we got there (8 a.m.). We went to a bridge outside the town and sat down on the wall. Monteith seemed to be looking for somebody. We went back to the town into a narrow street, when some placards caught his eye. He went over and knocked at the one closed and some one looked out of the open shop. We went in the shop, and *The Spark* caught his eye. He bought one. I spoke quietly to the man in the shop. He sent one of the girls away, and we went and got something to eat at Lavin's. We had breakfast there and went back to the shop, and he asked if the Commanding Officer had come yet. He was told "No," but to come inside and wait. Four men came in, not all at the same time, and some conversation took place between Monteith and them out of my hearing. I was given the suit I have on by a man in glasses; that was the man I was in the motor car with afterwards. Mr. Stack was one of the four in the shop. I did not hear if he was the Commanding Officer. Later on I was taken out of the shop by a man with glasses and a girl.

When we got to the Convent a motor car came up and stopped. The girl went back and we got in. Mr. Stack and the driver were in it. There was a parcel which I took to contain clothes in the car. Later on Mr. Stack asked me if I knew where "Mr. Rice" was. That name had been arranged by Sir Roger Casement. I said I could not locate the spot. They travelled the car about the roads looking for the place. We got a puncture at the end of a road going to the beach, where we were challenged by the police. They did not get out of the car before the police came; but then they mended puncture, and turned and went the road in the opposite direction from Tralee. They got out near a house at X roads, and Mr. Stack spoke to some one in the house. The sergeant came up again here and searched the car, and we went on straight to a little village, where we were stopped again by a young constable. We turned the car then and went to another small village where we were again searched by the police. I gave my name of David Mulcahy. The man with the glasses furnished me with his name. A revolver was taken from the man with the glasses. We then went on, and the car stopped. Mr. Stack and the other man got out and spoke to a man on the road with a bicycle. The latter went away and got a second bicycle, and brought me to a house, where I stopped the night. It was a house by itself, not in a village. In the morning he called again without a bicycle and directed me to a castle, where he told me to knock about, and he then left me. I remained there until a policeman came up and arrested me. When they put me out of the car they said nothing to me, but gave instructions to the man on bicycle. Stack said very little.

When on the submarine I overheard conversation from time to time that a small Wilson Liner was to be piloted from Fenit Pier. It had 20,000 rifles, with 5 rifles in each case, and over 1,000,000 rounds of ammunition. It was disguised as a timber ship. From what I heard there were 10 machine guns, 2 ready for action, and bombs and fire-bombs.

I heard that Dublin Castle was to be raided.

(Signed) D. Julian Bailey,
23rd April, 1916.

Appendix I.

EXHIBIT 32.

The Savoy, Denham, Bucks,
19th June, 1911.

Dear Sir Edward Grey,—I find it very hard to choose the words in which to make acknowledgment of the honour done me by the King.

I am much moved at the proof of confidence and appreciation of my services on the Putumayo conveyed to me by your letter, wherein you tell me that the King had been graciously pleased upon your recommendation to confer upon me the honour of a knighthood.

I am indeed grateful to you for this signal assurance of your personal esteem and support, and very deeply sensible of the honour done to me by His Majesty.

I would beg that my humble duty might be presented to His Majesty, when you may do me the honour to convey to him my deep appreciation of the honour he has been so graciously pleased to confer upon me.

I am, Dear Sir Edward,

Yours sincerely,

ROGER CASEMENT.

EXHIBIT 33.

CASEMENT, SIR ROGER, C.M.G.

Born September 1, 1864. Was in the service of the Niger Coast (Oil Rivers) Protectorate from July 31, 1892. Appointed H.M. Consul in the Portuguese Province of Lorenzo Marques, to reside at Lorenzo Marques, June 27, 1895; and Consul for the Portuguese Possessions in West Africa south of the Gulf of Guinea, to reside at Loanda; Consul in the Gaboon; and Consul to the Independent State of the Congo, July 29, 1898. Employed on special service at Cape Town during the war in South Africa, 1899-1900, and received the Queen's South African Medal. Transferred to Kinchassa, Congo State, August 20, 1900; and appointed, in addition, Consul for part of the French Congo Colony, August 6, 1901. Seconded for one year from December 31, 1904; and for six months from December 31, 1905. Made a C.M.G., June 30, 1905. Appointed Consul for the States of Sao Paulo and Parana, to reside at Santos, August 13, 1906. Transferred to Para, December 2, 1907. Promoted to be Consul-General at Rio de Janeiro, December 1, 1908. Received the honour of knighthood, June 20, 1911. Received the Coronation Medal, 1911. The State of Goyaz was added to the district of the Consulate-General at Rio de Janeiro, and a new Commission issued to Sir R. Casement, December 2, 1912. From 1909 to 1912 was employed while titular Consul-General at Rio de Janeiro in making certain inquiries relative to the rubber industry (Putumayo). Retired on pension, August 1, 1913. Pension ceased on September 30, 1914.

APPENDIX II.

PETITIONS ON BEHALF OF ROGER CASEMENT.

A Petition to the Prime Minister on behalf of Roger Casement. By Sir Arthur Conan Doyle.

To the Right Hon. H. H. Asquith,
Prime Minister.

Sir,—We, the undersigned, while entirely admitting the guilt of the prisoner Roger Casement, and the justice of his sentence, would desire to lay before you some reasons why the extreme sentence of the law should not be inflicted—

(1) We would call attention to the violent change which appears to have taken place in the prisoner's previous sentiments towards Great Britain (as shown, for example, in his letter to the King at the time of his knighthood) from those which he has exhibited during the war. Without going so far as to urge complete mental irresponsibility, we should desire to point out that the prisoner had for many years been exposed to severe strain during his honourable career of public service, that he had endured several tropical fevers, and that he had experienced the worry of two investigations which were of a peculiarly nerve-trying character. For these reasons it appears to us that some allowance may be made in his case for an abnormal physical and mental state.

(2) We would urge that his execution would be helpful to German policy, by accentuating the differences between us and some of our fellow subjects in Ireland. It would be used, however unjustly, as a weapon against us in the United States and other neutral countries. On the other hand, magnanimity upon the part of the British Government would soothe the bitter feelings in Ireland, and make a most favourable impression throughout the Empire and abroad.

(3) We would respectfully remind you of the object lesson afforded by the United States at the conclusion of their Civil War. The leaders of the South were entirely in the power of the North. Many of them were officers and officials who had sworn allegiance to the laws of the United States and had afterwards taken up arms and inflicted enormous losses upon her. None the less not one of these men was executed, and this policy of mercy was attended by such happy results that a breach which seemed to be irreparable has now been happily healed over.

Being ourselves deeply convinced of the wisdom of such a policy, we feel constrained to approach you with this petition, hoping that you may find yourself in agreement with the considerations which we advance.

We are, Sir,

Your obedient servants,

Sir T. Clifford Allbutt, K.C.B., Regius Professor of Physics at the University of Cambridge.

William Archer.

Appendix II.

Sir THOMAS BARLOW, Bart., K.C.V.O., President of the Royal College of Physicians, London.
HAROLD BEGBIE.
ARNOLD BENNETT.
ROBERT BLATCHFORD.
MUIRHEAD BONE.
HALL CAINE.
The Rev. R. J. CAMPBELL.
G. K. CHESTERTON.
The Rev. JOHN CLIFFORD.
EDWARD CLODD.
WILLIAM CROOKS.
Sir FRANCIS DARWIN (2 and 3).
W. BOYD DAWKINS.
Sir ARTHUR CONAN DOYLE.
JOHN DRINKWATER.
Sir JAMES G. FRAZER.
The Right Hon. Sir EDWARD FRY, G.C.B.
JOHN GALSWORTHY.
A. G. GARDINER.
ALICE B. GOMME.
G. P. GOOCH.
MAURICE HEWLETT.
SILAS K. HOCKING.
The Rev. ROBERT F. HORTON.
JEROME K. JEROME.
JOHN MASEFIELD.
H. W. MASSINGHAM.
Sir WILLIAM ROBERTSON NICOLL.
Sir SYDNEY OLIVIER.
The Rev. THOMAS PHILLIPS, President of the Baptist Union.
C. P. SCOTT, Editor, *The Manchester Guardian.*
CLEMENT SHORTER.
BEN TILLETT.
BEATRICE WEBB.
SIDNEY WEBB.
The Right Rev. the BISHOP OF WINCHESTER.
ISRAEL ZANGWILL.

Buswell's Hotel,
Dublin, 15th July, 1916.

Dear ,—Some Irish men and women who are deeply grieved at the events of the last few months propose to petition the Government to show mercy to Roger Casement. They are not influenced by any sympathy for his acts, but believe that any further shedding of blood will not tend to improve the relations between the two islands, or to smooth the irritation which unfortunately exists.

It is not proposed to prepare any monster petition at present; in this matter we must be guided by circumstances as they arise, and at present such a course does not seem advisable. The time available does not permit much delay for consultation, but we hope you will approve of the form of petition now drawn up. We propose that the present petition should go forward with only a limited number of signatures—those of people of note or influence in literature, art, &c. This will give it a separate distinct character and prevent the names being connected with those having strong political associations.

If you approve we shall be glad if you will return the petition signed so that it can be attached to others of the same nature.

Yours faithfully,

MAURICE MOORE.
AGNES O'FARRELLY.

Committee—

Rt. Rev. Monsignor A. Ryan.
Dr. Hyde, LL.D.
Rev. Matthew MacGuire.
Colonel Moore.
F. Allen, Esq.
Larcan Sherlock, Esq., late Lord Mayor, Dublin.

Mrs. Hutton.
Mrs. O'Nolan.
Miss O'Farrelly.
Miss Young.

The humble petition of the undersigned showeth—

1. The signers of this petition have no sympathy with the actions of Roger Casement in Germany, but they hope the Government will deeply consider not alone the legal aspect of the case, and the anger caused by acts hostile to the Empire in time of war, but also the larger and deeper considerations of policy which may result from the carrying out of the full measure of punishment which the legal tribunal has exacted. The relations of the Irish people to the Empire are of more importance than the personality of the man who has been arraigned for treason.

2. The capital city of Ireland has suffered severely as the result of the late disturbances; large areas of the city have been laid in ruins, and the material damage has produced widespread unemployment and distress. This distress has roused public feeling to a state of intense excitement, and a general feeling of unrest has spread to classes not previously affected.

3. In addition to the sufferings caused by the destruction of property in Dublin, a great number of people have been arrested both in Dublin and the Provinces, and deported to England. Their relatives and friends are uncertain as to their treatment, and in many cases their families have no means of support, so that the effects of the Rebellion, which was confined to Dublin and two small districts, have been spread into every corner of Ireland.

4. The actual leaders of the Rebellion in Ireland were executed immediately after its suppression, and a general feeling pervaded this country and abroad that enough blood had been shed. It is true that the special circumstances of Roger Casement's case make it impossible to differentiate in his favour; but time has elapsed since the acts of rebellion, and this, though not considered in law, makes a great human difference. The

reaction in public sentiment, which was undoubtedly caused by the punishments inflicted, ought to be allowed to settle. Your petitioners feel that another execution so long after will arouse popular feeling and prevent the quiet acceptance of the new measure for the government of Ireland. Whatever gratitude this measure might evoke will be countered by another act of severity, and the new Government will have new difficulties to face for which it is in no way responsible.

5. Inexcusable as Roger Casement's actions in this matter may be, it must be remembered that he has performed great services to the Empire and humanity by his work in the Congo and Putumayo. His life has been spent serving the country in fever-stricken regions in West Africa and Brazil, where his health was permanently impaired. Returning to Ireland sick and broken with disease after long years of exile, he found a state of affairs existing two or three years ago which might easily distract his mind and upset his judgment.

6. Your petitioners do not wish to draw any comparisons which might seem invidious, but they venture to express the belief that if clemency were shown it could be justified by abundant precedent.

7. Your petitioners therefore humbly pray that the extreme penalty of death may not be inflicted upon Roger Casement.

To the Right Honourable H. H. Asquith, K.C., M.P., Prime Minister.

Sir,—We, the undersigned, beg leave to place before you certain considerations affecting the case of Roger David Casement, now under sentence of death for high treason. Our object is to show reason why the sentence of the Court should not be executed.

We will not occupy your time with matters as well known to you as to ourselves, and on which your judgment cannot be challenged, such, for example, as the conspicuous public services of the condemned man and so forth. We address ourselves solely to points on which you may desire information as to the state of public opinion.

We assume that the penalty for high treason is peculiar in criminal law inasmuch as it depends for its sanction not on the general principle of the sacredness of law, but on its effect on the public peace. The conclusion is arrived at in every case by balancing the deterrent effect of carrying out the sentence against the conciliatory effect of remitting it. Recent events in South Africa have accustomed the public to this view. We therefore need trouble you with no apology for treating the decision as one of expediency only.

In our opinion, Casement had not, up to the time of his trial, any serious hold on the Irish people. His Nationalist writings were circulated in America, not in Ireland. His political projects, being those of an educated diplomatist, were too technical to be understood by such groups as the Republican Brotherhood and the irreconcilable section of Sinn Fein. We are confident that if during your recent visit to Ireland you inquired what Casement was driving at you did not receive a single well-informed reply. You certainly did not find him a national hero; and we venture to assume that you do not wish him to become a national hero.

There is, however, one infallible way in which that can be done; and that way is to hang him. His trial and sentence have already raised his status in Nationalist Ireland;

but it lacks the final consecration of death. We urge you very strongly not to effect that consecration. In the position of Mr. Arthur Lynch and General de Wet, Casement will be harmless, disabled by his own failure. On a British scaffold he will do endless mischief. The contrast between ruthless severity in his case, and conspicuous leniency—not to mention impunity—in others, will provide an overwhelming argument and illustration to the propagandists of hatred and revenge, whilst the halo which surrounds the national martyr will make a national faith of his beliefs and a gospel of his writings.

As against this nothing can be claimed except that other rebels may be intimidated. But the likelihood is all the other way. The Irish movement is not a solid phalanx of irreconcilables. The Casementites and Fenians were a negligible minority of it until the Rebellion. If, though still a minority, they are no longer negligible, it is precisely because of the policy of intimidation, of "giving Ireland a lesson," attempted by General Maxwell. The swing of the pendulum, not only in Ireland but in the neutral countries which are interested in Ireland, was immediate and unmistakable. But it has not been decisive. The Nationalist movement is still reasonable; and a friendly settlement is easy, provided no more executions take place. Even the crude notion that England owes Ireland a life for Mr. Skeffington's had better be respected.

You will observe that in putting the case thus before you, we have deprived ourselves of the support of those who see in the specific proposals of Casement a real hope for Irish independence, and who must therefore, within the limits imposed by common humanity, desire the strenuous impulse which would be given to his authority and influence by his death in an English prison as an Irish patriot. But you will hardly attach the less weight on that account to our urgent representation, which is prompted by a sincere desire for an unembittered settlement of the question which has occupied so large a share of the labours of your administration.

We are, Sir,

Your obedient Servants,

To the Right Honourable Herbert Louis Samuel, M.P.,
Secretary of State for the Home Department.

Sir,—We, the undersigned, have reason to believe that certain petitions are being presented to His Majesty the King praying for the remission of the capital sentence recently passed upon Roger Casement on the charge of high treason. We desire in this petition to ask that his work on behalf of subject races in the tropical regions of South America and Central Africa may also be taken into consideration. We beg to recall to you the tribute paid to this work by Lord Fitzmaurice and Lord Lansdowne in the House of Lords on the 3rd July, 1906. Lord Fitzmaurice (then Under-Secretary of State for Foreign Affairs) said—

> " . . . Mr. Casement had an exceedingly difficult task, and was subject to all those perils of flood and field which a man who has work to do in the interior of Africa has to encounter. He had, moreover, to carry on an inquiry which could not fail to be more or less disagreeable to those concerned, and to make him an object of suspicion and dislike to them. . . . That gentleman (Roger Casement) has been the object of many unjust attacks, and I am sure that I am giving utterance to the feelings of all here when I express the hope that Mr. Casement, whom

reasons of health have compelled to retire from an appointment which he held at Lisbon, will have an opportunity of adding further services to those with which his name is already associated."

The Marquess of Lansdowne supported this tribute in the following words :—

" . . . Then came the mission of Mr. Consul Casement, to whom my noble friend referred in terms of commendation which were thoroughly well deserved. Mr. Casement's report certainly had the effect of raising a corner of the curtain behind which was shrouded the iniquities that had been going on for many years."

These expressions referred, it is true, to his work in Central Africa, but they applied in every respect to a similar task, equally difficult and even more dangerous, which he accomplished in South America in a manner highly satisfactory to His Majesty's Government.

Those of us who laboured to counteract the evils exposed in both these charges found the investigations of Roger Casement of great assistance, and they helped more than anything else in securing for several millions of the child races of the world a large mitigation of the sufferings inflicted upon them by an unscrupulous exploitation. We desire also to emphasise that the questions submitted to Roger Casement for investigation were ultimately subjected to a searching scrutiny by impartial Committees, and in no case was the evidence secured by Roger Casement shaken in any way whatever.

We believe it will not be contested that the reports issued by Roger Casement during the period he served His Majesty's Government are regarded as displaying unusual skill and forming a valuable historical account of the treatment of native races.

We have the honour to be, Sir,

Your most obedient humble Servants,

To

The Right Honourable H. H. Asquith, K.C., M.P., Prime Minister.

The Right Honourable H. L. Samuel, M.P., Home Secretary.

Sirs,—We beg respectfully to urge that the sentence passed on Roger Casement should not be carried out.

We do not ask this for his sake, for he himself has not asked it.

We plead for clemency because of the grave effects which it is to be feared his execution would have on the relations between England and Ireland.

There are multitudes who feel that the knight-errant in the cause of suffering humanity in the Congo and the Putumayo cannot be treated as if he were on the moral level of a common murderer. Those who saw and heard him at his trial realised that his transgression of the law, however grave, left his own conscience clear. However much he may have outraged the instincts and principles which happily prevail where loyalty to one's own people and national aspirations is the same thing as loyalty to the State, he would walk to his death upright and unashamed.

Whatever may be said as to the necessity for swift, sharp measures in the heat of an armed insurrection, it might not be wise, when blood is cold, to press the utmost rigour of the criminal law against such a man, even if he stood alone and moral sentiment were strongly on the side of the law.

Sir Roger Casement.

But the danger is infinitely greater when there is a risk of a general divorce of moral sentiment from the law, especially in a case where the deepest and most sacred feelings of many people are concerned, as in the long struggle to preserve and uphold Irish Nationalism.

A large and growing number of Irish men and women would regard his execution, not as a just and necessary punishment of crime, but as a cruel act of vengeance.

The legal execution of persons who, however mistakenly, have broken the law and appealed to force in furtherance of a high cause has proved again and again to be the strongest stimulant to others to adopt similar aims and methods. Old John Brown's body troubled the slave-owners all the more when they had nailed his coffin down.

In Ireland, when devotion to country has paid the price of death, respect for the law is swept away by an intensity of sympathy which has never been generally understood in England.

At this moment that divorce of feeling from the established order has grown in Ireland with alarming rapidity. After years of hope, which seemed on the point of realisation, of friendship between England and Ireland, the estrangement of the two peoples is now in danger of becoming deeper and more bitter and more complete than before. Education has made it possible for disaffection to grow and spread in ways that were impossible fifty years ago. At this moment the one great hope in both countries has been of pacification and reconciliation between parties in Ireland and between England and Ireland. The possibility of this being brought about is now trembling in the balance, and we believe that the execution of Roger Casement would turn the scale in the direction of lawlessness and bitterness to such an extent that recovery could not take place in our generation.

For the sake of both England and Ireland we pray that that execution may not take place.

We have the honour to be, Sirs,

Your most obedient humble Servants,

Lightning Source UK Ltd.
Milton Keynes UK
UKHW011542030820
367624UK00001B/350